A Feminist Companion
to the Apocalypse of John

Feminist Companion to the New Testament
and Early Christian Writings, 13

Other title published in this series:

Forthcoming:

A Feminist Companion to

the Apocalypse of John

edited by
Amy-Jill Levine

with Maria Mayo Robbins

t&t clark

Published by T&T Clark International
A Continuum Imprint
The Tower Building, 11 York Road, London SE1 7NX
80 Maiden Lane, Suite 704, New York, NY 10038

www.continuumbooks.com

British Library Cataloguing-in-Publication Data
A catalogue record for this book is available from the British Library

Typeset by RefineCatch Limited, Bungay, Suffolk
Printed and bound in Great Britain by the MPG Books Group

ISBN: 978–0–8264–6650–1 (Hardback)
       978–0–8264–6651–8 (Paperback)

Contents

PREFACE

A Feminist Companion to the Apocalypse of John, along with its sister volumes on the other documents of the New Testament and early Christian literature, signals the extent to which feminist critique has become a core element of biblical, historical and theological study.

Letters of invitation to contribute to this series went well beyond scholars known from their contributions to explicitly feminist or women-identified collections, such as the two volumes of *Searching the Scriptures*[1] and the *Women's Bible Commentary*,[2] or from books and articles with 'feminist' in the title. Authors already established as having feminist interests were asked to suggest additional voices, and so interpreters at the beginning of their academic careers joined their senior colleagues in the pages of the volumes.

Invitations went beyond North America and Western Europe to East and South Asia, Africa, Eastern Europe, Central and South America, and Australia/New Zealand. Along with an intentional focus on cultural diversity, we targeted as well authors who might speak explicitly from two perspectives sometimes overlooked even in feminist biblical collections, namely, sexual identity (e.g., lesbian critique) and religious tradition (e.g., Evangelicals, Jews). Some chose to write explicitly from their social location, and some did not. For either new or previously published work not in English, Vanderbilt Divinity School/the Carpenter Program in Religion, Gender, and Sexuality provided funds for translation.

Not all those invited were able to contribute, but readers should be able to hear echoed in the footnotes – and by extension in the sources those notes utilize – numerous and diverse feminist voices speaking in other volumes and venues.

In addition to publishing select 'classics' in feminist analysis, the series invited numerous senior scholars to reconsider their earlier approaches and conclusions. Through their revisions, changes in feminist thought can be tracked. The series also sought contributions from biblical experts not known for feminist interests or even, in some cases, sympathies: 'write a "feminist" piece', we exhorted; when a few demurred ('I don't "do" feminist critique'; 'I don't know what feminist critique is'), we responded: 'You should find out about it; you should engage it; if you don't like it, explain why, for all disciplines can profit from engaged critique; if you do find it helpful, use it'.

We wish to thank Marianne Blickenstaff for help with the development of this project. We also wish to thank the Carpenter Program in Religion, Gender, and Sexuality at the Vanderbilt Divinity School for financial and technical support.

---

1 Elisabeth Schüssler Fiorenza (ed.), *Searching the Scriptures: A Feminist Introduction and Commentary* (2 vols; New York: Crossroad, 1993, 1994).
2 Carol A. Newsom and Sharon H. Ringe (eds), *The Women's Bible Commentary* (Louisville, KY: Westminster/John Knox Press, 1992; rev. edn, 1998).

It is our hope that this new series will quickly establish itself as a standard work of reference to scholars, students, and also to others who are interested in the New Testament and Christian Origins.

Amy-Jill Levine and Maria Mayo Robbins
Vanderbilt Divinity School and Graduate Department of Religion

ACKNOWLEDGMENTS

The editors and publisher are grateful to the following for permission to reproduce copyright material: *Biblical Interpretation* for 'Feminine Symbolism in the Book of Revelation' by A. Yarbro Collins, from *Biblical Interpretation* 1.1 (1993), pp. 20–33; Fortress Press for 'Ms.Calculating the Endtimes: Gender Styles of Apocalypse' by Catherine Keller, from *God and Power: Counter-Apocalyptic Journeys* (Minneapolis, MN: Fortress Press, 2005), pp. 53–65; Routledge for 'Hypermasculinity and Divinity', excerpted from Stephen D. Moore, *God's Gym: Divine Male Bodies of the Bible* (New York and London: Routledge, 1996).

Abbreviations

AAR	American Academy of Religion
AB	Anchor Bible
ABD	David Noel Freedman (ed.), *The Anchor Bible Dictionary* (6 vols; New York: Doubleday, 1992)
AJA	*American Journal of Archaeology*
ANRW	Hildegard Temporini and Wolfgang Haase (eds), *Aufstieg und Niedergang der römischen Welt: Geschichte und Kultur Roms im Spiegel der neueren Forschung* (Berlin: W. de Gruyter, 1972–)
Aug.	Suetonius, *Divus Augustus*
BETL	Bibliotheca Ephemeridum Theologicarum Lovaniensium
BGBE	Beiträge zur Geschichte der biblischen Exegese
BibInt	*Biblical Interpretation*
BR	*Bible Review*
BTB	*Biblical Theological Bulletin*
BZNW	Beihefte zur Zeitschrift für die neutestamentliche Wissenschaft
CBQ	*Catholic Biblical Quarterly*
CIL	*Corpus Inscriptionum Latinarum*
Dig.	*Digest* of Justinian
Dom.	Suetonius, *Life of Domitian* (*De Vita Caesarum*)
ErtFor	Erträge der Forschung
ESV	English Standard Version
FCB	Feminist Companion to the Bible
FRLANT	Forschungen zur Religion und Literatur des Alten und Neuen Testaments
GNS	Good News Series
HDR	Harvard Dissertations in Religion
HNT	Handbuch zum Neuen Testament
HTR	*Harvard Theological Review*
ICC	International Critical Commentary
JAAR	*Journal of the American Academy of Religion*
JBL	*Journal of Biblical Literature*
JFSR	*Journal of Feminist Studies in Religion*
JRelS	*Journal of Religious Studies*
JRS	*Journal of Roman Studies*
JSJ	*Journal for the Study of Judaism*
JSJSup	Supplements to the *Journal for the Study of Judaism*
JSNT	*Journal for the Study of the New Testament*
JSNTSup	*Journal for the Study of the New Testament*, Supplement Series
JSOTSup	*Journal for the Study of the Old Testament*, Supplement Series
KJV	King James Version
LCL	Loeb Classical Library
LSJ	Liddell–Scott–Jones *Greek–English Lexicon*
LXX	Septuagint
MT	Masoretic Text

NAB	New American Bible
NASB	New American Standard Bible
NCBC	The New Century Bible Commentary
NeoT	*Neotestamentica*
NIB	New Interpreter's Bible
NIBC	New International Biblical Commentary
NIBCNT	New International Biblical Commentary on the New Testament
NICNT	New International Commentary on the New Testament
NIGTC	New International Greek Testament Commentary
NIV	New International Version
NJB	New Jerusalem Bible
NJBC	*New Jerome Biblical Commentary*
NKJV	New King James Version
NovT	*Novum Testamentum*
NovTSup	*Novum Testamentum*, Supplements
NRSV	New Revised Standard Version
NTAbh	Neutestamentliche Abhandlungen
NTD	Das Neue Testament Deutsch
NTS	*New Testament Studies*
NTT	New Testament Theology
OTL	Old Testament Library
ÖTKNT	Ökumenischer Taschenbuch-Kommentar Neuen Testament
RSV	Revised Standard Version
SBL	Society of Biblical Literature
SBLDS	SBL Dissertation Series
SBLSP	*SBL Seminar Papers*
SBLSym	SBL Symposium Series
SC	Sources chrétiennes
SJLA	Studies in Judaism in Late Antiquity
TDNT/TWNT	*Theological Dictionary of the New Testament / Theologisches Wörterbuch zum Neuen Testament*
VT	*Vetus Testamentum*
WBC	Word Biblical Commentary
WE	Worldwide English (New Testament) (Willington, UK: SOON Educational Publishers, 1996)
WMANT	Wissenschaftliche Monographien zum Alten und Neuen Testament
WUNT	Wissenschaftliche Untersuchungen zum Neuen Testament
ZNW	*Zeitschrift für die neutestamentliche Wissenschaft*

LIST OF CONTRIBUTORS

David L. Barr, Wright State University, Dayton, OH, USA
Mary Ann Beavis, St Thomas More College, Saskatoon, SK, Canada
Greg Carey, Lancaster Theological Seminary, Lancaster, PA, USA
Adela Yarbro Collins, Yale Divinity School, New Haven, CT, USA
Lynn R. Huber, Elon University, Elon, NC, USA
Catherine Keller, Drew University, Madison, NJ, USA
John W. Marshall, University of Toronto, Toronto, ON, Canada
Stephen D. Moore, The Theological School, Drew University, Madison, NJ, USA
Jorunn Økland, University of Sheffield, Sheffield, UK
Hanna Stenström, Church of Sweden Research Unit and University of Uppsala, Uppsala, Sweden
Pamela Thimmes, University of Dayton, Dayton, OH, USA
Caroline Vander Stichele, University of Amsterdam, Amsterdam, The Netherlands

INTRODUCTION

AMY-JILL LEVINE

In the 1970s, when I entered college and began to take courses in New Testament Studies, I kept looking for women commentators. They were not represented in the hallowed halls of Pauline theology, and they were absent from studies of the Historical Jesus. But there, clustered around the book of Revelation, were published dissertations by women biblical scholars: Elisabeth Schüssler Fiorenza's 1972 *Priester für Gott; Studien zum Herrschafts- und Priestermotiv in der Apokalypse*[1] and A. Yarbro Collins's 1976 *The Combat Myth in the Book of Revelation.*[2] There was even an Anchor Bible Commentary written by a woman: J. Massyngberde Ford's 1975 contribution[3] (of course, it had to be pointed out to me that the J. of this book was a woman), as well as Collins's *The Apocalypse* in the New Testament Message series.[4] From this admittedly limited survey, I found myself with numerous questions: were women being channeled into studies of the Apocalypse because we were seen as unworthy to comment on the 'more important' books more often read in main-line churches? Or, did women biblical scholars find in Revelation a viable response to the power of imperial Rome and so to all oppressive, colonized (or pre-tenured) states? Were women compelled to write about Revelation because its images of women were so striking, or was it simply easier to stake out a place in Apocalyptic space rather than break into the bastions of Pauline studies or work on the Historical Jesus? Or was it simply accidental or idiosyncratic that these women scholars found themselves writing on Revelation: perhaps something in the text simply struck them as 'interesting'.

Thirty years later, studies of Revelation arise from numerous perspectives. Included in this collection are postcolonial criticism, cultural studies, millennial studies, commentary on performance art, psychological analysis, gender theory, intertextuality, cultural anthropology, Roman history, history of religion and rhetography. Conversation partners from outside biblical studies include Theodor Adorno, Homi Bhabha, Hélène Cixous, Paul de Man, Frantz Fanon, Michel Foucault, Sigmund Freud, Luce Irigaray, Carl Jung and Toril Moi; from within, the two major touchstones emerge in Elisabeth Schüssler Fiorenza's liberationist readings and Tina Pippin's less optimistic ones. The works of Barbara Rossing, Paul Duff and Steven Friesen are prominent, and the contributors to this volume frequently cite each other's work as well. New voices engage their predecessors, older

---

1 Elisabeth Schüssler Fiorenza, *Priester für Gott; Studien zum Herrschafts- und Priestermotiv in der Apokalypse* (NTAbh NF 7; Münster: Verlag Aschendorff, 1972).

2 A. Yarbro Collins, *The Combat Myth in the Book of Revelation* (HDR, 9; Missoula, MT: Scholars Press, 1976).

3 J. Massyngberde Ford, *Revelation, Introduction, Translation, Commentary* (AB, 38; Garden City, NY: Doubleday, 1975).

4 A. Yarbro Collins, *The Apocalypse* (New Testament Message, 22; Wilmington, DE: Michael Glazier, 1979).

theories are refined and newer ones tested. No consensus on the text is reached by all the writers; the gaps in historical knowledge and the spaces opened by multiple readers prevent the gates from closing.

Feminist studies of Revelation frequently focus on the female imagery: the Thyatiran prophet called 'Jezebel' (2.18–29), the 'Woman Clothed with the Sun' (12.1–17), the 'Whore of Babylon' (chs 17–19), and the 'Bride'/the 'Heavenly Jerusalem' (chs 19, 21, 22). Other images may display, or mask, female presence; there may (well) be women among the Nicolaitans or in the Synagogue of Satan, if not among the 144,000 virgins of ch. 14 and the inhabitants of the Heavenly Jerusalem. Here determination of women's presence depends on whether the masculine nouns and verbs are more than simple grammatical accidents. John describes the 144,000 as those 'who have not defiled themselves with women' (Rev. 14.4). The description could suggest a refusal to participate in the worship of the Whore via the cult of Roma or more broadly via engaging in Roman social life, and it could also indicate those who remain celibate because any contact with women is, for John, defiling. Some readers, finding in Revelation an alternative world in which God's justice prevails, take the apparent misogyny of the language here and elsewhere as pointing beyond actual men and women, and beyond gender roles. Others, unwilling to extricate the message from the medium, cannot so easily dismiss the sexualized violence by which Revelation's sense of 'justice' or 'liberation' is described. Revelation has been, and can be, read as liberating; it has been, and can be, read as marginalizing and oppressing.

Informed by postcolonial analysis, John W. Marshall's contribution locates the sources of Revelation's sexualized violence in the context of the traumas of 69–70 CE: the Roman War and the destruction of Jerusalem. Marshall finds that John's insistence on purity and strident efforts to differentiate himself from his proximate 'others' – 'Jezebel', the synagogue of Satan, Rome – are responses to the threats of hybridity faced by his subaltern, diaspora community. For Revelation the primary image of the threat, the 'conduit of contamination that compromises the purity of the saints', is the uncontrolled woman, both real and figurative. Epitomizing this role, the Whore and 'Jezebel' appear as bad mothers of demonic offspring, publicly active rather than contained and passive, deceptive and open to penetration rather than closed and pristine.

The complex figure of the Whore is simultaneously the city, its culture, a reminiscence of Scriptural invectives against other cities envisioned as women, a co-opting of Roman colonial propaganda in which conquered cities are depicted as women, and a parody of the goddess Roma (a point developed in Mary Ann Beavis's contribution), closely associated with the imperial cult in Asia Minor. Her destruction follows from her sexual transgressions as her lovers 'make her desolate and naked, and devour her flesh and burn her up with fire, for God has put it into their hearts to carry out this purpose' (Rev. 17.16–17). Modeling the pattern of double-mindedness described by Frantz Fanon, John thus both scorns and wants to displace/replace the colonizer.

Once Babylon is destroyed, John's triumphalistic Savior and his homosocial forces replace the false *Pax Romana* with the *Pax Christi*. John's co-optation by Roman ideology and rhetoric is well known, as is his inscription of eschatological hierarchy, his depiction of the New Jerusalem as a gated community, his pervasive and invasive patriarchalism, his imperially imposed peace ... this is no pure or pristine text; there is no empire without subordination. And yet, Marshall recognizes, there is peace nonetheless, and a 'healing of the nations' (21.24–27), as the Lamb with his own blood suffers for his people. Worse than empire may be anarchy; worse than divine justice may be no justice at all. Readers may reject John's rhetoric, but through Marshall's political contextualization of the Apocalypse, readers can better understand it and, perhaps, recuperate parts of his message.

Developing the interrelated depictions of purity, sexuality and female imagery, Hanna Stenström argues that medium and message, form and content, cannot be separated: John's mythopoetic language creates an internalized, negative image of women that cannot be argued away, and rejoicing over the death of the Whore has an effect on the reader. A symbol is not, ultimately, only a symbol; what is conventional cannot easily be dismissed. The good news then, for the feminist reader, is not the reclamation of the text; it is, instead, a reading that makes more visible the presuppositions for and patterns of oppression and thus strengthens the commitment to change them.

In Rev. 14.1–5, Stenström finds through inter- and extra-textual allusions a constructed world view in which the 144,000 represent the entire Christian community, the saved remnant of Israel. John defines this community as male (given their contrast to the 'women' in 14.4a); the purity language of 14.4a shows how impurity is connected with 'women' and purity with the male community; the conventional description of idolatry as sexual deviance then reinforces the point that the pure community is also a virginal one. Whereas women in subaltern groups typically represent and are even coerced into maintaining community purity, in Rev. 14.1–5 144,000 (male) virgins play this role. Marshall suggests that this shift may reflect the particularly intense situation prompted by Jerusalem's destruction; it may also reflect a concern to keep women in John's community pure (although this inclusion of women among the saints strikes me as a generous reading). Stenström offers a third reading: the reference to 'virgins' evokes the image of the 'good woman', but only men play this role.

Stenström then locates antecedent images of male purity and virginity in descriptions of the Temple priesthood and of soldiers in Holy War. Similarly reusing and combining imagery from Israel's Scriptures – purity language, female personification of cities, characterizations of the 'foreign woman' and 'prostitute', depiction of religious infidelity in terms of (what the text sees as) sexual deviance, and so forth – John constructs his 'women'. These allusions, especially when presented in Revelation's apocalyptic context, tend to meld, and the more the images coalesce, the more the delimitations of John's community are reinforced. In John's world, the pure, spotless, priestly, virgin, white-clad soldiers of the covenant community who participate in the holy stand against the impure, profane, sexually active, lying, alien women associated with the Beast and removed from the Heavenly Jerusalem.

In her study of Rev. 12.17–22, Stenström understands the Woman Clothed with the Sun as 'the Christian community' as well as the 'Israel from which the Messiah was born'. Thus, the community has become the 'Good Woman' and her children. Stenström also sees the Woman and so by implication the saints as disconnected to 'sexuality' and 'impurity' and as dichotomous with the prostitute Babylon. However, the Woman could be connected to both: childbirth can imply sexual intercourse (although the New Testament context does offer a virginal alternative), and parturition prompts a state of ritual impurity (Lev. 12.2–8). Given the openness of her body through childbirth, her hybrid wings (rather than being borne on eagle's wings, she sprouts her own), her flight, her female-savior (the Goddess) Mother Earth, and her freedom as she runs out of the text, she can be just as much a symbol of the chaotic as Babylon.

Extending her study to the letters to the seven churches, vice lists, depictions of the heavenly court, priestly imagery, and numerous other passages, Stenström demonstrates how Revelation's references, explicit and implicit, to concerns with purity function to create dualistic configurations of the saved 'Us' vs the damned 'Them'. Revelation makes 'no other room for women, neither in time nor in eternity, than to be the Others . . . "Women" are necessary for the construction of Christian identity but without any part in it'.

David L. Barr finds that all of John's female characters are 'symbolic constructs of the first order'. His approach to these 'Queens' is, first, to determine how John moved from history to myth and, second, to see if it is possible to retrace his steps and thereby disentangle, or deconstruct, Revelation's mythic images.

Beginning with Gaia/Earth, who 'opened her mouth and swallowed the river that the Dragon had poured from his mouth' (12.16), Barr finds a 'strictly mythic character', but one representing the 'original Queen Mother'. At this point, I wonder if the destabilizing of Revelation's images may have already occurred: if Gaia is 'strictly mythic', could the same be said for the Father on the throne? Next comes the equally mythic 'Queen Consort', also known as the 'Bride of the Lamb' and the 'Heavenly Jerusalem'. Barr's labeling the Bride as 'Queen', a step Revelation does not take, enables a more complete comparison between this figure and the Great Whore, whom he calls 'the Queen Ruler'. More might be made of the lack of royal titles accorded to, or royal homage paid to, any women; the heavenly system and the political system are, to use an overused term, 'patriarchal'.

History also comes into play, as the 'Queen Ruler' finds counterparts in John's world: Rome or (earthly) Jerusalem (albeit unlikely, given those Roman-identified seven hills) or both. But, as Barr notes, 'the undergirding myth seems to be that of the chaos monster Tiamat – the mother who would destroy her children and who is herself destroyed'. For other contributors to this collection, Tiamat is found instead in Gaia; given the fluidity, let alone the connection to fluids, of these images, the multiple connections may all be correct. The fourth mythic character, the 'Woman Clothed with the Sun', Barr titles 'Queen of Heaven'; her allusive connections range from Israel and the Church to Eve, Leto, Isis and Roma. Yet unlike Isis and her divine counterparts, worshiped under many names in multiple locations, this 'Queen of Heaven' has no name, no throne, no worshipers, and no caring consort. Barr sees her as a 'cosmic ruler', yet she rules nothing. At best, she, like the Queen Consort, has impressive accessories.

Finally comes 'Queen Jezebel', the one queen who disguises a historical counterpart, John's rival prophet from Thyatira, even as she invokes a historical counterpart, the ancient queen of Israel, herself already disguised and mythologized by Deuteronomic History. The name Jezebel conjures numerous usable markers: foreigners, whoredoms and sorceries, sexuality, dining with idol-worshipers, corruption. Whether John found his Thyatiran rival too powerful for a direct attack, as Barr proposes (I am not convinced: how many other candidates in Thyatira would there be for this role?), or whether the name-calling marginalizes through co-optation and objectification, her activities can be reconstructed: for example, she may well have advocated participation in the social and commercial life of Asia Minor, including eating meat offered to idols in pagan festivals (a point Thimmes develops).

How is this hand of five queens to be played? Or, as Barr asks, 'how might we as modern readers respond to the oppressive nature of these images?' Surveying a number of options, Barr simplifies them into two categories, 'discard' or 'dissect' (or, perhaps better, 'discard or fold'). Recognizing the irony of his male eyes offering women readers a new way of seeing, he opts for a new game: exploiting the gap between signifier and signified, words and meaning, speaker and hearer, and so considering 'the dialectical relation of history and myth as a reflection of the sign/signified gap'.

From history, Barr adduces the 'mythic theme of rebellion and the image of the "unsubmissive woman" undergirding "Jezebel" and Queen Ruler'. But contrary to Roman cultural–mythological conventions, these women are not slain by the True Ruler. Queen Ruler is slain by her allies and dependents; 'Jezebel's' expected demise is displaced onto her children (cf. 2 Sam. 12.18, wherein David and Bathsheba's son dies). Next, he cites the tradition of the loyal wife who legitimates succession (a point Huber develops); again Revelation adopts the mythic theme but subverts its political intent, for the role of Queen Consort is not to produce children, but to 'be' them as well as the place of their habitation. Similarly, the conventional Queen Mother becomes unconventional, in that she has no husband. These observations, coupled with an understanding of gender construction in antiquity – from the definition of woman as imperfect male to the possible loss of 'masculine identity' through loss of honor – open numerous interpretive possibilities. These include transgendered readings of the 144,000 celibate male virgins, and transvestite readings, given that Barr follows Catherine Keller in seeing the Ruler Queen as 'imperial patriarchy in drag'. Or, because three Queens relate to a reality inclusive of men and women – Queen Mother/Israel; Queen Ruler/Babylon; Queen Consort/John's community – and because John's male followers are to identify with the Queen Consort and the 'Good Woman' evoked by the 144,000 'virgins', could space for women's participation be opened? The deck is reshuffled; it is up to the reader to name the wild cards, fold, change the game, or take the risk of following the Queen Consort's command, 'Come!' (Rev. 22.17) and go all in.

Pamela Thimmes clearly sees the multiple stakes in reading Revelation. An expatriate living in Ireland, she sees from her new location the penetration of apocalyptic thought into US culture and thus its (her?) exports. A Christian 'believer', she struggles with Revelation's violence even as she seeks to honor its place in the canon and in liberationist circles. A scholar, she has various reading strategies that help her to construct meaning, to make sense of the text. A woman, she seeks herself in the visions. From these multiple perspectives she demonstrates John's attempt to appropriate 'Jezebel's' character (Rev. 2.18–29), sexualize it, brutalize it and contain it, and the attempts by which commentators, feminist and otherwise, respond.

As Thimmes shows, the Letter to Thyatira does not depict 'typical insider–outsider conflict'; it is, instead, an 'intra-Christian quarrel', and 'Jezebel' is, for the Thyatiran Church, an insider with clout. Thus, while Revelation is appropriately seen as 'resistance' literature responding to actual or perceived political repression, it is also literature on the offensive. John is, like Paul, an (itinerant?) outsider to the communities to whom he writes. He has, like Paul, supporters in those communities: those who display love, faith, service and endurance (2.19); 'my slaves' (2.20); 'the rest of you, who do not hold to ['Jezebel's'] teaching' [2.24]). And he has his enemies/rivals: the female teacher, whom John names 'Jezebel' (2.20). Her only self-identification, albeit one John mediates, is that 'she calls herself a prophet' (προφῆτιν [2.20]). The label masks her real name even as it attributes to her the characteristics of the notorious queen of 1 Kings 16–22, 2 Kings 9, whose real name is also suppressed. The original Jezebel's foreignness counteracts her namesake's insider status; her polytheism glosses the Thyatiran prophet's permission of eating food offered to idols; her unscrupulousness undergirds John's insistence that the female prophet pollutes her community; her royal authority, achieved through evil action, undercuts the authority of the female prophet; her marriage to Ahab and her sexualized death provide negative foils to John's vision of the 144,000, who have not defiled themselves with women.

John's describing his rival as 'beguiling' (πλανᾷ [2.20]; the term can mean 'deceive', but the sexualized 'beguile' is apt), promoting fornication and adultery (πορνεῦσαι [2.20], τοὺς μοιχεύοντας μετ' αὐτῆς [2.22], whether indicating the permitting of sexual intercourse or, metaphorically, participating in local cultic activities, or both), and permitting the eating of 'food sacrificed to idols' (2.20; cf. 1 Corinthians 8) shows the internal dimension of his polemic. It also shows John's consistency, for as Thimmes demonstrates, in John's hands the reference to food carries a sexual aftertaste even as it whets the appetite for the delicacies of the Whore and, less appetizingly, for the 'marriage supper' of flesh and blood. Through rhetoric, John attempts to assert both definition and control: to throw 'Jezebel' on a bed, similarly to punish her followers, and to 'strike her children dead' (2.23). Again, whether the children are literal, metaphorical, or both, goes unsaid. The language reflects, according to Thimmes, 'Jezebel's' constructed role as object of desire (a point developed in Carey's rhetographical study), object of fear, and foil for hostility against Rome. It is a language more violent, and more sexualized, than that applied to the other internal rival, 'Balaam' of the Church at Pergamum.

John does all he can to distance himself from 'Jezebel', but the efforts ultimately fail. Despite his attempts to erase the Thyatiran prophet, he has inscribed her existence, and in so doing has called forth, surely much to his horror, feminist responses. Thimmes shows how feminist understandings of the letters range from seeing them as offering a prophetic communication of revelation and thus establishing a counter-world to Roman imperialism, to a manifestation of 'pervasively constituted paranoia' in which John's concern is less Imperial Rome than it is a rival Christian teacher. To John's resistance literature, Thimmes herself comes as a resisting reader who rejects Revelation's pervasive violence, sexualized and objectified characterization of women, and exclusivist theology. She also resists total rejection of the letter. If Revelation is, as Thimmes argues, addressed to restless believers who willingly forgo old identities and loyalties, who live in the disequilibrium of the present, and who are waiting to be incorporated into a new and renewed community, then the future remains open. Perhaps it is not too late to find in it moments, however tentative, and vôices, however strange, that open upon dreams worth dreaming.

Coupling feminist theory with philological biblical criticism, Jorunn Økland excavates the disjunctions between the Bible's linguistic and cultural universes and those of its interpreters. Writing as the Bride, with informed mimicry and exposing the holes in the text as keyholes to new cultural universes and linguistic possibilities, she finds that the geography of Revelation's 'blissful "elsewhere"' is 'gendered' through the dynamics of segregation and hierarchy. But it is also open to possibilities yet unimagined.

Økland's map of the Heavenly location is constructed in part from the Heavenly inhabitants: the hypermasculine God and the gender-ambiguous Lamb who performs as the masculine lion and takes the male role in marriage to the 'Heavenly Miss Jerusalem'; the choir of 144,000 blameless virgins who emerge as exclusively male. Concerning the pure, nonpropagating παρθένοι with their echo of Matthew's infancy story, Økland notes that the term is not unambiguous. In antiquity παρθένος was not bordered by the status of the hymen (see e.g., 1 Cor. 7.25); today, the rendition 'virgin' is not restricted to men. That is, the meaning of the term remains unstable, as have been the various interpretations offered of the 144,000. One strategy to avoid understanding the 144,000 as male is to take the term as conventional and generic, and thus to distinguish between grammatical gender and sex. Another is to resist heterosexist presupposition – noting that παρθένος elsewhere usually denotes females – and take the 144,000 as women who have refrained from sexual contact with other women. Both views elide the androcentrism of the book, although at least the latter is not historically compelling.

Concerning Jerusalem the Bride who is also a city, Økland finds her to be a 'character' of a different kind than that of God, the lamb, or the 144,000. Partly implicated in, and partly distinguished from Mt Zion of Revelation 14, she is for Økland the Platonic *chora* seen through a feminist lens; she is 'place, home and accommodation rather than an inhabitant herself'. Not only city but also virgin-bride, she is necessarily unstable, and as both character and setting, fluidly flowing from one to the other, she speaks: with the Spirit, she exhorts, 'Come!' The single word could be her acceptance of the role within which Revelation's male discourse positions her: accepting and reinforcing her position as ready for penetration.

Yet according to Økland this mimetic role still holds open for Miss Jerusalem her own reserve; she is more than what she mimics. Miss Jerusalem escapes the *telos* of Revelation in the sense of having 'no end in herself'. She is not only open but also eternal; she is not confined to the text's *alpha* and *omega*; indeed, 'she has not yet taken place'. 'Whether she speaks this word only because it is expected of her within male discourse or whether she mimics and simultaneously speaks as the woman of a different "sexe", we cannot know'. In a text, and a world, of unstable gender identity, unstable language, and thus of unstable meaning, there is a freedom; in mimicry and in taking on an '"alien" posture', difference can challenge the dominant, without replacing it.

Like Økland, Caroline Vander Stichele recognizes that language and meaning cannot be separated, and thus she puts under increasing suspicion earlier feminist hopes for a redemptive reclamation of Revelation that severed the medium (the language) from the message (the meaning). Her 'Re-membering the Whore: The Fate of Babylon According to Revelation 17.16' begins by commenting upon approaches that seek to explain away or to justify John's violent rhetoric: the Whore is 'only' a city; the language is 'conventional'; the destruction wrought by the ten horns and the beast 'displays evil's self-destruction'. But more than metaphor is evoked by what Vander Stichele calls 'John's timeless rhetoric of war' in which the beast and its horns will 'hate the whore . . . make her desolate and naked . . . devour her flesh . . . burn her up with fire'. The Whore represents Babylon and so Rome, but she also represents a real woman. Gender cannot be detached from metaphor. The horror is too great, the images are too disturbing, their implications too dangerous.

According to Vander Stichele's lexical analysis, Revelation first presents readers with a female figure in 17.5; not until 17.18 is she identified with a city (πόλις). Thus the horrors to be perpetrated on the Whore are not, at first, associated with the city; they are associated with a woman (γυνή). Like Ezekiel 16, 23, Nahum 3, Isaiah 23 and other Scriptures in which the unfaithful woman/city is destroyed, Revelation presents the punishment as something the woman deserved. John's rhetoric is not original; Vander Stichele also adduces Isaiah 21, Jeremiah 51, and especially Isaiah 47, where Babylon is presented as a queen and where her punishment is to be stripped naked (47.3, see also Ezek. 16.39; 23.10, 29; Nah. 3.6; and compare Rev. 17.16). Thus biblically literate readers are less likely to be horrified by the violence, and more likely to condone it or at least excuse it. Connections of the 'Whore' to 'Jezebel' reinforce this judgment. And once the violence of 'Jezebel's' punishment too is explained (away), it becomes easier to address similar images in similar ways.

Supporting Vander Stichele's refusal to separate gender from metaphor are her observations about Revelation's context. Revelation would not have been as effective, and may have been (more) incomprehensible, had Babylon/Rome been depicted as a male: to compare the 'other' to a woman is to ridicule and denigrate, even as it reinforces the superiority of the (male) self. To describe a city as female is to present it as alien territory to be conquered. Military invasion is analogized to sexual penetration; the colonizer is male and the colonized female. These images are, as Vander Stichele states, more than matters of convention. Even more, the import of this rhetoric derives from the intended male identification with the raped woman: women's experience of sexual violence is therefore both co-opted and suppressed.

These observations continue in Vander Stichele's discussion of the language of 'prostitution'/'fornication'. Revelation 17–19 calls only the woman a 'whore' (πόρνη); her male partners – called 'kings', 'nations' and 'inhabitants of the earth' – participate in '*her* fornication' (πορνείας αὐτῆς). She, like 'Jezebel', has male victims, not male partners; she profits from their trade. Thus Revelation presents prostitution not as the desperate act of a starving woman, or the result of sexual abuse, or a role held by men as well, or even as a rational business decision.[5] Prostitution is presented

---

5 See, e.g., COYOTE, founded in 1973, an organization seeking repeal of laws against prostitution (i.e., decriminalization) and an end to the stigma associated with sex work, including not only prostitution but also stripping, phone sex, and porn actors. COYOTE also provides counseling, legal referrals, and various forms of aid to (mostly women) prostitutes. The organization's name is an acronym for 'Call Off Your Old Tired Ethics'. See also the 'International Committee for Prostitutes' Rights' and the 'Prostitutes' Education Network'.

not as a social reality but as a female-identified moral evil that must be extirpated. The metaphor depends upon and reinscribes gender relations even as it supports other systems of oppression.

Demonstrating this point, Vander Stichele also adopts a postcolonial perspective. As a citizen of Belgium, formerly a colonizing country, she finds herself identified with Babylon as 'the locus of colonial power and oppression'; one block from where she works is Amsterdam's 'red light' district, populated by women from Asia, Africa, South America and Eastern Europe, many of whom are enticed with false promises and entrapped into prostitution. The images converge as Babylon's fate (Rev. 17.16) recalls for Vander Stichele 'the violence done to the women who prostitute themselves'; the personal face and horrible fate she puts on this reminder show how Revelation 17, read from her perspective, creates not a *Sitz im Leben*, a setting in life, but a *Sitz im Tod*, a context of death. While the reader is supposed to rejoice in the death of the Whore, Vander Stichele concludes that 'not every reader does – at least not the resistant reader'.

Revelation recollects prophetic texts of Babylon's destruction and cities equated with women, and it recollects other texts as well; the texts cited then influence the interpretation constructed. A. Yarbro Collins situates the image of the 'Woman Clothed with the Sun' in its historical and cultural context and then complements this history-of-religion approach with an appeal to Jung (we must wait for Stephen D. Moore's essay for Freud's appearance). In Collins's analysis, the Woman in Revelation 12 is not (only) the Virgin Mary, as some traditional Catholic readings concluded, and she is not (only) the personified Israel, Jerusalem, or the covenant community rescued from Egypt, as found in antecedent Scripture. She is the exalted Mother Goddess. Her attributes, including the sun and the zodiac, are associated with Zeus as well as the Ephesian Goddesses (identified with Artemis and Diana), the Syrian Atargatis, and, especially, the Egyptian Isis as well as Leto. The Mother Goddess, in various appellations, was prominent in Asia Minor, and she would have been part of John's cultural context. Both Isis and Leto, like the Woman of Revelation 12, give birth, are persecuted, and are ultimately rescued. Collins then shows how John's narrative also draws upon a mythic pattern, widespread in the ancient Near East and the Greco-Roman world, depicting the defeat of a monster or dragon. According to Collins, this 'conflict may reflect cultural and political changes and struggles' experienced by the tellers of these myths, and they may also reflect 'the basic conflicts in human life and nature' such as between chaos and order, sterility and fertility, death and life.

However, Revelation 12 is not an account in which order is restored. The dragon will not be fully defeated until ch. 20. Here, at the 'sacred marriage' of the Lamb and the Heavenly Jerusalem, Collins sees a reappearance of the Woman of ch. 12. For Collins this figure is 'best understood as the Heavenly Israel', God's spouse 'whom he protects' and mother of the Messiah. The match is harmonious (see Huber's discussion of Roman marital ideals) in that both Bride and Lamb are characterized by power and weakness. The Woman's power resides in her role as Cosmic Queen (echoes sound here of Barr's contribution) and her ability to bear a son who will be the universal king. Her weakness is displayed in ch. 12: vulnerability to the Dragon's attack, inability to protect herself or her child, and dependence on a rescuing hero. Collins also sees in this composite figure a 'paradigm for the audience' of Revelation.

John's community has a heavenly identity: they are God's priests (1.6) and sealed in the book of life (3.5), and they are vulnerable to persecution and martyrdom.

For Collins, John's description of the restoration of order as a wedding not only provides a 'counterbalance' to the celibacy of Rev. 14.1–5, it also includes 'sexuality' as 'a symbol of the new creation, of wholeness, of the time of salvation'. But, less optimistically, the wedding of a city and a sheep may be one in which sexuality is displaced into the spiritual. Since the 'Bride' remains a bride (although see Huber's well-taken comments on her role as 'wife'), it is not clear that the relationship is consummated. Similarly, Collins suggests that John's appropriation of this ancient mythic consciousness indicates that 'he was forced to come to terms with the feminine aspect of the divine'. Or, less generously, perhaps John has co-opted the imagery and domesticated it, as Eve of Genesis 3 can be understood as a domestication of Ancient Near Eastern goddess traditions.

Approaching Revelation 17 still with history-of-religion concerns, Collins finds in the Whore not only the conventional personification of cities as women, but also 'an ancient Near Eastern understanding of goddesses as protectors of particular peoples or cities'. John's depiction of the Whore thus parodies Rome and its Goddess Roma, 'a prostitute who seduces the inhabitants of the earth'.

Finally, following Carl Jung and Erich Neumann (himself relying on J. J. Bachofen), Collins offers a psychological interpretation of these cultural symbols. She rehearses the 'evolution of consciousness' from the time the 'ego is contained in the unconscious', symbolized by the androgynous uroboros, 'the circular snake, the primeval mother, the primal dragon that begets, impregnates, and slays itself', and through subsequent stages, with their attendant myths – e.g., the Great Mother who both nurtures and destroys; the slaying of the dragon and the liberation of the female captive. In this psychological schema, the Woman of ch. 12 is the 'Great Mother' in her protective aspect; she 'represents a new feminine principle that incorporates consciousness and supports the patriarchate'. Her association with the sun and stars and her eagle's wings connect her to 'the masculine world of spirit and thought'. She and her son 'represent the spiritual masculine principle that is in danger of being swallowed by . . . the uroboric dragon that represents the maternal unconscious'. The Bride of ch. 20 plays, analogously, the role of 'female captive held by the dragon' and she who is rescued by her lover/son/consort/lord. Conversely, ch. 17 displays the 'Great Mother' in destructive mode; her seat upon 'many waters' (17.1) is a 'symbol of the feminine unconscious' (Vander Stichele, following Luzia Sutter Rehmann, suggests the image rather evokes the ports where prostitutes were found); her prostitute identity indicates the 'lure toward self-dissolution in the unconscious sea of participation, of non-individuation'. The beast that bears her is, of course, her 'phallic consort'. This Jungian perspective yields the conclusion that Revelation 17 signals Christianity to be a 'religion of individuation and consciousness' struggling to 'free itself from Greco-Roman culture and religion, which were more rooted in the participation mystique'. One might add, although Collins doesn't, that this same Jungian interpretation could be used to find in Christianity a struggle to free itself from the Great (and terrible) Mother of Judaism (phrased this way, the problematic aspects of such archetypal readings [should] become evident).

Also drawing upon Jung but drawing as well upon both her own fundamentalist Christian upbringing and historical-critical approaches to Revelation, Mary Ann

Beavis finds in John's invective and threats what Jung called 'the classical symptoms of chronic virtuousness'; like Jung, she regards his visions as 'sublimations of his fierce resentment of rival teachers and adamant rejection of paganism'. But Beavis rejects Jung's conclusion that the visions are an 'authentic experience of the fearsome side of God'. Instead, she diagnoses the precipitating cause as 'intense resentment and jealousy' of 'Jezebel' and through her of all powerful women.

Putting herself in 'Jezebel's' position (after all, even Paul, given certain circumstances, found no problem with eating meat offered to idols [cf. 1 Cor. 8.4,8], and the Thyatiran prophet's accommodationism is politically expedient [cf. 1 Pet. 1.17]), Beavis finds John's vindictive prophecies to be false and 'the charism of Rev. 22.21 . . . a more authentic expression of the best in Christianity'.

In a second redemptory move, she sees in the Bride/the New Jerusalem the presence of 'Dame Wisdom', and of the 'Hebrew Goddess' Chochmah/Sophia. She also sees, as does Collins, how the Woman Clothed with the Sun (12.1), the Earth (12.16), the Whore (17.1–6), and the Bride (19.7; 21.2, 9; 22.17) evoke ancient goddesses/the Goddess/the Queen of Heaven. The Sun Woman presents a synthesis of the Leto–Apollo–Python and Isis–Horus–Typhon stories, with perhaps allusions to the constellation Virgo and a pantheon of other goddesses. In Rev. 12.16, John states, 'And the Earth (γή) helped the woman.' The term γή appears 77 times in Revelation (an appropriate number), but in ch. 12 the term 'comes to life' to save a sister goddess. She 'swallowed the river which the Dragon had poured from his mouth' (Rev. 12.16). She is thus the voice of communion, of environmental healing. She is the symbol of integration, interdependence, or, to return to Marshall's point, of the very hybridity that John so abhors.

Despite John's attempt to suppress his female competitors real and allegorical – denying 'Jezebel' her real name; making the heavenly Jerusalem not a true bride but only 'like' one (ὡς νύμφην [Rev. 21.2]), masking the Goddess archetype behind the 'ancient serpent'; associating corrupt and destroyed Babylon with Roma; turning the ancient adulterous but now rehabilitated wife, Israel, once rescued from Egypt and Pharaoh into the gated New Jerusalem – the Goddess breaks out.

Through numerous critical approaches, 'Jezebel'/the Whore and the Woman Clothed with the Sun/the Bride/Heavenly Jerusalem can be seen as mirror images. But in his investigation of how Revelation employs rhetography – the rhetoric of the senses – in depicting the intertwined categories of wealth and gender, Greg Carey finds gaps in the comparison. In the sensory world John creates, Rome's acquisitiveness and exploitation contrast and compete with the purity and life-giving attributes of New Jerusalem. Rome may be opulent in its wealth, yet New Jerusalem is '*even more opulent*'. The distinction is in the *kinds* of wealth each city possesses, kinds that can be distinguished by sight, touch, taste, sound and smell.

Revelation codes Babylon the Whore and more broadly what Carey labels the 'Beast group' in the trappings of sensory materiality; the Whore's 'vibrant colors, rich tastes, fragrant odors, and melodic sounds' contrast with the 'white garments, "pure" or "clear" gold and precious stones, the tastes and smells of water and unspecified fruit, and a different array of sounds' of New Jerusalem and the 'Lamb group'. While Collins, since she finds no evidence of sexual desire in the description of Babylon/Rome, questions the claim that Revelation 17 is sadistic, erotic and pornographic, Carey's rhetographical study might nuance her conclusion.

In this 'ascetic aesthetic', abstraction, purity, and – to extend Carey's claims, perhaps spirit – triumph over specificity, sensuality and, by extension again, materiality. The pure, cold, hard New Jerusalem may be a bride, but she also bears a sense of virility. Babylon and the 'Beast group' share some of these masculine codes, but the rhetographical array codes this collective as soft and discordant, luxurious in scarlet and purple, intoxicated and intoxicating, absorbing rather than reflecting, unnatural (since her possessions can be stripped from her) and repulsive.

The sensory descriptions of Babylon and her cohort lead Carey to detect connections to the 'Strange Woman' of Proverbs 7; missing, however, for him is a connection between New Jerusalem and the 'Lamb group' and Woman Wisdom (Beavis, working through Goddess traditions, offers a different reading). Those 144,000 virgins not only do not defile themselves with human women or their metaphoric counterpart of Babylon/Rome, they do not even come into contact with Woman Wisdom. Thus, as Carey proposes, the text may well not only call the followers of the Lamb 'to abandon the social, cultural, commercial and religious systems of Roman imperial life', it may also call them away from wives and children, physical intimacy and delight in Creation. This observation then segues nicely into Huber's analysis of John's wedding imagery.

John's term 'Apocalypse' (ἀποκάλυψις) not only intimates the bringing of something hidden into the light, it also denotes the act of lifting the veil. It is similar linguistically to ἀνακάλυπσις, the lifting of the bride's veil at the wedding. Thus, as Lynn R. Huber observes, John's depiction of the wedding between Heavenly Jerusalem and the Lamb 'mimics Roman nuptial-familial rhetoric as part of his overall critique of the Roman Empire'. Huber's invocation of Roman imperial discourse and in particular Roman gender conventions complements the approaches to Revelation 19.1–8 which draw upon images from Israel's Scriptures (e.g., Ezekiel 16, Hosea 1–2, Isa. 61.10, and see Vander Stichele's contribution). Using familial and nuptial imagery – references to the Wife's having prepared herself (ἡ γυνὴ αὐτοῦ ἡτοίμασεν ἑαυτήν) and to the wedding (ὁ γάμος) of the Lamb, John's focus on the family offers an alternative to Roman family values, satirized as prostitution (τὴν πόρνην τὴν μεγάλην). At the same time, the traditional imagery threatens to maintain the status quo.

According to Huber, from the reign of Augustus onward (that is, from 27 BCE), family values was the watchword, if not the practice, of the Empire. Coinage, inscriptions, monumental art, legislation and cults promoted Caesar as the guardian of Rome's traditional values: piety to the gods, duty to the state, protection of the family (*familia*) and the household (*domus*, οἶκος), which were seen as essential to the maintenance of civic order. Roman marriage was seen as a partnership (*societas/* κοινωνία), based on mutual assent (*concordia*) and not a legal contract. In this configuration, woman's assent was to chastity and self-control (σωφροσύνης), maternal responsibility and spousal fidelity. Women were expected to marry (a point reinforced by the double meaning of γυνή as 'woman' and 'wife'), engage in cloth production and bear children.

If Revelation were composed during Domitian's reign, then Huber's study of Revelation's alternative family values becomes even more persuasive. Suetonius, who depicts Domitian as a philanderer, nevertheless mentions that the emperor sought to correct 'public morals' and that despite his own adulterous liaisons, he sought to enforce the laws forbidding adultery (*Dom.* 8). In the prevailing social discourse, the imperial family was meant to represent the ideal family, as Rome's *Arc Pacis* epitomizes and as numerous coins depicting Domitian and his wife, Domitia Longina (despite her own temporary exile for committing adultery), promote. More, imperial rhetoric depicted the royal household not only as the ideal, but also as divine, as part of the *domus divina*. Coinage from Domitian's reign depicts his divinized infant son sitting upon a globe. Thus Roman social discourse united political and familial imagery.

In Revelation's alternative vision, the divine family is not that of Domitian and Domitia Longina, but of the Lamb and the Heavenly Jerusalem. The counter-image is, Huber demonstrates, reinforced by tenses: in John's vision, the wedding is a present reality; it 'has come' (ἦλθεν [19.7]). The bride (*nova nupta*, νύμφη) has become a wife (γυνή [19.7]). In Roman society, this transition is symbolized by the *deduction*, the bride's journey from her (father's) home to the home of the groom. But, as Huber remarks, John offers no conclusion to the wedding. Rev. 21.1,10 envision the Bride (νύμφη) as still/always in the process of 'descending' (κατα-βαίνουσαν), in 'a state of perpetual *deductio*'.

This Bride is not simply a passive figure, and thus she serves as a fitting model for John's community, given a bit of gender-bending. Brides were expected to weave their own garment, the 'tunica recta'; in Revelation this becomes the fine linen, which is 'the just work of the saints' (19.8). Just as the Bride 'has prepared herself' (ἡτοίμασεν ἑαυτήν [19.7]), so too will John's community prepare to move from the world of the Whore to that of the Bride. Just as the garment is 'pure' (καθαρός [19.8]) – its weaving connotes the purity of the wife at her spindle – so the community will be chaste and faithful, pure virgin and loyal wife. But whereas the Roman wife was expected to bear children, the Bride of the Lamb, as Church or as member, would remain celibate. Images collapse into other images: members of the Church envision themselves as women, but the women do not fulfill their conventional roles; the female Bride and Heavenly Jerusalem become masculinized as they represent John's faithful ideal. As the wedding celebration continues, readers will determine how to understand their place in the reception.

Had Stephen D. Moore remained in either Cistercian sanctuary or Pentecostal prayer, the Beatific Vision and unending worship of the Divine (4.8–11; 5.13–14; 7.9–12,15; 8.3–4; 11.15–18; 14.1–3; 15.2–4; 19.1–18; 21.22–23; 22.3–5) might have been for him the grandest celebration and the most fitting reception. But as contemplation yields to Freud and charismatics to Derrida, Moore begins to query whether the relation of God to humanity is different in kind than that of Freud's powerful, dominant, large father to the small, powerless, dependent children, or whether transcendence trumps analogy. He asks, 'What if at the core of all these subtle scholastic formulations there were nothing but a superhuman being after all – an embarrassingly muscular being, insatiably hungry for adulation, but subjected to a stringent diet throughout centuries of (unsuccessful) Christian apologetics aimed at stripping away its all-too-robust flesh?' If metaphor is not 'only' metaphor, and if images are interpreted through our own cultural contexts then how might the Beatific Vision be understood, or analogized, in today's American culture? The answer, Moore suggests in a neat display of anachronistic anagogy, is in the spectacle of the bodybuilder. The sight is, as he reveals, replete with excesses and horrors, and we readers, 'his slaves' (Rev. 22.3), cannot look away.

The relation of Revelation to bodybuilding could have been anticipated, had critics but interpreted the signs correctly. Constantine (!) Daniel Vafiadis, one of the members of Mae West's Musclemen Review, took the name 'Dan Vadis' – one might imagine a brother named 'Quo' – and went on to star in such memorable Italian (Roman) epics as *Ercole l'invincibile* and *Spartaco e i dieci gladiatori*. The films have their fascist, hypermasculine, and perhaps ultimately impotent components, which returns us to Moore's essay and Revelation.

Moore highlights Revelation's own fascist components. Not merely presenting a simple reversal of Roman values, 'it represents the apotheosis of this imperial theology, its ascension to a transhistorical site'. In John's detailed descriptions of the accoutrements of the divine throne room, the attendants and their activities, Moore finds bigger and louder and grander recapitulations of the Roman imperial court, and in particular the court of the deified Domitian, 'our Lord and our God' (*dominus et deus noster*) and his 'preposterously phallic' cult. In this comparison, the 'Holy Other' emerges as distinct only in quantity, not quality; the Divine Empire is the Roman Empire with a different ruler and grander features. On the throne, almost aphasic (like the Bride, but we might listen with Økland's ears), the hypermasculine emperor is also impotent and increasingly feminized.

Moore ends his original article with a postscript on the Beatific Vision, narcissism and voyeurism, for 'the act of looking, watching, staring, gazing, gaping, gawking, gawping, ogling . . . eternally transmuted into an act of enraptured worship, defines the audience of the heavenly throne room no less than the stereotypical voyeur, crouched behind a bush and transfixed by his own Beatific Vision'. Translating this vision into 'a more contemporary idiom' or 'Beautific Vision', Moore moves from Go(l)d's Gym to reality television, and specifically to the theophanies and the 'great reveals' of *Extreme Makeovers* and *The Swan*: the suffering of the martyrs (to the cult of beauty) and their resurrection to the accolades ('oohs and aaahs') of the audience/adorers for whom Beauty equals Truth. Thus Revelation's great promise and reward is, as Moore observes, not to see God's truth or justice or mercy, but to see God's 'face' (Rev. 22.4). At the conclusion of his article, one would be hard- (or bench-) pressed to gaze at either Revelation, or 'reality television', in quite the same way.

With Catherine Keller's 'Ms.Calculating the Endtimes', the numerous themes sounded throughout this collection reappear: Virgins and Whores, Sex and Violence, Historical Contexts and Present Intertexts, Opulence and Oppression, Sublime Goddess and Silenced *Gyne*, Colonialism and Consumerism, Mimesis and Messianism. The themes are then heard more acutely, or seen with greater clarity, as Keller glosses her original chapter from her *God and Power: Counter-Apocalyptic Journeys* in response to editorial questions. Embedded in this reworking are also excerpts from other chapters in *God and Power*. The resultant conversation shows both the feminist process and the fruits of friendship.

Keller seeks to 'transcode the apocalyptic form of gender symbolism', by which she means both revealing John's binary, dualistic gender codes and interrupting them. The task is both political and theological; it recognizes that the apocalyptic emerges from positions (real or perceived) of marginality, adopts a revolutionary or reactionary stance, and is always threatened by being seduced by the rhetoric and stance of the group it opposes. Her own Counter-Apocalypse, like Moore's, proceeds with apt and apteral references to contemporary loci of spectacle and worship: *WrestleMania* and *Terminator* franchises, Arnold Schwarzenegger and militant machismo. But as she notes as well, 'at a certain historical angle, the apocalyptic Other turns out to be inseparable from the feminist self'. The women's movement has its origins in nineteenth-century millennialist rhetoric, and even oppositions to Christian apocalyptic ideology – from Marxist meta-narratives to Mary Daly's Metaethics – take on the 'demonizing dualism of apocalypse': hope against hope, righteous rage, purity of martyrs, eschatological urgency. Citing, inter alia, Shaker hymns, Frances Willard and Matilda Josyln Gage, Keller traces several female utopian visions that resisted apocalyptic masculinity from within apocalyptic discourse.

Feminist thought today tends to eschew the essentialisms that marked these earlier movements and discourses, save where essentialism is strategic. But as Keller shows, bits of apocalypse remain hidden in feminism. Her project, 'counter-apocalypse', seeks to counteract the dualism of the apocalyptic as well as its ascetic, heroic and dominating masculinity, without losing the justice for which it yearns and the alternative vision that sustains the critique of the present. The project is both complicated and enriched by Keller's attention to communities of readers. She describes, for example, how some 'liberation and third-world Christians have found in this text a stunning prophetic solidarity with the plight of the oppressed' and an exposure of 'the empire of late capitalist global economics'. But she also shows how this demonizing of global economy risks recapitulating the problems rather than working to resolve them (in divinity schools, 'globalism' is usually equated with exploitation, colonialism and elitism; in business schools, it is often seen as an opportunity for mutually beneficial cultural and economic exchange). The righteous anger of the liberation theologian does sometimes bleed into sexist and heterosexist (and, I might add, anti-Jewish) pieties; when John's violent rhetoric is seen as merely epiphenomenal, as having no intrinsic connection to the message of justice, such bleeding is facilitated. Meanwhile, 'the poor' may reject the politicized reading of Revelation, with its critique of global capital and colonialism; their preferential option may well be for Pentecostalism and the Prosperity Gospel exported along with the Pax Americana.

To envision a Counter-Apocalypse, Keller offers several possible moves, including parody, for already the Whore of Babylon is a parody of Roma, of the Roman Empire, of colonial power. The difficulty then becomes distinguishing between parody and colonial mimicry; the demand becomes determining who will, again, get hurt. A parody of the Iraq War, for example, might not be found amusing by the parents of a soldier killed in action. Another move is to anticipate, or listen for, the new, that which is 'coming', the Parousia of multiplicity and the gender-ambiguous Spirit to which our senses attend and to which we must be open and unveiled. Here Keller and Økland may be listening through the same keyhole.

The symbols of Revelation remain open, the wedding celebration is ongoing, and interpretations continue. Some readers will refuse to rejoice at the dismemberment of the Woman-who-is-Babylon; they will resist the (masochistic? infantile?) self-abasement before this imperial Deity who rules by patriarchal domination. Others will conclude that these descriptions are 'only' metaphors, separate form from substance, and worship the transcendent to which the metaphors imperfectly point. Some readers will understand, if not fully condone, John's rhetoric by seeking his political and social location; others will condone, if not fully understand, how the Apocalypse can provide comfort to those undergoing persecution or deprivation. Some readers may reject the coercive aspects of a choice between spending eternity in praise of the divine or being 'tortured [βασανισθῆναι] with fire and sulfur . . . the smoke of [one's] torment' ascending 'for ever and ever' (14.10–11; cf. 9.5; 20.15; 21.8); others may rejoice in their own salvation while believing that those being tortured deserve every pain inflicted upon them; still others may use mimicry or parody or anachronistic analogy to challenge, defang or replace John's message. What we find behind the veil may be beautiful, or terrifying, or both, but we cannot avert our eyes: John's vision is too influential today, in our own political climate, not to look for ourselves.

GENDER AND EMPIRE: SEXUALIZED VIOLENCE IN JOHN'S ANTI-IMPERIAL APOCALYPSE*

JOHN W. MARSHALL

Introduction

The two female figures who are the subject of violence and/or threats of violence in the book of Revelation, Jezebel and Babylon, are both portrayed negatively and in explicitly sexual terms. The shortest summary of the sexualized violence in Revelation might be 'Two whores, one John'. While the figure Babylon works fully in the realm of metaphor as a personification of the diabolically driven power of Rome, Jezebel may refer to an actual historical woman whom John condemns. These two female figures bear the weight of John's polemic against political, economic, religious and sexual morality in the larger Greco-Roman world (in the case of Babylon), and in the smaller community of people devoted to Jesus (in the case of Jezebel). In addition to their gender and to John's violent and sexually coded castigation of them, the two figures are related by a third factor, though as poles of a contrast: each polemic is deeply conditioned by the setting of the Apocalypse in a subaltern group in a colonial context. Understanding the relation of these three factors, this essay argues that the sexualized violence against female figures both within and without his community is a function of John's position as a resistant writer within a situation of colonialism. Moreover, it sees the character of his resistance as substantially formed by the phenomenon against which he writes. Recognizing how sexualized violence in Revelation is informed by postcolonial theory enables scholars to move beyond a reading that either valorizes or condemns John's Apocalypse to a reading that understands the role of gender in it as well as permits a distance from and critique of that role.

To that end, I treat first the situation of John's Apocalypse with a close eye to political circumstances. I then turn to readings of the Jezebel and Babylon passages which are conditioned by my understanding of John's political context and by the theoretical resources I find helpful in understanding that context, namely those of postcolonial theory.[1]

* This paper draws from John W. Marshall, 'Collateral Damage: Jesus and Jezebel in the Jewish War', in E. Leigh Gibson and Shelley Matthews (eds), *Violence in the New Testament* (London: T&T Clark, 2005), pp. 35–50 as well as *idem*, 'Who's on the Throne: Revelation in the Long Year', in Ra'anan S. Boustan and Annette Yoshiko Reed (eds), *Heavenly Realms and Earthly Realities in Late Antique Religions* (Cambridge, UK: Cambridge University Press, 2004), pp. 123–41.

1 On applications of postcolonialism within biblical studies, see R. S. Sugirtharajah, *Postcolonial Criticism and Biblical Interpretation* (Oxford: Oxford University Press, 2002); *idem*, *The Bible and the Third World: Precolonial, Colonial and Postcolonial Encounters* (Cambridge and New York: Cambridge University Press, 2001); *idem*, 'A Brief Memorandum on Postcolonialism and Biblical Studies', *JSNT* 73 (1999), pp. 3–5; R. S. Sugirtharajah (ed.), *Postcolonial Perspectives on the New Testament and its Interpretation*, *JSNT* 73 (1999), pp. 3–135; *idem*, *The Postcolonial Bible* (Sheffield:

Three questions set the agenda here: In what historical context did John compose? In what religious context did John formulate his vision? And in what political formation did the exigence for John's writing arise?[2] Thus I will first sketch a case for the wartime context of Revelation; second, I shall attempt to map the situation of Revelation in social and religious terms; third, I shall endeavor to bring to bear on Revelation a mode of historiography informed by postcolonial analyses that can illuminate a key cross-cultural phenomenon that conditions the book's entire setting, exigence and stance.

Axes of Violence

Violence in John's Apocalypse runs along several axes: Babylon and the angels, Michael and the Dragon, the two witnesses and the people of the Great City, the Son of God and the children of Jezebel, The Word of God and the Gentiles. These are all terms from within John's Apocalypse: transforming them to entities and relationships in John's social world is a complex undertaking. Overwhelmingly these depictions of violence elaborate a conflict between, on the one hand, the Holy City and its divine patron, and, on the other, the Great City – Babylon and Rome – of

---

Sheffield Academic Press, 1998); F. F. Segovia, *Decolonizing Biblical Studies: A View from the Margins* (Maryknoll, NY: Orbis Books, 2000); and 'Postcolonial and Diasporic Criticism in Biblical Studies: Focus, Parameters, Relevance', *Studies in World Christianity* 5 (1999), pp. 177–95; Musa W. Dube, *Postcolonial Feminist Interpretation of the Bible* (St. Louis, MO: Chalice Press, 2000). In the study of the Apocalypse, Tina Pippin, *Death and Desire: The Rhetoric of Gender in the Apocalypse of John* (Literary Currents in Biblical Interpretation; Louisville, KY: Westminster/John Knox Press, 1992) and Greg Carey, *Elusive Apocalypse: Reading Authority in the Revelation to John* (Macon, GA: Mercer University Press, 1999) make some of the first attempts to offer a postcolonial reading; Steven J. Friesen, *Imperial Cults and the Apocalypse of John: Reading Revelation in the Ruins* (Oxford: Oxford University Press, 2001), p. 17, argues against 'direct and detailed application of postcolonial methods'. See also Jean K. Kim, '"Uncovering Her Wickedness": An Inter (Con) Textual Reading of Revelation 17 from a Postcolonial Feminist Perspective', *JSNT* 73 (1999), pp. 61–81. Within the broad field of interpretative strategies with debts to postcolonial theory, I have tried to outline a historical-critical postcolonialism; see John W. Marshall, 'Postcolonialism and the Practice of History', in Caroline Vander Stichele and Todd Penner (eds), *Her Master's Tools? Feminist and Postcolonial Engagements of Historical-Critical Discourse* (Atlanta, GA: Society of Biblical Literature, 2005), pp. 93–108. For criticisms and response on postcolonialism and the study of early Christianity, see Amy-Jill Levine, 'The Disease of Postcolonial New Testament Studies and the Hermeneutics of Healing, with responses by Kwok Pui-lan, Musimbi Kanyoro, Adele Reinhartz, Hisako Kinukawa, Elaine Wainwright', *JFSR* 20/1 (2004), pp. 91–141.

2 As an aside, I should address how my case might function should a reader remain unconvinced of the particular timeframe within which I read Revelation. The aftermath of the Jewish War extends for generations after the cessation of the conflict itself. Indeed it may be argued that it was only the final failure of the Bar Cochba rebellion that put the Jewish War to rest, and even then it only transformed it into a larger narrative of worldly defeat and spiritual renewal of the Jewish covenants with the God of Abraham, Isaac, and Jacob. It is not possible to generalize the effect of the roughly 35-year gap between a dating in 69/70 CE and a dating in 95/96 CE. In either case, 'Christianity' and therefore also 'Jewish Christianity' is an unavailable category in the period under analysis, and the intensity of investment in God's care for his people and God's judgment on Rome remains vivid. Particulars of the *ex eventu* character of John's vision would need revision under an alternate dating, but his handling of gender and violence, and his position among a subject people in a colonial context, would retain substantially the same shape.

which Satan is the patron. Almost always, the violence in the Apocalypse is a recon-figuration of this conflict worked out through a variety of literary proxies.[3] Violence in Revelation is either the direct product of this clash of divine powers or it is the well-modulated and considered suffering permitted to the people of God in their destined fulfillment of the eschatological program. Rev. 6.10–11, in which 'the souls of those who had been slain for The Word of God' cry out for an answer of how long the suffering will continue and are told that it will be a little longer – until the appropriate number have been killed – stands as the paradigmatic example of such suffering that seems to be directly caused by the enemies of God but is portrayed as controlled by God.

The sole exception to the dominant pattern of inter-religious conflict is the struggle over false teachers in the messages to the seven assemblies in which figures named Jezebel and Balaam as well as a group called the Nicolaitans receive sharp condemnations. The threats of violence reach their apex with Jezebel. But even though the threat against Jezebel stands as a nearly singular depiction of intra-religious violence, I argue that the circumstances that generate the depiction of violence against the outsider (figured as Babylon) also generate the depiction of the violence against the insider (figured as Jezebel). In both cases, the violence against female figures is heavily inflected with sexual imagery. Sexualized violence against women is one of John's primary modes of depicting God's judgment.

Date

Dating the Apocalypse is a task fraught with uncertainty, and the more precise one's hypothesis, the smaller the circle of agreement it can command. Despite this eminently sensible observation, I find myself persuaded by quite a narrow window and quite a specific circumstance: the Jewish Diaspora in western Asia Minor during the latter stages of the Jewish War, in the long year, 69 CE, or immediately following. I have made a more extensive argument elsewhere[4]; here a brief sketch of the case must suffice. First, it is widely agreed that the reign of Nero and its chaotic aftermath provide the most plausible and simple referents for interpreting the numbering of emperors in ch. 17 and the gematria in ch. 13; there is no need for starting in the middle of the sequence or finding reasons to omit emperors. Second, the scene at the beginning of ch. 11 where the outer zones of the Holy City are given over to the Gentiles is to a great degree understandable in the midst of the Jewish War. Third, I find the arguments about the value of Irenaeus's poorly informed testimony in the latter half of the second century unpersuasive[5] and the use of the term 'Babylon'

3 While it is possible to treat all polemic as violent, the Apocalypse is so rich in depictions of acts causing physical pain, bodily injury, death and destruction, not to mention damnation, that for my purposes I use the term violence to refer to these acts as depicted in the text.

4 John W. Marshall, *Parables of War: Reading John's Jewish Apocalypse* (Waterloo, ON.: Wilfrid Laurier University Press, 2001), pp. 88–97.

5 Irenaeus writes near the end of the second century that the vision of the Apocalypse was seen 'almost in our own day, towards the end of Domitian's reign' (*Against Heresies* 5.30.3) and A. Yarbro Collins considers Domitian's testimony 'crucial' and the 'strongest external evidence' for dating Revelation (*Crisis and Catharsis: The Power of the Apocalypse* [Philadelphia, PA: Westminster/John Knox Press, 1984], pp. 57, 76).

insufficient to distinguish the aftermath of the war from its course. These are merely topics and do not constitute an argument, but they should illuminate the larger understanding that undergirds a date in late 69 or early 70 CE.[6]

Cultural and Political Context

Such a date is quite significant for Jewish communities in the ancient world. The armies of Rome had surrounded the Holy City and seemed to teeter between over-running the Temple of God and turning in on themselves in a storm of self-destruction, marching away from Jerusalem to continue the conflagration that engulfed northern Italy itself as emperor slew emperor in dizzying succession.[7] In the uncertainty of the long year, which Tacitus in a fit of Roman eschatological pessimism describes as looking by all accounts like the Empire's last,[8] John's community sought to make sense of Rome's violence upon Jerusalem and to recon-cile it with their hope in the power of their God and his Christ.

Beyond the particular political exigencies of the date under which I read Revelation, it is also necessary to consider larger political and cultural structures. Programmatically and historically I read the Roman Empire as a colonial empire and the Book of Revelation as a Jewish book.

The first position proceeds from understanding colonialism not as a phenomenon subject to narrow cultural and chronological borders but as constituted by broad features of political structure. Three factors indicate that the Roman Empire can be understood as a colonial empire and its political project as colonialist (as one descriptor among several justifiable): domination, exploitation and an ideology of natural domination. These three dimensions spread attention among the political, economic, cultural and discursive elements of colonialism.

First, colonization involves domination. One people rules over another. Military strength, deployed and threatened, is a significant factor in the maintenance of domination. The relationship between peoples is asymmetrical; the colonizers, for their own benefit, move populations into the colonized land. The colonized are displaced in various modes – internally, diasporically – again to the advantage of the colonizers but also to the benefit of local elites among the colonized. Politics too in colonized lands are deeply transformed either through enforced reformation or through the influence, direct or indirect, of a superordinate power.

Second, colonization involves exploitation, and this too takes many forms. The establishment of domination may entail the extraction of booty and the expropri-ation of land and resources. Tax and tribute may be paid in kind or in currencies. Structures of law favor the colonizers. Expropriation, tariffs, duties, levies and other forms of exploitation compound the extraction of wealth from the colony. Exploitation, however, spans a wider field than can be described with a balance

---

6 See recently George H. Van Kooten, 'The Year of the Four Emperors and the Revelation of John: The "pro-Neronian" Emperors Otho and Vitellius, and the Images and Colossus of Nero in Rome', *JSNT* 30 (2007), pp. 205–48.

7 See accounts in Tacitus and Suetonius as well as the standard treatment in Kenneth Wellesley, *The Long Year A.D. 69* (London: Paul Elek, 1975).

8 Tacitus, *Histories* 1.11.

sheet: it involves the restructuring and re-orientation of subordinate economies and cultures.

Third, colonialism propagates, in addition to its material effects, a discourse of hierarchy and right that justifies and contributes to the maintenance of colonial domination. This discourse, which has been the object of extensive theorization and critique, is one of the most culturally specific elements of colonialism: it is always articulated in relation to its contemporary ideological and epistemological framework. For example, the discourse of scientific racism that characterized later European colonialism was present neither in early European colonialism nor in the Roman context.

I also have argued elsewhere that the Book of Revelation is properly understood as a Jewish text. By this I mean a text that is a part of a Judaism that does not conceive itself as Christian and that cannot be understood as Christian within a polythetic and historical–critical understanding of the phenomenon of religion.[9] John's ethnic map is a Jewish map – a world of Jews and Gentiles – and his own name locates him in the Jewish territory of that map (Rev. 7.1–10; 10.11; 11.9; 17.15). His ideals of calendar and worship and his idealization of the heavenly Temple of the God of Israel situate him within Second Temple Judaism. So do his commitments to the 'commandments of God' (Rev. 12.17; 14.12). His care for purity is evident in descriptions of the Holy City (Rev. 21.27) and in his repeated emphasis on the washed and ritually pure robes of the saints (Rev. 7.4, 15.6; 19.8, 14; 22.14); conversely, Babylon is the haunt of the unclean spirits (Rev. 18.2). John's mythological heritage is that of the Hebrew Bible inflected by the wide experiences of Jews living in the Greco-Roman world.[10] All of this takes place in a time when 'Christian' is not an identity articulated as such. John and his audience see themselves as Jews through and through (cf. Rev. 2.9; 3.9) who keep the commandments, who are drawn from Israel, and whose destiny is God's Holy City.[11] Reading Revelation as Jewish and as in Roman colonial context is a basic responsibility of historical and critical reading.

Postcolonialism

John's Apocalypse depicts a chilling threat of violence against a fellow worshiper of Jesus. The following words are attributed to 'the Son of God', Jesus, in Rev. 2.22 and the beginning of v. 23:

---

9 Marshall, *Parables of War,* pp. 45–54; Jonathan Z. Smith, 'Fences and Neighbors: Some Contours of Early Judaism' in his *Imagining Religion: From Babylon to Jonestown* (Chicago, IL: University of Chicago Press, 1982), pp. 1–18.

10 A. Yarbro Collins, *The Combat Myth in the Book of Revelation* (HDR, 9; Missoula, MT: Scholars Press, 1976) and John W. Marshall, 'The Patriarchs and the Zodiac', in Richard S. Ascough (ed.), *Religious Rivalries and the Struggle for Success in Sardis and Smyrna* (Waterloo, ON.: Wilfrid Laurier University Press, 2005), pp. 186–213.

11 This form of argument on the Jewish character of John's Revelation is drawn from a more extensive presentation of it in John W. Marshall, 'John's Jewish (Christian?) Apocalypse', in Matt A. Jackson-McCabe (ed.), *Jewish Christianity Reconsidered: Rethinking Ancient Groups and Texts* (Minneapolis, MN: Fortress Press, 2007), pp. 233–56.

> Watch, I'll shove her on a bed, and make her lovers suffer terribly, unless they turn away from what she does. And I'm going to kill her children, dead.

Though this translation is accurate in its particulars and powerful in its vividness, it may not be as familiar as the Revised Standard Version's rendering:

> Behold, I will throw her on a sickbed, and those who commit adultery with her I will throw into great tribulation, unless they repent of her doings; and I will strike her children dead.[12]

In removing the liturgical Sunday-best that this text usually wears, I have attempted to make clear its violent intervention in a religious rivalry within a subaltern group. Jesus, referred to in this particular message as the Son of God (Rev. 2.18), is talking about a woman that the Book of Revelation calls 'Jezebel'. It is in this text, in this threat, that I see the situation of the Apocalypse exemplified, the conditions of its composition distilled, and the tableau of its origins brought into sharp focus.

Jezebel is not called a harlot or a whore in English translations of the text of Revelation, but the accusation is unmistakable both in Greek and in its echoes of the portrayal of Jezebel in 2 Kgs 9.22.[13] The action from which Jezebel was, according to Rev. 2.21, formerly given time to repent is her πορνείας. At its root, the term indicates the commerce of prostitution, but its meaning extends to the wider field of improper sexual activity.[14] By accusing Jezebel of πορνείας, Revelation casts her as a prostitute. I have gravitated to the set of English terms around 'whore' because the range of nouns, adjectives and verbs available from the same root in English closely matches the range of Greek terms based on πόρνη.

The accusation of whoring is no less bitter, and the threat of infanticide no less violent, than the times and circumstances in which John lived, and yet the bitterness of the condemnation and the intensity of the threat demand explanation. Traditional explanations dwell on the ways by which apocalyptic channels for the construction of knowledge and eschatological scenarios for the rectification of imperfection raise the stakes in argument. To see, or set, one's argument in the structure of the universe and the divine plan draws to a shrill pitch the conflicts that so regularly afflict new religious movements. Others have focused on the well-known fervor of insider conflict. Jonathan Z. Smith's description of the offense of the proximate other captures some of the heat generated in the crucible of insider conflict: 'While the "other" may be perceived as being either LIKE-US or NOT-LIKE-US, he is, in fact, most problematic when he is TOO-MUCH-LIKE-US, or when he claims to BE-US'.[15]

---

12 Translations are from the RSV unless noted.

13 See also Marshall, *Parables of War*, pp. 127–31.

14 See Paul Duff, *Who Rides the Beast? Prophetic Rivalry and the Rhetoric of Crisis in the Churches of the Apocalypse* (New York: Oxford University Press, 2001), p. 55, for a helpful analysis of the history and semantic field of πορνεία and related terms in their application to Jezebel.

15 Jonathan Z. Smith, 'What a Difference a Difference Makes', in J. Neusner and E. S. Frerichs (eds), *To See Ourselves as Others See Us: Christians, Jews, 'Others' in Late Antiquity* (Scholars Press Studies in the Humanities; Chico, CA: Scholars Press, 1985), pp. 3–48 (5, 47) [capitalization original].

Exploring John's strident efforts to differentiate himself from his 'other', specifically with regard to the 'synagogue of Satan' passages, David Frankfurter helpfully notes how proximate position and fuzzy borders generate a rhetoric of extreme distance and sharp borders.[16] We can connect these insights to John's specific chronological, geographical and cultural setting: 69 CE, during the larger Jewish War of 66–70 CE; the Jewish diaspora; a hybrid community in a colonial empire. This latest characterization of the cultural context invites the application of postcolonial theory.

Postcolonialism theorizes the phenomenon of colonization as a basic form of human interaction; it conditions particular circumstances as powerfully and pervasively as do the objects of other analyses: as pervasively as race, as powerfully as gender, as persistently as class. By and large postcolonial scholarship has been oriented to the last five centuries of Europe's colonial endeavor, a large part of it devoted to the reconsideration and re-interpretation of literary works – from both the colony and metropole – with a disciplined attention to colonization's historical and discursive dynamics. Other trajectories work in a more social-historical mode, most prominently the subaltern studies group focused especially on peasant politics of South Asia. The major theorists of this movement – revered, attacked, dismissed and cited – include Homi Bhabha, Gayatri Spivak, Ranjit Guha, Edward Said and Partha Chatterjee. Two analytical concepts elaborated by postcolonialists can illuminate the insider violence of John's Apocalypse: the first is hybridity; the second concerns the role of women as a topos of argumentation in colonial settings.

The notion of hybridity encompasses several locations in the literal and social geography of the colonial encounter. It is the condition of creative and contentious mixing of traditions and cultures that the colonized subject must negotiate.[17] It flowers in the colonial elite's value-laden embrace of elements of the subject culture seen also in a slightly less hierarchical mode in the foreignness of the expatriate community. 'Hybridity' also names the compromised condition of colonial authority. Diaspora is a paradigmatic location of hybridity as the dispersed negotiate what it means to be themselves in a new space. New spaces cannot support old selves, and the tensions of maintenance and modification – fraught always with questions of value and hypotheses of essence – afflict the colonized in the homeland and, just as surely, those in dispersion.[18]

16 David Frankfurter, 'Jews or Not? Reconstructing the "Other" in Rev 2:9 and 3:9', *HTR* 94 (2001), pp. 403–25.

17 Homi K. Bhabha, 'Signs Taken for Wonders: Questions of Ambivalence and Authority under a Tree Outside Delhi, May 1817', in his *The Location of Culture* (London: Routledge, 1994), pp. 102–22.

18 The literature of diasporic studies is substantial and within the phenomenon various forms of diaspora are commonly distinguished. The most common distinction is between populations dispersed under conditions of foreign rule and settler diasporas that are supportive of, allied with, and at least partially representative of the colonial power and its apparatus. The Jewish diaspora of antiquity was formed under a long span of time and a variety of conditions, of which foreign domination was one of the most frequent and significant. See John M. G. Barclay, *Jews in the Mediterranean Diaspora: From Alexander to Trajan* (Edinburgh: T&T Clark, 1996), and Eric S. Gruen, *Diaspora: Jews Amidst Greeks and Romans* (Cambridge, MA: Harvard University Press, 2002).

Postcolonial analyses deploy the concept of hybridity in a variety of situations. Homi Bhabha's influential development of the concept in 'Signs Taken for Wonders' focuses on the contradictory movements within strategies of maintaining colonial domination.[19] Hybridity names primarily the comprised condition of the colonizers' authority, but it also marks the changed circumstances of the colonized's subjectivity.[20]

The case that I have in mind here – the threats against Jezebel and her children – takes a different shape, but it can be illuminated by the second element of Bhabha's analytic apparatus; here we include a primary source that animated Bhabha's thinking on hybridity: Frantz Fanon's reflection on the colonial state of Algeria.[21] Fanon explored the agency and the possibilities that the colonized can deploy, with substantial attention to justifying the particular, and sometimes unpalatable, forms that colonial resistance may take. Fanon knows, and Bhabha learns from him and others, that the colonial situation is not simple and that the operation of desire in colonial contexts is thoroughly interwoven with relations of power. Fanon describes the colonial subject as double-minded, simultaneously scorning and wanting to displace and replace the colonizer; the colonized subject is in Fanon's words an 'envious man'.[22] Thus, the colonial context forces a 'dichotomy . . . upon the whole people'.[23] Most specifically relevant to the situations of John and Jezebel, Fanon acknowledges the *relation* of violence within the in-group as it struggles with the pressure of colonial domination.[24]

The conflict that animates the critique of Jezebel is well known to be 'eating food offered to idols' (Rev. 2.20). More than simply a practical concern, it is an emblematic concern for how much assimilation to the dominant (Roman) culture is to be deemed proper. Questions of what is licit to eat and what are the ramifications of transgressing the boundary of permissible food are raised to high stakes by the condition of the Jewish War and the Jewish diaspora's situation during that war, especially in a community that envisioned part of its identity as involving the integration of Gentiles and which engaged in communal eating as one of its central rituals. Josephus himself undertook a very extensive accommodation to Roman culture, but his writings make clear – even as they try to hide the fact – that strife

---

19 Bhabha, 'Signs Taken for Wonders', pp. 102, 107: 'the colonial presence is always ambivalent, split between its appearance as original and authoritative and its articulation as repetition and difference'. Bhabha's strategy for a political analysis of colonialism is modeled clearly on Derrida's analysis of the duplicity that afflicts the scene of writing itself (pp. 109–10).

20 Bhabha, 'Signs Taken for Wonders'.

21 Frantz Fanon, *The Wretched of the Earth* (trans. Constance Farrington; New York: Grove Press, 1968), p. 39.

22 Fanon, *Wretched of the Earth,* p. 39, cf. 52: 'When the native is confronted with the colonial order of things, he finds he is in a state of permanent tension. The settler's world is a hostile world, which spurns the native, but at the same time it is a world of which he is envious'.

23 Fanon, *Wretched of the Earth*, pp. 316, 45–46, cf. 41: 'The colonial world is a Manichean world'.

24 Fanon, *Wretched of the Earth*, p. 52: 'The colonized man will first manifest this aggressiveness which has been deposited in his bones against his own people. This is the period when niggers beat each other up, and the police and the magistrats do not know which way to turn when faced with the astonishing waves of crime in North Africa', cf. p. 43: 'thus collective autodestruction in a very concrete form is one of the ways in which the native's muscular tension is set free'.

between Jewish and Gentile communities during and after the Jewish War was a legitimate concern for Jews, and that the issues over which the conflicts took place were themselves matters of varied attitudes and practices among Jews.[25]

When the armies of the Empire are besieging the Holy City Jerusalem, how can a Jew conduct daily life in the Gentile cities without contamination or betrayal? There are more answers to this question than John is willing to countenance. The condition itself is comparable to other examples of the pressures diasporas face during war, and in this case it is a subset of the larger condition of colonial domination.[26] John, and his literary proxy the Son of God, focus such strident threats against Jezebel and her children because of the conflicted positions that characterize subaltern groups in colonial situations.

Jezebel

The underlying concern that gives currency to the question of eating food offered to idols is the topic of purity. In this intersection – perhaps 'collision' is the more accurate term – with the concept of hybridity, it becomes clear how John's commitment to purity[27] is a catalyst for conflict. Between John and Jezebel, this issue of food offered to idols stands as a divider, a litmus test of the authenticity of Judaism. For Jezebel, we must infer that, inasmuch as the accusation of eating food offered to idols is accurate, she did not understand that action to constitute a departure from authentic Judaism. Here are Celsus's squabbling frogs, arguing over food at a fevered pitch[28] when they stand together in a massive innovation within Judaism which treats Jesus as the viceroy of God. This conflict has too often been cast as a Paulinist configuration of devotion to Jesus against John's form of devotion, one less oriented to opening a wide path to Gentiles.[29] Perhaps this is the genealogy of the conflict between John and Jezebel. Its mechanics, its source of power, however, is the pressure of subalternity. Fanon's description of the self-destructive release of the native's 'muscular tension'[30] finds an ancient example in their conflict.

The second analytical avenue – formulated earlier as 'the role of women as a topos of argumentation in colonial settings' – proceeds from the gendered quality of the other accusation against Jezebel: the accusation that she undertakes illegitimate sexual unions, that she's a whore. In the colonial economy of representation, men often position women as the bearers of subaltern purity and authenticity. Women are cast as the bearers of morality, and they are positioned by men as symbols rather than as participants in anti-colonial discourse. In spite of this, the questions that scholars habitually ask concerning the charge against Jezebel – Is the accusation of sexual behavior a metaphor? Is this behavior a genuine feature of the opponents? Does the accusation hold a reality in addition to its metaphorical power? – do not

---

25 See Marshall, *Parables of War,* pp. 98–110 and, e.g., Josephus, *War* 2.398–400.

26 See Marshall, *Parables of War*, pp. 114–20 on other ancient diasporas during war.

27 See the purity of the New Jerusalem (Rev. 21.27), the role of white linen garments (Rev. 19.8, 14), the purity of the holy warriors on Zion (Rev. 14.4), etc.

28 *Contra Celsum* 4.23.

29 Frankfurter, 'Jews or Not?', pp. 403–25.

30 Fanon, *Wretched of the Earth*, p. 54.

interrogate the shape of the conflict in terms of gender *and* in combination with colonized subjectivity. Though the threats of the Son of God are formulated not only against Jezebel but also include those with whom she is said to have mixed illegitimately (τοὺς μοιχεύοντας μετ' αὐτῆς), the central object of the threat is Jezebel; she is singled out, she is named, she bears the bulk of the punishment. Not surprisingly, John focuses on the woman, and she stands as a topos of thought and argument in male discourse.

In the arena of civic politics, Kate Cooper's description of the process of 'thinking with virgins'[31] develops this insight: she argues that men of the Late Antique world articulated a new discourse of sexual morality to circumscribe an arena of power and competition in the face of the declining of civic participation. Postcolonial criticism understands the deployment of women as pretexts for colonial intervention, whether by contemporary theorists or colonial administrators, as one of the most vexing binds of the colonial and postcolonial situation.[32] In historical terms, this phenomenon is seen pre-eminently in the British opposition to the practice of *sati* (widow-burning) and strained combinations of denunciation, rationalization and explanation that followed in response.

John focuses his critique of insiders on the figure of Jezebel, formulating that critique vividly as a denunciation of a woman's sexual practice. This focus corresponds closely to the denunciations of the outsiders – the kings of the earth – in their relations to the Whore of Babylon which Revelation 17 narrates so extensively. John draws a female character as the conduit of contamination between the insider community and the contaminating influence of the outside, the other. Jezebel broaches the border that ought not to be crossed. In his focus on woman's sexuality and on a woman as a conduit of contamination in the colonial encounter, John engages a recurrent trope of colonial relations. We see the reverse of this trope in the exhortation of 1 Tim. 5.14 that 'young women should marry, bear children, and keep house so that the enemy should have no occasion to criticize'. In 1 Timothy, the outsider's gaze – the Greco-Roman gaze – is the motive for rectitude among young women whom the author positions as the community's bearers of virtue; in Revelation, censure of a female character's sexual activity is the most prominent criticism of practice. Whether as good wives or as paradigmatic adulteresses, female characters are representatives of ideals formulated by and on behalf of males in a discourse written by and primarily for men with reference to the wider situation of the colonial empire.

The insider conflict in Revelation is seen not only in the depiction of Jezebel but also in the denunciations of the figure (presumably male) of Balaam and in condemnations of the teaching of the Nicolaitans. Though the message of 'him who has the two-edged sword' (Rev. 2.12) to the angel of the assembly at Pergamum briefly

---

31 Kate Cooper, *The Virgin and the Bride: Idealized Womanhood in Late Antiquity* (Cambridge, MA: Harvard University Press, 1996). See also the response by Shelley Matthews, 'Thinking of Thecla: Issues in Feminist Historiography', *JFSR* 17 (2001), pp. 39–55.

32 Leela Gandhi, *Postcolonial Theory: A Critical Introduction* (New York: Columbia University Press, 1998); Gayatri C. Spivak, 'Can the Subaltern Speak?', in C. Nelson and L. Grossberg (eds), *Marxism and the Interpretation of Culture* (Urbana: University of Illinois Press, 1988), pp. 271–313.

threatens to fight the opponents of the assembly, the threats of violence find their most elaborate form in the bullying of Jezebel and her followers.

The opposition of male as pure to female as impure is certainly wider than the colonial context. But Revelation's version of that highly gendered opposition is overwhelmingly oriented to John's understanding of a conflict between the forces of God and Jerusalem on the one hand and the forces of the Devil and Rome on the other. The Son of God is the purveyor of purity who promises white garments and a heavenly abode to his followers and who leads saints who have not 'defiled themselves with women' (Rev. 14.4) in a war against the fornicating Empire. Jezebel, figured as female and impure, represents a hybridity that John cannot tolerate because his understanding of the stakes of the conflict between Jerusalem and Rome, literally as well as figuratively, makes essential difference, the difference between purity and impurity, absolutely necessary. John's Jesus has no tolerance for Jezebel and the less starkly drawn border she represents for him.[33]

Babylon

Where the explicit threats against Jezebel and her followers are isolated to a few verses in Revelation 2, John's tirade against Babylon stretches from her appearance in Rev. 14.8 to her destruction in 18.20–24 and the destruction of her beast and her lovers in 19.19–21. The motifs of conflict in colonial contexts that facilitated an understanding of the shape of the conflict that John portrays between Jesus and Jezebel also illuminate the polemic against Babylon. Paul Duff has done the major work of explicating the ways in which John connects Jezebel and Babylon. In addition to the obvious accusation of whoring discussed above, Duff notes the parallels in their roles as mothers of morally dubious, if not demonic, offspring, their untoward disposition to activity rather than passivity, their deceptiveness, and their consumption of defiling food.[34] These accusations are, as Duff argues, programmatic for John's conflicts, both within his community and without.

In John's vision, Babylon notoriously stands as a figure for Rome and simultaneously for the personification of Rome through the goddess Roma, who was closely associated with the Imperial cult in Asia Minor. Together with Augustus and/or current emperors, Roma, as the mother of the city, received the worship of subject provincials, especially urban elites.[35] John's depicting Rome/Roma as Babylon was also based on the long tradition of casting enemy capitals as whores.[36] The choice of a female representation of Rome also reverses Roman statuary and coinage's traditional representation of Rome as male and conquered nations

---

33 Paul Duff's summary of the contrast between John's disposition towards the world and that of Jezebel is apt. To paraphrase Duff, Jezebel sees a continuum where John sees oil and water. Duff, *Who Rides the Beast?*, pp. xiii, 189, 131–32.

34 Duff, *Who Rides the Beast?*, pp. xiii, 189, 89–92.

35 Friesen, *Imperial Cults and the Apocalypse of John*, pp. xiii, 285, 25–103.

36 Duff, *Who Rides the Beast?*, pp. xiii, 189, 20; Ulrike Sals, *Die Biographie der 'Hure Babylon'* (Tübingen: Mohr Siebeck, 2004).

as female.[37] Elisabeth Schüssler Fiorenza's declaration that the depiction of cities as female was 'conventional'[38] is accurate, but it interrogates neither the effect of the gender convention nor the complexity of John's whole-hearted entry into that convention; he reverses elements of it that suit his polemic, but he is in no sense innocent of it.

John follows his vision of the impure Babylon with the pure lamb, the Bride of Revelation 19. The women that precede Babylon are Jezebel, Revelation 12's Woman Clothed with the Sun, and the women from whom the 144,000 virginal men of 14.4 have kept themselves pure. These preceding women are not specified as 'pure', and childbirth entails a breach of purity that requires purifying action. The Woman Clothed with the Sun, last seen in Rev. 12.6 and described as protected by God for 1,260 days, does not appear beyond ch. 12. It is unclear whether those 1,260 days were intended to carry beyond the present of the book's intended audience. Purity, however, does not seem to be the focus of John's narrative of the woman.

A hermeneutic attuned to the anxieties of hybridity can read Rev. 14.1–5 profitably: women in subaltern groups often bear the burden (or banner) of purity in relation to the outside world, but in Revelation 14, men do so. This may indicate a particularly intense anxiety, such as the circumstances of the Jewish War might present. It may also be that for the protagonist males – the 144,000 'male virgins' of 14.1–4 – to keep pure from protagonist women is also to keep protagonist women pure. That is, it keeps them in a state that declares that the protagonist society has not been overrun and defiled.[39] A. Yarbro Collins's analysis of the role of the holy war tradition in relation to the virginal purity of the 144,000 is apposite,[40] but, as I have argued elsewhere, her reading of Revelation 14 needs to be intensified by the understanding of John's stake in the purity of the Jerusalem Temple and by the crisis that the Jewish War constituted. The performance of purity that John envisioned as his local community's role in Asia Minor during the Jewish War sets the stage for the elaborate portrayal of impurity that follows as Babylon takes the stage in Rev. 14.8.

After the portrayal of the 144,000 holy warriors on Zion and the following angelic announcement to the Gentiles, an angel pronounces judgment on Babylon: 'Fallen, fallen is Babylon the great, who from the wine of her lusty whoring made all the nations to drink' (Rev. 14.8).[41] This first portrayal of Babylon combines John's anxieties about purity with the sexualized depiction of moral or immoral action that

---

37 Friesen, *Imperial Cults and the Apocalypse of John,* pp. xiii, 285, 86–95, treats statuary in Aphrodisias. The notorious Judea Capta coin series depicting a male Roman soldier standing over a defeated female representing Judea only slightly after John's Apocalypse, on my dating, represents the opposite configuration of parties in the same conflict that John treats. Carlos Castán and Carlos Fuster, *La moneda imperial romana: Julio César, 100 a.C.–Rómulo Augusto, 476 d.C* (Madrid: Graficinco, 1996), p. 77.

38 Elisabeth Schüssler Fiorenza, *Revelation: Vision of a Just World* (Proclamation Commentaries; Minneapolis, MN: Fortress Press, 1991), p. 95.

39 Alison M. Keith, *Engendering Rome: Women in Latin Epic* (Cambridge, UK: Cambridge University Press, 2000); Carol Dougherty, *The Poetics of Colonization: From City to Text in Archaic Greece* (Oxford: Oxford University Press, 1993).

40 Collins, *Crisis and Catharsis,* pp. 160–63.

41 My translation, cf. 17.2–3.

is so characteristic of his vision. In contrast to Babylon's wine, God has his own vintage: the harvest of Rev. 14.15–16 begins it. In the wine press of the wrath of God, the harvest of the earth is squeezed until blood flows in incredible quantities. Babylon's crime is paradoxically also her punishment. In response to the transgression of her impurity, she is forced to drink blood, the ultimate impurity in its synecdoche of the ultimate taboo: cannibalism. As the punishment of Babylon is extended to those who associated with her in the series of bowls in Revelation 16, an angel makes the (il)logic of matching crime and punishment clear:

> And I heard the angel of water say, 'You are just in your judgments, you who is and was, O Holy One. For men have shed the blood of saints and prophets, and you have given them blood to drink. It is their due!' And I heard the altar cry, 'Yes, Lord God the Almighty, your judgments are true and just!' (Rev. 16.5–7)

To her utter destruction as a city, Babylon is forced to drain the cup of God's wrath (Rev. 16.19–21). The drinking of blood is a punishment by God (in a telling contrast to the significance of drinking Christ's blood in ritual remembrance of his death). Whose blood is not made clear, nor does John address whether the blood is defiling, though the punishment context makes it seem likely.

In Revelation's cycle of woes and judgments purity and impurity spring from a variety of sources, but they attach to characters on the basis of the judgment that the text explicitly or implicitly pronounces on those characters: impurity from God and his followers attaches to Babylon, and impurity from Babylon attaches to Babylon; in the former case the destination is to blame, in the latter case the source. Babylon the whore forces the nations to 'drink the wine of her passion of her whorings' – but the wine is wine (Rev. 14.8). On the other hand the wine of God's anger is blood (Rev. 14.20). God's angels deliver punishments that are instances of impurity – sores, the blood of the dead, blood outside the body (Rev. 16.2–4). Finally the dwellers of the earth are drunk with the wine of the whorings of the kings of the earth with Babylon, and Babylon holds a cup of the impurities of her whorings and is said to be drunk on the blood of the saints and witnesses of Jesus. The contents of the cup and the source of her drunkenness do not match well, but the logic of the text is not tight here: what God does is good even if he is a source of impurities.

After the destruction of the city of Babylon which concludes the sequence of the seven bowls of God's wrath, Babylon's judgment begins. Her sins are indwelling demons, harlotry (Rev. 18.7), a pride specifically cast as an evasion of widowhood with its ideal of sexual restraint, and further fornication with the kings of the earth. All are sexually inflected sins: the notion that women who transgressed sexual boundaries were demon-possessed served both to intensify social sanction and to undercut embarrassment on the part of cuckolded husbands. The judgment of Babylon climaxes as her former lovers turn on her in hatred; according to the angel, 'they will make her desolate and naked, and devour her flesh and burn her up with fire, for God has put it into their hearts to carry out this purpose' (Rev. 17.16–17). The cannibalism – oddly, it seems eating precedes cooking here – that God requires as punishment is no longer merely implicit in the cup of blood, though it remains associated with John's sexualized critique. The violent action to which God compels the beast and the kings is parallel to that which is required of the followers of Jezebel: to repudiate their leader figured as illegitimate sexual partner, i.e., whore. Jezebel's time is up, and the Son of God in 2.22 is committed to killing her children and doing God-knows-what to Jezebel.[42] Presumably the repudiation that Jezebel's colleagues/lovers are urged to undertake will yield forgiveness; conversely, the turning of the beast and kings against Babylon yields only a temporary stay of execution.

The elaborate mourning over Babylon that the merchants, sailors and kings undertake in great detail cements the association of the metaphorical whore/city with Rome and its economic and colonial practices. Their cries make more dense the weaving of sexual, political and economic critiques of Rome.[43] In addition to the mourning of the clients of Rome, a voice from heaven urges:

> Render to her as she herself has rendered, and repay her double for her deeds; mix a double draught for her in the cup she mixed. As she glorified herself and played the wanton, so give her a like measure of torment and mourning. (Rev. 18.6–7)

The punishment exceeds the crime. Babylon is destroyed in Rev. 18.21–24, but the portrait of the violence against her comes into relief in contrast with the scene that follows.

Just as the sexual purity of the holy men in Rev. 14.4 provides one bookend to the voyeuristic portrayal of Babylon's sexualized impurity, the marriage supper of the lamb closes the scene with a counterposed image of sexual purity and passivity. The supper that begins in Revelation 19 commences with a celebration of the accomplishments of the Groom's Father: he has destroyed the Harlot and 'has avenged on her the blood of his servants' (Rev. 19.2). After the narrator (a master of ceremonies in a narratological sense) celebrates the Father, comments briefly on the beauty of the Bride's attire (Rev. 19.8), and puts in a kind word concerning the guests (Rev. 19.9), the encomium focuses on the Groom. A military man of sorts, the Groom surpasses any warrior or leader in the conflicts that wracked the Roman world. The visionary's epideictic description is so dense that any paraphrase would vitiate its force.

> Then I saw heaven opened, and behold, a white horse. He who sat upon it is called Faithful and True, and in righteousness he judges and makes war. His eyes are like a flame of fire, and on his head are many diadems; and he has a name inscribed which no one knows but himself. He is clad in a robe dipped in blood, and the name by which he is called is The Word of God. And the armies of heaven, arrayed in fine linen, white and pure, followed him on white horses. From his mouth issues a sharp sword with which to smite the nations, and he will rule them with a rod of iron; he will tread the wine press of the fury of the wrath of God the Almighty. On his robe and on his thigh he has a name inscribed, King of Kings and Lord of Lords. (Rev. 19.11–16)

---

42 Duff, *Who Rides the Beast?*, p. 99, notes that John was not interested in resocializing 'Jezebel' and her core constituency.

43 The literature on the mourning songs of Revelation 18 is vast. See Richard J. Bauckham, 'The Economic Critique of Rome in Revelation 18', in L. Alexander (ed.), *Images of Empire* (Sheffield: Sheffield Academic Press, 1991), pp. 47–90, for analysis and bibliography.

The Groom is an international man of mystery of sorts, followed by an immense wedding party of holy warriors – no women in sight.[44] His entry completes the conditions necessary for dinner to start. The angel announces the 'great supper of God'. On the menu will be the rival suitors and their retinues: kings, captains, mighty men, horses and their riders, the slaves and the free, the small and the great (Rev. 19.18). Notably, the Groom is not the carver for this meal, but rather the butcher, slaughtering those listed on the menu by the 'sword of his mouth' (Rev. 19.19). With the exception of two delicacies deep fried in the lake of burning sulfur, namely the False Prophet and the Beast, the menu is served raw, though by this point only the birds have retained their appetite (Rev. 19.19–20).

Emphasizing the peculiarity of this wedding prompts the question of what drove John to the contortions such a scene contains. No mystical union of Christ and the assembly of his followers is in focus here. This is a celebration of victory in rivalry: the warrior of the God of Israel victorious first of all over the Whore who seemed to be so distracting to his followers and subsequently over the Beast and his legates in heaven and on earth. It is a celebration of the prowess of the Groom, of his family and his retinue, and the 'Church' is his trophy wife. No other female figures are present at what looks suspiciously like a shotgun, or spearpoint, wedding.[45]

In the spirit of bonhomie that a wedding supper can stimulate, Revelation's remaining text has as one of its major functions peacemaking. Like the Pax Romana, John's Pax Christi is a peace imposed by a victor, but a peace nonetheless. Though Satan is chained in the abyss for a millennium to come, and though some types of people – 'the cowardly, the faithless, the polluted . . . murderers, whoremongers, sorcerers, idolaters, and all liars'[46] – are exiled to the lake of burning sulfur (Rev. 21.8), John's Holy City includes a prominent place for reconciliation. The conversion of at least some of the kings of the earth is one witness to this reconciliation motif (Rev. 21.24); the declaration that the leaves of the trees that line the river of the central street of the Holy City are 'for the healing of the nations' is another (Rev. 21.24–27). Who can be healed of what under what conditions is ambiguous, but John's conviction that innumerable Gentiles will be healed and brought into God's people is clear.

Conclusion

The contrast between Jezebel and Babylon on the one hand and on the other hand the Queen of Heaven and the Lamb/Bride is the contrast between active woman and passive woman, between impure and pure, between the woman condemned by God to suffer sexual violence and the woman protected therefrom by divine and male power, between the woman engaged in human political and cultural contest and the woman on whose behalf a man acts, the contrast between the whore and the virginal bride/idealized mother. As problematic as these contrasts are in their restriction of

---

44 'The armies of heaven, arrayed in fine linen . . . ' (Rev. 19.14), cf. 14.1–4. For arguments concerning the status of the 144,000 of Rev. 14.1–4, to which the army of 19.14 clearly corresponds, see Collins, *Crisis and Catharsis*, pp. 127–32 and Marshall, *Parables of War*, pp. 140–41, 151–52, 160–63.

45 Andrew Alföldi, 'Hasta-Summa Imperii: The Spear as Embodiment of Sovereignty in Rome', *AJA* 63 (1959), pp. 1–27.

46 Where the RSV translates πόρνοις as 'fornicators', I have rendered it as 'whoremongers'.

options for women to the extremities of virtue or depravity, they are basic to John's vision of an ideal future and his critique of an imperial present.

Revelation is a document of resistance to Rome's colonial empire, but despite the intensity of his desire for purity and despite the depth of his anxieties over contamination, John does not resist from a position of purity the structures that sustain colonialism. He makes his own, dwells in, embraces, deploys, expresses, believes in, and is constituted by the habitual acceptance of sexualized violence against women that is so broadly characteristic of patriarchal societies. Such an awkward list is meant to emphasize that there is no kernel of the 'real John' that can be purified of this disposition. This is who he is. The conditions of empire and imperial domination exacerbate this quality in John. In significant measure, he is what he opposed. He is a hybrid man in a condition where it would be utterly exceptional that he could be otherwise. Substantial truth lies in Tina Pippin's declaration:

> In the Apocalypse narrative, gender oppression is left untouched by the sword of God. The tale of the Apocalypse is not a tale of the liberation of female consciousness. The Apocalypse is not a tale for women.[47]

Given Pippin's apt caution, it is not possible to say with Elisabeth Schüssler Fiorenza that 'Revelation never pictures any serfs and subjects of this reign. No oppressive rulership and subordination but the life-giving and life-sustaining power of God characterizes God's eschatological reign and empire.'[48] The text is littered with slaves before, during, and after God's eschatological victory;[49] beyond the firmly intact gender hierarchy, there is no kingdom or empire without subordination. At the same time as John imagines a kingdom where all are priests and where Temple is as omnipresent as God, he imagines a hierarchy of thrones, elders and slaves.[50] A feminist analysis that minimizes the hierarchical and patriarchal elements of the Apocalypse abets an ahistorical scripturalizing, i.e., a positioning of the text as authoritative and normative and by definition in conformance with the values readers who treat the text as Scripture hold as true. On the contrary, by emphasizing the elements of imperialism, hierarchy and gendered violence which remain integral to John's vision, and by attending to the conditions of hybridity that make these mixtures endemic to the colonial (and human) condition, I hope to understand the forces that shaped John's discourse historically. Such an understanding is by no means a call for acceptance and in no way endorses an essentialism that sifts the elements of his message into either morally suspect and therefore epiphenomenal or morally validated and therefore essential. Sexualized violence is integral to John's anti-colonial, or more accurately anti-Roman, cry for justice and to his vision of an immolated Lamb who with his own blood will purchase the oppressed for God. The contradiction is that painful.

---

47 Pippin, *Death and Desire*, p. 105.

48 Schüssler Fiorenza also embraces the term 'empire' to characterize what has usually been discussed under the title 'kingdom of God' (*Vision of a Just World*, p. 113).

49 Rev. 1.1; 2.20; 6.11; 15.3; 19.2, 5, 10; 22.3, 6, 9.

50 Priests: Rev. 1.5; 5.10; 20.6; omnipresent temple: Rev. 21.22; hierarchy of thrones etc.: Rev. 4.4; 11.16.

'THEY HAVE NOT DEFILED THEMSELVES WITH WOMEN . . .'
CHRISTIAN IDENTITY ACCORDING TO THE BOOK OF REVELATION*

HANNA STENSTRÖM

The Book of Revelation is often read as a text that creates an alternative[1] symbolic universe for its audience, thereby also constructing for them an identity safely anchored within, and legitimated by, this universe.[2]

This article presents some observations concerning the construction of Christian identity in Revelation. I take as my point of departure Rev. 14.1–5, and in particular 14.4a, where purity language as well as female and sexual imagery describe the Christians as a collective of male virgins.[3] Even a cursory reading of Revelation shows that female imagery, which is also often sexual imagery, is used recurrently. Whereas feminist[4] and non-feminist[5] scholars alike have attended to the female

* This article is a revised version of Chapter 1 of my (unpublished) dissertation, 'The Book of Revelation. A Vision of the Ultimate Liberation or the Ultimate Backlash? A study in 20th century interpretations of Rev 14:1–5, with special emphasis on feminist exegesis' (Uppsala University, 1999). I want to thank Amy-Jill Levine for constructive criticism of a first sketch for this article, and for encouragement, and Lone Fatum for useful and encouraging criticism of a first more developed draft. The responsibility for the final shape of this article—composed in 2000—is, however, solely mine.

1 'Alternative' both in the sense that it differs from the symbolic universe of the society where it was written and that it differs from the symbolic universe of other Christian communities in its time and context, i.e. Asia Minor in the late 90s CE.

2 See, e.g., Pablo Richard, *Apocalypse. The People's Commentary on the Book of Revelation* (The Bible & Liberation Series; Maryknoll, NY: Orbis Books, 1995); Elisabeth Schüssler Fiorenza, 'Visionary Rhetoric and Social-Political Situation' in *eadem, The Book of Revelation: Justice and Judgment* (Philadelphia, PA: Fortress Press, 1985), esp. pp. 181–203; *Revelation: Vision of a Just World* (Proclamation Commentaries; Minneapolis, MN: Fortress Press, 1991).

3 This is not due to the use of masculine grammatical forms, since these could be used inclusively, but to the contrast between 'the 144,000' and 'women'. So also, e.g., David E. Aune, *Revelation 6–16* (WBC, 52B; Nashville, TN: Thomas Nelson Publishers, 1998), p. 811. Compare Tina Pippin, *Death and Desire: The Rhetoric of Gender in the Apocalypse of John* (Literary Currents in Biblical Interpretation; Louisville, KY: Westminster/John Knox Press, 1992), p. 50.

4 See Susan R. Garrett, 'Revelation', in Carol A. Newsom and Sharon H. Ringe (eds), *The Women's Bible Commentary* (Louisville, KY: Westminster John Knox Press, 1992), pp. 377– 82; Jean K. Kim, '"Uncovering Her Wickedness": An Inter(Con)textual Reading of Revelation 17 from a Postcolonial Feminist Perspective', *JSNT* 73 (1999), pp. 61–81; Tina Pippin's *Apocalyptic Bodies: The Biblical End of the World in Text and Image* (London and New York: Routledge, 1999), pp. 64–77, 92–97, 117–25; *eadem, Death and Desire* and 'The Revelation to John', in Elisabeth Schüssler Fiorenza (ed.), *Searching the Scriptures,* Volume Two: *A Feminist Commentary* (New York; Crossroad, 1994), pp. 109–30; Schüssler Fiorenza, 'Visionary Rhetoric', p. 199; *eadem, Vision of a Just World*, pp. 12–15, 130–31; Luzia Sutter Rehmann, 'Die Offenbarung des Johannes. Inspirationen aus Patmos', in Luise Schottroff and Marie-Theres Wacker (eds), *Kompendium Feministische Bibelauslegung* (2nd edn, Gütersloh: Chr. Kaiser/Gütersloher Verlagshaus, 1998), pp. 725–41.

5 For a non-feminist study that pays attention to the function of the female imagery see L. L. Thompson, *The Book of Revelation: Apocalypse and Empire* (New York: Oxford

imagery, the use of purity language has not been given the attention I think it deserves.[6] The use of purity language, and the connections between purity/impurity and the female imagery, have not been the focus of feminist critical assessment of Revelation with the notable exception of some comments by A. Yarbro Collins,[7] Tina Pippin[8] and Susan Garrett.[9]

Therefore, my contribution to this *Feminist Companion* is a brief presentation of the use of female and sexual imagery and purity language in the construction of Christian identity and in the construction of a world in Revelation.

Presuppositions

In this article, I do not use Revelation as a source for historical information,[10] asking, for example, if Rev. 14.4a bears witness to an actual ascetic, all-male, community.[11] I refrain from asking historical questions for several reasons. One is the methodological difficulty connected with such a use of Revelation. The Apocalypse is not the kind of text that gives straightforward answers to historical questions. Even more important for me is that attention solely to the text itself makes it possible to keep the focus on the use of gender, more specifically on symbolic gender and gendered symbolism.[12]

University Press, 1990), pp. 79–83, 90. See also David L. Barr, *Tales of the End. A Narrative Commentary on the Book of Revelation* (Santa Rosa, CA: Polebridge Press, 1998), pp. 109, 111–14; Arthur W. Wainwright, *Mysterious Apocalypse: Interpreting the Book of Revelation* (Nashville, TN: Abingdon Press, 1993), p. 115, and my discussion of how non-feminist scholars have read Rev. 14.4 in Stenström, 'Ultimate Liberation or Ultimate Backlash?', pp. 120–49, esp. 123–41.

6 It is generally recognized that 'purity' is a basic element in some of the most important categories used for describing Christians in Revelation, as 'priests' and 'soldiers in the Holy War'. See E. Schüssler Fiorenza, *Priester für Gott. Studien zum Herrschafts- und Priestermotiv in der Apokalypse* (NTAbh NF 7; Münster: Verlag Aschendorff, 1972). I have not found studies that make 'purity' a key concept for reading Revelation.

7 A. Yarbro Collins, *Crisis and Catharsis: The Power of the Apocalypse* (Philadelphia, PA: Westminster Press, 1984), pp. 159–61, includes very sharp critical remarks about the misogyny and the negative attitude towards the human body implied in the connection between women and defilement in Rev. 14.4a. *Eadem*, 'Women's History and the Book of Revelation', in *SBLSP* 26 (1987), pp. 80–91, discusses the use of purity language in Rev.14.4a, offers a short feminist critique, and explores strategies for transforming purity language 'into attitudes more affirming of femaleness' (p. 90).

8 Pippin, *Death and Desire*, pp. 50, 70, criticizes Collins for not taking her own understanding of purity in Revelation to its utmost consequence, namely that the New Jerusalem excludes females.

9 Garrett, 'Revelation', p. 382.

10 One of the unsolved issues in studies of Revelation is whether the text's description of the present as a time of severe persecution is to be taken at face value or if it is rather to be taken as a generic feature of apocalypses. There is hardly any external evidence for a persecution of Christians in Asia Minor in the 90s. When I in the following write about the present of the author and his community I try to do justice to the descriptions the text gives, not to the actual historical realities behind the text. See Schüssler Fiorenza, *Vision of a Just World*, esp. pp. 124–29; Thompson, *Book of Revelation*, esp. pp. 171–201; Collins, *Crisis and Catharsis*, esp. pp. 84–110.

11 In Stenström, 'Ultimate Liberation or Ultimate Backlash?', pp. 97–105, I sketch a 'possible historical context for Rev. 14.1–5'. I use David L. Barr, 'Elephants and Holograms: From Metaphor to Methodology in the Study of John's Apocalypse', in *SBLSP* 25 (1986), pp. 400–411 but develop the argumentation somewhat further.

12 For a similar approach see Tina Pippin, *Death and Desire*, esp. pp. 16, 53.

Some words may be necessary about my understanding of gender. I assume, with feminist theory in general, that 'gender' is a many-dimensional, socially and historically variable construction. Theoretically – and for pedagogical reasons – one may distinguish among biological, social and symbolic dimensions, although these dimensions are in practice very closely connected and difficult to separate. Analysis of symbolic gender is a central feminist task, and – in the case of Revelation – perhaps the only possible one. Revelation is certainly one of these texts that are 'not "about" women but . . . use(s) women figuratively to make a point about something else . . . [it] "us(es) women to think with" '.[13]

Two specific features of gender as a symbolic category (in antiquity and throughout Western history) are relevant for analysis of Revelation. The first concerns the connections made between the male–female-dualism and a number of dualisms that have nothing to do with sex and bodies. For example, 'rationality' is connected with masculine and male, 'irrationality' with femininity and female, as are 'spirit/matter', 'mind/body' and 'culture/nature'. The concepts may be seen as complementary or antagonistic, but in both cases they are hierarchically ordered, with the 'female' part connected with the lower element. 'Woman', 'womanly' and 'female' could therefore be used as synonyms for what is imperfect, maybe also evil; 'man', 'manly' and 'male' in turn represent what is perfect, maybe also good.[14]

Second, oppositions between women are created and charged with symbolic meanings. Women are put in opposition to each other as 'sensuous roses or virginal lilies, pedestalled goddesses or downtrodden slaves, Eves or Marys, Madonnas or Magdalenes, damned whores or God's police'.[15] Both kinds of women are part of the system, since they presuppose one another in acquiring their meaning as 'Good' and 'Bad'. The 'Good' cannot therefore be treated in isolation, as a thunderbolt from a feminist heaven into the patriarchal system.

The creation of oppositions between different kinds of women in Revelation's social context is also visible in the honor-and-shame value-system.[16] Although

---

13 From Elizabeth A. Castelli, 'Romans', in Elisabeth Schüssler Fiorenza (ed.), *Searching the Scriptures: A Feminist Introduction and Commentary* (2 vols; New York: Crossroad, 1993, 1994), vol. 2, pp. 272–300, where 'us(es) women to think with' is attributed to Karen King. Castelli does not mention the source for the quotation. A similar formulation, 'using gender to think with', is attributed to Karen King in G. Aichele, et al., *The Postmodern Bible* (The Bible and Culture Collective; New Haven, CT: Yale University Press, 1995).

14 This is common feminist knowledge. See, e.g., Kerstin Aspegren, *The Male Woman. A Feminine Ideal in the Early Church* (ed. René Kieffer; *Acta Universitatis Upsaliensis, Uppsala Women's Studies, Women in Religion, 4;* Stockholm and Uppsala: Almqvist & Wiksell, 1990), pp. 11–12; Marie J. Giblin, 'Dualism', in Letty M. Russell and J. Shannon Clarkson (eds), *Dictionary of Feminist Theologies* (Louisville, KY: Westminster/John Knox Press, 1996), p. 74; Elaine L. Graham, *Making the Difference. Gender, Personhood and Theology* (London: Mowbray, 1995), pp. 4, 11–14.

15 This is also common feminist knowledge, but I owe the formulation to Kenneth Knowles Ruthven, *Feminist Literary Studies: An Introduction* (Cambridge, UK: Cambridge University Press, 1984), p. 82.

16 On the 'honor and shame value system' see Bruce Malina, *New Testament World. Insights from Cultural Anthropology* (rev. edn, Louisville, KY: Westminster/John Knox Press, 1993), pp. 28–62; Halvor Moxnes, 'Honor and Shame', *BTB* 23.4 (1993), pp. 167–76. Moxnes uses Revelation as an example of how the value system is operative in the New Testament (p. 174).

acquiring and preserving honor[17] was central for both women and men, honor meant different things for them. In the moral division of labor,[18] male honor was connected with 'authority over the family, willingness to defend one's reputation, refusal to submit to humiliation',[19] while female honor was characterized by 'sexual exclusiveness, discretion, shyness, restraint and timidity'.[20] Women not under male authority were seen not only as stripped of their female honor, but also as sexually (and in other senses) aggressive and dangerous.[21]

For both men and women, 'shame' was a positive value: a concern for one's honor. However, in life marked by the moral division of labor, 'honor' was connected to the male and 'shame' to the female. A woman was honorable if she had concern for shame, a concern exercised in shyness, restraint, sexual exclusiveness and submission to authority.[22] This female shame acquires a meaning close to 'goodness'.[23] When shame is lost it cannot be regained. Prostitutes were seen as permanently shameless, since they did not respect the lines drawn through sexual exclusiveness. A female prostitute therefore fittingly symbolized the chaotic.

I use the term 'purity language'[24] with reference to words from a wide semantic field which originally had different meanings but can be subsumed under the abstract notion of 'purity/impurity', and I presuppose the understanding of 'purity' first formulated by Mary Douglas and now standard in social-science exegesis.[25] The field covers the spectrum of meanings from concrete cleanness and dirt to the purity connected with the Temple (holiness) and its opposite, the cultically impure or profane. The words in Revelation which belong to the field are, on the positive side: ἅγιος, ἄμωμοι, ὅσιος, and on the negative side: κοινός, ἀκάθαρτος, μολύνω and ῥυπαρός.

I also find it reasonable to assume that Revelation is influenced by the changes of the use of 'purity/impurity' in Early Judaism. There was a gradual dissolution of the connection between purity and the Temple cult. Purity language took on more of a spiritual and ethical meaning, making 'to be pure' almost synonymous with 'being virtuous', that is, living in accordance with the will of God. 'Impurity' could be used

---

17 Honor is 'the value of a person in his or her own eyes plus the value of the person in his or her social group' (Malina, *New Testament World*, p. 145).

18 Malina, *New Testament World*, pp. 48–55.

19 Malina, *New Testament World*, p. 49.

20 Malina, *New Testament World*, p. 49.

21 Malina, *New Testament World*, p. 50.

22 Malina, *New Testament World*, pp. 50–53.

23 Malina, *New Testament World*, p. 53.

24 Here I follow Jerome H. Neyrey, 'Unclean, Common, Polluted and Taboo. A Short Reading Guide', *Forum* 4/4 (1988), pp. 72–82. I have adjusted the specific focus words to make the choice fit what we meet in Revelation, excluding some words Neyrey mentions and including others.

25 See Mary Douglas, *Purity and Danger: An Analysis of the Concepts of Pollution and Taboo* (London: Routledge and Kegan Paul, 1966); *eadem*, 'Critique and Commentary', in Jacob Neusner (ed.), *The Idea of Purity In Ancient Judaism* (SJLA, 1; Leiden: E. J. Brill, 1973), pp. 137–42; *eadem*, *In the Wilderness: The Doctrine of Defilement in the Book of Numbers* (JSOTSup, 158; Sheffield: Sheffield Academic Press, 1993). A more developed work with 'purity' in Revelation must take the developments of the understanding of purity in more and more recent works into account, but this understanding and literature suffice for this article.

with reference to almost everything considered to be a sign that a person had rejected God (or was rejected by God), be it worship of other gods, sexual acts considered illegitimate or immoral deeds. At the same time, 'sectarian' groups could use purity language, including Temple imagery, with reference to themselves.[26]

Finally, some words may be necessary about my understanding of genre[27] and language. When I read Revelation as an apocalypse, I read it as a text that transmits an interpretation of a specific situation from a certain perspective, written to influence its receivers to adopt this interpretation and to act in accordance with it. I also assume that if the text were received in the sense that was intended, it would be seen as heavy with significance, since it is a message from God and thereby a revelation of a knowledge about reality that is invisible in day-to-day life.

Furthermore, I have learned from Elisabeth Schüssler Fiorenza[28] that Revelation does things with and to its readers through the power of its mythopoetic language, a language that uses a number of inherited symbols charged with meaning, power and associations. This mythopoetic language reaches us at levels deeper than the merely intellectual; it shapes our attitudes and influences our actions and choices. This language works through its openness, ambiguities and many possible meanings. What it says cannot be fully translated into one clearly definable meaning.

Like all Jewish and Christian apocalypses from the beginning of the first century CE, Revelation reuses images from older texts, especially from the Hebrew Bible. To this heritage belong the purity language mentioned earlier, female imagery (often with a strong sexual element), and the use of words for (what was considered) sexual deviance in a transferred sense for different kinds of (what was considered) cultic and religious deviance.[29] The personification of cities as women, including hostile cities personified as prostitutes, is part of this heritage.[30]

---

26 Neusner, *Idea of Purity*, pp. 13–15.

27 I do not intend to give a definition of the genre but to mention some features of it relevant for my reading. On the genre see D. E. Aune, 'The Apocalypse of John and the Problem of Genre', *Semeia* 36 (1986), pp. 65–96; John J. Collins, 'Introduction: Towards the Morphology of a Genre', *Semeia* 14 (1979), pp. 1–20; *idem*, 'The Genre Apocalypse in Hellenistic Judaism', in David Hellholm (ed.), *Apocalypticism in the Mediterranean World and the Near East* (Tübingen: Mohr Siebeck, 1989), pp. 531–48; Lars Hartman, 'Survey of the Problem of the Apocalyptic Genre', in Hellholm (ed.), *Apocalypticism*, pp. 329–43; D. Hellholm, 'The Problem of Apocalyptic Genre and the Apocalypse of John', *Semeia* 36 (1986), pp. 13–64; Thompson, *Book of Revelation*, pp. 18–34.

28 See Schüssler Fiorenza, *Vision of a Just World*, pp. 19–32; 'Visionary Rhetoric', esp. pp. 186–88.

29 The use of this female imagery has been subjected to much feminist research and reflection. Examples include Leonie Archer, 'The "Evil Women" in Apocryphal and Pseudepigraphical Writings', in *Proceedings of the Ninth World Congress of Jewish Studies. Division A: The Period of the Bible* (Jerusalem: World Union of Jewish Studies, 1986), pp. 239–46; Phyllis Bird, 'To Play the Harlot: An Inquiry into an Old Testament Metaphor', in Peggy L. Day (ed.), *Gender and Difference in Ancient Israel* (Minneapolis, MN: Augsburg Fortress Press, 1989), pp. 75–94; Claudia V. Camp, 'What is So Strange about the Strange Woman?', in David Jobling, Peggy L. Day and Gerald T. Shephard (eds), *The Bible and the Politics of Exegesis* (Cleveland, OH: Pilgrim Press, 1988), pp. 17–31; T. Drorah Setel, 'Prophets and Pornography', in Letty M. Russell (ed.), *Feminist Interpretation of the Bible* (Philadelphia, PA: Westminster Press, 1985), pp. 86–95. See also Athalya Brenner (ed.), *A Feminist Companion to the Latter Prophets* (FCB, 8; Sheffield: Sheffield Academic Press, 1995).

30 See e.g. Isa. 1.21; 23.15–18; Nah. 3.4–5.

Although there are texts wherein specific forms of this imagery are easily identified ('foreign woman', 'adulteress', 'prostitute'), the images gradually became more
and more mixed. In texts from around the beginning of the first century, it is often
difficult to decide whether the sexually tempting woman is 'foreign' or 'prostitute' or
the neighbor's wife. All women are, at least potentially, prostitutes or adulteresses,
seductive, dangerous and strange. In this increasingly misogynistic imagery, the
sexually tempting woman gradually came to represent those chaotic, lethal powers
that lead men away from God.[31]

Christian Identity in Revelation

If we look for the understanding of Christian identity in Revelation, the inter-
connected four visions of groups, 7.1–8, 9–17; 14.1–5 and 15.2–3 – which can be
understood as visions of Christians – are a possible point of departure.[32] All four are
inserted between passages that depict the present as a time of eschatological woes
(when those faithful to God suffer terribly) and the immediate future (when God's
wrath will strike the earth and judgment will be passed). The function of the visions
in these literary contexts[33] is to reassure the audience that God will protect them
from the coming wrath.[34] At the same time, they emphasize the necessity of adhering
to a certain form of Christian praxis.

Some recurrent motifs in Revelation show important aspects of Christian identity.
For example, the number 144,000 – 12,000 from each of Israel's twelve tribes (7.4–8;
14.1) – suggests that the Christian community is the restored, eschatological Israel.[35]
Rev. 7.3 may also, when read in the context of the Apocalypse as a whole, evoke
associations with Ezekiel 9, where those who have rejected idolatry receive on their

---

31 I owe the description of the development to Archer, 'Evil Women', p. 245. For examples see
Hosea 1–3; Ezekiel 16; 23; Jeremiah 2–5; Prov. 2.16–19; 4Q184; *T. Reu.* 5.1.

32 Issues about the relations among these four groups and the identification of the respective
groups have received much scholarly discussion. Whether 'the 144,000' in 7.1–8 and 14.1–5 are
identical has been questioned, but the connection today is the scholarly consensus. The 144,000 as an
anti-image of the followers of the Beast must also be identical to those mentioned in 15.2. The most
difficult issue is whether the limited 144,000 and the countless multitude can be identical, although
there are good reasons to assume that both are the Christians, described under different aspects. For
elaborated discussions that also give arguments to support my reading, see Aune, *Revelation 6–16*,
pp. 434, 439–48, 460–61; Barr, *Tales*, pp. 74, 87–88; Charles H. Giblin, *The Book of Revelation: The
Open Book of Prophecy* (GNS, 34; Collegeville, MN: Liturgical Press, 1991), pp. 90–91; Schüssler
Fiorenza, 'Visionary Rhetoric', pp. 188–89. For the opinion that the 144,000 and the countless
multitude are not to be understood as identical, but as a group among the Christians and the totality,
see A. Yarbro Collins, 'Apocalypse (The Revelation of John)', *NJBC*, pp. 996–1016 (1005, 1009).

33 For more detail on how Rev. 7.1–8, 9–17 and 14.1–5 fulfill virtually the same functions in their
respective literary contexts, see Hellholm, 'Apocalyptic Genre', pp. 49–50. See also Schüssler
Fiorenza, 'Visionary Rhetoric', p. 171, for the argument that all four visions belong to a series of
visions of eschatological protection, along with 11.15–19; 12.10; 19.1–9 and 20.4–6.

34 I here follow Schüssler Fiorenza, *Vision of a Just World*, pp. 66–67.

35 That Rev. 7.1–8 describes the Church as 'New Israel' (or 'True' or 'Restored' Israel) is assumed
in, e.g., Aune, *Revelation 6–16*, pp. 436, 460; Barr, *Tales*, p. 87; Robert Henry Charles, *A Critical and
Exegetical Commentary on the Revelation of St. John vol. I* (ICC; Edinburgh: T&T Clark, 1920),
pp. 206–07; Giblin, *Open Book*, p. 67; Schüssler Fiorenza, *Vision of a Just World*, p. 67.

foreheads a mark that will protect them from divine wrath.[36] This interpretation implies that the 144,000 are the Christians as a totality, not a certain group within the community.[37] That these Christians are identified as Israel is reinforced, although with slight variations, through their description in 14.1 as being on Mount Zion. This reference echoes Joel 3.4–5, where a saved remnant of Israel is gathered on Zion immediately before the Lord's Day.[38] Revelation invites Christians to understand themselves as the remnant of Israel, and thus as Israel in its totality; the Others are in John's eyes no longer part of Israel, whatever they may think about themselves. The allusion to Joel also reinforces the impression that not only 7.3–4 but also 14.1–5 describes the Christian as protected by God from the forthcoming wrath and judgment.

The similarities among 7.9–17; 14.1–5; and 15.2–3 are striking: all three passages describe the Christians as participating in worship. Such recurrent cultic imagery, mainly from the Temple cult in Jerusalem, may well be the most important category for interpreting Christian identity and describing salvation in Revelation.

There are therefore good reasons for approaching the construction of Christian identity in Revelation through 7.1–8, 9–17; 14.1–5 and 15.2–3. Of these four visions, Rev. 7.9–17 and 14.1–5 give the most elaborate interpretation of the group seen in the vision, in vv. 14b–17 and vv. 4–5 respectively. However, I find 14.1–5 to be the best place to start. Revelation's literary structure is extremely complicated and no consensus exists on how it should be understood, but 10.1–15.4 may be seen as the center of the central part, 4.1–22.5.[39] Chapters 12 to 14 may be understood as its core. Some scholars even regard Rev. 14.1–5 as the central text in the text's central part.[40] Rev. 14.1–5 presents the 144,000 as an anti-image of the followers of the Beast.[41] Through this contrast, the audience is persuaded to stand firmly committed

---

36 Collins, 'Apocalypse (The Revelation to John)', p. 1005.

37 So, e.g., Charles, *Revelation,* p. 199; Barr, *Tales,* pp. 87–88; Giblin, *Open Book,* p. 137; Akira Satake, *Die Gemeindeordnung in der Johannesapokalypse* (WMANT; Neukirchen-Vlyn: Neukirchener Verlag, 1966), pp. 41–47. See also Aune, *Revelation 6–16,* p. 440–48, esp. p. 447. Aune presents different readings of the texts. See Collins, 'Apocalypse (The Revelation to John)', pp. 1005, 1009 for a different opinion, namely, that 'the 144,000' are a specific group, a kind of 'elite'.

38 So, e.g., Schüssler Fiorenza, *Vision of A Just World,* p. 87.

39 So, e.g., Schüssler Fiorenza, *Vision of A Just World,* p. 35.

40 So, e.g., Giblin, *Open Book,* p. 15; Richard, *People's Commentary,* p. 117.

41 See e. g., D. E. Aune, *Revelation 6–16,* pp. 795–96; Eduard Lohse, *Die Offenbarung des Johannes* (NTD; Göttingen: Vandenhoeck and Ruprecht, 1983), p. 82; Schüssler Fiorenza, 'Visionary Rhetoric', p. 189; *eadem, Vision of A Just World,* pp. 87–88; A. Yarbro Collins, *The Apocalypse* (New Testament Message, 22; Wilmington, DE: Michael Glazier, 1979), p. 101. The points of correspondence are numerous. The formulaic introduction Καὶ εἶδον in 14.1 has parallels in 13.1, 11; Mount Zion (14.1) where the Lamb stands is a contrast to 'the Sea' (13.1) which is the home of Chaos and anti-godly forces; the Beast in 13.3 is described as an anti-image of the Lamb (cf. 5.6). That the 144,000 participate in worship of the Lamb makes them a deliberate contrast to those who worship the Beast in 13.8, 12. Having the name of the Lamb and of God on their foreheads makes the People of God a contrast to the followers of the Beast who carry the mark of the Beast (cf. 13.16–17). Rev. 13.3–4, 8, 12, 14 also reinforce the point that the Beast has a universal following, in contrast to the Lamb, who is followed by a group of a specific number. If the 144,000 are contrasted to the followers of the Beast, we have an image in Rev. 14.1–5 of those who 'are written in the Book of the Lamb' (13.8), the 'Holy Ones' described in 13.10.

to their form of Christian faith and praxis. To do otherwise is to commit to a Beast from the Abyss.[42] The text both comforts those who have chosen 'the Lamb' and reinforces for the hesitant the importance of choosing. It thus has a central function in John's project, and its description of the 144,000 must be central in the identity he constructs for his community.[43]

Rev. 14.1–5

Rev. 14.1–5 falls into two parts: the first, vv. 1–3, is a vision; the second, vv. 4–5, is its interpretation. The vision in vv. 1–3 may itself be divided into two parts, since v. 1 refers to something seen and vv. 2–3 to something heard.[44] Serving as a bridge between the vision and the interpretation, Rev. 14.3 repeats the mention of the 144,000 from v. 1 and describes the group with an expression that appears in a slightly varied form in 4c, οἱ ἠγορασμένοι ἀπὸ τῆς γῆς. The emphasis falls on the elaborate interpretation of vv. 4–5, that is, on the identity and characteristics of these 144,000.[45]

The description of the 144,000 in vv. 4–5 has four elements. The first three are parallel (all begin with οὗτοι).The fourth breaks the pattern, but also connects to the first, since both are followed by an explanatory addition. They can therefore be understood as parallels that create an *inclusio*.[46]

(1) οὗτοί εἰσιν οἳ μετὰ γυναικῶν οὐκ ἐμολύνθησαν, παρθένοι γάρ εἰσιν.
(2) οὗτοι οἱ ἀκολουθοῦντες τῷ ἀρνίῳ ὅπου ἂν ὑπάγῃ.
(3) οὗτοι ἠγοράσθησαν ἀπὸ τῶν ἀνθρώπων ἀπαρχὴ τῷ θεῷ καὶ τῷ ἀρνίῳ,
(4) καὶ ἐν τῷ στόματι αὐτῶν οὐχ εὑρέθη ψεῦδος; ἄμωμοί εἰσιν.

The actions of the 144,000 are emphasized in the first, second and final part of the description. A certain praxis is necessary for a share among those who will be saved, although the imagery in 14.1 also speaks about the 144,000 as protected by God and vv. 3 and 4c say that God has intervened on their behalf ('bought them free'). As God's property, they are expected to live according to the high standards God requires and defines. Perhaps Rev. 14.1–5 is best described as one of those New Testament texts where deeds are required for 'staying in' but not for 'getting in'.[47]

All four elements of the description use inherited symbols that open to many

---

42 So e.g., Schüssler Fiorenza, 'Visionary Rhetoric', pp. 191–92.

43 Cf. Schüssler Fiorenza, 'Visionary Rhetoric', which shows convincingly that 14.1–5 is well integrated in Revelation as a whole, has a decisive function in the whole, and can be used as a key text for understanding Revelation.

44 Schüssler Fiorenza, 'Visionary Rhetoric', p. 181.

45 So, e.g., Schüssler Fiorenza, 'Visionary Rhetoric', p. 181.

46 So, e.g., Aune, *Revelation 6–16*, p. 810.

47 For a reading that stresses the necessity of deeds in Rev. 14.1–5 but not the interweaving of deeds of God and deeds of Christians see Schüssler Fiorenza, 'Visionary Rhetoric', p. 191.

possible meanings. This is not the place for a complete survey,[48] but I shall point to some central elements in the description and to some of their meanings.

First, the 144,000 are described as males. This reading is not primarily dependent on masculine, grammatical forms that may be used inclusively of men and women. Rather, the contrast between 144,000 and 'women' in 14.4a logically makes the 144,000 a male community.[49] At the same time, their designation as 'virgins' creates associations with the Good Woman, with concern for her shame.

In the description of Christians in 14.4a, 'purity' is basic.[50] Impurity is connected with 'women', 'purity' with the male community.[51] The language is also strikingly sexual: defilement occurs through sexual intercourse, and therefore faithful Christians are 'virgins'. Since to use expressions of (what was considered) sexual deviance with reference to cultic–religious deviance is conventional, persons who always keep their faith may be called 'virgins'.[52] The 'defiling women' in Rev. 14.4a are not easy placed in a specific category, e.g., 'wives of other men' or 'foreign women'. We have here an example of how all women could be seen as tempting, dangerous, defiling and used as descriptions for what leads men away from God.

Rev. 14.4a also evokes a number of associations to older texts that explain how 'pure male virgins' could function as a description of Christians. First are images of what the Christians are, or ought to be, namely priests[53] and/or soldiers in Holy War.[54] To be pure and allowed to serve in the cult or in Holy War, priests and soldiers were to refrain from sexual intercourse. A people of constantly worshiping priests or an army always ready for battle must therefore remain virgins.[55] Associations can also be made to Exodus 19, where members of the priestly people (Exod. 19.6) are not allowed to touch women (Exod. 19.15) when they wait for God at Sinai.[56]

---

48 For studies that cover Rev. 14.1–5, its functions in Revelation and its interpretations see Aune, *Revelation 6–16*, pp. 783–86, 794–96, 803–23; C. H. Lindijer, 'Die Jungfrauen in der Offenbarung des Johannes XIV 4', in *Studies in John: Festschrift Presented to J.N. Sevenster on the Occasion of His Seventieth Birthday* (NovTSup, 24; Leiden: E. J. Brill, 1970), pp. 124–42; Daniel C. Olson, '"Those Who Have Not Defiled Themselves With Women": Revelation 14.4 and the Book of Enoch', *CBQ* 59 (1997), pp. 492–510; Satake, *Gemeindeordnung*, pp. 39–47; Schüssler Fiorenza, 'Visionary Rhetoric'. About different interpretations of 'the 144,000' in New Testament research see Otto Böcher, *Die Johannesapokalypse* (ErtFor, 41; Darmstadt: Wissenschaftliche Gesellschaft, 1975), pp. 56–63.

49 So, e.g., Aune, *Revelation 6–16*, p. 811.

50 Μολύνω means 'to soil, smear' with dirt. It can also refer to 'defile' in a transferred sense and be related to the cult. See Aune, *Revelation 6–16*, pp. 810–11.

51 For feminist criticism, see Pippin, *Death and Desire*, pp. 50, 70; Collins, *Crisis and Catharsis*, pp. 159–60.

52 So, e.g., Garrett, 'Revelation', p. 377; Lohse, *Offenbarung*, p. 83, Christopher Rowland, 'The Book of Revelation: Introduction, Commentary and Reflections', *NIB* XII, pp. 502–736 (664).

53 So, e.g., Satake, *Gemeindeordnung*, pp. 45–46; Collins, *Apocalypse*, p. 100; Rowland, 'Revelation', pp. 664–65. Schüssler Fiorenza, 'Visionary Rhetoric', p. 190, describes the purity of the 144,000 as 'cultic'. See surveys of discussion that mentions this interpretation in Aune, *Revelation 6–16*, pp. 812, 819–22; Olson, '14:4 and Enoch', p. 494.

54 So, e.g., Barr, *Tales*, pp. 113–16, 128–30; Giblin, *Open Book*, pp. 24–34; Rowland, 'Revelation', pp. 665; Satake, *Gemeindeordnung*, pp. 45–46; Collins, *Apocalypse*, p. 100. Cf. Aune, *Revelation 6–16*, p. 812; Olson, '14.4 and Enoch', p. 494. As these examples show, 'priestly' and 'military' interpretations are not mutually exclusive.

55 Cf. Garrett, 'Revelation', p. 380.

56 Aune, *Revelation 6–16*, p. 822; Rowland, 'Revelation', p. 664.

Second, there are possible associations to negative images that provide a contrast to the 144,000. One is that the 144,000 are a deliberate contrast to the Watchers in *1 Enoch* who defiled themselves with human women and became fathers of the giants.[57] Another is that the male collective in 14.1–5 is the positive counter-image of the People of God in Ezra 9 and Mal. 2.11.

The priestly interpretation has the advantage of being closely connected with Revelation as a whole, where cultic imagery is generally ubiquitous and where the People of God are recurrently envisioned as participants in worship. Three times Revelation also explicitly calls the Christians 'priests' (1.6; 5.10; 20.6). The role of the 'Holy War' motif in Revelation is, on the other hand, contested. Some scholars see it as *the* motif undergirding the Apocalypse;[58] others are not convinced.[59] The imagery of the Watchers is less easy to relate to Revelation, since it is not overtly present elsewhere; however, one may argue that the imagery implies that the Christians are angels who participate in heavenly worship, perhaps even taking the place of the Watchers.[60] An understanding of the 144,000 as the opposite of a people that defiles itself through marriage with foreign women could, perhaps, be related to the presence in Revelation of the foreign woman par excellence, Jezebel, who has seduced some members of the community in Thyatira.

Both the explicit use of purity language and the use of imagery suggesting 'purity' hold 14.1–5 together and point towards a number of other texts in Revelation. In addition to 14.4a, the last part of the description, 14.5, uses explicit purity language, ἄμωμοι. The word denotes 'without spots, clean', but it may also be used in the ethical sense of 'blameless' and with reference to the perfection required of sacrificial animals. In other words, it is another example of cultic imagery.[61]

The phrase καὶ ἐν τῷ στόματι αὐτῶν οὐχ εὑρέθη ψεῦδος in 14.5 can be understood in light of the connection the Hebrew Bible often makes between God and truth, lie and idolatry. To refuse to 'worship the Beast' and to refrain from 'lying' can therefore possibly function synonymously.[62]

'Purity' is also used implicitly. That the 144,000 are on Mount Zion, the place where God is present, presupposes purity. That they carry the name of the Lamb and his Father on their foreheads (v.1) alludes to Exod. 28.36–38; 39.30–31. Thus, they are described as priests who, in 14.2–3 also participate in worship, which requires

---

57 See Collins, 'Women's History', pp. 88–89 and 'Apocalypse (The Revelation of John)', p. 1010; Olson, '14.4 and 1 Enoch', esp. pp. 496–498, 505–507. See also Lindijer, 'Jungfrauen', p. 127, who mentions what must be a form of this hypothesis and calls it 'die originelle Hypothese von Tambayah', with reference to an article by a T. I. Tambayah, published in *The Expository Times*, 1920/1921.

58 Richard Bauckham, *The Theology of the Book of Revelation* (NTT; Cambridge, UK: Cambridge University Press, 1993); Giblin, *Open Book*; cf. Barr, *Tales*, pp. 101–49, although the reading of Rev. 11.19–22.21 as a war story is not only in terms of biblical Holy War but also as a story about cosmic war in more general, mythic terms.

59 Aune, *Revelation 6–16*, p. 819.

60 Olson, '14.4 and 1 Enoch', pp. 505–507. See also a somewhat different understanding of how this '144,000 as opposite to Watchers' can be related to Revelation as a whole in Collins, 'Apocalypse (The Revelation to John)', p. 1010.

61 Aune, *Revelation 6–16*, pp. 822–23. Cf. Schüssler Fiorenza, 'Visionary Rhetoric', p. 190.

62 Aune, *Revelation 6–16*, p. 823.

'purity'.[63] This priestly imagery reinforces the maleness of the 144,000 mentioned in 14.4a. In 14.4b, ἀπαρχή can be understood as sacrificial language and so as yet another way of describing the 144,000 as pure (cultically fit).[64] Thus, Rev. 14.1–5 draws a clear line of purity around the group, and 'purity' is basic to the construction of Christian identity, a purity connected with males who form a deliberate contrast to defiling women.

Rev. 14.1–5 also shapes Christian identity through the use of contrasts. The 144,000 are 'bought free' from 'earth' and 'humankind', and thus they represent a wholly new species, destined to live on a new earth. They are contrasted not only to 'women' in 14.4a, but also, implicitly, to men who have 'defiled themselves with women'. They have also kept themselves free from 'lie'. The parallels indicate that 'earth', 'humankind', 'women' and 'lie' are to be understood either as different aspects of an evil from which the Christians have been delivered and actively reject, or as different ways of talking about the same thing. 'Earth' and 'humankind' may in this context be understood as those who have chosen the Beast and not the Lamb, as 'idolaters' (see 13.3, 8, 12, 14). 'Lie' may also have associations of 'idolatry'. To defile oneself with women is therefore another way of speaking about 'idolatry', consistent with the established use of sexual language for cultic and religious deviance. Finally, 14.1–5 is a deliberate contrast to ch. 13. 'Women' and 'the followers of the Beast' are both ways of negatively defining the People of God; they are images of that from which Christians must distance themselves and in contrast to which they must form their identity.

Having seen how Rev. 14.1–5 depicts Christians, we briefly return to the earlier visions to see some further similarities between them. First, Rev. 7.5–8 is often read as describing a mustering of the soldiers who will fight the final Holy War.[65] Second, 7.9–17 introduces another image connected with purity, namely 'clothes' that are white, clean or made clean. This image opens to a number of interpretations and associations. The στολὰς λευκάς (7.9) may be understood as a reference to the clothing of heavenly beings and of those worthy of heaven.[66] The motif is varied in 7.14, where the clothes are made white in the blood of the Lamb.[67] That blood makes something pure is cultic, sacrificial, imagery. The passage may also be taken as an allusion to Exod. 19.10, 14, which exhorts the (priestly) people to make their clothes clean before they meet God. Thus, 'have made one's clothes clean' is a presupposition for being allowed into the divine presence.[68] L. L. Thompson shows how 'white' is used,[69] homologously, for 'proper garments, righteous deeds

---

63 Schüssler Fiorenza, 'Visionary Rhetoric', p. 190.

64 See, e.g., Aune, *Revelation 6–16*, pp. 814–18; Thompson, *Book of Revelation*, p. 78. There has been much scholarly discussion about the proper understanding of ἀπαρχή in Rev. 14.4b and the relation between the ἀπαρχή and 'humanity' in this verse. However, the common understanding of it as 'sacrificial language' is sufficient for my purposes here.

65 So e.g., Bauckham, *Theology of Revelation*, pp. 78, 90; Giblin, *Open Book*, pp. 28–29, 226. See also how this reading is questioned in Aune, *Revelation 6–16*, p. 436.

66 See, e.g., Aune, *Revelation 6–16*, p. 468, with brief discussion and further references.

67 For possible associations evoked by 7.14c, see Aune, *Revelation 6–16*, pp. 474–75.

68 Schüssler Fiorenza, *Priester für Gott*, pp. 394–95.

69 Thompson, *Book of Revelation*, pp. 78–79. Thompson uses 'homologues' to 'refer to any correspondence of structure, position or character in the different dimensions in John's world', p. 78.

and holiness'[70], and how therefore the clothing imagery in Rev. 7.9, 14 is intimately connected to passages where purity language – words for 'holy' – describes God (e.g., 15.4) and God's deeds as well as certain humans (οἱ ἅγιοι) and their actions.[71]

Female Imagery in Rev. 12.17–22

In Rev. 14.4a, female imagery creates a contrast between 'the 144,000' and 'women'. Therefore, the next group of texts I approach are those that use female imagery, which is often also connected with sexual imagery and purity language, as is the case in Rev. 14.4a.[72]

In the central part of Revelation, in ch. 12, we encounter another vision of the Christian Community, this time in female form: the extremely complex image of the Woman Clothed with the Sun.[73] Among the many possible meanings of this figure, I choose to read her as the Christian Community, which understands itself as true Israel, threatened by evil and protected by God. At the same time, she is the Israel from which the Messiah was born. The continuity between Israel and the Christians is stressed.[74] Thus, the understanding of the Christians as Israel in Rev. 7.1–8 and 14.1–5 is also present here.

In Revelation 12 the Christians are not a male collective resembling a Good Woman in their concern for shame (guarding their virginity); instead, they are embodied as a woman and her children. Although this female figure bears some resemblance to a goddess and Queen of Heaven, she may also be seen as a primarily passive figure who conforms to her culture's ideal of femininity.[75] Neither sexuality nor impurity is connected with her. In a feminist reading of Revelation 12, Tina Pippin emphasizes that the Sun Woman is both marginalized in the text and left behind in the desert without any further information given of her fate, while the text describes in detail the fates of both the Bride and, especially, the Prostitute.[76]

If the Woman Clothed with the Sun is another image for the Christian Community, the prominent grandiose opposing female images – The Prostitute

---

70 Thompson, *Book of Revelation*, p. 79.

71 The white clothes may also, especially in combination with the palm branches, be seen as symbols of victory. See Barr, *Tales*, pp. 74, 85; cf. Aune, *Revelation 6–16*, pp. 468–70.

72 For a feminist reading focusing on the use of dichotomized images of women, see Garrett, 'Revelation'. My reading is similar to hers. See also Pippin, *Death and Desire*, esp. pp. 57–86.

73 On Revelation 12 see Böcher, *Die Johannesapokalypse*, pp 68–76; Pierre Prigent, *Apocalypse 12. Histoire de l'exégese* (BGBE, 2; Tübingen: J. C. B. Mohr, 1959). See also Aune, *Revelation 6–16*, pp. 660–713; Garrett, 'Revelation', pp. 379–80; A. Yarbro Collins, *The Combat Myth in the Book of Revelation* (HDR, 9; Missoula, MT: Scholars Press, 1976).

74 So e.g., Garrett, 'Revelation', p. 379, and, with slight variations, Giblin, *Open Book,* pp. 125–26. Schüssler Fiorenza, *Vision of a Just World*, p. 81, identifies the woman as 'the messianic community', and connects it to other texts about the protection of the Christians: 7.1–8; 11.1–2; Charles, *Revelation of St. John*, p. 315.

75 So Barr, *Tales*, pp. 111–12, although he further claims that the Sun Woman is also a powerful, queenly figure and thus more than the stereotypical passive female waiting for someone who can rescue her.

76 Pippin, *Death and Desire*, pp. 53, 74–76. See also pp. 77–80, 84.

Babylon[77] (Revelation 17–18)[78] and Jerusalem the Bride (Revelation 19, 21) – represent two worlds: one that must be left and destroyed; another that will come and where Christians will live forever. There are also similarities in formulations which make them counter-images.[79] The Sun Woman may even be seen as a contrast to the Prostitute, surpassing her in glory.

Depicting the dichotomy between Bad and Good Woman,[80] Revelation counterposes the figure without concern for shame, Babylon, to the figure that has all the concern for shame for which one could possibly wish, Jerusalem. Babylon the Prostitute also fulfills, to the utmost degree, the expectations of how women who are not under male authority behave: she is dangerous, and her sexual activities know no limits. She symbolizes all that is chaotic, and she personifies the opposite of God and the order God institutes.[81]

In this way, female imagery shows a vision of the world as divided, and Revelation draws lines to a high degree between the impure and the pure. The destruction of the impure – the female prostitute – is the very presupposition for the coming of salvation and the new world, envisioned as pure, as Bride.[82]

The envisioning in Revelation 17–18 of Babylon as a Prostitute makes the use of sexual language inevitable. The porn-cognates become catchwords in 17.1–19.10[83] (see 17.1–2, 4–5, 15–16; 18.3, 9; 19.2). Purity language (17.4; 18.2) and forms of βδελυγ- (17.4) are used, and impurity is also implicit in excessive, illicit sexuality. Thus, Babylon is depicted as an epitome of impurity. Descriptions of her unrestricted sexuality also imply impurity. In 18.2, where the image of prostitute vanishes and the image of city remains, Babylon is described as a home for demons and impure animals. Thus, Babylon is a sharp contrast to Jerusalem where nothing κοινόν will enter (21.27).

Revelation's female and sexual imagery works not only through the use of contrasts but also through a system of homologies in which constructions of Christian identity and of the world merge.[84] Babylon the Prostitute is a homologue to Jezebel (Rev. 2.20–23), who becomes on a smaller scale what Babylon is on the worldwide

77 On Babylon as enemy of God in prophetic texts and the demonization of Babylon see, e.g., Psalm 137, esp. vv. 8–9; Isaiah 47; Jeremiah 50–51. For a study of these texts see David J. Reimer, *The Oracles against Babylon in Jeremiah 50–51: A Horror among the Nations* (San Francisco, CA: Mellen Research University Press, 1993).

78 D. E. Aune, *Revelation 17–22* (WBC, 52C; Nashville, TN: Thomas Nelson Publishers, 1998), pp. 925–27, 928–33, 935–37 for comparative material relevant for the image of the Whore in Revelation.

79 Compare Rev. 17.1–2 and 21.9–10. See, e.g., Aune, *Revelation 17–22,* pp. 1144–46 and Celia Deutsch, 'Transformation of Symbols: The New Jerusalem in Rv 21,1–22,5', *ZNW* 78 (1987), pp. 106–26 (122–24), for systematic presentations of the similarities of the descriptions of Jerusalem and Babylon.

80 Garrett, 'Revelation', pp. 377, 381–82 emphasizes the use of dichotomized 'women' in Revelation, and a criticism of these images is central in her criticism of the book.

81 Moxnes, 'Honor and Shame', p. 174. Cf. Garrett, 'Revelation', pp. 377, 382.

82 Cf. Garrett, 'Revelation', who argues that 'purity' is the central point of the metaphor 'bride of the Lamb', although without following 'purity' throughout Revelation.

83 Aune, *Revelation 17–22,* p. 916.

84 Numerous works mention many of these relations; I am in the following particularly indebted to Thompson, *Book of Revelation*, pp. 89–91.

scene.[85] The description in Rev. 14.4 of the 144,000 as παρθένοι, virgins, fits this pattern. They are a homologue to Jerusalem the Bride as Jezebel is to Babylon the Prostitute.[86] They are as pure as the ideal Bride and as committed to God as the ideal Bride to her husband. At the same time, their description as 'undefiled by women' makes them the opposite of 'those who fornicate with Jezebel', of the kings of the earth who were Babylon's sexual partners, and of the πόρνοι excluded from the New Jerusalem (21.8).

An understanding of the πόρνοι not as sexually deviant males in general but as male prostitutes[87] makes the parallel even more clear. Babylon and the condemned are prostitutes; Jerusalem and the saved are virgins. At the same time, this understanding would make the androcentrism of Revelation even more total. Not only the Good ones but also the Bad are described as males.

The Letters to the Churches in 2–3 and the Visions of New Jerusalem in 21–22

Rev. 14.1–5 creates contrasts between Us and Them, and purity language draws those lines. There are two other parts of Revelation where the lines between 'Us and Them', or perhaps better 'Insiders and Outsiders',[88] are very sharply drawn: the seven letters to the communities in Revelation 2–3,[89] and the vision of the New Jerusalem in 21–22.[90]

The parallels between Revelation 2–3 and 21–22 are evident.[91] Those whom chs 2–3 describe as 'inside' the community are presented in virtually the same way as those 'inside' New Jerusalem in chs 21–22.[92] The lines around the community – the lines drawn between the pure and the impure – seem to coincide with the lines dividing the cosmos, the New Jerusalem from the horrors Outside. Therefore, chs 2–3 and 21–22 may also provide material for understanding Christian identity in Revelation. In these texts, the audience meets open categories with which they are invited to identify or exhorted to eschew. At the same time, a number of specific

---

85 Thompson, *Book of Revelation*, p. 90.

86 Thompson, *Book of Revelation*, p. 90. Cf. Lohse, *Offenbarung*, p. 83; Schüssler Fiorenza, 'Visionary Rhetoric', p. 190.

87 This is the ordinary meaning of the word in non-biblical Greek. The understanding is proposed in Aune, *Revelation 17–22*, pp. 1223–24 and mentioned in Stephen D. Moore, *God's Gym. Divine Male Bodies of the Bible* (New York and London: Routledge, 1996), p. 129, with reference to commentaries that mention this possible meaning. Cf. Pippin, *Apocalyptic Bodies*, p. 125.

88 Cf. A. Yarbro Collins, 'Insiders and Outsiders in the Book of Revelation and Its Social Contexts', in J. Neusner and Ernest S. Frerichs (eds), *'To See Ourselves as Others See Us': Christians, Jews, 'Others' in Late Antiquity* (Scholars Press Studies in the Humanities; Chico, CA: Scholars Press, 1985), pp. 187–218.

89 So, e.g., Barr, 'Elephants', p. 410.

90 Cf., e.g., Barr, *Tales*, p. 117; Pippin, *Death and Desire*, p. 50.

91 The descriptions of the 'Insiders' in New Jerusalem are reminiscent of the promises given to the faithful (in other words, the 'Insiders') in Revelation 2–3. Compare Rev. 2.7 with 22.2; 2.11 with 21.8; 2.26 with 22.5; 3.12 with 21.1; 22.4, and see Barr, *Tales*, pp. 54–55. Deutsch, 'Transformation', p. 124; Thompson, *Book of Revelation*, p. 90. Revelation thus reinforces the impression that the outsiders to New Jerusalem are outsiders to John's group and that the insiders to the group are insiders to New Jerusalem.

92 Cf. Thompson, *Book of Revelation*, p. 90.

'opponents' in the communities are turned into 'idolaters', 'fornicators'; 'followers of Balaam' and 'Jezebel'.

Revelation 2–3 presents outbursts against 'Nicolaitans', 'followers of Balaam' and 'those who fornicate with Jezebel' (2.14, 20–23).[93] Although words meaning 'impure' are not used for the opponents, they are presented as doing things that are tantamount to impurity, namely eating 'meat sacrificed to idols' and committing sexual acts described as illicit (2.14, 20). Rev. 2.20–23 labels someone 'Jezebel' and turns her into a personification of the evil woman who does everything in her power to lead the faithful astray. Jezebel is an example of the 'women' with whom the 144,000 have not defiled themselves.

In the letters, we also meet the theme 'lie', which we found in 14.5. The first passage in Revelation concerning 'liars' is 3.9, which mentions the 'so-called Jews'. The passage might refer to actual Jews since John claims that those who acknowledge Jesus as Messiah, as resurrected Savior, are the 'true Jews', true Israel.[94] Although the word is not used, 'lie' is implicit in 2.2, 9.

Rev. 3.4–5, 18 also offers examples of 'clothes' used in a metaphorical sense. Reusing inherited symbolism, 'soiled clothing' refers to a sinful life, while 'clean clothes' symbolize a life of righteousness, deliverance from sin, and the reward for virtuous living.[95] These images are part of the symbol system where 'white' and 'clean' clothes correspond to the 'holiness' characteristic of God and humans connected with God, a holiness enacted in deeds. Once again, 'purity' is basic to the understanding of Christian identity, an understanding closely connected with the understanding of God and salvation.

Rev. 3.12 uses Temple imagery, implying purity, when the victor (cf. 15.2) is promised to be a pillar in the Temple. Since visions of judgment and the redeemed world make values clear,[96] it is important for our view of Revelation's basic values that what has a share in the New Jerusalem in 21–22 is described as pure. That which will be excluded is described as impure.[97] Rev. 21.27 clearly places emphasis on the purity of Jerusalem and its inhabitants: καὶ οὐ μὴ εἰσέλθῃ εἰς αὐτὴν πᾶν κοινὸν καὶ [ὁ] ποιῶν βδέλυγμα.

Purity is also implied in the description of New Jerusalem by means of terms that recollect the Temple, although there is no Temple in the city since all of New

---

93 About Revelation 2–3, with discussions about the historical circumstances interpreted in the text, see Barr, 'Elephants', p. 410; *Tales*, pp. 42–46, 50–51; E. Schüssler Fiorenza, 'Apocalyptic and Gnosis in Revelation and in Paul', in *eadem, Justice and Judgment*, pp. 114–32; *Vision of a Just World*, pp. 132–36; Thompson, *Book of Revelation*, pp. 116–45; Collins, *Crisis and Catharsis*, pp. 84–88, 132–38.

94 So, e.g., Barr, *Tales*, p. 56; Charles, *Revelation*, pp. 56–57; Giblin, *Open Book*, pp. 55–56; Schüssler Fiorenza, *Vision of a Just World*, pp. 135–36 (with developed discussion); Collins, 'Apocalypse (The Revelation to John)', p. 1002, cf. *eadem*, 'Insiders and Outsiders', pp. 204–10.

95 Cf. Isa. 64.5, Zech. 3.3–4.

96 J. J. Collins, *The Apocalyptic Imagination* (New York: Crossroad Continuum, 1984), p. 7.

97 Cf. Deutsch, 'Transformation', pp. 118–22, esp. pp. 121–22. About Insiders–Outsiders to New Jerusalem, and the paradox that, on the one hand, Rev. 21.25 states that the gates to New Jerusalem are never shut and, on the other, that there is clearly an Outside, see Barr, *Tales*, p. 117.

Jerusalem is the Holy Place where God abides.[98] Its inhabitants are also described as priests. In 22.3–4 God's slaves (οἱ δοῦλοι αὐτοῦ)[99] are constantly close to him, worshiping (λατρεύσουσιν). The description of these slaves in 22.3–4 also leads to associations with the high priests.[100] In 22.14, the imagery of 'washed clothes' appears again, with wording similar to Rev. 7.14: those who have a share in New Jerusalem are 'those who have washed their robes'.[101] If the Insiders are thus described as priests and the new world is conceived in terms of purity, the Outsiders are, basically, impure and thus form a contrast to the 144,000 of 14.1–5.[102]

These Outsiders are described in vice lists[103] that all seem to be variations of the same list. The first list appears in 21.8; the context, Rev. 21.5–8, depicts God as speaking directly about the division between Outsiders and Insiders. As a speech put in the very mouth of God, 21.5–8 has extreme significance. The vices are the major ones in the Hebrew Bible and Early Judaism: idolatry, murder, sexual immorality and lying.[104] They are also connected with impurity and bear associations with what is not allowed in the Temple: ἐβδελυγμένοι, πόρνοι, φάρμακοι, εἰδωλολάτραι. As πόρνοι the condemned are an obvious anti-image of the 144,000 παρθένοι. In Rev. 14.5 the 144,000 are also said to be free from lies, and 21.8 places liars among the condemned.[105]

The other catalog of those who will be left outside, 22.15, is almost identical: ἔξω οἱ κύνες καὶ οἱ φάρμακοι καὶ οἱ πόρνοι καὶ οἱ φονεῖς καὶ οἱ εἰδωλολάτραι καὶ πᾶς φιλῶν καὶ ποιῶν ψεῦδος ('outside are the dogs and sorcerers and fornicators and murderers and idolaters, and everyone who loves and practices falsehood'). They too are an anti-image of the 144,000 in 14.1–5. 'Impurity' is the characteristic that holds the list together.

As mentioned, πόρνοι can be understood as referring specifically to male prostitutes. If 22.15 is read in the light of Deut. 23.17–18,[106] κύνες – which can be taken in a more general sense as 'wicked persons' – can also refer to 'male

---

98 Rev. 21.3, 9–27 implies that the New Jerusalem is a Temple, as a comparison between Rev. 21.16 and 1 Kgs 6.20; 2 Chron. 3.8ff; Ezek. 43.16; 45.2; 48.20 suggests. The emphasis on the purity of New Jerusalem implies that the city fulfills the requirements of purity – as the Temple should do – to the utmost degree. On the motif 'New Jerusalem as Temple', or perhaps rather as making the Temple unnecessary, see Deutsch, 'Transformation', pp. 113–15, 121–22, 125–26 and Collins, 'Apocalypse (The Revelation to John)', p. 1015. See also Aune, *Revelation 17–22*, pp. 1015, 1166–68, 1187–91, who places the concepts of 'New Jerusalem' and 'eschatological Temple' in the context of Early Judaism.

99 Christians are described as δοῦλοι τοῦ θεοῦ in Rev. 2.20; 7.3; 19.2, 5; 22.3, 6. In some passages, a certain person is identified as a δοῦλος τοῦ θεοῦ: 1.1, where the designation refers to John, and 15.3 where it refers to Moses. See also Rev. 10.7; 11.18 where the prophets are called δοῦλοι τοῦ θεοῦ. On this theme in Revelation see Satake, *Gemeindeordnung*, pp. 86–97.

100 Cf. Rev. 22.3–4 and Exod. 28.36, 38. See Schüssler Fiorenza, *Priester für Gott*, pp. 384–89.

101 For a detailed presentation of the similarities between Rev. 7.9–17 and the visions of New Jerusalem in 21.1–22.5, see Aune, *Revelation 6–16*, pp. 437–38.

102 So, e.g., Pippin, *Death and Desire*, p. 50, who also emphasizes the implication that the insiders are male.

103 For detailed discussion of these vice lists see Aune, *Revelation 17–22*, pp. 1130–32, 1222–24.

104 Aune, *Revelation 6–16*, p. 823.

105 So, e.g., Rowland, 'Revelation', p. 722.

106 See Aune, *Revelation 17–22*, pp. 1222–23.

prostitutes'. Revelation thus envisions both the saved[107] and the condemned as males.

Additional Texts

Finally, I add some other observations that support my thesis that 'male and pure' is a basic understanding of Christians in Revelation. As is well known, cultic imagery – which implies purity – is recurrent throughout this text. When the imagery is specified to the degree that the inherited designation 'people of priests' or simply 'priests' describes the Christians, the imagery becomes gendered. We meet the explicit designation 'priest' three times: 1.6; 5.10; and 20.6.

An integral part of purity language is 'holiness', and οἱ ἅγιοι is also a recurrent, basic designation for Christians. Normally, it refers to the group as a whole, not to an elite subset or to special individuals.[108] The connections between Revelation and the Law of Holiness are obvious: God is Holy and therefore the People of God are obliged to be holy. Thereby, a homology is created between God and certain humans,[109] a homology that is also evident when the deeds of both God (15.4) and humans (19.8) are described as δικαιώματα. '"Holy humans" . . . thus function on the human plane as God's holiness on the divine plane.'[110] The imagery of 'clothing' is part of this: in 19.8, βύσσινον λαμπρὸν καθαρόν is the clothing of the Bride, but the words are immediately interpreted as the τὰ δικαιώματα τῶν ἁγιῶν, the righteous deeds of the saints.

A text that also shows the condemned as the opposite of the ideal Christians in Rev. 14.1–5 (read in light of ch. 13 and 15.2–3) is 9.20–21. Having parallels to the vice lists in Revelation 21–22, Rev. 9.20 is a long, stereotypical description of idolaters and the insufficiency of 'idols'. The 'idolaters' are persons who do not turn away from their πορνεία, murder, magic, theft. Again, the difference between Us and the Others is the difference between virgins and fornicators.

Conclusions

Purity language, and thus conceptions of purity, as well as female and sexual imagery, are basic to Revelation's construction of Christian identity. Revelation provides a textbook example of how 'purity' can structure a symbolic universe. The lines that divide the cosmos can be seen as coinciding with the lines that separate Us (the Insiders of one's group) from Them, the Others (the Outsiders to one's group).

---

107 Cf. Pippin, *Death and Desire*, pp. 50,70–71. Pippin also concludes that the Insiders to New Jerusalem are all males.

108 The term ἅγιοι is used 26 times in Revelation: four times about the Holy City, once about Christ, once about an angel, twice about God. (God is also twice called ὅσιος, Rev. 15.4; 16.5.) Of the 16 times when it describes Christians it is once used in a macarism (20.6) and once (22.11) with reference to a Christian Anyone. Here, where ὁ ἀδικῶν καὶ ὁ ῥυπαρός is contrasted with ὁ δίκαιος καὶ ὁ ἅγιος, we have another instance of purity language, which is used to describe both the Good person and his opposite. Cf. Satake, *Gemeindeordnung*, pp. 26–34.

109 Following Thompson, *Book of Revelation*, p. 78.

110 Thompson, *Book of Revelation*, p. 78.

The dichotomized female images fit well into this creation of a world. The evil, hostile power Babylon is portrayed as the Great Prostitute, chaotic, uncontrolled and impure; the Good World to come is Jerusalem the Bride, who keeps to her place, is controlled and pure. And those who have a share in the redeemed world (the Insiders of the author's community) must be like her, while those who are like Babylon are outsiders to the community and will be outside of salvation.

Revelation presents the dualism characteristic of apocalypses and the apocalyptic through the use of dualisms connected with gender. However, Revelation does not, as far as I have seen, use the male–female dualism connected with spirit/matter, reason/feeling and other constructions that are often ontological. Even if the men/women contrast in Rev. 14.4a could be related to the connection between women and matter (or other features of this doomed world), the connection is not developed. This has to do with the fact that, even if the dualisms in Revelation may tend toward the ontological, they are primarily ethical. Revelation is not concerned with liberation from matter, imperfection and the like.

But a kind of ethical dualism, a fight between Good and Evil, God and the Devil, is basic. Human beings must choose sides. To describe this kind of dualism, the dichotomized images of women, as they are shaped within the honor–shame value system, is useful. 'Good' human beings or institutions in Revelation are under the control of their Lord, obedient. Someone or something that is at its proper place – in other words, pure – is Good. This is what was expected from women, and this is what Revelation expects from Christians.[111]

What is 'evil', then, are persons or human institutions who refuse to be controlled by the Lord, who are disobedient. Since they do not stay at their place in the order they are impure. This refusal and so its attendant evil and impurity are characteristic of 'bad' women, and characteristic of the Others, those who do not conform to the ways of believing and living which John finds 'Christian'.

The many diverse images of Christians are held together through 'purity', explicitly mentioned or implicit. Since 'impurity' and 'female' may be seen as connected in Revelation, in the texts reused (e.g., Exodus 19), and in the cultural context, the emphasis on purity as a basic characteristic of what has a share in salvation suggests that the saved ones are male.[112] The imagery used to describe Christians also often implies through other means – and in Rev. 14.4a says in plain words – that they are males. If we stay within the text and the world created through the text, there is no other room for women, neither in time nor in eternity, than to be the Others, the ones the Christian has refused along with lies, Beast worship or murder. 'Women' are necessary for the construction of Christian identity but without any part in it.

However, there is a paradox in the maleness of this normative Christian.[113] He is

---

111 Cf. Garrett, 'Revelation', pp. 377, 382 for a similar reading.

112 So Pippin, *Death and Desire*, pp. 50, 70.

113 Pippin, *Apocalyptic Bodies*, pp. 121–25, argues that the Christians, who are in her opinion envisioned as a male collective, are supposed to identify with Jerusalem the Bride, and thereby become females, in order to marry the Lamb. Pippin also concludes (p. 123) that, in Revelation, heaven is a 'sanitized place where the only role for the female is played by men', a conclusion similar to my own but reached in a different way.

supposed to model his behavior after the paradigm of the Good Woman, and thus, in all his masculinity, he takes on female traits. According to Revelation, Christians are a collective of undefiled males who resemble the Good Woman.

Of course, the ideal prescribed for men might as well be enacted by women. The role of the 'male woman' may also be implicit in Revelation,[114] but it is not explicit in the text. In fact, Revelation has no concern for real women; it is solely concerned with formulating an understanding of the world and of Christian identity, an identity that is male. Women are only used to think with, and as a means for expressing an understanding of Self and of the Other.

Concluding Discussion

I have presented a reading of Revelation which focuses on the problematic features of the text for feminist readers, to a high degree confirming the readings by Tina Pippin and Susan Garrett. It may seem to be the case that Revelation is simply impossible for feminists. However, there are also other ways to read. In the 1990s, feminist analysis and evaluation became a site not only for different readings of Revelation but also for discussions of central issues with relevance far beyond the interpretation of this text.[115]

The main participants in this discussion are Elisabeth Schüssler Fiorenza and Tina Pippin.[116] Another critical, at least deeply ambivalent, reader is Susan Garrett.[117] Luzia Sutter Rehman forms her own reading, which is more optimistic about the possibility of reading Revelation as a vision of liberation, in relation to Garrett.[118] Since space is limited, I have chosen to focus on Schüssler Fiorenza and Pippin.[119]

Schüssler Fiorenza reads Revelation in a liberation-theological tradition as a vision of the just world God will create for all the oppressed.[120] Pippin finds the text suitable for reading with gender as an analytical tool, since many textual meanings

---

114 See, e.g., Aspegren, *Male Woman*.

115 See Pippin, *Death and Desire*, esp. pp. 50–53; Schüssler Fiorenza, *Vision of A Just World*, esp. pp. 12–15, 130, 131; *eadem*, 'Epilogue' in *The Book of Revelation: Justice and Judgment* (2nd ed., Philadelphia, PA: Fortress Press, 1998), pp. 205–36; *eadem*, *Sharing Her Word: Feminist Biblical Interpretation in Context* (Boston, MA: Beacon Press, 1998), pp. 93–95, 99–101. See also Catherine Keller, *Apocalypse Now and Then: A Feminist Guide to the End of the World* (Boston, MA: Beacon Press, 1996), pp. 46, 74, 324–25 n. 125. For examples of how feminist strategies developed for work with Revelation are given a more general relevance see E. Schüssler Fiorenza, *But She Said: Feminist Practices of Biblical Interpretation* (Boston, MA: Beacon Press, 1992), pp. 41–43 and the criticism of this passage by the Bible and Culture Collective, G. Aichele et al., *The Postmodern Bible* (The Bible and Culture Collective; New Haven, CT: Yale University Press, 1995), pp. 260–67 (parts of this discussion refer to other parts of *But She Said*). See also the response to the criticism in Schüssler Fiorenza, *Sharing Her Word*, pp. 16–21.

116 See Pippin, *Death and Desire*, pp. 47, 51–53, 63; Schüssler Fiorenza, *Vision of a Just World*, pp. 12–15, 130–31; 'Epilogue', pp. 208–209, 216–19; *Sharing Her Word*, pp. 93–95, 99–101.

117 Garrett, 'Revelation', esp. pp. 377, 382.

118 Sutter Rehmann, 'Offenbarung', esp. pp. 727, 735–36.

119 For a more developed presentation and discussion of feminist readings of Revelation with additional examples, see Stenström, 'Ultimate Liberation or Ultimate Backlash?'; Sutter Rehman, 'Offenbarung', came to my attention too late to integrate discussion of it in the dissertation.

120 This is visible throughout Schüssler Fiorenza, *Vision of A Just World*, esp. pp. 5–6, 14–15, 27–29, 109–14, 131, 139.

become visible through such an analysis. As a result of what such an analysis makes clear, she finds it impossible to read Revelation as liberating for women.[121] Where Schüssler Fiorenza sees in Revelation a vision of a future for liberated women, Pippin sees a future liberated from women.

Schüssler Fiorenza is well aware of the problems inherent in the female imagery and finds a feminist critique of it necessary.[122] However, she still finds it possible to reclaim the text for women. The gendered meaning of the female imagery should, in her opinion, not be seen as primary. Masculine grammatical gender is to be seen as inclusive, until it is made clear that a gender-specific meaning is intended. The female imagery is to be understood as conventional, a kind of dead metaphor that can be translated into another language, a living language that does not reproduce the androcentrism and misogyny of the original. Thus translated, the images may speak clearly again, not about how horrible women are but about a God who is on the side of the oppressed in their struggle for liberation, a language that exhorts us to choose the same side as God in this struggle.[123]

I think my reading intimates that I am one of the pessimists.[124] Presupposing the commonly recognized insight that the form and content of a text cannot be separated, as a box and its contents, I am skeptical about the proposal that the content, the message, of e.g. 14.4a, can be separated from its language.

Furthermore, Schüssler Fiorenza has convinced me that the rhetoric of Revelation and its mythopoetic language do something to the reader/hearer and evoke a number of possible meanings. She has taught me that the language is not fully translatable and that it reaches us at a level deeper than the mere intellectual. Therefore, I am very sceptical of her translation strategy, which I fear may stay at the intellectual level. I cannot get rid of the feeling that she is actually in conflict with her own basic understanding of the language of Revelation in her strivings to reclaim the text for women.

When I try to relate Revelation to myself and other contemporary female readers, I find it highly relevant to ask which deeply internalized, negative images of women this text touches in us, images of which I may not be fully conscious. I am worried about what this may do to me, for example, when I am invited to rejoice over the death of the Whore. My brain may be able to criticize the imagery and then translate it into a message about the downfall of the oppressor. But what happens deep down in me, where even I may have internalized the contempt for 'the Whore'?[125]

It is no solution for me that this female imagery, including Rev. 14.4a, is symbolic, since the symbolic dimension is basic in the construction of gender. When it comes to gendered symbols, none of them is 'only a symbol'. They all participate in the construction of gender. I am also convinced that even conventional language – the sexist and heterosexist jokes, the anti-Semitic caricatures of Jews, all kinds of

121 This is basic throughout Pippin, *Death and Desire*. See esp. pp. 53, 56, 80, 105.

122 Schüssler Fiorenza, *Vision of a Just World*, pp. 14, 130–31; 'Visionary Rhetoric', p. 199.

123 Schüssler Fiorenza, 'Visionary Rhetoric', pp. 13–15.

124 I admit all similarities between my own understanding of Revelation and the ones found in Garrett, 'Revelation', as well as works by Pippin.

125 Cf. Pippin, *Death and Desire*, pp. 81–82.

prejudices, to take only some examples – hurts, and it participates in oppressive structures.[126]

I do not think that the author of Revelation primarily intended to express his opinions about women. In my reading and feminist evaluation of the text, I take it as self-evident that John wanted to interpret his time, to show what he considered good and what he found evil, and to influence the beliefs and praxis of his audience. My criticism has nothing to do with taking the language literally in a simple sense as referring, for example, to actual women. The point is that when John communicated his interpretation to his audience and tried to influence them, he used a language provided by his culture, a language where one 'uses women to think with' and where speech about women and sexuality can make points about something else. He also uses a purity language where impurity is connected with women and sexuality. This makes Revelation deeply problematic (to say the least) for those who do not accept, for example, the dichotomizing of women into Good and Bad or those culturally conditioned meanings of 'women' which make it possible to describe a firm commitment to Christian beliefs and praxis as keeping oneself undefiled from (sexual intercourse with) women.

However, I am more optimistic than Schüssler Fiorenza on one issue. I do not think that a gender analysis of Revelation which does not lead to reclaiming through translation necessarily leads to a reinforcement of stereotypes or leads us away from politics. Making oppressive patterns visible might well give rise to protest and strengthen the commitment to struggle for change.

My brief, tentative and descriptive presentation of the uses of purity language, female and sexual imagery, and understanding of Christian identity in Revelation points to further tasks for feminist scholars. It evokes a number of questions that are not new, but that may be approached anew with the findings presented as the point of departure. There are ongoing discussions where feminist biblical scholars may find a place, both in the sense of being influenced and of influencing. There must be room for further and more sophisticated analyses of the texts I have highlighted, with a number of theoretical tools. The description of Christian identity above also evokes the questions of how this identity, the symbolic understandings of the self as individual and collective, is realized in practice. How is the vertical relation to God actualized in horizontal relations, to other humans inside and outside the community? Revelation and its reception are also rewarding objects of study for feminists who want to scrutinize constructions of gender and analyze how symbolic speech about women can be a speech about virtue and vice, good and evil in all arenas of life.[127] It is here, I think, that feminist study of Revelation finds one of its most important contexts.

Other early Christian texts have similarities to Revelation, although they are parallel developments from the same cultural presuppositions rather than examples of direct literary influence.[128] For example, Rev. 14.4a is interesting as part of a pattern

---

126 Cf. Garrett, 'Revelation', p. 381.

127 See, e.g., Pippin on the Jezebel image in history, in *Apocalyptic Bodies*, pp. 32–42.

128 For New Testament texts, see 2 Cor. 11.2 (a parallel mentioned by, e.g., Aune, *Revelation 6–16*, p. 812; Lohse, *Offenbarung*, p. 83; Garrett, 'Revelation', p. 378) and the Church as bride imagery in Ephesians 5.

of ideas in its cultural context. The understanding of the 'virginal man' as the perfect human, or the faithful Jew, has been found elsewhere. Kerstin Aspegren mentions the root in Plato and Philo for the connection 'male–perfect–virginal' which will appear in Christian texts.[129] There are texts of debated dating and provenance (Christian or Jewish?) which provide other examples of the male virgin as an image of a person faithful to God, namely *Joseph and Aseneth*, where παρθένος is also used (4.7; 8.1), and the *Testament of Joseph*, where παρθένος is not used but where Joseph's fidelity towards his God is enacted through his defending himself against the seductions of Potiphar's wife. Thus, my reading of Revelation points towards a broader study of 'the virginal male'.[130]

The virginal men in Revelation ought to model their lives after the ideal of the Good Woman. This motif has also been found elsewhere, such as in the *Acts of Thomas*.[131] Therefore, the image of the ideal Christian in Revelation may also contribute to a study of the 'female man' in early Christianity, a character that must be as interesting a subject of study as is his sister, the 'male woman'.

Feminist exegetical work along these lines, where the understanding of Christian identity in Revelation is placed in a wider, cultural and historical context, makes it possible to draw lines from the past to our own time, to ourselves. Such a work may contribute to the understanding of how we got the societies and gender constructions that we have, an understanding that is the presupposition for all work for change.

---

129 Aspegren, *Male Woman*, p. 14.
130 See, e.g., the reuse of Rev. 14.1–5 in Methodius, *Symposion*, Discourse 1, ch. 5, where Christ is the ἀρχιπαρθένος, who leads the choir of the virgins.
131 See Aspegren, *Male Woman*, p. 133.

Women in Myth and History:
Deconstructing John's Characterizations*

David L. Barr

'Jezebel' may be as good an example as any of Susan Suleiman's observation that 'The cultural significance of the female body is not only (not even first and foremost) that of a flesh-and-blood entity, but of a symbolic construct.'[1] Consider this riff from Tom Robbins's novel *Skinny Legs and All*; it comes in an exchange between Buddy Winkler (a fundamentalist preacher willing to precipitate World War Three if it will hasten the Second Coming) and Patsy Charles, a member of his church who is just a bit irreverent. Buddy has come for dinner; he had earlier called Ellen Charles, Patsy's grown daughter, 'Jezebel' for using makeup, and Patsy goads him into explaining what he meant:

'It is written in the Book of Revelation, chapter two, verse eighteen, that God Almighty sent a message to the church in Thyatira—'
'Where?'
'Thyatira.'
'Where's that?'
'It don't matter! It don't exist anymore. God said unto them, "I have a few things against thee, because thou sufferest a woman named Jezebel, which calleth herself a prophetess, to teach and to seduce my servants to commit fornication."'
'So she didn't do the fornicating herself. She tried to get other folks to do it.'
'Patsy, you're missin' the point. Jezebel was a prophetess of Baal. She was a pagan fanatic; she was a filthy idolator who led the Is-raelites away from Jehovah. For twenty-seven years, that woman used her power as queen to try to overthrow Jehovah and replace him with the idols of her native country.'
'What was the king doing all this time?'
'Ahab was under her thumb. It's the same ol' story. A connivin' woman influencin' a weak man to commit crimes he never woulda had the gumption to commit by hisself.'
'Uh-huh.'
'She wanted to convert Is-ra-el to Baal worship. I'm talkin' the gold calf, Patsy. You know what I'm talkin'? I'm talkin' strange shrines in the woods. I'm talking nekkidness and orgy and human sacrifice. Little children by the hundreds sacrificed to some stupid, smelly dairy animal. Babies hacked to pieces on a greasy altar in the moonlight—'
'Gross!' Patsy suddenly held the plumping pork chops in vomitous regard. 'I don't wanna hear about dead babies.'
'Oh, we hear a heap of ugly thing when we speak of Jezebel. Her lies sent an innocent neighbor to a horrible end so that Ahab could annex his vineyards.'
'Hubby's little helper went too far, you say? But tell me now, Bud, where does the makeup figger in?'

* An earlier version of this paper was presented to the Section on John's Apocalypse at the Society of Biblical Literature Annual Meeting, Toronto, 26 November 2002.
1 Susan R. Suleiman, 'Introduction', in *eadem* (ed.), *The Female Body in Western Culture* (Cambridge, MA: Harvard University Press, 1986), p. 2.

'The makeup?'

'You know, the painted woman thing. Isn't that what she's remembered for?'

'Patsy, have you ever seen a baboon's bottom?'

'I thought we agreed not to spoil our supper.'

'A baboon's rump is redder than your apron. Sometimes there's yellow and blue thrown in. Why does your baboon have a colored rump? To attract other baboons to mate with it. Why did Jezebel color her face? I'll wager you can make the obvious connection.'

When Patsy later passes this information on to her daughter, who had asked her to find out, Ellen responds, 'I'm delighted to learn that I've been compared to a heathen fornication instructor, a husband corrupter, and a baboon's ass, all in one lump.'[2]

Jezebel, in Robbins's story, turns out to be an even more complex lump, as a significant theme of the novel is how the daughter learns to read Jezebel differently. But Jezebel is a pretty big lump in John's story as well.

First, I think the woman John calls Jezebel is a real person, even though it is not likely that any woman bore such a name in John's time. She is located in a particular city; specific actions are alleged of her; she is assumed to have significant authority; John presumes the audience will know who he means. But this mingling of historical and mythical images is characteristic of the Apocalypse. John has so dressed his women in mythic guise that they no longer appear to be mere mortals. I want to think about the fact that all John's female characters are symbolic constructs of the first order, to ask how he got from history to myth, and to ask as well whether it is possible to retrace his steps.

John's story is about the hidden world of apocalyptic truth, and the women who appear in this story are not real women. The purpose of his story is not to depict women but to create a scenario that allows his audience to overcome Roman oppression.[3] Nevertheless, his story does intersect with the lives of real women in the real world, most often in oppressive fashion.[4] To understand this contradiction and disentangle the liberating and oppressive aspects of the work, this essay will first review John's four main women characters for their historical and mythic dimensions. It will then briefly explore the function of myth and the dialectic between signifier and signified, and finally, it will attempt a deconstructive reading of the mythic images.

John's story can certainly be read as an instance of patriarchal misogyny; that may in fact appear to us to be a natural reading. Perhaps so. But it is also capable of an unnatural reading, one that enables us to view John's images of women Otherwise.

---

2 Tom Robbins, *Skinny Legs and All* (New York: Bantam, 1995), pp. 32–33.

3 Barbara R. Rossing argues that the two women are not used in an individualist, moralistic, sense but with a corporate, political, meaning. See her *The Choice Between Two Cities: Whore, Bride, and Empire in the Apocalypse* (Harvard Theological Studies; Harrisburg, PA: Trinity Press International, 1999), p. 164.

4 While I disagree with her solution, I quite agree with Tina Pippin's analysis of the problems of Revelation and the role it assigns to women: passive objects of men's desires. See *Death and Desire: The Rhetoric of Gender in the Apocalypse of John* (Literary Currents in Biblical Interpretation; Louisville, KY: Westminster/John Knox Press, 1992) and *Apocalyptic Bodies: The Biblical End of the World in Text and Image* (London and New York: Routledge, 1999).

Women in Myth and History

What I am addressing here is not unique to John's treatment of women. It is the function of an apocalypse to see the universal in (and behind) the particular, to see through history to myth.[5] We thus seek to uncover the dialectic between John's mythic story of women and the women of his historical situation.

Gaia/Earth

There are four or five female characters in John's story; the one most often over-looked plays only a minor role and can be quickly summarized. She is Gaia/Earth, who defended another woman whom the Dragon was trying to destroy in a flood: Gaia/Earth 'opened her mouth and swallowed the river that the Dragon had poured from his mouth' (12.11). While I suspect – what with this mouth-to-mouth exchange of fluids – there is some room for Freud in this story, I only observe that Gaia/Earth is a strictly mythic character. That Gaia is the original Queen Mother will interest us later, for all the other characters seem to be queens as well. The other four women are well known and widely treated, so I will be brief, working backwards as I often do.[6]

The Queen Consort

Better known as the Bride of the Lamb, this last of the four major female characters in the Apocalypse is the least interesting. We barely glimpse her as the angel promises to show John 'the bride, the wife of the Lamb', but what he sees is 'the holy city Jerusalem coming down out of heaven from God'. The remaining description is of the city. Of course it was traditional to picture cities as women; there are countless feminine images of both Rome/Roma as regal women and of conquered cities portrayed as captive women. So it does not surprise us that a city is pictured as a bride, but it is a little odd for a bride to be pictured as a city. The literary strategy here is profoundly opposite from that in John's portrayal of Babylon/Rome, where the female image is maintained up to the very last moment; here the female image is abandoned immediately. This has the effect of de-sexualizing the image, and it may reflect John's uneasiness with sex itself (as does the rather disconcerting image of the community as 'virgins' who 'have not defiled themselves with women' at 14.4).

This image of the city as bride perhaps owes something to the scriptural metaphors of Israel as God's bride/wife (e.g., Isa. 49.18; Ezek. 16.8–14), but as A. Yarbro Collins has shown, it also fits nicely with the structure of the Holy War mythology. There are many versions of the myth, but the general dénouement

---

5 Of the many excellent discussions of myth and apocalyptic, see Paul D. Hanson, *The Dawn of Apocalyptic: The Historical and Sociological Roots of Jewish Apocalyptic Eschatology* (rev. edn, Philadelphia, PA: Fortress Press, 1979) and A. Yarbro Collins, *The Combat Myth in the Book of Revelation* (HDR, 9; Chico, CA: Scholars Press, 1976).

6 In addition to Rossing, *Choice Between Two Cities*, and Pippin, *Death and Desire* and *Apocalyptic Bodies*, see Edith M. Humphrey, *The Ladies and the Cities: Transformation and Apocalyptic Identity in Joseph and Aseneth, 4 Ezra, The Apocalypse, and the Shepherd of Hermas* (Sheffield: Sheffield Academic Press, 1995); Catherine Keller, *Apocalypse Now and Then: A Feminist Guide to the End of the World* (Boston, MA: Beacon Press, 1996); and Paul Duff, *Who Rides the Beast? Prophetic Rivalry and the Rhetoric of Crisis in the Churches of the Apocalypse* (New York: Oxford University Press, 2001).

includes a final battle, renewed order and fertility, procession and victory shout, temple dedication, wedding banquet, and universal rule of the champion.[7] It is clear that the author's real interest is the city, and the bride image is necessitated only by the underlying mythic structure.[8]

This mythic image is enhanced by its location on a great high mountain (21.10), surely the sacred center of the universe. The Queen Consort is entirely a mythic image and corresponds to no historical feminine reality; it represents at best a cosmic image of the faithful community.

The Queen Ruler
Better known as the Great Whore or the Whore of Babylon, the Queen Ruler is a far more complex image. The character is more fully drawn, there is a narrative sequence, and the image remains a woman until the very end when, like the bride image, it is suddenly a city. Marla Selvidge comments on the 'irony' of John's portrayals, wherein the depictions of opposing women are active, creative and powerful, whereas the women who do not oppose him are rendered as passive, dull and 'almost boring'.[9]

This woman is hardly boring; even John is 'amazed' (θαύμαζω = to be awed by a spectacle; 17.6). She is described as being dressed as a ruler (in scarlet and purple) and carrying a gold cup – she is clearly a lady. But no. She is drunk, and her cup is full of the impurities of her sexual transgressions, a revolting if not entirely clear image. Even more revolting, her drunkenness is caused by her drinking of the blood of the witnesses of Jesus.[10] Her power seems to rest in part in her sexual seductiveness, for the kings of the earth have 'committed fornication with her' (18.3). She seems to be riding high, supported by the scarlet beast with ten horns. She proclaims her own invulnerability: 'I rule as a queen; I am no widow, and I will never see grief.'[11]

Then things turn ugly. The beast and its allies desert the Queen Ruler, strip her naked, eat her and burn her up. The proud and haughty queen is reduced to food for beasts, reduced to ashes.

Unlike the Queen Consort, the historical reference(s) here is clear, more or less: the Queen Ruler is most often identified with Rome; she is less often but vigorously

---

7 See the discussion in Chapter 5 of Collins, *Combat Myth*, and S. H. Hooke, 'The Myth and Ritual Pattern in Jewish and Christian Apocalyptic' in *idem*, *The Labyrinth: Further Studies on the Relationship Between Myth and Ritual in the Ancient World* (New York: Macmillan, 1935), pp. 213–33.

8 The image also serves John's story, where she is the counterfoil to the Queen Ruler of ch. 17 (compare 17.1 with 21.9) and the correlate to the Queen of Heaven in ch. 12. There is no Temple dedication in John's story because there is no Temple in the New Jerusalem (21.22). The marriage and wedding banquet are described in 19.7 and following. The extraordinary fertility of the new order is indicated at 22.2.

9 Marla J. Selvidge, 'Powerful and Powerless Women in the Apocalypse', *NeoT* 26 (1992), pp. 157–67 (167). The situation is reminiscent of Milton's *Paradise Lost*, where Satan proves to be a more fully drawn character than God.

10 Purity notions pervade these images, wherein the human body replicates the social body. Women are impure when they discharge blood; this woman drinks blood. Consumption of any kind of blood was to result in expulsion from the community (Lev. 7.26–27). The whole world here is perverted.

11 Rev. 18.7; see the precursor at Isa. 47.8.

defined as Jerusalem.[12] On the one hand, she is certainly the ruler over the nations, and this figure can only be Rome in John's time. But on the other hand, she is the great city destroyed, and so is, certainly, Jerusalem (John earlier identified Jerusalem as the great city [11.8]). This is, in other words, a complex symbol. The Queen Ruler is clearly Rome, the city that sat atop the world in John's time, but she is seen by one from Judea[13] whose own city once sat atop the world. Jerusalem too tried to ride on imperial power (or so the priestly cooperation with Rome must have seemed to one like John), and look what happened to her.

That is, John is not only thinking historically, he is thinking mythically, and in myth historical realities merge. The undergirding myth of the Queen Ruler seems to be that of Chaos; in a myth already two millennia old in John's time, the original Queen of the Gods, Tiamat, sought to destroy the created order but was herself destroyed. Versions of the Chaos myth existed in all cultures – Egyptian, Greek, Roman, Jewish – and elements of this myth have been mediated to John in a Jewish guise that I will come to below.

This image of the Queen Ruler is very powerful and it is quite surprising, as Caroline Vander Stichele has shown, that she is never represented in art from antiquity (which concentrated on the peaceful and triumphal motifs of the Apocalypse) and rarely in the medieval tradition outside illuminated manuscripts. Only in the modern period is her sexuality emphasized; apparently she does not appear naked until 1993.[14] I suspect that these images play a far different role in our culture than they did in antiquity.

The Queen of Heaven

The next woman I will describe occurs suddenly and dramatically in the story – out of thin air, we might say – for John looks into the sky and there sees her, the Queen of Heaven (Revelation 12). She is clearly a mythic character: clothed with the sun, the moon beneath her, twelve stars crowning her head. What is not so clear is just which mythic character she is; among the suggestions: Israel, the Church, Eve, Leto, Isis, Roma, all the above.[15] What we (post-) moderns fail to grasp is that, mythologically

12 For the dominant view see David E. Aune, *Revelation 6–16* (WBC, 52B; Nashville, TN: Thomas Nelson Publishers, 1998), p. 959, and the bibliography there. For the minority view that sees her as Jerusalem see Alan James Beagley, *The 'Sitz Im Leben' of the Apocalypse with Particular Reference to the Role of the Church's Enemies* (BZNW, 50; Berlin: de Gruyter, 1987). There may also be some malicious delight in the echo of the popular image of the wife of Claudius, Messalina, as a wanton queen; see J. Edgar Burns, 'Contrasted Women of Apocalypse 12 and 17', *CBQ* 26 (1964), pp. 459–63.

13 On the possible background of John, see A. Yarbro Collins, *Crisis and Catharsis: The Power of the Apocalypse* (Philadelphia, PA: Westminster Press, 1984), pp. 25–50; for an overview and bibliography see David E. Aune, *Revelation 1–5* (WBC, 52A; Nashville, TN: Thomas Nelson Publishers, 1998), pp. xlvii–lvi.

14 Caroline Vander Stichele, 'Apocalypse, Art and Abjection: Images of the Great Whore', in George Aichele (ed.), *Culture, Entertainment and the Bible* (Sheffield: Sheffield Academic Press, 2000), pp. 124–38 (131).

15 Collins discusses the various versions of this myth and concludes that John's telling is closest to the Leto myth (*Combat Myth*, p. 67). While this is true of the form of the story, the basic mythic tradition seems to be that of Eve, the one whose son would crush the serpent's head (Gen. 3.15). While the Pauline tradition blamed Eve for failing (1 Tim. 2.11–14), John's use of the myth is entirely positive.

speaking, these are not so much alternatives as aspects. There's that wonderful scene in the *Metamorphosis* where Lucius address the Goddess in her diverse appearances. He first salutes her as the bountiful Earth (Ceres), then as the heavenly star (Venus), then as the genetrix of life (Artemis), and finally as the associate of death (Proserpina). We might think he had covered his bases. But when she replies, she extends his list, saying she is called: Pessinuntine Mother of the Gods, Cecropian Minerva, Paphian Venus, Dictynna Diana, Ortygian Proserpina, Attic Ceres, Juno, Bellona, Hecate, Rhamnusia, before insisting on her real name, which is Queen Isis.[16]

I am not, of course, suggesting that John would agree with this list; I make the more basic point that mythological thinking is not much concerned with discrete identities. Our nameless woman is just that: woman, unnamed. Her traits suggest a conflation of the various Queen of Heaven myths with the stories of Israel and Eve, mother of the future king. Our woman is not only shown as a cosmic ruler herself; she is pregnant with a future ruler. The Dragon, who knows the woman's son to be his own death warrant (as the God of Genesis had promised Eve, Gen 3.15), waits to devour him. The child is snatched up to heaven while the woman flies away to the desert. There she is attacked, but she is preserved by her ally Earth, who opens her mouth and swallows the flood (a rare instance of woman rescuing woman). The Dragon, and thus the storyteller, now loses interest in her, and the story shifts to the war on her 'seed', which seems an odd choice of terms since ancient cultures generally thought the seed came from the man and was planted in the field of the woman. The Queen of Heaven's sojourn in the wilderness is said to be temporary (12.14), but she disappears from the story.

Again, the mythic portrayal has overwhelmed the historical. To the degree that history can be found here, the dominant image is that of Israel in the wilderness after the Exodus escape through the flood waters that destroy the pursuing army.[17]

Queen Jezebel

The last character I will examine is also a mother, but not a proper mother like the Queen of Heaven. Now this is a really interesting woman. She seems to have been a rival to John in the city of Thyatira, whom John chooses to disguise in the mythic figure of Queen Jezebel. However, the mythic Jezebel was originally a historical figure. Daughter of King Ethbaal of Sidon, wife of King Ahab of Israel, and mother of King Joram of Israel, this woman made a name for herself.[18] And what a name. While the charges against the historical Jezebel are serious – they involve the murder of the innocent Naboth to claim his vineyard and the execution of prophets of Yahweh – these are not what mark her image. Making only subliminal use of any notion of usurpation of power, John concentrates instead on her sexuality. There is nothing in the record about Jezebel committing any acts of sexual indiscretion (though the man who is about to murder her accuses her of 'whoredoms and

---

16 Lucius Apuleius, *The Golden Ass* (trans. Stephen G. Adlington; London: Heinemann, 1915), p. 547.

17 The eagle's wings and wilderness protection recall Exod. 19.4; Pharaoh has been replaced by Satan and the Egyptian army by a flood, but such substitutions are the essence of myth.

18 Jezebel's story is told through the eyes of the Deuteronomic Historian in 1 Kings 18, 21, and 2 Kings 9.

sorceries' [2 Kgs 9.22]); to the contrary, she appears to be quite a faithful wife and mother. What I cannot tell is whether John invented the sexual charges or whether they had become part of the image of Jezebel already; I suspect the latter.[19]

In either case, what makes Jezebel a useful image for John is her sponsorship of prophets inspired by the Goddess Asherah (Astarte) and her consort Baal (900 of them ate at her table, according to 1 Kgs 18.19). This illicit table is also useful to John, for in his judgment the table of his rival at Thyatira is also faulty: she eats idolatrous food. More in a moment. But as we attempt to move back toward history – from the mythic Jezebel to the rival prophet of Thyatira – we need to raise two questions. Why does John not address his rival by name? And how does John manage to force her from her soapbox into the bedroom; that is, why the sex?

Everyone agrees that John's opponent is not actually named Jezebel, but few have raised the issue of why John hides her real name. To my mind the closest to an answer, and the most convincing one, comes from Paul Duff:[20] she was likely too powerful to attack directly. Those who followed her were probably the wealthiest and most influential members of the assemblies. John needed to move cautiously or risk alienating important people. John is thus not hiding her identity any more than he is hiding Rome's identity. Any competent reader would know of whom he speaks. His attack on his powerful rival must be indirect; he must present the image of the opponent in such a way that the reader condemns it.

This need also explains the sexual innuendo, for what better way to ruin a woman's reputation? It is extremely unlikely that the rival prophet engaged in any kind of sexual misconduct, so how does John manage the allegation? All the material he needed lay readily at hand in the Hebrew prophets, especially Hosea, Ezekiel and Jeremiah.[21] Consider Hos. 2.2–5:

> Plead with your mother, plead – for she is not my wife, and I am not her husband – that she put away her whoring from her face, and her adultery from between her breasts, or I will strip her naked and expose her as in the day she was born, and make her like a wilderness, and turn her into a parched land, and kill her with thirst. Upon her children also I will have no pity, because they are children of whoredom. For their mother has played the whore; she who conceived them has acted shamefully.

Hosea does go on to indicate directly that he is talking about Israel and the worship of Baal (2.8). The equation of idolatry and adultery became a commonplace; John's genius – an evil genius to be sure – was to use it against an actual woman.[22]

---

19 For an excellent discussion of the Jezebel narrative, including the sexualization of the figure, see Judith E. McKinlay, 'Negotiating the Frame for Viewing the Death of Jezebel', *BibInt* 10.3 (2002), pp. 305–23. Peter R. Ackroyd suggested that the portrayal of Jezebel in Kings already attempts to 'frame' her with characteristics of the mother goddess; see his 'Goddesses, Women, and Jezebel', in Averil Cameron and Amélie Kuhrt (eds), *Images of Women in Antiquity* (Detroit, MI: Wayne State University Press, 1983), pp. 245–59 (258).

20 Duff, *Who Rides the Beast?*

21 See Marla J. Selvidge, 'Reflections on Violence and Pornography: Misogyny in the Apocalypse and Ancient Hebrew Prophecy', in Athalya Brenner (ed.), *A Feminist Companion to the Hebrew Bible in the New Testament* (FCB, 10; Sheffield: Sheffield Academic Press, 1996), pp. 274–85.

22 As we will see, Jezebel is the anti-image of the Queen Consort, making the 'wife' imagery of Hosea seem appropriate, including the death of her children (Rev. 2.22–23).

What then can we conclude about the historical woman, the prophet of Thyatira? Were she really the sexual profligate that John paints, there would have been little need to warn the Thyatirans not to tolerate her. Almost certainly her pornography is of the spirit, and John sees her commensality with idolaters as symbolic adultery. John wishes his readers to see her as a factional leader who advocates accommodation to Greco-Roman culture with all its attendant immorality – the ultimate guilt by association.

If we try to read through John's judgment, we might conclude that she was a woman who did advocate participation in the social and commercial life of Asia Minor.[23] Perhaps a follower of Paul, she at least adopts a similar strategy: eating the idol-tainted food of the pagans and practicing her craft. Her followers would be able to participate in the economic life of the cities. If we go a step further and ask how she presented herself, the answer becomes evident. No less than John, she claimed the prophetic word.

Despite John's polemic, then, it is doubtful that she shared anything with Israel's Jezebel: she did not worship the Goddess; she did not sponsor prophets to some other divinity; she did not murder anyone; she did not attack rival prophets as John does. The myth obscures the history.

Perhaps the 'history' shapes the myth, for two motifs from the Jezebel story appear in the characterization of the Queen Ruler: her supporters turn against her (Jezebel thrown from her balcony by her own eunuchs), and she is eaten by the beasts (her body left in the street to be eaten by the dogs; 2 Kgs 9.33–36). In addition, like the Ruler Queen, the historical Jezebel's hands are bloody with the lives of the prophets of Yahweh.

In summary, John uses women's bodies as symbolic constructs by portraying four mythic queens. Two are good: the Queen Mother and the Queen Consort, both of whom are depicted in positive relationship to their male protector, son or husband. The Queen Mother is preserved in the wilderness, and the Dragon who sought her destruction is destroyed by her son. A bride prepared for her wedding, the Queen Consort awaits the victorious son. These images correspond in only a general way to the historical reality of the community of the faithful, whether Israel or the church. They have only an accidental gender identity: they are not historically female. Still, John has chosen to construct his image of the faithful community on the female body.

The other two queens are bad women who conform to the stereotypical perception of sexually coded women as wicked. The bad women look a lot alike on the mythic level (both are rulers, both have bloody hands, both are sexually tainted, both support foreign deities), but they bear very little resemblance on the historical level. That is, one is an empire; the other is an actual woman – and none of the traits accorded them is true of the actual woman, so far as we can see.

John's strategy works on two fronts. His primary aim is to persuade the audience to see Rome as the oppressor;[24] a sub-theme is to see the prophet of Thyatira as Rome's alter ego.[25] He succeeds brilliantly at both – so brilliantly that scholars have

---

23 Again, Duff's argument is convincing; see *Who Rides the Beast?*, esp. chapters 5 and 10.
24 Collins, *Crisis and Catharsis*, p. 141.
25 Duff, *Who Rides the Beast?*, pp. 89–92.

invented a Domitianic persecution and condemned Jezebel's apostasy, with no real evidence for either outside John's rhetoric.[26]

I do not wish in this essay to explore further the world behind the text – to ask after the politics of the Roman economy or the power relations at Thyatira – I wish rather to consider the world in front of the text. How might we as modern readers respond to the oppressive nature of these images? This question is most powerfully put by Tina Pippin's autobiographical response: 'Having studied the evils of Roman imperial policy in the colonies, I find the violent destruction of Babylon very cathartic. But when I looked into the face of Babylon, I saw a woman.'[27]

I find this a disturbing and compelling conclusion. I come finally to adopt the dual premise: that the positive images of women in the work are hardly liberating, and that the negative images are oppressive and degrading.[28] So I ask: what are we to do then?

Two options have been vigorously presented and cogently argued. Pippin has insisted on confronting these images directly and condemning the book as – among other labels – a 'pornoapocalypse'.[29] Marla Selvidge would seem to agree.[30] The logic of this approach is to reject the book and, if possible, discard it. I admit to being tempted by this approach, and I have never recommended that my daughter read it (though I hope she has read my book about it!).

But I have finally decided that the Apocalypse is too powerful to be ignored: it is powerful both in its own images and story and powerful in its influence on American culture and politics. This leads to the other option: to read the Apocalypse against the grain. Yet this option also presents difficulties for me. Most notable here is the work of Elisabeth Schüssler Fiorenza, who argues that it is a mistake to read the gender inscriptions of the text as descriptions of actual genders.[31] Schüssler Fiorenza insists on interpreting the Apocalypse from the perspective of its dominant theme, which she sees as liberation from forces of domination. Like her, I find great potential in this theme, but I am not quite able to ignore the gendered images in which it is cast.

Catherine Keller has also proposed a 'counter-apocalyptic reading' that holds up its liberating intentions while criticizing its sexism.[32] She is amused, I think, by the ambivalence of 'a women's movement still inspired by a master myth that can hardly tolerate the sex of women'.[33] Her own reading is a kind of poetic, postmodern meditation, which I find quite moving, but I am never quite able to discover its hermeneutical strategy.

---

26 On persecution see Leonard L. Thompson, *The Book of Revelation: Apocalypse and Empire* (New York: Oxford University Press, 1990).

27 Pippin, *Death and Desire*, p. 80.

28 Not that John's presentation of opponents as male figures is any better. If there is a female Jezebel, there is also a male Balaam (2.14); if there is a female Queen Ruler, she sits astride a male beast (17.3). Unlike the dragon of ancient mythology, John's dragon is male.

29 Pippin, *Apocalyptic Bodies*, p. 92.

30 Selvidge, 'Reflections'.

31 Elisabeth Schüssler Fiorenza, *Revelation: Vision of a Just World* (Proclamation Commentaries; Minneapolis, MN: Fortress Press, 1991) p. 13.

32 Keller, *Apocalypse Now and Then*.

33 Keller, *Apocalypse Now and Then*, p. 224.

In reading women in the Apocalypse I find myself unable either to find a comfortable reading strategy or to ignore this powerful text. At the very least the book should come with a warning label: 'Women, take note: this book could be hazardous to your mental health.'[34] As I have reflected on the issues involved I have phrased a question thus: is there any place for women and men to stand from which they can read this story without internalizing its hostile images of women? Can women read John's text without being forced to see themselves only through John's eyes? Can men read John's text without being forced to see women in these images?

I recognize the irony of my male voice and eyes here and so want to be clear that what I am proposing is not what women might or ought to say. I seek only to open some space in the text through which women might be heard. I have noted already that there is a gap between John's mythic world and the historical world of Asia Minor. I now want to explore that space.

Mything the Point: The Gap between Signifier and Signified

Christine Brook-Rose has written a provocative essay, 'Woman as Semiotic Object',[35] that shows how women's silence and value as objects of exchange have marked Western discourse and explores how language changes as women speak (a rather nice paradigm for what has happened in Apocalypse studies in the last decade, but I pass over that). The essay concludes with an example of how social paradigms construct meaning. Consider the ambiguity of the sentence: 'John sleeps with his wife twice a week, and so does Bill.'[36] Why is that sentence so much more ambiguous than the linguistically identical 'John mows his lawn twice a week, and so does Bill'? The answer is clear: meaning resides not simply in texts or words but also in the cultural constructs in which and from which we read them. We have a ready cultural construct of the adulterous triangle, but none – so far as I know – of men secretly mowing each other's lawns.

Brook-Rose's essay leads me to two fundamental points. The first is that meaning results from the complex interaction of the intent of the speaker, the actual words chosen, the cultural constructs in which those words are cast, the cultural constructs with which the words are taken, the meanings attached to those words, and the intentions of the hearers. It is, in other words, a bit more complicated than it may first appear.

My second point is that even in the simplest communication meaning often goes astray because of the inevitable asymmetry between speaker and hearer. I have found this most often true when trying to talk to my teenagers, but I suspect it is happening right now; that is, what you think you're reading is not necessarily what I think I'm writing. At the most basic level, words do not mean the same thing to different people, and attempts to make sure there can be no misunderstanding result in the

---

34 A similar label could be applied for men, both in regard to their treatment of women and, more pervasively, to the use of violence. But that is a topic for another time.

35 Christine Brook-Rose, 'Woman as a Semiotic Object', in Susan R. Suleiman (ed.), *The Female Body in Western Culture* (Cambridge, MA: Harvard University Press, 1986), pp. 305–316.

36 Brook-Rose, 'Woman as a Semiotic Object', p. 314.

sort of prose found in insurance policies, which is so 'clear' it is almost impossible to understand. But even at a trivial level, were I to tell you about the cat I watched playing in the ruins at Ephesus, not only would we have multiple images of those ruins (it was in the upper agora), but perhaps a dozen or so different cats (it was a brown mackerel tabby, but even that will only help some of you imagine my cat).

There is always a gap between the signifier and the signified. This is an inherent problem of all communication. But it is also an opportunity, for it is in just that space that I suggest we can find a place to stand. Let's consider the dialectical relation of history and myth as a reflection of sign/signified gap.

Deconstructing Myth, Constructing Women
Steven Friesen points out two notable parallels between the use of myth in Revelation and in the Imperial Cult, both with gaps. First, according to Friesen, 'One of the most striking agreements in the mythic methods of Revelation and the imperial cults surfaces in the subject of violence related to gender imagery.'[37] He gives the specific example of the many images that present corporate entities as women who are attacked and destroyed by masculine figures, such as Claudius's conquest of Britannia.[38]

The mythic theme of rebellion and the image of the unsubmissive woman undergird both Queen Jezebel and Queen Ruler. But John also constructs differences from these imperial images. In the case of the Ruler Queen it is not the True Ruler who slays her, as in the Imperial propaganda, but her own allies and dependents. In the case of Jezebel, she is neither destroyed nor threatened with destruction; it is her children that risen Jesus threatens to kill (2.23). Now this is a truly repugnant idea, morally, but it is reminiscent of the biblical God's dealing with David's adultery

37 Steven J. Friesen, *Imperial Cults and the Apocalypse of John: Reading Revelation in the Ruins* (New York: Oxford University Press, 2001), p. 177.
38 Friesen, *Imperial Cults*, p. 173, presents a photo. The photo here, taken by the author, represents the imperial conquest of a nation, figured as a woman.

(2 Samuel 11–12). There are also many instances in myth (e.g., the Minotaur) and in history (e.g., with rival claimants to a throne), where the children are killed because of the deeds of the parent. More to the point, it is ironically parallel to the action of the Dragon who, when he fails to kill the Queen Mother, turns to make war on her children (12.17). In both cases the mythic 'children' are those who follow the same path as the mother.

John's myth of the unsubmissive female is parallel to but asymmetrical with the myth of his culture. Still, that cultural myth provides the likely construct from which to read John's images.

A second shared theme to which Friesen points is the faithful wife. But again, differences appear. In the Imperial Cult bridal imagery supported hegemony, especially the succession of emperors.[39] Revelation shares the mythic theme but not this political intent, for the Queen Consort in the Apocalypse does not legitimate succession; rather, she functions as a way of portraying the union of human and divine. Or, if there is legitimation here in the fulfilling of the pattern of the holy warrior now wed, the legitimation supports the current ruler rather than insures succession. Again the replication is asymmetrical.

Some of these aspects, especially the ideas of providing the legitimate heir to the throne, are evident in the Queen Mother image of ch. 12.[40] There is also a lack of symmetry, since the Queen Mother does not have a husband present. Again, John's use of these myths leaves some opening, a gap we may be able to utilize.

I segue into my final point by asking why these issues have only arisen recently. An obvious part of the answer is that only recently have significant numbers of women been involved in the study of the text. This has been an enormous benefit to the field. But why did men fail to notice? It is not that men did not identify with the images. In fact, these are images made by and for men, and I don't mean just in the voyeuristic sense. Men saw themselves in these female images. David Stern has argued that the Rabbis used the image of the captive woman 'as a kind of foundational myth upon which they represented their own relationship to the pagan world in which they lived'.[41]

This notice of identification leads me to ask a more obvious question: would upper-class Roman women have identified with these mythic images? Would they, like Pippin, have looked at the imperial propaganda showing the emperor assaulting a captive woman and identified with the woman? Almost certainly not. I suspect that upper-class woman could see themselves in the role of the faithful wife perhaps, but not in the image of the captive woman. So how is it that men could see themselves in this image but women could not? Maybe sex isn't all it's cracked up to be.

We are accustomed to the idea that our gender identity is formed by the culture in which we live. We are simply not the men/women that our grandparents were. In John's world women's reality was an embedded reality. Socially, women were contained in a male reality.

---

39 Friesen, *Imperial Cult*, p. 178.
40 Her son is the 'male child, who is to rule all the nations with a rod of iron' (12.5).
41 David Stern, 'The Captive Woman: Hellenization, Greco-Roman Erotic Narrative, and Rabbinic Literature', *Poetics Today* 19/1 (1998), pp. 91–127.

But this is also true of women's biological identity. Biologically, physiologically if you will, women were not a separate sex in antiquity. It seems obvious to us that there are two biological categories, men and women. It is only 'common sense'. 'Man' and 'woman' seem like natural categories – we noticed certain differences between ourselves and our sisters/brothers when we were very small. Yet this system of two opposite classifications is a recent invention – the ancients did not regard women as a separate category of human but only as imperfect males. According to Aristotle and most subsequent physicians,[42] women's genitalia were identical to male genitalia, only they remained undeveloped and internal. Thus the very notion of male/female is a cultural (i.e., male) construct. This point is seen quite dramatically in the current debate about homosexuality.

What started me thinking along these lines of fluid identity was Catherine Keller's comment that the Ruler Queen is really a 'drag queen', imperial patriarchy in drag.[43] A male reality is portrayed in female guise. While at first this description may seem only mildly amusing, it does begin to destabilize our perception of the text's gender categories. And much the same can be said of the Queen Consort, for the earlier symbolization of the community was as celibate male virgins (14.1–4).

So three of our four mythic queens relate to an historical reality that is inclusive of men and women but dominated by men: Israel (the Queen Mother[44]), the Roman Empire (the Queen Ruler), and the Johannine community (the Queen Consort). Only Queen Jezebel corresponds to an historical female, the prophet of Thyatira. At the least, this semiotic gap between signifier and signified suggests that Elisabeth Schüssler Fiorenza is right in her insistence that we should not read the gender inscriptions of the text literally.[45] These female images are employed as images with which men were expected to identify. There is a dramatic gap between the mythic reality and the historical. Still, this does not eliminate the misogyny apparent in the story John tells.

Or so it must appear to us, given our cultural paradigms. I have argued that John's culture had different paradigms, both of the nature of sexual identity (one sex not two) and of ready myths of female place (the myth of the unsubmissive woman and the myth of the faithful wife). John both replicates and distorts these myths in his own telling. I suggest that by raising these paradigms and myths to the level of consciousness we might learn to read John differently.

By the end of Tom Robbins's novel, Ellen Charles learns to read Jezebel differently. She learns, in fact, to embrace the insult hurled at her by Buddy Winkler, for she has learned to see Jezebel not just through the patriarchal tradition but through her own eyes. Jezebel's careful application of her make-up before she confronts her accuser becomes not an act of seduction, but an act of dignity. More important, Jezebel embraces the goddess that those like Buddy seek to obliterate.

---

42 See the very provocative study by Thomas Laqueur, *Making Sex: Body and Gender from the Greeks to Freud* (Cambridge, MA: Harvard University Press, 1990).

43 Keller, *Apocalypse Now and Then*, p. 77.

44 It is a vast oversimplification to identify this woman with Israel, for many other mythic realities are combined in the image; nevertheless, Israel is the most apparent source of the messiah.

45 Schüssler Fiorenza, *Vision of a Just World*, p. 13.

John's use of Jezebel is clearly closer to that of Buddy than that of Ellen, and there is no room for the Goddess in John's story. Or is there? There is at least the dim reflection of the Goddess in John's female images: Queen of Heaven, Queen Ruler, Queen Consort. The mythic image is blurred by the overarching misogyny of the story; still it may be possible to see our own bodies in the symbolic construct of hers.

'TEACHING AND BEGUILING MY SERVANTS':
THE LETTER TO THYATIRA (REV. 2.18–29)*

PAMELA THIMMES

Myth ends up having our hides. Logos opens up its great maw and swallows us whole.[1]

A good story knows more than its teller.[2]

For those willing to let themselves feel it, any story leaves behind an uneasiness, sometimes at the center, other times at the edge of perception . . . it must be carried.[3]

Cixous, O'Donohue and Hirschfield have something to say about the Apocalypse of John, although none of them is speaking about that work. Their assertions about myth, story and uncertainty are instructive, particularly when approaching a slippery text like the Apocalypse that devours and regenerates itself as the story unfolds.

Few works have garnered the audience or the imaginative interpretations of John's Apocalypse; few works have produced such iconic images (the Lamb, the four horsemen, the Whore of Babylon, the beasts and a dragon, 666, the Bride, the New Jerusalem) or have been and continue to be as culturally pervasive or provocative. To be sure, this is a liminal text, and the liminal space is always restless, a mixture of betwixt and between. In texts that put the characters and the reader in boundary or threshold situations, the old center is destabilized and the margins become the center; the shift from insider to outsider necessitates a new meaning of community, and spaces of darkness and light are as confusing as they are revelatory. Written in the language of the liminal, the Apocalypse is a restless book, addressed to restless readers (/believers) who willingly let old identities and loyalties dissolve and who live in the disequilibrium and ambiguity of the present, so as to be incorporated into a new and renewed community.

In truth, for most of my academic career I had no interest in the Apocalypse. It was my students and adult faith-community groups that forced me to confront the narrative and allow it to confront me. Every encounter with the text remains a struggle, and I continue to be a resistant reader. I resist the pervasive violence, the way women are characterized, stereotyped and excluded, the moral and theological

* An earlier version of this article appeared as 'Women Reading Women in the Apocalypse: Reading Scenario 1, the Letter to Thyatira (Rev. 2:18–29)', *Currents in Biblical Research* 2:1 (October 2003), pp. 128–44.

1 Hélène Cixous, *Coming to Writing and Other Essays* (eds D. Jenson, S. R. Suleiman and S. Cornell; trans. A. Liddle and S. Sellers; Cambridge, MA: Harvard University Press, 1992), p. 23.

2 John O'Donohue, as quoted by Emily Hanlon on the site, 'Fiction Writing: The Passionate Journey' (http://www.thefictionwritersjourney.com/archives/2004_03_01_thefictionwritersjourney_archive.html [accessed 14 January 2009]).

3 Jane Hirschfield, 'Poetry and Uncertainty', *American Poetry Review* 34.6 (November/December 2005), pp. 63–72 (68).

exclusivity and absolutism. Pippin finds a 'discourse of war inscribed in the text',[4] observing that 'The violence of the book is startling; violence is done to nature and people and supernatural beings. There are swords and slaughter and hunger and martyrs.'[5]

The Apocalypse is also a war story, and as Barr wryly notes, 'war stories are not polite reading'.[6] It is a book teeming with monarchical language, threats, battles, war and symbols of war, violence and death. It is a textworld populated with only four key or notable female or female-identified characters:[7] the Thyatiran prophet whom John labels Jezebel in 2.18–29, the Woman Clothed with the Sun in 12.1–17, the great city personified as the Whore of Babylon in chs 17–19, and the Bride (i.e., the city of Jerusalem) in chs 19, 21 and 22. Each of these female or female-identified characters is drawn in mythological language: they are fantasized, criticized, protected and rescued, demonized and destroyed, and/or perfected (or is that purified? or idealized? certainly spiritualized). John's women – and they are 'his' women for he has constructed them and controls them – generally inhabit earthly locales, and they are excluded from the New Jerusalem (as are all women!).[8] These observations are not meant to dismiss or ignore the fact that male characters or male-identified characters in the Apocalypse are also stereotyped, vilified, criticized or idealized; they are.[9] That said, male characters are rarely 'typed' with the explicit sexual signifiers and venomous rhetoric reserved for and about female characters.

We never encounter a text 'cold'. We always read from somewhere, from perspectives that can be simultaneously conscious and unconscious. As a reader I am aware of certain lenses or reading strategies that I bring to the text. For example, as an American, I am aware of the way Jewish and Christian apocalyptic ideas, but particularly images from the Apocalypse, were embedded in the narratives, attitudes and aspirations of those who explored, colonized, settled and established what is now known as the United States of America;[10] as an expat (now living in Ireland),

---

4 Tina Pippin, *Death and Desire: The Rhetoric of Gender in the Apocalypse of John* (Literary Currents in Biblical Interpretation; Louisville, KY: Westminster/John Knox Press, 1992), p. 97.

5 Pippin, *Death and Desire*, p. 99.

6 David L. Barr, 'Towards an Ethical Reading of the Apocalypse: Reflections on John's Use of Power, Violence, and Misogyny', *SBLSP* 36 (1997), pp. 358–73 (363). He also writes, 'John portrayed a community at war, fighting for their very lives.'

7 Barr suggests there is a fifth female (female-identified) character, Gaia, the Earth, in 12.16. See David L. Barr, 'Jezebel's Skinny Legs: (De)Constructing the Four Queens of the Apocalypse', at http://www.wright.edu/~dbarr/jezebel.htm (accessed 14 January 2009). See also his article in this volume, 'Women in Myth and History: Deconstructing John's Characterizations', pp. 55–68.

8 See Pippin's comments on this in her 'Eros and the End: Reading for Gender in the Apocalypse of John', *Semeia* 59 (1992), pp. 193–210, and 'The Joy of (Apocalyptic) Sex', in B. E. Brasher and L. Quinby (eds), *Gender and Apocalyptic Desire* (Millennialism and Society Series, 1; London: Equinox Publishing, 2006), pp. 64–75.

9 Barr demonstrates that it is John's practice to pair an evil woman with an evil man, for example Jezebel/Balaam, the Whore/Beast. See his 'Towards an Ethical Reading of the Apocalypse', p. 365.

10 See Catherine Keller, *Apocalypse Now and Then: A Feminist Guide to the End of the World* (Boston, MA: Beacon Press, 1996), p. 159; and 'The Breast, the Apocalypse, and the Colonial Journey', in C. B. Strozier and M. Flynn (eds), *The Year 2000* (New York: New York University Press, 1997), pp. 42–58. Among the best studies from U.S. historians see John Leddy Phelan, *The Millennial Kingdom of the Franciscans in the New World*, 2nd revised ed. (Berkeley: University of

I see in a different way and from this location how apocalyptic thought continues to pervade U.S. culture and is exported in all forms of media, art, economic and public policy throughout the world;[11] as a believer I struggle with the violence in the text and toil to understand the ethical complexity of the work, while honoring the place the book has in Christian faith communities as a spiritual touchstone for hope and an antidote to fundamentalism and fear;[12] as a scholar I employ a toolbox of methodologies in an attempt to make sense of both the intricacy and density of the worlds represented by and in this text (Barr's description of the three worlds implicit in any text – 'the world within the text, the world behind the text, and the world in front of the text'[13] – is a concise and helpful articulation of exegetical practice); and as a woman I look for myself – that is, for women – in the text. I look for how identity is constructed, by whom and to what end, what is recorded and what is not recorded, because the category of gender is an essential component for analysis in any reading strategy, but particularly in works where women are drawn to type, theologically and ideologically, as they are in the Apocalypse. While the text itself

California Press, 1970) and Lois Parkinson Zamora, *Writing the Apocalypse: Historical Vision in Contemporary U.S. and Latin American Literature* (Cambridge, UK: Cambridge University Press, 1993). Zamora, following on and enlarging Phelan's work, briefly documents the legacy of apocalyptic thinking brought to the 'New World' by European colonialism from the beginnings of the period of exploration. Examples include Christopher Columbus, in whose letters and diaries are quotations describing 'a new heaven and a new earth' from the Book of Revelation and Isaiah through which he understands his mission. She writes that in Spanish explorations and conquest of the Americas 'apocalyptic optimism pervaded the Age of Discovery in Spain. Explorers, statesmen and clergy alike viewed the events of geographical exploration and colonization of America as a fulfillment of the prophecies of Revelation – that is as necessary prerequisites to the end of the world' (p. 7). Seventeenth-century Puritans in New England, interpreting Revelation literally, saw the location of the 'new heaven and new earth' as America, the place promising both spiritual renewal and political and institutional freedom. 'The earliest Puritan texts attest to constant attempts to unite apocalyptic theology and American history: The New World is directly associated with the culmination of history' (pp. 8–9).

11 Zamora, *Writing the Apocalypse*, p. 9. One of the legacies apocalyptic thinking/belief and the Apocalypse itself has had in U.S. history and commerce can be seen on the U.S. dollar bill, on which is printed the motto, *Novus Ordo Seclorum*, A New World Order (p. 9). Consider also the popularity of films like *Apocalypse Now* (1979), *Independence Day* (1996), *The Matrix* (1999), *Armageddon* (1999), *The Day after Tomorrow* (2004). Quinby notes that the contemporary period is marked by an 'elasticity of apocalyptic belief' where there is a fusion between popular culture and apocalyptic belief that she calls 'techno-fundamentalism or fundamentalist pop'. In addition she notes that the killing spree at Columbine High School, near Littleton, Colorado in 1999, shows the darker side of 'how secular and religious apocalypticism are part of the cultural fabric for today's youth. . . . The title of the Columbine High School yearbook encapsulates the way American teenagers in general embrace such a blurring: 'The Rebelations'''. See Lee Quinby, 'The Deployment of Apocalyptic Masculinity', in B. Brasher and L. Quinby (eds), *The Journal of Millennial Studies*, special issue, *Engendering the Millennium*, 2.1 (Summer 1999).

12 On a pastoral note, a survey of the Revised Common Lectionary and the Roman Catholic Lectionary shows that none of the letters or portions of the letters to the seven churches is used in the three-year cycle of Sunday readings.

13 David L. Barr, 'Beyond Genre: The Expectations of Apocalypse,' in *idem* (ed.), *The Reality of Apocalypse: Rhetoric and Politics in the Book of Revelation* (SBLSym, 39; Atlanta, GA: Society of Biblical Literature, 2006), pp. 71–90 (71).

travels in multiple directions at the same time (it is liminal, it is a war story, etc.), so does my reading of it.

This study, divided into two broadly conceived sections, is not meant to be a detailed and exhaustive study of the letter to Thyatira (2.18–29). Instead, it is meant to suggest ways to think about and examine particular aspects of the letter. Section 1 examines the conflicts/rivalries between John and the community (or a portion of the community) at Thyatira. At the center of this conflict is a Thyatiran teacher and prophet John labels 'Jezebel'. Her character is drawn to type ideologically and theologically and marked with explicit sexual signifiers. He accuses her of 'teaching' (διδάσκει, 2.20) and 'beguiling' (πλανᾷ, 2.20) the community to practice 'immorality/fornication' (2.20, πορνεῦσαι), that is, eating food sacrificed to idols. Further, John charges her, and those who support her, with 'committing adultery' (τοὺς μοιχεύοντας μετ' αὐτῆς, 2.22). Of the four key female characters found in the Apocalypse only the Thyatiran prophet seems to have any relation to an actual human woman, but that claim is tenuous. 'Jezebel' may be a member of the church community in Thyatira, but John does his best to malign and exclude her and her followers from the community.

Section 2 highlights the direct links John makes to the triad of women, sex and food in the text, a connection not made with male characters in the Apocalypse. Anthropological studies regularly find the triad linked in a variety of cultures in significant ways. John's sexualization of the female is repeatedly connected with food. John's language is code language – Jezebel is a code, food is a code, sexuality is a code – that plays on archetypes and stereotypes, defines social relations, determines inclusion and exclusion, and determines boundaries and transgressions in the community vis-à-vis the culture. To be clear, the conflict in Thyatira is a rivalry for authority in the community between John and Jezebel, expressed in a *rhetoric of conflict* that serves to defend the community from spiritual and cultural corruption from within and without. For John, the enemy in Thyatira is 'Jezebel'. She is a female with spiritual authority (and a following) who, in John's view, accommodates the culture, and such females are dangerous, uncontrollable and bring death (e.g., Jezebel, the Whore of Babylon). 'Eating culture', then, marks a connection between apostasy and uncontrollability.

Section 1: John and 'Jezebel'

Introduction
Recent scholarship recognizes that the Apocalypse cannot be understood or explored in relation to any one, particular literary genre; instead it is a hybrid genre,[14] a highly intertextual work, a book of mixed generic conventions,[15] variously described as a work that 'constantly overruns any boundaries placed around it. It

---

14 Gregory L. Linton, 'Reading the Apocalypse as Apocalypse', in D. L. Barr (ed.), *The Reality of Apocalypse: Rhetoric and Politics in the Book of Revelation* (Atlanta, GA: Society of Biblical Literature, 2006), pp. 9–42 (10).
15 Linton, 'Reading the Apocalypse', p. 39.

refuses to stay inbounds',[16] as 'a writerly text or an open work',[17] and as a polyvalent text that 'provides simultaneous frustration and pleasure to the reader'.[18]

Yet at the beginning of the work John uses the letter genre, an ancient and familiar form, to address seven churches in western Asia Minor. These seven letters form an epistolary introduction to the whole work while expressing John's cultural, political, theological and spiritual concerns in the dualistic language of threat and promised rewards. Schüssler Fiorenza sees the letters as 'a work of visionary rhetoric' that weaves together 'poetic and rhetorical elements'[19] for the purpose of encouraging the Asian Christian communities. While Schüssler Fiorenza reads the letters as the 'main objective' for the purpose of 'prophetic communication of the revelation',[20] Carpenter finds a less neutral interest on John's part. She suggests a 'pervasively constituted paranoia'[21] in the letters, where 'encouragement is entirely secondary to the *warnings* that the church members are under constant surveillance, that judgment could come at any moment'.[22] She writes,

> The introductory epistles are, then, like Gothic texts, replete with 'hints' of all kinds of sinfulness, abomination, and violence, with the allure of 'secret truths', and with the perpetual constitution of the subjective as 'transparent to and often under the compulsion of, another male'. They thus construct an appropriate staging for what Elizabeth Cady Stanton called 'visions which make the blood curdle'.[23]

The comments of Schüssler Fiorenza and Carpenter provide important observations because 'visionary rhetoric' and the prophetic nature of the revelation do not imply neutrality; rather, the prophetic (word) is *always* perspectival – it is uttered in language (metaphoric/symbolic/code) meant to illumine, judge, persuade and/or transform the individual, the community, and/or societal structures in the *present*, and uttered in relation to particular actions or events. John's 'visionary rhetoric' is aligned in simple polarities – the language of fidelity and apostasy, of life and death, the language of competing thrones; that is, a rhetoric of conflict. It is language that is simple, direct and uncompromising; in fact, extreme. The letters, like the book itself, attack anyone or anything that hints of Roman accommodation; that is, of the Empire, which in the Mediterranean world of early Christianity was the universal and complex network of religious, cultural, political and economic relationships, each thoroughly implicated with the other.

16 Linton, 'Reading the Apocalypse', p. 40

17 Linton, 'Reading the Apocalypse', p. 40.

18 Linton, 'Reading the Apocalypse', p. 41.

19 Elisabeth Schüssler Fiorenza, *The Book of Revelation: Justice and Judgment* (2nd edn, Minneapolis, MN: Fortress Press, 1998), p. 187.

20 Schüssler Fiorenza, *Book of Revelation*, p. 140.

21 Mary Wilson Carpenter, 'Representing Apocalypse: Sexual Politics and the Violence of Revelation', in Richard Dellamora (ed.), *Postmodern Apocalypse: Theory and Cultural Practice at the End* (Philadelphia: University of Pennsylvania Press, 1995), pp. 107–35 (116).

22 Carpenter, 'Representing Apocalypse', p. 116.

23 Carpenter, 'Representing Apocalypse', p. 116.

The Text – General Assessment of the Community
The community is praised for its love, faith, service and patient endurance (2.19).
The praise is followed with three issues and three threats and rewards.

Three issues:
1. 'you tolerate that woman Jezebel who calls herself a prophet' (2.20).
2. The prophet 'is teaching and beguiling my servants to practice fornication
3. and to eat food sacrificed to idols' (2.20).

Three threats and rewards:
1. 'I am throwing her on a bed,[24] and those who commit adultery with her I am throwing into great distress, unless they repent of her doings' (2.22).
2. 'I will strike her children dead' (2.23).
3. 'To everyone who conquers and continues to do my works to the end, I will give authority over the nations; to rule them with an iron rod, as when clay pots are shattered' (2.26b–27).

Pippin, building on Collins's early arguments, reads apocalyptic literature as a response to political repression, with revolution as the political agenda. In other words, apocalyptic literature is 'resistance literature'.[25] Collins argues repeatedly that the Apocalypse is a response to Roman oppression, although to a perceived crisis rather than an actual one.

> This interpretation makes sense of a perceived crisis which involves conflict with Jews, mutual antipathy toward neighboring Gentiles (pagans), conflict over wealth, and precarious relations with Rome. The book also deals with experiences of trauma, including the destruction of Jerusalem (a symbolic center for Christians as well as Jews), Nero's police-action against Christians in Rome, the offense of the ruler-cult to Christian messianism (Christ, not Caesar, is God incarnate), the execution of Antipas (Rev. 2.13), and the banishment of John. These elements of perceived crisis and trauma were interpreted by the construction of a symbolic system which is the inverse of the Roman ideology.[26]

I agree that John understands Rome as an oppressive presence whose immanence is pervasive, but I find a different kind of conflict portrayed in the letter to Thyatira. This is not a typical insider–outsider conflict (perceived or real), or the result of the kinds of external forces that Collins enumerates. Rather it is an example of an intra-Christian quarrel, based in issues of power and authority, including gender dynamics and sexual politics; it is a conflict over different interpretations of what it meant to be

---

24 The Greek expression, εἰς κλίνην, is rendered in the NRSV as 'on a bed', in the RSV as 'on a sick bed', and in the NJB as 'to a bed of pain'. Because of the sexualized language in the pericope, I suspect, many scholars (and translators) have chosen to render κλίνην as 'sick bed'. Perhaps the allusion to fornication in the previous verse, and a bed and adultery in this verse, all connected with Jezebel herself and those who associate with her, were such graphic allusions, leaving much to the imagination, that translators tried to defuse the rhetoric.

25 Pippin, *Death and Desire*, p. 28; A. Yarbro Collins, *Crisis and Catharsis: The Power of the Apocalypse* (Philadelphia, PA: Westminster Press, 1984), pp. 84–110.

26 A. Yarbro Collins, 'Reading the Book of Revelation in the Twentieth Century', *Interpretation* 40.3 (1986), pp. 229–42 (240–41).

(i.e., how to live and act as) a Christian. The conflict in the letter to Thyatira is not unlike the conflicts reflected in the Gospel of John, 3 John, the letters of Paul, or the *Didache*'s constructions of and teaching about the authentic prophet.

Perhaps one way to understand the dynamics at play in the text is to reflect on how communities work, how authority is constituted (and contended), and how texts reflect the internal and external realities of negotiating disparate worldviews. This list represents some internal factors that, when contended, can find externalization in texts:

1. In the face of uncertainty, ambiguity, dangerous and contentious situations, communities [and authors] create symbols to bridge these situations – symbols that ease dissonance, resolve confusion, increase predictability, provide direction and anchor hope and faith.
2. Texts can represent communities and/or individuals, but fundamentally they probably represent coalitions of various individuals or interest groups that explicitly or implicitly demonstrate that the communities and the texts they create are vibrant political arenas, often with unambiguous and enduring differences.
3. Community dynamics often revolve around resources and the allocation of resources. If authority, leadership and power are seen as basic resources, and they are restricted or understood as privileged, then these basic community resources are *in* and *under* contention.
4. Privileged resources and declared, maintained, and enduring differences give *conflict* a central role in community dynamics [and narrative dynamics], transforming authority, leadership and power issues into critical resources.
5. Conflict is particularly likely to occur at the boundaries, with issues like class, status, gender and theology.
6. In real life and real time, communities can initiate strategies for negotiating conflict, but texts have little or no need for negotiation – texts frequently function as the 'party platform' which in turn is understood and argued as articulating the authorized, revealed and traditional position.[27]

Letters addressed to seven different communities, located in seven different Asian cities, seem to indicate that John knew these churches, at least by reputation. But there is nothing in any of the letters to indicate that he was the 'founder' of or a leader/prophet or congregational member in any of the churches. In other words, the only evidence of John's connections to these churches is the series of letters that he is commanded to write.

While John initially praises the Thyatiran community for its love, faith, service and patient endurance (2.19), all of that is quickly forgotten. The remainder of the message is a diatribe against a woman he names Jezebel, those who support her, what she does to them, what will happen to her, and what will happen to them. One of the more interesting aspects about this conflict is the issue of distance and location – John is writing *from* Patmos; Jezebel is *in* Thyatira.

As is generally the case with apocalyptic literature, questions of identity (or

---

27 This list is based loosely on a list in Lee G. Bolman and Terrence E. Deal, *Reframing Organizations: Artistry, Choice, and Leadership* (2nd edn, San Francisco, CA: Jossey-Bass, 1997), p. 163.

identities) remain open. Primary questions for the reader include: Who is this John; and is he trustworthy? The work provides no historical or biographical background for the visionary, John, no specific information about his ministry, not even his connection to the seven churches. He never indicates how he knows specific features about the cities and individual churches to which the letters are addressed,[28] nor, as noted above, does he indicate that he is either a founder of these communities or resident in any one particular community. One must presume that, whether 'John' was a historical person or a symbolic figure representing a particular under-standing of what it meant to be Christian, either his audience already knew him and accepted him as a spiritual authority or the power of his charismatic authority and authenticity, articulated through his (written) visions, was meant to convince readers without any need of further verification. Nevertheless, the text indicates two aspects about this 'John' meant to establish his spiritual credentials and authenticity as a true prophet: (1) he is some distance away from the churches, on the island of Patmos 'because of the word of God and the testimony of Jesus' (διὰ τὸν λόγον τοῦ θεοῦ καὶ τὴν μαρτυρίαν Ἰησοῦ, 1.9),[29] and (2) as the result of a striking and terrifying foundational vision of the exalted Christ (1.9–20), he claims prophetic authority for the visions he is commanded to write (1.3; 22.7, 10, 18, 19).

Collins sees the conflict between John and Jezebel as one between itinerant prophets over power and values, not only for 'the leadership of the various con-gregations, but also for the hospitality of those able to provide it'.[30] Whoever/whatever/wherever this John is, in some respects his dilemma is akin to that of Paul. As a prophet, he is a resident of no community, a citizen without roots. Just as Paul confronts opponents in his communities by letter, John does the same. Just as Paul had local supporters, so John had his. John's words indicate that there are two groups in the Thyatiran community: those who follow John are identified as 'my servants' (2.20); those who follow Jezebel are identified as 'the rest of you, who do not hold this teaching' (2.24).

In the face of the textual silence about John's identity I choose to understand him in the tradition of the charismatic, itinerant, Christian missionary (i.e., like Paul and the wandering prophets/teachers mentioned in the *Didache* 11–13). Even though the seven churches in the Apocalypse are all within a rather restricted geographic area, quite unlike the geographic reach of Paul's activity, I take John to be an itinerant prophet because that was a common pattern among early Christian evangelists who depended on two kinds of authority: heavenly authority as a result of a direct, personal call from God, and the authority that individual groups of believers/communities invested in them after listening to their preaching and paraenesis.

---

28 This is accomplished by making John the prophetic amanuensis of Christ's revelation. He is told to write what he sees (1.9).

29 Many scholars now doubt the traditional interpretation that John had been exiled to Patmos by Roman authorities because of his witnessing to Christ. There is nothing in the historical record to indicate that Rome used Patmos as a penal colony at the end of the first or the beginning of the second century CE.

30 A. Yarbro Collins, 'Insiders and Outsiders in the Book of Revelation and Its Social Context', in J. Neusner and E. S. Frerichs (eds), *To See Ourselves as Others See Us: Christians, Jews, 'Others' in Late Antiquity* (Scholars Press Studies in the Humanities; Chico, CA: Scholars Press, 1985), pp. 187–218 (217).

Thus, I understand John to be an itinerant *outsider* to the Thyatiran community, and Jezebel, the resident *insider*. In fact, one of the easiest ways to construct a discourse is with opposites and contraries. Schüssler Fiorenza argues that the prophet called Jezebel belongs to the community of Thyatira[31] and that John labels her an opponent because 'her authority equaled that of John whom, in turn, she might have perceived as a false prophet'.[32] The text affirms that John sees Jezebel as part of the Thyatiran community. She is obviously an *insider* with clout; otherwise, why allow her figure to dominate the letter? The letters, then, provide an interesting arena in which to examine simplistic polarities, and at the same time they provide a glimpse into the insider–outsider conflict structured according to the *outsider's* viewpoint. In order to maintain his own authority John portrays Jezebel in ways that discredit her local and spiritual authority and show her actions to be outside of acceptable boundaries. Then he uses his own authority to threaten her and her supporters with a violent end.

When the Insider is a Woman and the Outsider is a Man

The Apocalypse is a textual landscape of naming and name-calling. One general feature of apocalyptic literature is its pseudonymity. Not only does John engage in name-calling, but in an unusual twist, he actually names himself. Whether the name 'John' is a pseudonym is unclear, but the author's practice of using pseudonyms for his characters is a general feature in the work, so why not for himself?

To combat Jezebel and reclaim her followers for himself John employs a *rhetoric of conflict*: he engages in name-calling and he associates 'Jezebel' with the activities of teaching (διδάσκει, 2.20) and beguiling, deceiving (πλανᾷ, 2.20), fornication/ sexual immorality (πορνεῦσαι, 2.20), eating food sacrificed to idols (φαγεῖν εἰδωλόθυτα, 2.20), and leading others to commit adultery (τοὺς μοιχεύοντας, 2.22). According to John, though, she calls herself a prophet (προφῆτιν, 2.20). In other words, she claims the same prophetic authority as he does. While he is willing to acknowledge her claim, his name-calling response is his technique to delegitimate and distort that claim.

The phrase, the *rhetoric of conflict*, refers to the language or narrative strategies of persuasion and exhortation used to influence outcomes. Language and texts are cultural constructs best understood as 'cultural conventions or sociopolitical practices that enable speakers and hearers, writers and readers, to negotiate linguistic ambiguities and to create meaning in specific rhetorical contexts and sociopolitical locations'.[33] A text is a product, and the discourse of conflict is composed and used for a particular audience to elicit an outcome; it is expressed in ways that will maximize its appeal to that audience. The *rhetoric of conflict* can include expressions like speech as competition, speech as violence, speech as control, speech as exclusion, speech as blame. It is propagandistic and frequently intertwined with gender, relationships, sociocultural and theological boundaries, authority, power and

---

31 Schüssler Fiorenza, *Book of Revelation*, p. 116.

32 Elisabeth Schüssler Fiorenza, *In Memory of Her: A Feminist Theological Reconstruction of Christian Origins* (New York: Crossroad, 1984), pp. 55, 78.

33 Elisabeth Schüssler Fiorenza, *Rhetoric and Ethic: The Politics of Biblical Studies* (Minneapolis, MN: Fortress Press, 1999), p. 92.

prestige (or status). In this respect, the *rhetoric of conflict* in biblical texts is used as a theological and political instrument in the service of ideological interests. Glenn's study of classical rhetoric exposes elements that have relevance for understanding the impact of John's rhetoric in the letter to Thyatira:

> For the past twenty-five hundred years in Western culture, the ideal woman has been disciplined by cultural codes that require a closed mouth (silence), a closed body (chastity), and an enclosed life (domestic confinement). Little wonder, then, that women have been closed out of the rhetorical tradition, a tradition of vocal, virile, public – and therefore privileged – men.[34]

> Rhetoric always inscribes the relation of language and power at a particular moment (including who may speak, who may listen or who will agree to listen, and what can be said); therefore, canonical rhetorical history has represented the experience of males, powerful males, with no provision or allowance for females. In short, rhetorical history has replicated the power politics of gender, with men in the highest cultural role and social rank. And our view of rhetoric has remained one of a gendered landscape . . .[35]

John refers to the members of the community who support Jezebel as 'my servants' (τοὺς ἐμοὺς δούλους).[36] Another way to translate δούλους is as 'slaves' (2.20). Is this a case where John uses verbal and dramatic irony at the same time? I do not think so; instead, the emphasis should be on the possessive 'my' (ἐμούς), not on the translation of 'servant/slave'. John understands the Thyatiran community in the possessive sense, and this is an important linguistic indicator of what is a critical issue for John: his authority has been superseded by a female teacher and prophet.

Comparison of John's invective against 'Jezebel' with his complaints against characters in other churches such as Pergamum – a congregation in which John's authority is also contended – suggests that Jezebel's position (teacher and prophet) and her gender motivate harsher and sexualized rhetoric. The letter to Pergamum is noteworthy for three things: John says Satan's throne is there and Satan dwells there (2.13), he refers to 'Antipas my witness', who was killed among them (2.13), and he mentions the teaching (τὴν διδαχήν, 2.14) of 'Balaam', who is associated with eating idol food and practicing fornication/sexual immorality (φαγεῖν εἰδωλόθυτα καὶ πορνεῦσαι, 2.14). The name Balaam is another example of John's name-calling. Like Jezebel he is labeled with the name of a character from the Hebrew Bible, and John uses some of the same vocabulary for Jezebel's activity (πορνεῦσαι καὶ φαγεῖν εἰδωλόθυτα, 2.20) as he had for Balaam. But there are some striking differences: John does not refer to Balaam as a prophet, and he does not use the sexualized and violence-laden language in describing Balaam's threat in Pergamum that he does with Jezebel's threat in Thyatira. In the letter to Pergamum there is reference to a war (2.16), the sword of my mouth (v. 16, an aspect of the exalted Christ in the intro-ductory vision), and the conqueror receiving hidden manna (v. 17), but there is no reference to beguiling/deceiving (v. 20), a bed (v. 22), adultery (v. 22), tribulation

---

34 Cheryl Glenn, *Rhetoric Retold: Regendering the Tradition from Antiquity through the Renaissance* (Carbondale: Southern Illinois University Press, 1997), p. 1.

35 Glenn, *Rhetoric Retold*, p. 2.

36 John speaks of his supporters as 'my servants', yet those associated with Jezebel he calls 'children' (and they will be struck dead).

(v. 22), striking children dead (v. 23), power over the nations (v 26), ruling with a rod of iron (v. 27), or pots broken in pieces (v. 27) as found in the letter to Thyatira. What separates these two labeled or branded (by name) individuals is that Jezebel is a teacher *and* a prophet and she is a female, the *only* female named in the letters. She holds two recognized roles or offices[37] in the Thyatiran community, while Balaam is identified only as a teacher. Granted, John singles out each for breaching the same boundaries – eating idol food and practicing fornication – but he contends Jezebel's authority in a way that he does not contend Balaam's. As a prophet, she is a peer; Balaam is not. But, John's Jezebel is silent. She can provide no oracles, no visions, no prophetic word. Unlike John, she is a teacher and prophet without a voice; she cannot teach, prophesy or provide any defense against John's vilification and threats.

It is impossible to separate John's naming of the woman prophet from his critique of her (and her followers), and his threats. The rhetoric of conflict always *brands* the combatants, using naming or name-calling as a means of definition, power and control. John not only calls his characters names – Balaam, Jezebel, Woman Clothed with the Sun, Whore, Beast, Babylon, 666 (616), Bride – he literally *brands* some.[38] In the case of the Thyatiran letter, the pseudonym for the woman prophet is that of an Israelite queen. In naming her as such the archetypes and stereotypes associated with Queen Jezebel of 1 and 2 Kings[39] are now associated with John's Jezebel: she is a foreigner, an outsider, a polytheist, a treacherous, wicked and unscrupulous woman who compromised Israelite monotheism with the power of the throne. John uses her archetypically, representing the female who, with overwhelming power, deceives, destroys and/or devours the male; in literature she is often portrayed as a poisonous or venomous woman because association with her led to death and/or destruction.[40]

John is not the first to 'play' with the name. Jezebel is a name 'at play' in the Hebrew Bible. Appler notes that the name means 'where is Baal'.[41] Yee claims that in the MT 'the name Jezebel is probably a two-layered parody. The original name *'îzĕbûl* ("Where is the Prince?") first became *'î-zĕbûl* ("No nobility"). *Zĕbûl*, a title of Baal, was then distorted into *zebel* ("dung"; cf. 2 Kgs 9.37).'[42] Is this play on the name intentional in the Apocalypse? There is no way to determine whether the author is playing with the parody and using 'Jezebel' in the broader sense of the

---

37 1 Cor. 12.4f. (χαρισμάτων, gifts) and Eph. 4.7–11 (τῆς δωρεᾶς τοῦ Χριστοῦ, gifts of Christ) use different terms, but both refer to these roles or offices as 'gifts'.

38 In six different texts John brands characters on their foreheads (and/or hands) with seals, marks, writings or names: 7.3; 9.4; 13.16; 14.1, 9; 17.5. Neyrey defines labelling as a 'symbolic action that encodes considerable information about the way the labelers view the world'. He also speaks about the rationale of this practice and sees it as a way to categorize what is unclean, common, polluted and taboo. See Jerome Neyrey, 'Clean/Unclean, Pure/Polluted, and Holy/Profane: The Idea of the System of Purity', in R. L. Rohrbaugh (ed.), *The Social Sciences and New Testament Interpretation* (Peabody, MA: Hendrickson, 1996), pp. 80–104 (87).

39 Reign of King Ahab and Queen Jezebel, 1 Kgs 16.29–22.40; death of Queen Jezebel, 2 Kgs 9.30–37.

40 She was said to persecute and pursue prophetic rivals of Baal (1 Kgs 18.4) and was complicit in the death of Naboth (1 Kings 21).

41 Deborah A. Appler, 'From Queen to Cuisine: Food Imagery in the Jezebel Narrative', *Semeia* 86 (1999), pp. 55–73 (58).

42 Gale A. Yee, 'Jezebel', *ABD* 3, pp. 848–49 (848).

archetypal wicked woman.[43] Regardless, 'Jezebel' is John's term of derision. John exerts his control on the text and the Thyatiran community by naming an otherwise anonymous female character Jezebel; in this way he attempts to define her, to control his argument, and control any interpretation of her. 'Jezebel', the name, is used as a moral marker meant to isolate, vilify and scorn. His name-calling labels her an enemy outsider, a death-dealing female. Margaret Hallissy's study of the deadly, 'poisonous' or 'venomous' woman in literature finds that

> Writers . . . are allusive, highly conscious of their antecedents in mythology and earlier literature, so no work can be seen in isolation from what has gone before. While creating their own character, writers in the tradition are anxious to remind the reader of all the past poison ladies.[44]

> The image of the woman who uses poison or is venomous is, above all, an image of female power and male fear of that power. . . . Women do not see themselves as poison ladies; men see them that way. All the misogynistic notions related to the image are manifestations of male fear of domination by a woman.[45]

> . . . the most threatening combination of all is the woman who combines the morally venomous power of female sexuality with the asexual power of the mind. In this literature, the smart and sexy woman is the most terrifying of all. The male protagonist's task is at least to survive her, at most to subdue her – in other words, by showing his power to control her, to become a hero.[46]

Anything but a symbolic name for the Thyatiran prophet would risk marginalizing John's own argument and would not allow him to control the interpretation of her. Like the phrase he uses of the community, '*my* servants', she belongs to him; he has named her, he has constructed her, he has objectified her. Sankovitch cautions,

> When women pop up in the books of male myths it is under names they themselves do not recognize, springing from an alien naming, and clad in deceptive images equally alien . . . their presence is a mock presence. Women are really absent from them, since only false names, false icons, inane and without reverberation or deep radiance, pretend to represent women.[47]

---

43 As with archetypal representation, or even simple stereotyping, it is difficult, if not impossible, to tease truth from fiction. For studies on Queen Jezebel see Athalya Brenner, *The Israelite Woman: Social Role and Literary Type in Biblical Narrative* (Sheffield: Sheffield Academic Press, 1985); Eleanor Ferris Beach, *The Jezebel Letters: Religion and Politics in Ninth-Century Israel* (Minneapolis, MN: Augsburg Fortress Press, 2005).

44 Margaret Hallissy, *Venomous Woman: Fear of the Female in Literature* (New York: Greenwood Press, 1987), p. xiii. Hallissy clarifies why female stereotypes and archetypes are so dangerous: 'Of course, men who poison are frightening too, but when men poison, it is not seen as an action expressing malign qualities peculiar to masculinity. The notion of the venomous woman is misogynistic in the sense in which Andrée Kahn Blumstein uses the term in *Misogyny and Idealization in the Courtly Romance* (Studien zur Germanistik, Anglistik und Komparatistik; Bonn: Bouvier, 1977) in that from the "shortcomings of an individual woman" is drawn a generalization applying to all women' (p. xii).

45 Hallissy, *Venomous Woman*, p. xiv.

46 Hallissy, *Venomous Woman*, p. xv.

47 Tilde Sankovitch, *French Women Writers and the Book: Myths of Access and Desire* (Syracuse, NY: Syracuse University Press, 1988), pp. 3–4.

Caird seems to recognize John's manoeuvre when he notes that John is playing Elijah to *his* Jezebel.[48] But even at that, the name is problematic: clearly this Thyatiran woman is not a queen and Queen Jezebel was not a teacher or a prophet; what fuses them is that both women constitute a threat. Furthermore, the Deuteronomic historian's thoroughly negative portrayal of Queen Jezebel in 1 and 2 Kings creates a symbol of the powerful, dangerous woman. The name 'Jezebel' is an ideological weapon in his rhetoric of war, used in a strategic way to link and transfer to his female character a history of interpretation replete with assignations and monstrous, death-dealing conduct.

While the pseudonym Jezebel is meant to undercut and distort her authority and reputation as a teacher and prophet in the Thyatiran community, and to generate fear of her, she remains a part of the community John praised: 'your latter works exceed the first' (2.19). The community would not know her as Jezebel, an enemy outsider. And if this female character represents an actual woman, an actual prophet with a leadership position in the community, would the reader see John's praise of the community as anything but a commendation for the leaders, including her? The opening verse of the letter, 'I know your works – your love, faith, service, and patient endurance. I know that your last works are greater than the first' (2.19, NRSV) does not restrict these qualities only to John's 'servants'.

Barr calls John's rhetoric 'performance language',[49] and if John is playing Elijah to his Jezebel, this is exactly the performance he wants. Just as Elijah ordered the capture and slaughter of the prophets of Baal[50] (1 Kgs 18.40), John promises violence against Jezebel and those who follow her: striking her children dead (2.23), ruling them with a rod of iron and breaking them like earthen pots (2.27). John's naming has misogynistic implications. By linking her with Queen Jezebel, John uses the broad, archetypic and stereotypic brush: this female, like her namesake, is treacherous, evil, poisonous, venomous; she brings tribulation (θλῖψιν, 2.22), destruction and death (they will be shattered, 2.27). Margaret Hallissy suggests:

> Every poison lady in literature owes her full significance to archetypes and stereotypes, characters from the literature of the past summoned like shades from Hades to add greater dimension to her characterization and notions about women in general upon which men base judgments of individual women. These archetypes and stereotypes influence the reader's responses to the venomous-woman character, including whether we take her seriously.[51]

> The image of the venomous woman depends on a combination of misogynistic notions and traditional role expectations; in other words, evil women stand as representatives for all women.[52]

---

48 G. B. Caird, *The Revelation of St. John* (Black's New Testament Commentary, 19; New York: Harper and Row, 1987), p. 45.

49 David L. Barr, *Tales of the End: A Narrative Commentary on the Book of Revelation* (Santa Rosa, CA: Polebridge Press, 1998), p. 178.

50 It should not be lost on the reader that Jezebel's position as Baal's 'high priestess was integral to her authority as queen'; Yee, 'Jezebel', p. 849.

51 Hallissy, *Venomous Woman*, p. 1.

52 Hallissy, *Venomous Woman*, p. 10.

Duff understands Jezebel as a critical figure in John's larger narrative arc, noticing that name-calling and association with an infamous queen is but John's opening act for Jezebel. He argues that 'all of the . . . female characters in the Apocalypse are keyed to the figure of "Babylon"',[53] and they 'serve the interest of John's rhetoric of innuendo, that is, his strategy of *indirectly* accusing his rival of monstrous deeds'.[54] Further, he notes that

> John shares with his male contemporaries in Greco-Roman society the fear that each and every woman presented a danger to the integrity of society. . . . John plays on those cultural stereotypes that depict women as out of place in the public sphere. . . . Women operating in traditionally masculine roles within the public sphere were, for the most part, neither trusted nor tolerated because they were believed to lack such self-control (σωφροσύνη).[55]

Name-calling/labeling is not a strategy of indirection. It is a well-used, direct practice to establish equivalence and coherence between two disparate characters; it is one way that John establishes boundaries and polarities. It is his way of controlling his female and female-identified characters (Jezebel, the Whore, the Bride) and controlling how they are interpreted. They do not have real names, only symbolic names.

Section 2: Women, Sex and Food

Introduction

Anthropological literature is filled with studies that link women, sex and food. John links the same triad:

1. *Woman*: John, in the person of Christ, accuses the Thyatiran teacher and prophet (2.20) and promises to strike dead her children if she does not repent (2.23);
2. *Sex*: He accuses her of beguiling (bewitching, deceiving) members of the community to practice πορνεῦσαι, fornication/sexual immorality (2.20); she refuses to repent of her own πορνείας, sexual immorality (2.21); those who follow her are accused of τοὺς μοιχεύοντας μετ' αὐτῆς, committing adultery with her (2.22); and
3. *Food*: she encourages members of the community to eat food sacrificed to idols (2.20).

Section 1 noted that women with authority – like Jezebel the Queen and Jezebel the Thyatiran teacher and prophet – are both desired and feared; women with authority over men are viewed by men (and sometimes by other women) as a threat, and women who have authority are often depicted in the sexualized language of seduction. Such archetypic and stereotypic characterizations can result in violence against the woman and those associated with her. The letter to Thyatira makes two violent

---

53 That is, the Whore of Babylon. Paul Duff, *Who Rides the Beast? Prophetic Rivalry and the Rhetoric of Crisis in the Churches of the Apocalypse* (New York: Oxford University Press, 2001), p. 85.
54 Duff, *Who Rides the Beast?*, p. 85.
55 Duff, *Who Rides the Beast?*, pp. 107–108.

threats against the woman: 'I will throw her on a bed' (2.22) and 'I will strike her children dead' (2.23), and a string of threats leveled against those who support her: they will be thrown into tribulation (2.22), they will be ruled with a rod of iron and broken as earthen pots (2.27). This section considers how the three aspects of the triad interact and how John employs these aspects in the Thyatiran letter.

Women, Sex and Food

Anthropologists treat food as both a filter and a mirror: food absorbs and reflects numerous cultural phenomena, and it mirrors social organization at the most intimate as well as most universal levels. In countless cultures eating is a sexual and gendered experience; gender and eating as well as sex and eating are seen as overlapping metaphors because food is a code, a language that contributes to the organization of a social world.[56] Mary Douglas notes,

> If food is treated as a code, the message it encodes will be found in the pattern of social relations being expressed. The message is about different degrees of hierarchy, inclusion and exclusion, boundaries and transactions across the boundaries.[57]

Appler's study of the Jezebel narrative in 1 Kings 17 to 2 Kings 9 demonstrates that food is a symbol used to link Jezebel with the societal structures of the period: the monarchy, its subjects, the nations and the cult(s) – Baal and YHWH. Throughout the history of interpretation, 'the story about Jezebel and food becomes interpreted by scholars as a story about Jezebel and sexual promiscuity'.[58] Yet there is nothing in the Jezebel narrative to associate her with sexual promiscuity, vis-à-vis her husband, although in 1 Kgs 9.22 Jehu accuses her of 'whoredoms and sorceries', accusations that are euphemisms for her participation in the Baal cult. As seen in Section 1, the archetypic and stereotypic representations of Queen Jezebel are linked with John's Jezebel, including the association of food and eating practices (eating idol food) with sexual promiscuity (2.20).

As a reminder, John's use of the phrase to 'eat food sacrificed to idols' is found in both the letter to Pergamum and the letter to Thyatira. Apart from Acts 15.29; 21.25 and 1 Corinthians 8.1, 4, 7, 10, 19, the term εἰδωλόθυτον (idol food) appears in the Apocalypse, associated with only Balaam and with Jezebel. Coupled with eating idol food, Jezebel is also accused of *beguiling*; Balaam is not. The English term 'beguile' is the translator's lexical choice. The Greek verb πλανάω may be translated as 'to deceive', 'to beguile', 'to lead astray', and it is a term used in the Apocalypse of those characters (male and female) whose deception brings death and who will be destroyed and defeated.[59] However, the fact that the majority of recent English

56 Carol M. Counihan, *The Anthropology of Food and Body: Gender, Meaning, and Power* (New York: Routledge, 1999), pp. 6, 19.

57 Mary Douglas, 'Deciphering a Meal', in *eadem, Implicit Meanings: Selected Essays in Anthropology* (2nd edn, New York: Routledge, 1999), pp. 249–75 (249).

58 Appler, 'From Queen to Cuisine', p. 55.

59 Rev 2.20 of Jezebel; 12.19; 20.3, 8, 10 of the Great Dragon called the Devil and Satan; 13.4, of the Beast of the earth; 18.23 of the city of Babylon; 19.20 of the Beast; 20.3 of the Dragon.

translations choose to render the verb in a sexualized manner[60] – as 'beguile' – reveals how effective John's name-calling practice is when a female character is the one labeled. This example proves the adage that every translation *is* an interpretation!

John's use of sexualized language – πορνεῦσαι (to practice fornication/sexual immorality, 2.20),[61] πορνείας (fornicate, 2.21),[62] and τοὺς μοιχεύοντας μετ' αὐτῆς (those who commit adultery with her, 2.22)[63] – brackets the accusation of φαγεῖν εἰδωλόθυτα (to eat idol food, 2.20). Whether fornication/sexual immorality and adultery are euphemisms for eating idol food is unclear. The terms represent a range of activities that could have quite different meanings, and they could represent accusations of some form of sexual misconduct in the community (including the community in Pergamum since πορνεῦσαι is used in 2.14). But that seems unlikely, particularly given the commendation to the community for its love, faith, service and patient endurance as well as Paul's repeated use of the phrase in 1 Corinthians 8. There the subject is idol food and the threats and risks associated with participation in local cultural activities.[64]

The link between food and sex is natural as both are instinctive, human drives with overlapping symbolic associations that link cultural and political hierarchies – they are boundary issues. For example, eating may represent copulation, and food may represent sexuality.[65] Food and sex are linked in the portrayal of Queen Jezebel in 1 and 2 Kings and the depiction of Jezebel and the community at Thyatira. They also link Jezebel and Babylon [the Great Harlot/Whore]. From Genesis through the Apocalypse, the reader is reminded that food and 'food choices have consequences. Food decides who is inside, who is outside'.[66] Eating with others lies at the heart of social relations and indicates one's place in the social system – with whom you eat, where you eat, what you eat.[67] Individuals and groups identify with others by eating the same food in the same way. Anthropology understands the connection between sex and food:

---

60 E.g., the RSV and NRSV read 'beguiling'; the NJB reads 'luring'; the NIV and NIB-British read 'misleads'; the New American reads 'misleads'; the KJV, NKJV, and the ESV read 'seduce'.

61 Used of Balaam's teaching in 2.14; of the Whore in 17.2; of the nations' and kings' association with the Whore, 18.3, 9.

62 Also used of humankind (τῶν ἀνθρώπων) who did not repent after the sixth trumpet in 9.20–21; of the Whore/Babylon the Great in 14.8; 17.2, 4; 19.2; of the nations' and kings' association with the Whore, 18.3.

63 Used only here in the Apocalypse.

64 For studies on Paul's use of the term see Peter D. Gooch, *Dangerous Food: 1 Corinthians 8–10 in Its Context* (Studies in Judaism and Christianity, 5; Waterloo, ON.: Canadian Corporation for Studies in Religion, 1993); Alex T. Cheung, *Idol Food in Corinth: Jewish Background and Pauline Legacy* (JSNTSup, 176; Sheffield: Sheffield Academic Press, 1999); John Fotopolous, *Food Offered to Idols in Roman Corinth: A Socio-Rhetorical Reconsideration of 1 Cor 8:1–11:1* (Tübingen: Mohr Siebeck, 2003).

65 Counihan, *Anthropology of Food and Body*, p. 9.

66 Jean Soler, 'The Semiotics of Food in the Bible', in C. Counihan and P. van Esterik (eds), *Food and Culture: A Reader* (New York: Routledge, 1997), pp. 55–66 (56).

67 Counihan, *Anthropology of Food and Body*, pp. 6, 8; Douglas, 'Deciphering a Meal', p. 240.

Precisely because eating and intercourse involve intimacy, they can be dangerous when carried out with the wrong person or under the wrong conditions. Hence food and sex are surrounded with rules and taboos that both regulate their use and reinforce beliefs basic to the social order, most notably beliefs associated with gender.[68]

Food and sex are aspects of bodily culture, the backdrop against which play out an assortment of associations, symbols, human interactions and cultural boundaries. The body is a bounded system that can represent all kinds of transactions across boundaries as well as the breaching of boundaries. Duff argues that for males in the Greco-Roman world women were feared and thought unstable and uncontrollable precisely because their bodily boundaries were so easily breached.

> ... every female body – to some degree or another – resists its own bounds. For instance, the female bodily boundaries are penetrated in the course of the sexual act. A woman consequently conceives (by the deposit of a foreign element) and then the boundaries of her body are stretched by pregnancy and penetrated a second time (this time from the inside) by the birthing process. As Anne Carson has graphically suggested, '[w]oman's boundaries are pliant, porous, mutable. Her power to control them is inadequate, her concern for them unreliable. Deformation attends her. She swells, she shrinks, she leaks, she is penetrated, she suffers metamorphoses'.[69]

Penetration of the body, either through intercourse or eating food, is an intimate experience, what anthropology calls social merging. All kinds of hierarchies (class, race, gender) are maintained through dietary rules[70] and rules about the body and sexual activity. Quite literally, women are food – for their unborn fetuses and for their infants. Traditionally, women have been responsible for the daily preparation of food, which also means they have been involved with the economics of food since food is a primary focus of much economic activity.

In the Apocalypse every female character is associated with sex and food. Duff, studying the particular connections between Jezebel and Babylon, highlights the economic and alimentary comparisons and contrasts between the two: he links Jezebel to imperial commerce,[71] and he examines the specific connections between the two characters with regard to the mouth, nourishment, food and self-control, sexuality and self-control, and the female body in sexual imagery and as boundary.[72] He argues:

> The sheer number of alimentary images in the document, especially those connected with danger and death, suggest the importance of the issue of social boundaries and the role that the issue of εἰδωλόθυτα plays in constructing those boundaries. By emphasizing the role of food in the visions of the Apocalypse, John is able to advocate implicitly the importance

---

68 Counihan, *Anthropology of Food and Body*, p. 3.

69 Duff, *Who Rides the Beast?*, p. 107; Anne Carson, 'Putting Her in Her Place: Women, Dirt, and Desire', in D. M. Halperin, J. T. Winkler and F. I. Zeitlin (eds); *Before Sexuality: The Construction of Erotic Experience in the Ancient Greek World* (Princeton, NJ: Princeton University Press, 1990), pp. 135–70 (154).

70 Counihan, *Anthropology of Food and Body*, p. 9.

71 Duff, *Who Rides the Beast?*, pp. 61–70.

72 Duff, *Who Rides the Beast?*, pp. 99–111.

of boundaries in his community. As the individual physical body is vulnerable to what enters it through the mouth, so the social body of Christians needs to be wary of its own points of vulnerability.[73]

In Thyatira and throughout the Roman world, trade groups, clubs and associations expressed social connections, common causes and private friendships with banquets or cultic meals that shored up some boundaries while extending others. Participation in such meals provided a way of protecting and expanding economic interests, prosperity and business partnerships with other guild members while legitimating the patronage system and the privileges of the elite. To do otherwise would have compromised social, civic and economic self-interests. The meat used in these meals came from animals slaughtered on pagan altars (probably to the patron deity of the butchers' guild).[74] Other Christian leaders in Asia, including the author of 1 Peter, the author of the Pastorals, Polycarp of Smyrna, and Melito of Sardis encouraged Christians to engage in civic practices that would earn praise from outsiders 'while also lessening group-society tensions',[75] but John does not.

Cultural knowledge is inside knowledge, and John seems intent on marking sharp, exclusive, sectarian boundaries that restrict participating in the culture. His position is uncompromising. He understands these kinds of social intercourse as 'eating food sacrificed to idols' (2.20). Participation in such meals was apostasy because the food was a form of intercourse, a literal and spiritual participation in the social, religious and economic practices of the Empire. In other words, what we eat (as well as where and with whom) is symbolic of who we are, of identity and loyalties. As Freud noted, 'To eat and drink with someone was at the same time a symbol and a confirmation of social community and of the assumption of mutual obligations.'[76] For John, Thyatirans are literally 'eating culture',[77] that is, those who follow Jezebel are complicit in the social and economic oppression and brutality that is Rome. Women, food and sex are all real entities in Thyatira; they are boundary issues. In short, they are indicators of community self-definition and the social, religious and cultural values of the community.

Conclusion

Keller notes that the 'apocalypse always charges its batteries with sex/gender images. . . . the lascivious sex of a powerful woman is inscribed in the object of all end-time hatred – whether or not literal Jezebels were around to provoke a particular prophet'.[78] The conflict represented in Thyatira is a conflict for authority, a conflict

73 Duff, *Who Rides the Beast?*, p. 100.

74 Barr, *Tales of the End*, p. 58.

75 Philip A. Harland, 'Honouring the Emperor or Assailing the Beast: Participation in Civic Life among Associations (Jewish, Christian and Other) in Asia Minor and the Apocalypse of John', *JSNT* 77 (2000), pp. 99–121 (115).

76 Sigmund Freud, *Totem and Taboo* (trans. A. A. Brill; New York: Vintage, 1918), p. 174.

77 The title of the work seems an appropriate metaphor for John's argument. R. Scapp and B. Seitz (eds), *Eating Culture* (Albany: State University of New York Press, 1998).

78 Keller, *Apocalypse Now and Then*, p. 253.

over who will set and maintain group boundaries. Protecting the solidarity of the group and defending it from outsiders was a male duty, so the Thyatiran prophet posed complex problems and multiple threats for John: she was a female, she was a peer, she was an insider and he was the outsider, she had internal support, her boundaries were different from his.

For John this was a conflict about survival, the survival of the Christianity he envisioned which included the exclusion of anything associated with Roman power or oppression. John sees danger in anything associated with Rome, and his attempts to restrict the social and civic lives of these communities could have had enormous implications for incipient Christianity. At the same time, John sees danger in the feminine. The female and female-identified characters include two whores (Jezebel and Babylon the Great), a mother (the Woman Clothed with the Sun), and a virgin (the Bride/the New Jerusalem), all of whom are subject to male control, and none of whom will be in the New Jerusalem (the Bride becomes the New Jerusalem, into whom stream 144,000 male virgins!). Pippin argues that the exploitation of female images in the Apocalypse is part of male desire: 'The unconscious desires of the male reader, not only for the destruction of the dominant political and economic power but for the destruction of the sexual power of the female, are found in the ideology of desire in the text.'[79] John's Jezebel is a fantasy woman constructed as the object of desire, the object of fear, and as a foil for hostility against the Empire. The ferocity of the language used against the Thyatiran teacher and prophet, as well as those who follow her, is surpassed only by the vehemence against Babylon, the Great Harlot/Whore. John's rhetoric of conflict is a language that cannibalizes and consumes; it is language that permits no response or rebuttal.

Picking carefully among John's textual shards, I am unable to find a woman I recognize in the Apocalypse; prophets are not quiet in the assembly! This story knows more than it tells, and it tells more than it knows. As a reader I am left to linger in that ambiguous and destabilized liminal space where darkness and light remain confusing and revelatory. The story leaves behind an immense uneasiness . . . it must be carried.

---

79 Pippin, *Death and Desire*, p. 84.

WHY CAN'T THE HEAVENLY MISS JERUSALEM JUST SHUT UP?*

JORUNN ØKLAND

Within the last decade feminist biblical scholarship has relocated its point of departure. Feminist scholars no longer must begin by pointing out that our sources are androcentric and that androcentric scholarship represents a limited perspective. Instead, many now take gender theory as a point of departure and explore what this theoretical approach might contribute to an understanding of biblical texts. This shift is not just a result of biblical gender studies becoming more established and, hence, now in a position to set its own agenda. It also relates to 'the linguistic turn' of the humanities, which returns the spotlight to the complicated process of reading texts. Nevertheless, as Helge Jordheim points out, in this linguistic turn language as a historical, material, located phenomenon ironically got lost again, not least through the subsumption of 'philology' under 'theory' as expressed most clearly by Paul de Man,[1] whose understanding of philology as 'an examination of the structure of language prior to the meaning it produces'[2] owes more to structuralist method than to traditional, historical–critical philology with its sensitivity towards the fact that texts are written in particular languages under particular historical and material constraints that affect *both* the linguistic structures *and* their meaning-content. Thus, even the most universalizing theory is linguistically embedded, although this is not always admitted or recognized. Theories or theologies formulated in one language are necessarily dependent on the possibilities of that language. When applied to different linguistic systems they may tease out what is unexpressed or suppressed, but it is equally plausible that they render important possibilities in that other language invisible. For feminism this is a problem because feminism began as a Western movement for equality, but unless feminist theories are applied with critical care towards geographical, linguistic and historical difference they could serve as just another tool in the continuing Western colonization of 'hearts and minds' around the globe. Thus, the turn to a more explicitly feminist-theoretical agenda potentially has its problems – even if as a feminist I mainly welcome such a turn.

This essay is to some extent inspired by Toril Moi, who sometimes includes reflections on linguistic differences among American English, French and Norwegian in

* I am grateful to John Marshall for posing the devastating question as to why the bride is speaking if she is *only* the receptacle, as she was so situated in an earlier phase of this work. This essay is a minimally modified version of my 'Why Can't the Heavenly Miss Jerusalem Just Shut Up?', first printed in Caroline Vander Stichele and Todd Penner (eds), *Her Master's Tools? Feminist and Postcolonial Engagements of Historical-Critical Discourse* (Global Perspectives on Biblical Scholarship; Atlanta, GA/Leiden: Society of Biblical Literature/Brill, 2005), pp. 311–32.

1 For this argument, see Helge Jordheim, *Lesningens Vitenskap: Utkast til en ny filologi* (Oslo: Universitetsforlaget, 2001), pp. 94–101. He discusses Paul de Man, 'The Return to Philology', in *idem*, *The Resistance to Theory* (Minneapolis: University of Minnesota Press, 1986), pp. 21–26.

2 de Man, *Resistance to Theory*, p. 24.

her study of literature, although she does not explore these differences systematic-ally.[3] It is also inspired by Theodor Adorno, who used foreign words frequently in his writings as an 'explosive force'.[4] In Sinkwan Cheng's words, 'this "explosive" power comes precisely from the way the *Fremdwort* functions as an outlaw in the land of linguistic purity and organicity – as an outlaw which nonetheless promises to be the founder of a new law in the world "to come"'.[5] Whether the presence of foreign words is perceived as elitist–exclusivist, or as underground lingo reinforcing group boundaries or just lacking mastery of the main language depends on the perceived relationship between the social location of the sender and the receiver. But neither of these is adequate to describe Adorno's use of *Fremdwörter*, since his use of them is not grounded in his lacking mastery of English, not an attempt to create an alternative lingo for a particular group, nor an elitist expectation that everyone will – or should – understand their meaning. Their whole point is on a linguistic level to create rupture and protest against a hegemonic–cultural demand that difference be concealed.

Gender Theory, Philology and Linguistic Difference

A coherent and smooth text in only one language might eliminate the 'distraction' that foreign languages and universes of meaning represent in order to facilitate a firm focus on the content or theory. But it would also render invisible the difference of the linguistic and cultural universes that the biblical texts represent, that the theories I use to interpret them represent, and that my own Norwegian background represents – and thus it would undermine its own content. Therefore, the variety of languages upon which biblical scholars are dependent will be exposed rather than concealed through transcriptions and translations that mimic the essay's main language[6] (even if I – as the Bride [see below] – will for the most part adhere to this strategy). With foreign alphabets and words constantly interrupting and leaving fissures and channels into other universes of language and meaning, the result is a fractured text that exposes difference, alienation and mimicry in both its form and content.[7] In Adorno's words, 'Wörter aus der Fremde'[8] 'have their legitimacy as an

3 One exercise in the translingual versatility of feminist concepts and theories might be to compare the first chapter of her book *What is a Woman?* with its Norwegian version from the year before: '*What is a Woman?' and Other Essays* (New York: Oxford University Press, 1999); *Hva er en kvinne? Kjønn og kropp i feministisk teori* (Oslo: Gyldendal, 1998).

4 Theodor W. Adorno, 'On the Use of Foreign Words', in R. Tiedemann (ed.), *Notes to Literature* (trans. S. W. Nicholson; 2 vols; New York: Columbia University Press, 1991), vol. 2, pp. 286–91 (286).

5 Sinkwan Cheng, '*Fremdwörter* as "The Jews of Language" and Adorno's Politics of Exile', in M. O'Neill (ed.), *Adorno, Culture and Feminism* (London: Sage, 1999), pp. 75–103 (77).

6 The notion of mimicry, and how one can thereby speak sensibly within one discourse/language and simultaneously say something entirely 'different', is developed below in relation to Luce Irigaray and to the incident wherein the Woman/Bride utters male discourse.

7 Thereby hopefully attention is also drawn to how colonialism and alienation affect the very language of our texts, not merely their content.

8 Cheng discusses the problem of translating into English the title of Adorno's other article on the topic, 'Wörter aus der Fremde'. She prefers the title 'Alien Words' to 'Words from Abroad', which is the name under which this piece is published in English (Cheng, '*Fremdwörter*', pp. 77, 95).

expression of alienation itself'.[9] But as 'holes' in the text they also have the potential to work the other way round, to serve the reader as openings to other worlds of meaning, to be keyholes through which to unlock the default readings of the text, to hear suppressed voices.

Traditional NT scholarship has often been acutely aware of linguistic difference, although it is often hopelessly uncritical in its application of philological knowledge. For example, it is quick to use Greek terms and refer to their meanings according to the lexicon, as if this would in itself explain the text. Also traditionally, in British scholarship at least, there is a tendency to use this lexical information merely to paraphrase the text, not to use it to engage in a longer dialogue or argument over the views expressed in it.[10] That is why a coupling of critical feminist theory with more conventional, philological biblical criticism could bring out the best in both. For this purpose I find Luce Irigaray particularly apt, because much of her theory is developed through close readings of historical texts. She has repeatedly pointed out how passage through the master discourse and rigorous interpretation of its phallogocratism[11] down to the level of syntax and grammar are indispensable *before* a different syntax, grammar and metaphor can develop.[12] In her main work, *Speculum de l'autre femme*,[13] Irigaray has interrogated the stranglehold of ancient male discourse on history and pointed out its fissures, from where one could sometimes, perhaps, hear the other (mainly understood as 'woman') speaking.[14]

Finally, before moving on to Revelation, I will point out some particularities of the languages hitherto noted compared to the main language of this essay, English. I take this step to show how language and meaning cannot be separated, and why therefore I find it a problem that much anglophone feminist theory is not always aware of the difference that linguistic difference makes. In an anglophone feminist-theoretical context, the distinction between sex and gender was invented, and it has been very productive.[15] 'Sex' in this context may denote biology, materiality, or even

---

9 Adorno, 'On the Use of Foreign Words', p. 289.

10 This is a general criticism of British NT scholarship that John Riches launched in a stunning main lecture at the British New Testament Conference 2007, entitled 'Reception History as Literary History'. I hope it will be made available in writing very soon.

11 I.e., the reign of the phallus and the logos in combination, i.e., a logic, argument and sexed vocabulary that presupposes male supremacy and reinforces it.

12 See, e.g., Luce Irigaray, *Ce Sexe qui n'en est pas un* (Paris: Minuit, 1977), p. 157.

13 Luce Irigaray, *Speculum de l'autre femme* (Paris: Minuit, 1974). My references to works in languages other than English are necessarily inconsistent in this essay. In the case of Irigaray, where I refer to *her* writing or where the French is important in itself I use the French text. Where I use Irigaray to construct meaning in the English text, I will rely on the English translations by Gillian Gill and Catherine Porter/Carolyn Burke (see Luce Irigaray, *This Sex which is not One* [trans. Catherine Porter with Carolyn Burke; Ithaca, NY: Cornell University Press, 1985], and *Speculum of the Other Woman* [trans. Gillian Gill; Ithaca, NY: Cornell University Press, 1985]).

14 I leave aside for the moment the closely related but much larger hermeneutical problem of how to understand ancient Greek and Hebrew texts at all within modern cultural and linguistic contexts, since this is constantly dealt with by traditional biblical scholarship.

15 When anglophone post-structuralist feminist theorists such as Judith Butler started to question the distinction, non-anglophone theorists found this particular aspect of her theorizing less ground-breaking since it dismantled a distinction that had been operative mainly in English language anyway. See discussion in Toril Moi, *What is a Woman?*, pp. 10–45.

essential mental characteristics[16] that some believe to be innate to men and women. 'Gender' is the socioculturally constructed system of roles and identities that sorts people into two groups, men and women, and attributes to them a role that influences their self-understanding, mentality and possibilities from birth.

French and Scandinavian languages do not have the English distinction between sex and gender. On this basis, Toril Moi, from the same small language community as myself, points out that English-language critics, *including* the post-structuralists, have misread the French feminists, above all Simone de Beauvoir, through the lens of the sex/gender distinction: 'English-language post-structuralists have largely failed to see how the more inclusive approach to subjectivity and the body could be found in de Beauvoir and other feminists writing in languages that do not operate with such a distinction.'[17] Similarly, when, in the English translation, Irigaray's *sexué* is translated as 'sexualized' (see below), the latter term in English carries very different connotations than 'gendered', which in my view would have covered the French term better (although not perfectly). On the other hand, the linguistic system into which Scandinavian feminists read the English sex–gender distinction only has one term for the various types of differences between men and women – 'kjønn/kön' – which does not thereby mean that they are unable to distinguish among physiology, social roles and metaphors *when necessary*. For the moment, this observation only means that my use of the term 'gender' will mimic English, while denoting the semantic fields of Norwegian 'kjønn' or French 'sexe'; this usage allows me to approach Revelation's bodies in their interpreted state without getting caught in the endless anglophone feminist-theoretical debates on what is more important: sex or gender. This approach means that 'gender' must be read as something more comprehensive than 'gender as opposed to sex'. 'Gender' in this 'foreign' sense has a material side, but its materiality cannot always be pinned down and defined. Luckily, such terminological recirculation is a possibility in the highly versatile and complex English language, which recently has been hailed as Esperanto's true heir and fulfillment.[18]

Another particularity of Scandinavian languages compared to English is that there are linguistic alternatives to the silent, unstable inclusion of women under a masculine/generic term. In the hegemonic languages of feminist theory today, English and French, women can sometimes be included in the masculine term 'man' or *homme*, which then takes on generic meaning. For current French thinkers this possibility of using *homme* in both a masculine and a generic sense represents the core of phallogocentrism.[19] 'Woman' is sometimes presupposed within the generic term, other times not. Her inclusion does not make a visible or 'hearable' difference

16 That these concepts are at least as elusive as 'sex' itself only fuels current debates. I will not go into the discussion of all the different entities to which 'biological body' can refer. See further Elsa Almås and Espen Esther Pirelli Benestad, *Kjønn i bevegelse* (Oslo: Universitetsforlaget, 2001), pp. 19–31; Anne Fausto-Sterling, *Sexing the Body: Gender Politics and the Construction of Sexuality* (New York: Basic Books, 2000). I will also not discuss the complicated relationship between modern 'biology' and ancient Greek φύσις, an equally elusive term.

17 Moi, *What is a Woman?*, p. 5.

18 Mark Abley, *Spoken Here: Travels among Threatened Languages* (London: Heinemann, 2003), pp. 93–94.

19 I am particularly relying on Irigaray (*Speculum de l'autre femme*, esp. pp. 58–61) for the idea that the world is understood according to λόγος, an order defined by the masculine.

to the term,[20] and she is rarely mentioned explicitly. For 'man' or *homme*, woman is the difference without which the term could not make claims to universality. Woman becomes the necessary support of the universality of 'man', operating within the latter term as a constant shadow that cannot be dialectically absorbed – neither obliterated nor fully assumed. This ambiguity was particularly convenient in post-revolutionary France when it came to teasing out what *Droits de l'homme* ('Rights of Man') should mean in practice. The linguistic ambiguity made it easier not to give women equal rights with men even if they were sometimes subsumed under the *homme*-terminology, thereby loading that designation with universal meaning.[21]

Germanic (including Dutch and Scandinavian) languages preserve the ancient Greek distinction between generic ἄνθρωπος and masculine ἀνήρ. That is, they have a separate word for 'human being' as individuals and as a whole that both English and French lack. I am not thereby suggesting that phallogocentrism is a French and English phenomenon only or that the generic signifier in Greek and Germanic languages is not frequently used in an exclusively masculine sense too. But this difference accounts for some of the distinct directions gender studies take in the various language communities. In what follows, I pursue the issue of linguistic difference, but now focus more specifically on the issue of gender and language, engaging whether 'woman' can be spoken in any phallogocentric language at all or whether the 'organicity' of the phallogocentric text conceals the difference of woman.

Male and Female Virgins

Drawing on the gender-critical and philological observations developed in the previous section, I will now explore some of the virginal characters in Revelation's blissful 'elsewhere',[22] with its odd relationships between lovers, between humans and sheep, and between men and women in general. The book as a whole is dressed in the language of war and conquest, imperial rulership and worship, purity and danger.[23]

---

20 This is a problem not only of anthropological terminology, but of much Western philosophical discourse more generally: Derrida's invention, the term *différance*, which when pronounced in French sounds like the correctly spelled *différence*, illustrates this ambiguous (graphic) difference that does not make a (audible) difference. See Jacques Derrida, 'Différance', in his *Margins of Philosophy* (trans. A. Bass; Chicago, IL: University of Chicago Press, 1982), pp. 3–27.

21 See Joan W. Scott, *Only Paradoxes to Offer: French Feminists and the Rights of Man* (Cambridge, MA: Harvard University Press, 1996).

22 One could call this place neither 'heaven' nor 'new earth' because the texts simply imply that it moves around (i.e., it is mobile). Under the influence of Theo Angelopoulos's 'Το μετέωρο βήμα του πελαργού' ('The Suspended Step of the Stork'; Athens, Greece: Greek Film Centre, 1991) and also Irigaray (e.g., in 'Le Miroir, de l'autre côté', in *Ce Sexe*, p. 16), I have chosen the term 'elsewhere' (αλλού; 'ailleurs'/'autre côté'), a term that encompasses all these possibilities.

23 For language of war and conquest, see in particular Catherine Keller, *Apocalypse Now and Then: A Feminist Guide to the End of the World* (Boston, MA: Beacon, 1996); and Stephen D. Moore, 'Revolting Revelations', in I. R. Kitzberger (ed.), *The Personal Voice in Biblical Interpretation* (London and New York: Routledge, 1999), pp. 183–200. For imperial ideology and worship, see, e.g., David Aune, 'The Influence of Roman Imperial Court Ceremonial on the Apocalypse of John', *BR* 18 (1983), pp. 5–26. Purity issues are touched upon by most feminist readers: see in particular A. Yarbro Collins, 'Feminine Symbolism in the Book of Revelation', in *BibInt* 1 (1993), pp. 20–33 and Hanna Stenström, 'The Book of Revelation: A Vision of the Ultimate Liberation or the Ultimate Backlash? A Study in 20th Century Interpretations of Rev 14.1–5, with Special Emphasis on Feminist Exegesis' (PhD dissertation, Uppsala University, 1999).

I will show how the characters in question and their mutual relations represent the blissful 'elsewhere' as a specific gendered place.

Feminist biblical scholars have studied Revelation from various perspectives, but a common question seems to arise repeatedly: can Revelation be saved or reclaimed as sacred Scripture for Christian women? As Stenström demonstrates particularly clearly in her thesis, both men and women have looked to Revelation as a writing of Christian hope – which is why many feminist biblical scholars cannot just write it off as a misogynist text, but must try to come up with gender-sensitive interpretations of it instead.[24] They have also shown a special interest in the various females of Revelation. Among scholars who draw on feminist and other gender theory in their interpretations of Revelation, the level at which they activate such theory and its outcome varies considerably. Elisabeth Schüssler Fiorenza and A. Yarbro Collins remain largely within the historical-critical paradigm in their work on Revelation, albeit with gender awareness.[25] Stephen D. Moore relates closely – and broadly – to literary and gender theories, and he constantly draws attention to language as I also attempt here, although he does so in such a way that one probably has to be a native speaker of English in order fully to appreciate the results.[26]

Catherine Keller, Tina Pippin and Hanna Stenström are more interested in the social functions and consequences Revelation has or might have for women, and they also engage more systemically with feminist theory.[27] Stenström points out that in Revelation 'women' can be used as a 'rhetorical means to designate Evil when the topic is the struggle between Good and Evil and the necessity to take sides in the struggle'.[28] Pippin's comment concerning the Bride, the Lamb and the 144,000 is fundamental to the argument here: the 'scene is disturbing because the imagery is that of mass intercourse'.[29] These readings focus on the *influence* of the gender structures of the text on real, embodied women, as analyzed with the help of feminist theory. As a result, they also take cultural location more fully into account.[30]

---

24 See, e.g., Stenström, 'Book of Revelation', pp. 32, 240.

25 Among their numerous publications on Revelation, the following are the most important for this essay: A. Yarbro Collins, *The Combat Myth in the Book of Revelation* (HDR, 9; Missoula, MT: Scholars Press, 1976); *eadem*, 'Feminine Symbolism'; Elisabeth Schüssler Fiorenza, *Revelation: Vision of a Just World* (Proclamation Commentaries; Minneapolis, MN: Augsburg Fortress Press, 1991).

26 Stephen D. Moore, *God's Gym: Divine Male Bodies of the Bible* (New York and London: Routledge, 1996).

27 Stenström, 'Book of Revelation'; Keller, *Apocalypse*. It should be noted that Keller is more a theologian than an exegete; hence her approach is mentioned, but used less actively here. See also Tina Pippin, *Death and Desire: The Rhetoric of Gender in the Apocalypse of John* (Literary Currents in Biblical Interpretation; Louisville, KY: Westminster/John Knox Press, 1992); and *eadem*, *Apocalyptic Bodies: The Biblical End of the World in Text and Image* (New York: Routledge, 1999).

28 Stenström, 'Book of Revelation', p. 316.

29 Pippin, *Death and Desire*, p. 80.

30 In particular, Pippin's *Apocalyptic Bodies* challenges me to think through my own relationship to Revelation. In my upbringing within the context of the Lutheran state church of Norway, Revelation was a book 'not to be read' – it was too liminal, too imaginative. Revelation challenged the relatively happy, tempered, grace-filled marriage between social democracy and Lutheranism. Revelation is hopelessly socially un-democratic, and it distorts the rational structures of Lutheran dogmatics – especially in relation to grace and the life hereafter. Like the wedding at Cana incident in John 2, where Jesus turned water into wine, my cultural religious background had a particular way of viewing such incidents: 'Me vett de é der, men me liga de ikkje' – 'we know it's there, but we don't like it'.

In relation to these various ways of activating feminist theory, I will combine the tools of traditional philology and feminist theory in order to focus narrowly on how the characters in the scenes of the 'elsewhere' contribute to the 'kjønning'/gendering of this place. I will then ask if the difference of 'elsewhere' can be expressed at all within the language of 'here'. I resist mainstream discourse and its penchant for asking what is figurative and literal speech – a question that I often find sidetracking important discussions of the structures of meaning in the book of Revelation. The gender of the various heavenly characters and the text's concern for the purity of these *male* and *female* bodies will thus be approached with a presupposition borrowed from Swedish sociologist Yvonne Hirdman, namely that the characters represented in the various spaces contribute to or reflect a gendered discourse of the place in question.[31]

According to Hirdman, the 'gender system' operates according to two dynamics: segregation and hierarchy. Hirdman underscores their unique structuring abilities: they *make* sense. She shows how character, action and place are intimately linked and stand in a legitimizing, reinforcing, dialectical relationship with each other.[32]

In Revelation, the most important places are the old world and the new world (coming down from heaven). We learn a lot about these places through the characters that inhabit them. The characters in/from heaven, on which I focus here, are presented at more or less regular intervals throughout the book, such as in chs 4–5, 7, 14 and 20.11–22.5. The main characters are God and the Lamb. As Stephen D. Moore demonstrates, God (θεός), who mostly sits on the throne in heaven (e.g., 4.2–3; 7.11; 11.16; 16.11; 22.1), is described in hypermasculine metaphors and grammar; Moore finds that Revelation's heaven parallels the modern gym where the male bodybuilder (God), 'the supreme embodiment of hegemonic hyper-masculinity',[33] is 'mirrored' by the multitudes lining the interior walls of the heavenly city/gym.

The Lamb (ἀρνίον), a somewhat gender-ambiguous character (cf. Rev. 5.6–8; 14.1–4; 19.7), is generic and grammatically neuter. If we read Revelation 'with the grain' within a heterosexual framework, however, we observe that, since the Lamb is eventually married to the Bride, the holy Jerusalem, it must be male. This is not the only possible reading, but it is perhaps most adequate if one reads with the gender ideologies of Revelation's historical setting in mind. Indeed, as Steve Moyise demonstrates, this Lamb is rather unstable;[34] it performs as a masculine lion (λέον).

The 144,000 παρθένοι

Rev. 14.1–3 describes a group of no fewer than 144,000 who stand on Mount Zion together with the Lamb. They sing a new song before the throne, which no one can

31 The argument behind this assertion can be found in my *Women in their Place: Paul and the Corinthian Discourse of Gender and Sanctuary Space* (JSNTSup, 269; New York: Continuum, 2004).

32 Yvonne Hirdman, 'Genussystemet–reflexioner kring kvinnors sociala underordning', *Kvinnovetenskapelig tidsskrift* 3 (1988), pp. 49–63 (52).

33 Moore, *God's Gym*, p. 139.

34 Steve Moyise, 'Does the Lion Lie down with the Lamb?', in *idem* (ed.), *Studies in the Book of Revelation* (Edinburgh: T&T Clark, 2001), pp. 181–94.

learn except the 144,000. They are described as 'virgins' (παρθένοι; 14.4) and also as 'blameless' (ἄμωμοι; 14.5) and as 'first fruits' (ἀπαρχή; 14.4), the latter designations borrowed from the sphere of ritual sacrifice. Revelation 14.4 includes them among the heavenly bodies: 'It is these who have not defiled themselves with women, for they are virgins; these follow the Lamb wherever he goes. They have been redeemed from humankind as first fruits for God and the Lamb' (NRSV).

The same group is also encountered earlier in Rev. 7.4–8. There they still seem to be on earth, where they are about to be sealed on their forehead by an angel with the seal of the living God (7.2). The resonance with the Passover story (Exodus 12) is not to be missed, although in the latter 600,000 men are mentioned alongside the phrase 'in addition women and children' (Exod. 12.37), which means that in Exodus the 600,000 are clearly male and adult. In a similar way as in the Passover story, the seal should prevent the 144,000 from being harmed when God's angels go out to punish (Rev. 7.3). The gender-status of the 144,000 is more ambiguous than the 600,000 men from Exodus since women and children are not mentioned separately, but there may be other reasons for that, as we shall see. In any case, they are described in masculine grammatical terms, and they are taken from each of the tribes of the *sons of Israel* that are named in the list (Rev. 7.5–8) – 12,000 from each tribe. Israel and his sons were male, and usually only men were counted in lists of this kind.

By ch. 14 the 144,000 are redeemed from the old earth. In the narrative, it is uncertain up to this point whether they are male or female, as the lack of female designations in ch. 7 may be a result of normal phallogocentric speech where the female is invisibly subsumed under the grammatically male proper names, tribes and categories. However, the sealing seems to be the differentiating act that makes maleness definitive. The ambiguity of the possibly phallogocentric speech in ch. 7 is removed by the clear reference to the group's avoidance of defilement by women. In Stenström's words, 'the sense of exclusive maleness is rather due to the fact that the group is put in contrast to "women" . . . The real name of the believer is a name in masculine'.[35]

Rev. 14.1 also gives more information about the seal that the 144,000 received in ch. 7: the seal bears the names of the Lamb and the Father. The 144,000 have not been 'inscribed' by women and other defiling agents: they have kept themselves pure by not having sexual relations with women. So what the 144,000 have in common are both the presence and absence of inscriptions on their body – foreheads and penises are sealed with the seal of the Father, but women's defilations are absent from their skin.

Because both their number and the reference to the seal on their forehead are repeated, I believe, along with the majority of scholars, that the references in Revelation 7 and 14 are to the same group. From a narrative point of view, characterization of two distinctive entities by means of the same referents would be less than elegant. Thus, modern readers may find theologically problematic Revelation's apparent presupposition that there are no women inhabitants in its 'elsewhere', most often

---

35 Stenström, 'Book of Revelation', p. 72.

described as 'heaven' or 'the New Jerusalem'.[36] Yet, if the 144,000 are male, the use of the term παρθένος also becomes odd, for παρθένος usually denoted the female (translated 'virgin').[37]

The modern mainstream scholarly silence concerning the gender of the heavenly inhabitants in Rev. 7.2–8 and 14.1–5 could be seen as an ordinary consequence of androcentrism: as long as the interpreters are male and men inhabit Revelation's 'elsewhere', the interpreters do not see any problems, or prefer not to open what in a modern context is a potential can of worms. Before gender had become a burning issue, Ronald Preston and Anthony Hanson could, however, innocently and matter-of-factly state that, 'if taken literally it means that only male celibates can be saved!'[38] Thus, in contrast to subsequent interpreters, they acknowledged that there was a gender problem and accounted for how they dispensed with the letter and inter-preted the expression according to what they felt made better sense. But in the face of the growing feminist criticism of the Bible, such accountability became increasingly problematic: it would imply the denouement of the irredeemably sexist plot of Revelation, which is, after all, part of the Bible, whose authority and reliability were already under attack from so many other angles. Instead, a rather apologetic, gender-blind inclusivism took over. More recently again, feminist scholars have pointed out the theological problem of the exclusion of women in the expression, especially Tina Pippin, who sees it as symptomatic of the Apocalypse as a whole.[39] More or less implicitly, the demand for male virginity is seen as a symptom of the text's misogynist ideology: women are seen as defiling, so men who want to be redeemed must not even have touched one.[40] Before returning to alternative solutions, I will, as promised, question what philology might have to contribute to the issue at hand.

Historical–critical exegesis is highly sensitive towards the problems of translating παρθένος. It is commonly known that Matthew, in his fatal (because of the effective history of its interpretation) designation of Jesus' mother as παρθένος (Matt. 1.23), was just quoting the Septuagint translation of the Hebrew עלמה (Isa. 7.14), meaning 'young girl'. The Septuagint translator had not chosen the closest Greek

---

36 In early Christianity this absence of women is unlikely to have caused many problems, as it was believed that virtuous, Christ-believing women were resurrected as men (e.g., Tertullian, *De cultu feminarum* 1,2). It is a recurring theme in Kari Børresen's scholarship that Augustine is the first early Christian author to argue that women are resurrected as women. When Augustine argues that 'the Lord said that there would be no marriage in the resurrection, not that there would be no women' (Latin: *nuptias ergo dominus futuras negavit esse in resurrectione, non feminas*; for edition see Marie Turcan [ed.], *Tertullian: De cultu feminarum / La toilette des femmes* [SC, 173; Paris: Cerf, 1971]), he thus disputes with Tertullian, Jerome and the Encratites who all believed women would be resur-rected as males, or angelic males (Kari Børresen, 'Patristic "Feminism": The Case of Augustine', in Ø. Norderval and K. L. Ore (eds), *From Patristics to Matristics: Selected Articles on Christian Gender Models by Kari E. Børresen* (Rome: Herder, 2002), pp. 33–47 (42).

37 'Virgin' has in modern times lost much of its ancient medical connotations, and its experiential meaning has been extended to include also men who have not had sexual intercourse.

38 Ronald Preston and Anthony T. Hanson, *The Revelation of Saint John the Divine* (London: SCM Press, 1949), p. 100.

39 Pippin, *Death and Desire*, pp. 70, 86.

40 Pippin, *Death and Desire*, pp. 70, 81; cf. Stenström, 'Book of Revelation', pp. 285, 314.

equivalents, κόρη or νεᾶνις,[41] but this other term, παρθένος, which more often than the Hebrew original referred to the state of not yet having engaged in sexual intercourse. He was blissfully unaware of the effects and consequences his insensitive translation would have, through the endorsement of the Gospel author, for later dogmatic concerns and views of sexuality. From the outset, however, παρθένος was not an unambiguous description of a bodily state either. As Delling pointed out, the ancient Greek use of the term was in no way limited to girls with an unbroken hymen even if this state may represent one out of the many elements upon which the use of the term is contingent.[42] For Delling, the term clearly denotes a mature young woman – he remarks that the bodily state is one option alongside many others – but he also admits that it is difficult to 'assign a specific meaning to each occurrence' of the word, given that its various nuances intermingle.[43] In the religious context of the Bible, there are frequent references to a 'virgin' who bears a divine child.[44] But, again, Delling pleads for attention to semantic nuance: 'one has to ask in *each* case what specific ideas are bound up with the statement.'[45] Delling goes on to point out that there is no emphasis on virginity in the Hebrew use of עלמה and that its translation as παρθένος is odd; indeed, even the Septuagint use of παρθένος covers everything from chastity, youth and young girls to virginity in a more narrow sense (it can even be used for a raped girl as it is in Gen. 34.3).[46] In true philological fashion, he emphasizes that the 'well-known' figure of The Virgin is an abstraction of religious history.[47]

I cite Delling in detail here because, as with many articles in *TWNT/TDNT* (the chosen representative of philological, historical–critical approaches for my argument here), his article destabilizes what many readers perceive as the 'meaning' of the term in question. His critical *Begriffsgeschichte* thus approaches the deconstructive method. He demonstrates the variety of meanings for παρθένος in ancient Greek, and how arbitrary the later preoccupation with the hymen of the 'mother of god' is. Nevertheless, having done away with any fixed meaning of the term, he still 'short-circuits' when he comes to the use of the word in Revelation: here it is suddenly used

---

41 For the latter possibility, see Kristin de Troyer, 'Septuagint and Gender Studies: The Very Beginning of a Promising Liaison', in A. Brenner and C. Fontaine (eds), *A Feminist Companion to Reading the Bible: Approaches, Methods and Strategies* (Sheffield: Sheffield Academic Press, 1997), pp. 326–43 (337).

42 Gerhard Delling, 'παρθένος', *TDNT* 5, pp. 826–37. Cf. LSJ, s.v. παρθένος/εια. From the examples they mention, the term also seems more closely linked to female gender than to sexual status.

43 Trans. G. W. Bromiley. Delling, 'παρθένος', p. 825: 'die verschiedenen Klangfarben mischen sich zum Teil in den Aussagen, so daß nicht jedes Vorkommen auf eine bestimmte festlegbar ist.'

44 Context here understood as Mediterranean context. Delling discusses particularly Plutarch's theories of the conception of Plato by Apollo, and virgin goddesses who bear divine children, such as Isis and Persephone. In a footnote he points out that further east one cannot find examples of the virgin mother-goddess.

45 Trans. G. W. Bromiley. Delling, 'παρθένος', p. 827: 'Indessen ist in jedem Falle zu prüfen, welche besonderen Auffassungen sich mit der Aussage verbinden.'

46 Delling, 'παρθένος', p. 831.

47 Delling, 'παρθένος', p. 830: 'die "bekannte" Gestalt der Jungfrau ist eine religionsgeschichtliche Abstraktion.'

only figuratively (*nur bildlich*), like πόρνη.[48] Having just deconstructed any 'literal' meaning of the term by listing all its possible meanings, why does Delling have this sudden change of mind? The '*only* figurative' explanation is the scholarly safety valve, blown when scholars are uncomfortable with Revelation's statements and want to avoid the problems with its meanings.

If none of the aforementioned elements is indispensable and thus none can determine the use of the term παρθένος, its usage for men does not have to be classified as 'figurative'. Thus, its appearance in Revelation is probably contingent on elements other than the physiological feature that became so crucial in the production of the dogma of incarnation in a later period when asceticism had become an ideal. In other words, Revelation's usage of παρθένος for men is only metaphorical to the extent that all language is metaphorical. This perception is reflected in modern English translations such as *Good News for Modern Man*, which translates παρθένος as 'they are unmarried' or 'chaste'. Yet, however philologically and modern-contextually adequate these translations may be, they are not representative of the importance attached to a physiological, 'literal' understanding when women are designated as such elsewhere in the New Testament. If παρθένος in the verses concerning Mary in Mt. 1.23 and Lk. 1.27 had been translated in similarly flexible ways, exegetes would definitely have had less to discuss, and the church would have produced fewer 'heretics'.

Even if παρθένος is mostly used for females, Revelation is not the only Christian writing to use this term for men. In the phrase περὶ δὲ τῶν παρθένων (concerning the virgins) in 1 Cor. 7.25, the genitive plural is adequate both for masculine and feminine grammatical gender, and because of 7.26 it is reasonable to believe that the plural refers to both male and female virgins: 'I think it is good for a human being (ἀνθρώπῳ) to be/remain like that', i.e., a virgin. It is even possible that the author of Revelation is alluding to this saying, because the valorization of lifelong virginity is rather foreign to most other ancient Mediterranean discourses on which Revelation otherwise draws. Even the relatively conceptually close Temple Scroll from Qumran states the following about entrance into the New Jerusalem: 'a man who lies with his wife and has an ejaculation, *for three days* shall not enter the whole city of the temple in which I shall cause my name to dwell',[49] which is very different from Paul's advice about lifelong abstinence.

Having established that any problems with the male παρθένοι are theological rather than linguistic–philological, we return to the discussion of alternative reading

48 Delling, 'παρθένος', p. 835.

49 Florentino García Martínez, *The Dead Sea Scrolls Translated: The Qumran Texts in English* (trans. W. G. E. Watson; 2nd edn, Grand Rapids, MI: Eerdmans, 1996). 11Q19 (*Temple Scroll*[a]) 45, 11–12. In some later rabbinic texts it seems rather to be agreed that not to have a wife is 'to diminish the image of God' (for this expression see *t. Yeb.* 8:7; comp. concerning the issue of getting the priorities right, e.g., *Qidd.* 29b); still, the balancing of marriage and family duties with Torah study is represented as difficult. See a full discussion of these and other examples in Daniel Boyarin, *Carnal Israel: Reading Sex in Talmudic Culture* (Berkeley and Los Angeles: University of California Press, 1993), pp. 134–66. Among these options, the church fathers seem to follow Paul's preference for the unmarried state most of the time.

strategies. To avoid understanding the 144,000 as male, one alternative strategy is to read male names, male categories – like the notion of the first fruit, which in terms of animal sacrifice meant male victims – and the masculine grammar of the Greek as generic and conventional, a reading strategy also applied to other parts of the New Testament. This approach is taken by Schüssler Fiorenza, who emphasizes that grammatical gender is not the same as sex, and that masculine pronouns do not imply that something is imagined as male. Therefore women can read Revelation as gender-inclusive.[50] This interpretation is possible on the basis of two distinctions: between literal and symbolic/metaphorical, and between sex and gender. Schüssler Fiorenza is aware of the gendered dualisms and the androcentrism of both Revelation and the context in which it was produced, but gendered dualisms, in her view, should not be taken in 'a literalist sense'.[51] Within the rhetoric of Revelation, 'sexual language is used metaphorically', in this case that is to say that the 144,000 have not participated in the idolatry of the imperial cult.[52]

I do not contest this reading, which keeps a firm focus on what is probably an overall message of the book. But since Schüssler Fiorenza has taught me so much about the 'hermeneutics of suspicion' and unmasked the naturalized truths of centuries of kyriocentric dominance in other contexts, I find her approach to Revelation's gendered language rather surprising. Not only does she not see it as decisive for the Apocalypse's message, she also suggests that the relation between grammatical gender and sex is arbitrary. I agree that in languages like German, Norwegian and Greek, where all nouns are gendered masculine, feminine or neuter, the reasons why something is grammatically gendered one way or the other do not always conform to modern thinking about sex and gender. That cities, countries and many natural phenomena (like tornadoes) are gendered feminine rather than neutral is not rational according to such measures, but it is explicable, because in a pre-modern world view – where everything in the cosmos was conceived of as having gender qualities – being hospitable, reproductive and accommodating were feminine qualities that women and cities and the soil embodied; moreover, hosting uncontrollable natural forces was something women had in common with natural phenomena. There is often a cultural–historical explanation behind grammatical gender, but the fact that there is not always such an explanation does not mean that it is illegitimate to question the gender designation.

In fact, I find such questioning a passageway into ancient webs of gender discourse that are otherwise invisible to the modern feminist gaze, which tends to look for men and women and nothing else. Whereas I strongly agree with Schüssler Fiorenza that masculine grammatical forms can include women, for me this does not make Revelation a potentially women-inclusive writing. Rather, it only demonstrates the problem of phallogocentric discourse: it *can* include women, but no one knows exactly when it does because women are not worthy of representation separately from the male. On other occasions, Revelation expresses gender so explicitly that

50 Schüssler Fiorenza, *Vision of a Just World*, pp. 14, 130–31.

51 Schüssler Fiorenza, *Vision of a Just World*, pp. 13–14, 88.

52 Extensive arguments against this approach have been presented by Pippin and Stenström, so I will only pursue my philological issue here.

I end up concluding with Pippin that Revelation resists a generic reading of its anthropology altogether.

Another alternative interpretive strategy would be to read 14.1–5 outside of a heterosexist framework and take seriously that παρθένος elsewhere more often than not denotes the female. In that case, these παρθένοι are women who have not defiled themselves by having sex with other women. If so, it is sexual contact between women, not women *per se*, that is seen as impurity. But such a reading of the 144,000 παρθένοι would presuppose a gynocentric imaginary and a rather unrestrained way of talking about women who are erotically attracted to other women, but still able to control themselves. This would be highly unusual in an ancient literary context[53] and would, in my view, not fit with the masculine grammatical forms and the andro-centric approach found elsewhere in the book.

Miss Jerusalem

One could argue that Jerusalem, the Bride, must be female (e.g., Rev. 19.7; 21.9). But she is also a city.[54] The question is thus whether she is a 'heavenly character' in line with God, the Lamb, and the 144,000. If so, what does she contribute to the gendering of the 'elsewhere' that I am exploring here?

Like Athena, born from the forehead of her omnipotent Father Zeus after he had swallowed her mother, so Miss Jerusalem is similarly born from her Father, the Omnipotent (21.22), after he has ridden himself of 'the Great Whore', Babylon. In the ancient world, cities were often gendered female through grammar and/or the connection with a city goddess.[55] As in much androcentric discourse concerning women, the femininity of cities could be perceived as either promiscuous or virginal, although in a Greco-Roman context the femininity of cities seems mostly to be a way of expressing their maternal role as home and nurturer. In Revelation, Babylon is the whore and the New Jerusalem is the pure bride (21.2, 9). Thus, holiness is associated with virginity and wholeness, and it is dissociated from fragmentation and broken-ness. The formerly holy earthly Jerusalem has to disappear, for she has fulfilled her duty and is defiled through evil invasion/penetration.[56]

---

53 Bernadette Brooten has combed ancient texts for references to female homoeroticism in her *Love Between Women: Early Christian Responses to Female Homoeroticism* (Chicago, IL: University of Chicago Press, 1996), esp. pp. 62–64. The references are hard to find, veiled in obscure language, and adopt an extremely hostile stance towards the phenomenon.

54 The text leads the reader to identify the Bride with the holy city, the New Jerusalem (21.2). The New Jerusalem is obviously contrasted with (the Old) Jerusalem; whether the Zion of 14.1 is identical to the New Jerusalem (with the exception that she is not yet descended to the new earth) is less clear. However, because of their similar characterization as the place for the redeemed, I choose to treat them as identical. Augustine suggested that the Bride in Revelation 21 is rather to be identified with the woman of ch. 12 (followed by Luther and more recently Lohmeyer, the idea seems to be that all biblical women look the same and they all prefigure the church). See counterarguments in Collins, *Combat Myth*, p. 132 and Mikael Koch, *Drachenkampf und Sonnenfrau: Zur Funktion des Mythischen in der Johannesapokalypse am Beispiel von Apk 12* (WUNT, 184; Tübingen: Mohr Siebeck, 2004), p. 222.

55 This motif is also mentioned in Collins, 'Feminine Symbolism', pp. 26–27.

56 Moving from imagery to possible text-external realities, the Roman invasion of the city could be seen as a kind of rape.

Is Miss Jerusalem a character inhabiting the 'elsewhere' like the others? Or is her presence of a different kind? If we look at Revelation 14, we notice that she is not missing entirely, being partly implicated in, partly distinguished from the 'Mount Zion' on which the 144,000 stand. She is a brilliant example of Luce Irigaray's 'woman who has not yet taken (a) place', which is the *chora*:[57]

> Woman is still the place, the whole of the place in which she cannot take possession of herself as such. She is experienced as all-powerful precisely insofar as her indifferentiation makes her radically powerless. She is never here and now because it is she who sets up that eternal elsewhere from which the 'subject' continues to draw his reserves.[58]

The preliminary answer must therefore be that she seems to be place, home and accommodation rather than an inhabitant herself with the possibility to act, move and make (right) choices, as the other heavenly characters. The virgin Bride is possessed by God and the Lamb and becomes inhabited by them; they do not even need their own temple to dwell in because they are constantly in her, and her space is accommodating them well enough. Also, they whose names have been recorded in the Lamb's Book of Life are allowed to enter her (22.27). The New Jerusalem may be female, but she does not inhabit herself.

This instability in the characterization of Jerusalem as both city and human virgin bride is more comprehensible. In her article 'Bodies-Cities', feminist theorist Elizabeth Grosz explores the constitutive and mutually defining relations between corporeality and the metropolis. She points out that 'the body is psychically, socially, sexually, and discursively or representationally produced, and . . . in turn, bodies reinscribe and project themselves onto their sociocultural environment so that this environment both produces and reflects the form and interests of the body'.[59] Humans do not *make* cities (contrary to humanist and Marxist views) any more than cities 'produce the bodies of their inhabitants as particular and distinctive types of bodies'.[60] There is thus a fluidity between the concepts of the city and the human body. In Revelation, Miss Jerusalem is a city described in a language that explores the multivalent, metaphorical potential of a human female body. However, after 21 chapters, all of which contain attempts to excise the dangerous and unreliably vulnerable females, in 22.17 the only female left, the city Jerusalem, starts to speak!

---

57 Explained briefly, the philosophical use of the term goes back to Plato's *Timaeus* (50D–52D), which understands Space/Place (χώρα) as present at the birth of the cosmos alongside Being and Becoming, representing a triad or the three Kinds. *Chora* (χώρα) is the space that all bodies occupy and is the substance of which they are made: it is the ever-existing, all-receptive place/space, the amorphous and formless imprint-bearer that nevertheless prevents the imitations from being identical to their origin. Concerning the revitalization of this ancient Greek term, see my 'Men are from Mars and Women are from Venus', in T. Beattie and U. King (eds), *Gender, Religion, and Diversity: Cross-Cultural Approaches* (New York: Continuum, 2004), pp. 152–61.

58 Irigaray, *Speculum of the Other Woman*, p. 227.

59 Elizabeth Grosz, 'Bodies-Cities', in B. Colomina (ed.), *Sexuality and Space* (Princeton Papers on Architecture; Princeton, NJ: Princeton Architectural Press, 1992), pp. 241–53 (242).

60 Grosz, 'Bodies-Cities', p. 250.

Her vital function as χώρα means she cannot be allowed to be extinct like the others. With the Spirit, she says ἔρχου ('come').[61]

In Revelation, as in many other ancient writings, speech belongs to males alone. Women give birth, suffer, are acted upon, but they do not speak. It is as if the Bride's one word is a message to her readers that she has survived the treatment given to her in the previous chapters. But if males own the discourse, does this speech (re)constitute the Bride as a man too? Does the one word spoken by the Bride actually construct her as a speaking character in the book as a whole, thus undermining the representation of her as the χώρα in the Zion/Jerusalem passages?

Irigaray reflects on the fact that 'women' (which cannot be identified), in order to speak intelligently, have to speak as *sexué* males or as *asexué*.[62] As part of male discourse, the Bride's ἔρχου would indeed be *parler-homme*, one of the few lines that the discourse 'needs' its female character to utter in order for it to appear to itself as non-rapist. Within such structures of meaning, this single word expresses the Bride's acceptance of the role male discourse grants her – as submissive, sexually available, ready for the nuptial chamber of the Lamb and his 144,000 brothers. A woman's *parler-homme* still does not make her male in the same way as them.

But this word ἔρχου (a present imperative, second-person singular verb), in itself a complete finite sentence, the shortest possible one, is not able to mimic any other hierarchy than that between the commanding, speaking subject and the 'thou', the second-person singular pronoun that is supposed to follow the imperative. Spoken in Greek, its grammatical gender is open, and the fact that it is spoken together with the gender-neutral Spirit does not clarify it any further. In the text, the neutral Spirit and the female Bride command, and the male hearer (ὁ ἀκούων) is commanded to repeat after them. But who is to come? Might it not be the Lamb, but an Other?

At this point the text takes a strange step. One would expect that 'come' is what the bride says to Jesus *alias* the Lamb, who identifies himself in the previous verse. But in the context of 22.17, the imperative is repeated a third time, only this time in the third person, and the one commanded to follow the Bride's imperative is specified as 'the one thirsting' (ὁ διψῶν), still in grammatically masculine terms. This theme of thirst, fluid and saturation opens up other ranges of meaning that cannot be fully explored here.[63] Important for the moment, however, is that ὁ διψῶν is much more ambiguous than the 'come Lord Jesus' of v. 20, an ambiguity that allows for the coming of many, not only of the Lord Jesus.

To display how the 'eschatology' of Irigaray and that of John the Seer could

---

61 This reading presupposes that the end is an inherent part of the text of Revelation, not just a postscript more or less detached from the rest of the text, so that 'the bride' in 22.17 refers to the same bride as in 21.2, 9, 'Miss Jerusalem'. If this is *not* the case, and the book's ending is either a later addition or an unrelated postscript by the same author, then John's heaven is an all-male place sustaining itself on a female, unspeaking χώρα.

62 Irigaray, *Ce Sexe*, pp. 133; 145–46; see discussion of these terms above. For woman as not being an identifiable entity, see Irigaray, *Speculum de l'autre femme*, p. 285.

63 Amy-Jill Levine has pointed out in personal communication that this theme further reinforces connections to the Fourth Gospel. This very good point could only be explored in responsible detail in a more intertextual reading than the one presented here.

be seen as touching each other at this point, I will use Irigaray's notion of *parler-femme*, literally, 'speaking woman'. The expression is, as often with Irigaray, highly ambiguous and carries a range of meanings. Its English translation, 'speaking (as) woman', is somewhat narrower, even if the 'as' is put in brackets. However, if woman has not yet taken place, how can one already speak as woman? Are speaking and writing[64] *causes* or *effects* of a different 'sexe'? In the case of the ideology of sexual difference of the 'here and now' (labeled phallogocentrism, phallocratism, etc.), Irigaray sees writing that does not question its relation to this ideology as both producer and product (thus both *cause* and *effect*) in the current economy of meaning.[65] Similarly, concerning a different 'sexe' she would not limit herself to only one of these options: the creative Word can bring a different 'sexe' into being, but it can also be the effect of such a creation.

Thus, in Irigaray's notion of *parler-femme* there is a tension between 'already' and 'not yet'. Both Irigaray and John the Seer speak of the elsewhere *to come*, and both put this speech into the words and discourses available here and now. John the Seer claims already to speak from 'elsewhere' back into this world, but his words and discourse sound depressingly familiar – depressingly 'here'. Irigaray on the other hand states explicitly that speaking from the other side is not yet possible, and I am tempted to suggest that she diagnoses the problems with John's reversed 'elsewhere' precisely: 'We do not escape so easily from reversal . . . There is no simple manageable way to leap to the outside of phallogocentrism, nor any possible way to situate oneself there, that would result from the simple fact of being a woman.'[66] However, exactly for this reason she sees it as important to traverse the male imaginary and the dominant phallogocentric discourse in order 'to provide a place for the "other" as feminine'.[67]

In order to start *parler-femme*, then, it is necessary to go back into the nuptial chamber and 'destroy, but . . . with nuptial tools. The tool is not a feminine attribute. But woman may re-utilize its marks on her, in her'.[68] If we now look at Miss Jerusalem again, in many ways she reminds us of Irigaray's *femme* (wife or woman) of the philosopher.[69] By the end of Revelation she is the bride in the nuptial chamber: what remained for her in order to arrive at speech was to do the wedding (night)[70] with the great multitude, gods and men, and fulfill the role of matter, χώρα, and city for them. And, as does Irigaray, we can assume that this enterprise was not an easy one. When she arrives at speech, she mimics the line given her by the male

---

64 In her discussion of writing, Irigaray gives speech primacy over writing (in contrast to Derrida). A different writing may be an 'effect' of *parler-femme*.

65 Irigaray, *Ce Sexe*, p. 129.

66 Irigaray, *This Sex,* p. 162.

67 Irigaray, *Ce Sexe*, p. 133.

68 Irigaray, *Ce Sexe*, p. 150.

69 Irigaray, *Ce Sexe*, pp. 147–48. By this term she hints at how philosophers describe their wives or women in general in gross stereotypes and without a self. To a certain extent the wives become mediators or foils for the philosophers' celebrations of their selves, but Irigaray hints that the wife who has insider knowledge about the philosophers can use this knowledge to come into being as her own self.

70 The nuptial connotations of *faire la noce avec les philosophes* is lost in the English translation; cf. Irigaray, *Ce Sexe*, p. 147.

discourse in the nuptial chamber. This is fine, however, for still, according to Irigaray, *mimicry* is the one path to which the female condition is assigned. However, she continues: 'But this [i.e., mimetic] role itself is complex, for it supposedly lends itself to everything, if not to everyone. That one can copy anything at all, anyone at all, can receive all impressions, *without appropriating them to oneself* . . . If she can play that role so well, if it does not kill her, quite, it is because she keeps something in reserve . . . she still subsists, otherwise and *elsewhere* than there where she mimes so well what is asked of her.'[71]

Through *mimétisme* the bride can simultaneously deal with male discourse in order to uncover its mechanisms, and at the same time re-utilize the marks these mechanisms leave on her to create space for the other woman to come. *Parler-femme* thus remains a possibility through its specific relation to the *otherwise* and *elsewhere*, in a different discourse without any closure of *arché* and *télos*, beginning and end[72] – or, to put it in Revelation's words, ἄλφα and ὦ (22.13; transliterated: *alpha* and *omega*). Whereas Revelation's author seeks to define the *télos*[73] of time, of men, and of God's transactions with himself through the media of the Lamb and the Bride, the Bride herself has no *télos* within this book, in the sense of a closure and end. Her gates are never closed (21.25) and, as she is just a place, she can have no end in herself. But her openness and infinity somehow make her more eternal than the men who come (and go), and for whom she functions as a receptacle. Hence, seen from a modern perspective, she is not confined to the book of Revelation, she is not confined inside the alpha and omega of the hard cover of the Bible either; indeed, she has not yet taken place.

As Pippin points out in her reading of Heaven from the perspective of the Bottom-less Pit: 'the tree and waters of life in the New Jerusalem are repetitions of their Eden versions in Genesis.'[74] Similarly, the Bride's *parler-femme*, speaking 'come', can only be likened to the first page of the Bible where God, who is helplessly confined within its hard cover and within the logics of its discourse, proclaims, 'Let there be light!' (Gen. 1.3). I am impressed with the astonishing effects of his creative proclamation – still it sounds like the cry of a claustrophobic who has just entered a narrow, dark room. The bidding of the Bride – 'come' – may be wholly in accordance with the discourse of the narrow, dark nuptial chamber it is spoken within, and yet it is wholly other too, as the creative word bringing the phantasmic becoming-woman into life, here, there or 'elsewhere'.

Conclusion

I have tried to use feminist theory in combination with philology to investigate how male and female virgins in the book of Revelation contribute to its construction of

---

71 Modified English quote from Irigaray, *This Sex*, pp. 151–52.

72 Irigaray, *Ce Sexe*, p. 149.

73 τέλος not only denotes end as such, but the purposeful, ultimate aim/fulfillment. See LSJ, s.v. 'τέλος'.

74 Tina Pippin, 'Peering into the Abyss: A Postmodern Reading of the Biblical Bottomless Pit', in E. S. Malbon and E. V. McKnight (eds), *The New Literary Criticism and the New Testament* (JSNTSup, 109; Sheffield: Sheffield Academic Press, 1994), pp. 251–67 (259).

the 'elsewhere', but my broader concern has been to investigate how difference (sexual, linguistic or other) can speak through a dominant language (which, one could argue, in a most universalizing way, is always non-identical to itself anyway). I have argued for two main ways in which this is accomplished – through mimicry and through taking on an 'alien' posture – but because my overall goal is awareness I am hesitant to conclude that one is better than or can manage without the other.[75]

As should be clear by now, in my view Revelation's 'elsewhere' is a gendered place in that a group of males lives on and off the female ground. Revelation has been much explored in terms of intertextuality in recent years with conflicting notions both of intertextuality and of which texts could be linked to Revelation in an inter-textually sensible way.[76] One of the intertextual echoes that I hear in Revelation's 'elsewhere' is the resonance from Hesiod's account of the paradisiacal existence of ἄνθρωποι ('human beings', definitively used in a male sense since they are contrasted with women) before the arrival of the γένος ('species') of women. Absence of women does not mean that there was no feminine entity surrounding them and accommodating them, for, until the arrival of the devastating Pandora, they lived happily on and off γαῖα ('the earth') and what *she* constantly had to offer them. None of this makes the masculinity of Revelation's 144,000 any more stable. Knowing that femininity is usually lurking somewhere just under the surface of the term παρθένος, the use of this term of men is a bit queer. I wrote about Jerusalem as being possessed (by God and the Lamb), but these 144,000 are not their own either. They were purchased and sealed, just like slaves. They are described as first fruits and as blameless, like appropriate but powerless victims bought for animal sacrifice in the heavenly Temple. In this way then, their masculinity does not imply any kind of control over the discourse.

Further, the Bride, Miss Jerusalem, goes into the nuptial chamber. Whether she speaks this word only because it is expected of her within male discourse or whether she mimics and simultaneously speaks as the woman of a different 'sexe', we cannot know. But the attentive listener to the sound coming from the other side may hear . . . the Bride, Jerusalem, the 'phantasmic "becoming-woman"' not (yet) leaping outside of the Seer's discourse, but situating herself at its borders, on the Bible's very last page, and moving continuously from the inside to the outside,[77] through the canonical Bible cover and beyond, where she can come and become.

---

75 Biblical scholars are in a good position to reflect upon such issues, as they study texts in different languages; they do not speak only one language – many use English in heteroglossic ways that mimic other languages. Such practices have their problems (of fragmented and inconsistent textual surfaces and misunderstandings), but they also create possibilities.

76 See, e.g., David Aune, 'Intertextuality and the Genre of the Apocalypse', *SBLSP* 30 (1991), pp. 142–60; Alison M. Jack, *Texts Reading Texts, Sacred and Secular: Two Postmodern Perspectives* (JSNTSup, 179; Sheffield: Sheffield Academic Press, 1999); and Steve Moyise, *The Old Testament in the Book of Revelation* (JSNTSup, 115; Sheffield: Sheffield Academic Press, 1995).

77 Paraphrasing Irigaray, *This Sex*, pp. 122, 141.

RE-MEMBERING THE WHORE: THE FATE OF BABYLON ACCORDING TO REVELATION 17.16*

CAROLINE VANDER STICHELE

The woman/whore called Babylon in Revelation 17–19 has often been interpreted as representing the Evil Empire.[1] Such interpretations are founded on the perception that this woman represents something other than a human being. To be certain, the text seems to point in that direction, when it states in 17.18: 'The woman you saw is the great city that rules over the kings of the earth.'[2]

This revelation of the meaning of this female character stands at the end of a long episode in which one of the seven angels featured in the previous scene first introduces (17.1–3a), then describes (17.3b–6), and finally explains (17.7–18) the vision of the whore.[3] The woman's identity as city is more specifically disclosed after her impending annihilation has been announced and justified as part of God's purpose: 'And the ten horns that you saw, they and the beast will hate the whore; they will make her desolate and naked; they will devour her flesh and burn her up with fire. For God has put it into their hearts to carry out his purpose by agreeing to give their kingdom to the beast, until the words of God will be fulfilled' (vv. 16–17).

Commentary on these verses often displays a disturbing tendency to explain away or justify their more troubling aspects.[4] For example, some interpreters stress that the

---

* An earlier version of this article has been presented in the 'Feminist Hermeneutics of the Bible Section' at the Annual SBL Meeting in Boston (1999) and appeared in *lectio difficilior. European Electronic Journal for Feminist Exegesis* 2000/1 under the title 'Just a Whore: The Annihilation of Babylon According to Revelation 17:16' (www.lectio.unibe.ch00_1/j.htm). I would like to express my gratitude to Todd Penner for his stimulating feedback and comments on a previous version of this piece.

1 So for instance James L. Resseguie, *Revelation Unsealed: A Narrative Critical Approach to John's Apocalypse* (*BibInt*, 32; Leiden: Brill, 1998), p. 137: 'The characterization of evil as a whore portrays the beguiling, stupefying side to evil's Janus-face – one side is ugly and repugnant, while the other side is attractive and desirous.' And Gregory K. Beale, *The Book of Revelation* (NIGTC; Grand Rapids, MI/Cambridge, UK: Eerdmans; Carlisle: Paternoster, 1999), p. 888: 'She includes the entire evil economic-religious system of the world throughout history. She receives power from the devil himself.'

2 Unless stated otherwise, citations from the Bible come from the NRSV.

3 The angel is introduced in Rev. 17.1 as 'one of the seven angels who had the seven bowls'. This refers back to the scene related in Revelation 16. The angel serves more concretely as *angelus interpres*. As David E. Aune observes, this is the only time in Revelation that John actually receives an explanation of what he sees. 'This may reveal the importance of Revelation 17 in the estimation of the author-editor, who emphasizes the revelatory role of the *angelus interpres* at the beginning and end of the book (1.1; 22.6, 8–9), although this angel in fact appears only in Revelation 17.1–18; 19.9–10 and (if it is the same angel) in 21.9–22.9' (*Revelation 17–22* [WBC, 52C; Nashville, TN: Thomas Nelson Publishers, 1998], p. 919).

4 A similar observation is also made by Stephen D. Moore, who notes that 'the phrase "they will devour her flesh" trips a tad too lightly off the tongues of most commentators on Revelation' (Stephen D. Moore, *God's Beauty Parlor and Other Queer Spaces in and around the Bible* [Stanford, CA: Stanford University Press, 2001], p. 196).

sentence concerns Babylon as a city.[5] To support this point, they refer to texts from the Hebrew Bible that pass the same judgment on other cities, be they Jerusalem, Tyre or Nineveh. A similar observation concerns the executors of this sentence, namely, the ten horns and the beast. Their actions against the whore are often understood to show the self-destroying power of evil.[6] As I will demonstrate, however, these interpretations are problematic insofar as they tend to obscure other implications also present in these verses.

In Revelation's dualistic world view, Babylon appears on the wrong side as one of the enemies ultimately facing annihilation. In accord with what can be seen as the timeless rhetoric of war, 'the enemy' is literally stripped of her humanity and presented as an incarnation of evil. Studying the text's rhetorical strategy unveils how this effect is reached. In what follows, I focus on Rev. 17.16, which describes how Babylon is demolished. In my view this disturbing scene resists a facile reduction of the woman/whore to 'just a metaphor'.[7] What makes her deserve such a gruesome fate? How is this murder motivated, legitimated, and thus covered up in the text? Rather than averting the eyes, one has to face the horror of it all.

From Whore to City

With its escalating violence, the scene unfolding could be a shot from an action movie, such as *End of Days* or *Terminator*. Together, the beast and its horns will undertake four actions against the whore: they 'will hate the whore'; 'they will make her desolate and naked'; 'they will devour her flesh'; and they will 'burn her up with fire'. The predictions of hating the whore, making her naked, and devouring her flesh either explicitly state or presume a person as object. The two other statements, making her desolate and burning her up with fire, are more ambiguous. They also recur with respect to the city in ch. 18, which mentions both her desolation (18.17, 19) and her being burned (18.8, 9, 18; 19.3).[8] As I will show, 17.16 still belongs to the

---

5 So, e.g., Ulrich B. Müller, who speaks about 'die Zerstörung Roms, der Hure Babylon. Dies schildert der Verfasser in Vers 16–18 und weist damit auf Kap. 18 voraus' (*Die Offenbarung des Johannes* [ÖTKNT, 19; Gütersloh/Würzburg: G. Mohn/Echter Verlag, 1984], p. 296). Anne J. Visser understands 'make naked' to refer to thorough plundering and 'devouring her flesh' to the total extermination of all the inhabitants of Rome (*De openbaring van Johannes* [De prediking van het Nieuwe Testament; Nijkerk: Callenbach, 1972], p. 199). Aune (*Revelation 17–22*, p. 957) states that 'since the whore is a city, the phrase ἠρημωμένην ποιήσουσιν αὐτήν, "they will make her desolate," i.e. depopulate her, is appropriate'.

6 So for instance George B. Caird, *The Revelation of St. John the Divine* (Black's New Testament Commentary, 19; London: A. & C. Black, 1966), p. 221; Charles H. Giblin, *The Book of Revelation: The Open Book of Prophecy* (GNS, 34; Collegeville, MN: Liturgical Press, 1991), p. 166; Robert W. Wall, *Revelation* (NIBCNT, 18; Peabody, MA: Hendrickson), p. 209; Resseguie, *Revelation Unsealed*, p. 140; Beale, *Book of Revelation*, p. 887.

7 Such a metaphorization of the whore's punishment is, for instance, undertaken by Beale, when he writes: 'Perhaps three metaphors have been combined in the description: Babylon's nakedness is exposed like that of a whore, she is devoured like a victim of a fierce beast, and she is burned like a city' (*Book of Revelation*, p. 883).

8 Burning could also apply to a person. According to Lev. 21.9, the daughter of a priest who has prostituted herself is to be burned to death. For Lambertus J. Lietaert Peerbolte, the similarities between this text and Rev. 17.16 'should probably lead to the conclusion that the author of

first part of the section about Babylon, in which the image of the woman/whore dominates (17.1–18). In the second part (Revelation 18), the image of Babylon as city takes center stage.[9]

The identification of the woman with the great city (ἡ γυνὴ ἔστιν ἡ πόλις ἡ μεγάλη) is made explicit only in 17.18, which thus forms the turning point between chs 17 and 18. This shift is confirmed by lexical data. To describe the whore, the context preceding 17.16 has already used the term 'woman' (γυνή) five times and the term 'whore' (πόρνη) four (vv. 1, 5, 15, 16).[10] In the following context, by contrast, the term 'woman' is absent and 'whore' appears only once, at the end of this section (19.2), where she is mentioned for the last time as 'the great whore' (ἡ πόρνη ἡ μεγάλη). This expression corresponds with the one in 17.1, the opening verse, thus forming an inclusio framing the whole section.

While Babylon is named 'woman' only in the context preceding 17.18, the reverse holds true for Babylon as city. The term 'city' (πόλις) is used for the first time in 17.18 and occurs further only in the following context (18.10, 16, 18, 19, 21). In Revelation's narrative logic, therefore, the reader is first confronted with a female character, called Babylon in 17.5, which is only identified in v. 18 with 'the great city'.[11] Rev. 17.18 thus also forms a turning point in the representation of Babylon, because precisely here the identification of the 'woman' with the 'great city' is explicitly made. Verse 16, by consequence, still belongs to the section that pre-dominantly describes Babylon as a woman. Moreover, 'the whore' is explicitly named as object and several elements in the sentence presume a human being as the main character referent. In sum, taking into consideration both the context and the content of Rev. 17.16, it does not seem justified either to limit the meaning of this verse to Babylon as city or to state that the judgment of the great whore, announced in 17.2, refers to ch. 18 rather than 17.[12]

Revelation depicts the fate of the Harlot as her well-deserved punishment prescribed by the Mosaic Law' (*The Antecedents of Antichrist. A Tradition-Historical Study of the Earliest Christian Views on Eschatological Opponents* [JSJSup, 49; Leiden: Brill, 1996], p. 163). In my view, however, the correspondence between these two texts is too limited to be convincing. As I will demonstrate below, other texts from the Hebrew Bible play a far greater role.

9 See also A. Yarbro Collins, 'Revelation 18: Taunt-Song or Dirge?', in Jan Lambrecht (ed.), *L'Apocalypse johannique et l'Apocalyptique dans le Nouveau Testament* (BETL, 53; Leuven/Gembloux: University Press/Duculot, 1980), pp. 185–204 (198).

10 In Rev. 17.5 Babylon is in fact identified as ἡ μήτηρ τῶν πορνῶν. According to Aune (*Revelation 17–22*, p. 937), this could be understood in an archetypical sense, meaning that she is the source of the whoredom of others, or in a superlative sense, meaning 'the most depraved whore'. However, her being called 'mother' can also be related to the preceding Babylon 'the great' (ἡ μεγάλη). In that case, the whore appears not just as mother, but as a representation of the Great Mother. A psychological (Jungian) interpretation of this image is offered by A. Yarbro Collins. According to her 'the great prostitute of ch. 17 is the Terrible Mother. Her character as a prostitute symbolizes the seductive and charming power of the Great Mother's lure toward self-dissolution in the unconscious sea of participation, of non-individuation.' 'Feminine Symbolism in the Book of Revelation', *BibInt* 1 (1993), pp. 20–33 (30); 'Feminine Symbolism in the Book of Revelation', reprinted in this volume, pp. 121–30.

11 As Aune (*Revelation 17–22*, p. 959) points out, the order of the elements mentioned by the angel in v. 7 is reversed in what follows. First, the beast, the seven heads and ten horns are explained and only at the very end, in v. 18, does the woman appear.

12 According to Aune, 'the judgment of the great whore refers not primarily to Rev 17 (though her judgment is briefly mentioned in 17:16) but to Rev 18' (*Revelation 17–22*, p. 916).

The name Babylon further identifies the whore with the city, an identification already cultivated in the preceding context. In 14.8 an angel announces: 'Fallen, fallen is Babylon the great! She has made all nations drink of the wine of the wrath of her fornication.' The expression 'Babylon the great' (Βαβυλὼν ἡ μεγάλη) occurs again in ch. 16, where God is said to remember 'great Babylon' and give her the wine-cup of the fury of his wrath (v. 19). 'Babylon the great' also appears on the forehead of the whore riding the beast: 'Babylon the great, mother of whores and of earth's abominations' (17.5); it appears as well in the following chapter regarding the destruction of the city (18.2, 10, 21). And yet, this name is a 'chiffre', a mystery, because both 'the great whore' and 'Babylon the great' in fact refer to a third party, hinted at but never explicitly named.[13] The majority of commentators point to Rome as the most likely candidate for this title.[14] If this is the case, then the term πόλις (city) used in 17.18ff. is to be taken in its literal sense, while the terms γυνή (woman) / πορνή (whore) and Βαβυλών (Babylon) refer to Rome metaphorically. The image thus evoked by the metaphors is one of seduction and sexual perversion in the first case and of domination by a colonial power in the second. The great whore/mighty city is clearly depicted as evil, but her end is already in sight.

From City to Whore

At one level, the metaphorical use of the term 'whore' comes as no surprise, as earlier prophetic books also address and condemn cities as whores.[15] Brenner uses the term 'pornoprophetics' to denote this particular type of literature.[16] Ezekiel 16 and 23, which picture Jerusalem as a whore undergoing a similar fate, offer the closest parallel to the demise of the whore in Rev. 17.16.[17] In both Revelation and Ezekiel, the punishment is presented as reflecting God's will, although, in both as well, others will execute the sentence. In Ezekiel this is done by the woman's lovers; in Revelation by the beast and its horns. Less elaborate parallels can also be found in Nah. 3.1–7, where Nineveh is first addressed as a city and then compared with a prostitute, and in

---

13 I consider it more likely that μυστήριον (mystery) is part of the introduction to the title rather than part of the title itself. This interpretation is also supported by v. 7, where the angel announces that he will explain 'the mystery of the woman' (τὸ μυστήριον τῆς γυναικός). In both cases, however, 'it describes a hidden meaning of Babylon the Great that needs further revelatory interpretation' (Beale, *Book of Revelation*, p. 859).

14 According to Beale, however, not just Rome is meant, but 'the apostate church and unbelieving Israel are included inasmuch as they have become part of that sinful world system' (Beale, *Book of Revelation*, p. 886). Other authors suggest that not Rome, but Jerusalem is intended. So, e.g., J. Massyngberde Ford, *Revelation* (AB, 38; Garden City, NY: Doubleday, 1975), p. 285.

15 As Gail Corrington Streete observes: 'The prophets of the exile . . . are particularly jealous for the honor of JHWH, which becomes symbolic of their own, a point illustrated by the fact that by far the largest number of occurrences of the terminology of adultery (thirty-four) are found in the writings of the exilic prophet Ezekiel, who is also the prophet with the most graphic and violent imagery of sexual punishment' (*The Strange Woman: Power and Sex in the Bible* [Louisville, KY: Westminster/John Knox Press, 1997], pp. 79–80).

16 Athalya Brenner, *The Intercourse of Knowledge: On Gendering Desire and 'Sexuality' in the Hebrew Bible* (BibInt, 26; Leiden: Brill, 1997), pp. 153–74.

17 In other prophetic texts Israel and Judah are presented as whores (e.g., Hosea 2; Jer. 2.20–3.20). The accusation of prostitution also occurs in Jer. 13.20–27 with respect to Judah/Jerusalem.

Isa. 23.15–17, which compares Tyre's fate to that of a whore, but no judgment or sentence follows the comparison.[18] A disturbing correspondence between these prophetic traditions and Revelation exists as far as their rhetorical strategy is concerned, because the depiction of the women makes their punishment look to be something they deserve.[19]

Most of the images Rev. 17.16 employs to describe the whore's fate are also present in the earlier texts. In Ezekiel 16, God through the prophet directly addresses Jerusalem as a woman (v. 3); the city is depicted as a whore in vv. 15–41, and her fate is announced in v. 35: 'Therefore, O whore, hear the word of the Lord.' The following verses elaborate: her clothes will be stripped and she will be left naked (v. 39); she will be stoned and cut to pieces (v. 40); her houses will be burned (v. 41). Both her being made naked and the burning of her houses correspond to elements in Rev. 17.16.

Later, Ezekiel introduces two more women who are first specified as Oholah and Oholibah and then identified with Samaria and Jerusalem (23.2–4). They too are criticized for playing the whore and are judged accordingly.[20] In Ezek. 23.9, Oholah has already been delivered to her lovers, who have made her naked and killed her with the sword (v. 10). In v. 22, Oholibah is addressed: 'Therefore, O Oholibah, thus says the Lord God . . . '. She will undergo a similar fate to that of her sister (vv. 22–35): her nose and ears will be cut off (v. 25); she will be hated and left naked (v. 29). Both Oholah and Oholibah will thus be made objects of terror and of plunder (v. 46), and the houses of their sons and daughters will burn up (v. 47). Again the parallels with Rev. 17.16 are striking, specifically the mention of hatred (v. 29), being made naked (vv. 10, 29), and the burning (v. 29).[21] A further correspondence is that the names of the women are symbolic, insofar as they do not disclose the identity of the referents. In Ezek. 23.4 Oholah and Oholibah are identified as Samaria and Jerusalem.[22] In Revelation Babylon is also a symbolic name, but the identity of the

---

18 See also Isa. 47.1–3, where Babylon and Chaldea are addressed as women facing divine vengeance.

19 Many commentators uncritically reproduce this view. So, for instance, Jean-Pierre Ruiz writes: 'In Rev 17,16 the devouring of the Prostitute's flesh is part of the punishment *justly* inflicted because of her crimes' (*Ezekiel in the Apocalypse: The Transformation of Prophetic Language in Revelation 16,17–19,10* [European University Studies Series, XXIII. Theology Vol. 376; Frankfurt am Main: Peter Lang, 1989], p. 366 [italics added]).

20 As Fokkelien van Dijk-Hemmes remarks, 'The intention is probably to strengthen the audience's resolve that both metaphorical women, so perverse since their very maidenhood, indeed deserve the utterly degrading and devastating treatment to which they are to be exposed' ('The Metaphorization of Woman in Prophetic Speech: An Analysis of Ezekiel 23', in Athalya Brenner and Fokkelien van Dijk-Hemmes, *On Gendering Texts: Female and Male Voices in the Hebrew Bible* [BibInt, 1; Leiden: Brill, 1993], pp. 167–76 [175]).

21 As Ruiz (*Ezekiel in the Apocalypse*, p. 365) argues, 'in all three texts (Ezekiel 16; 23; Revelation 17) the metaphors are so constructed that the language[s] of hating, stripping/devastating and burning serve on the sociopolitical stratum as they would in describing the fate of a woman punished for sexual misconduct'. However, in his view, Rev. 17.16 differs from the parallel texts in Ezekiel insofar as: (1) different cities are in view and (2) 'devouring her flesh' is absent in Ezekiel 16 and 23. As a third difference I would add that the notion of sexual infidelity/adultery present in Ezekiel 16 and 23 is absent in Revelation 17, where no partner is mentioned.

22 See also Van Dijk-Hemmes: 'Oholah, which is traditionally understood to mean "(she who has) her own tent (i.e. sanctuary)," metaphorizes the capital of Northern Israel Samaria while Oholibah, "My tent (is) in her," metaphorizes Jerusalem' ('Metaphorization of Woman', p. 172).

envisioned party is never disclosed. Moreover, Babylon is not a fictional name but an existing one used as a codeword for a different entity. The choice of Babylon seems largely motivated by its role in Israel's history as narrated in the Hebrew Bible and by the characteristics it shares with (presumably) Rome: being a foreign colonial empire; destroying Jerusalem and its temple; having an (envisioned) downfall.[23]

While Ezekiel focuses on God's own people, other prophetic books condemn non-Israelite cities as whores. In Nah. 3.1–7 Nineveh is first addressed as a city (v. 1) and later compared with a prostitute. Her fate is announced: 'I will let nations look on your nakedness and kingdoms on your shame' (3.5). She will be made a spectacle: 'Then all who see you will shrink from you and say, "Nineveh is devastated; who will bemoan her?"' (v. 7). Nahum offers the opposite order from that found in Ezekiel, for it first addresses Nineveh as a city and only then compares the city to a whore. The image of the city resurfaces in the following context, which describes her being devoured by fire (Nah. 3.13, 15). Elements found in both Ezekiel and Revelation also recur here: nakedness, devastation and burning. Isa. 23.15 compares Tyre's fate with that of a whore. The comparison is repeated in v. 17, which states that Tyre 'will prostitute herself with all the kingdoms of the world on the face of the earth', but no judgment or sentence follows the comparison.[24]

Both Nah. 3.1–7 and Isa. 23.15–17 thus share with Ezekiel and Rev. 17.16 the theme of cities being condemned as whores. Concerning Nineveh, the same elements are mentioned as part of her punishment: she will be made naked, devastated and burned. A major difference from Ezekiel, however, is that in Nahum and Isaiah the notion of adultery is absent. Nineveh and Tyre are foreign cities and consequently, no relationship between these cities and YHWH is presumed. This is also the case with Babylon in Revelation 17, where the issue of adultery is also absent. Babylon is presented as committing fornication with the kings of the earth, but no (betrayed) divine husband is in sight.

Alongside texts that condemn cities as whores, another cluster of texts also seems to have inspired the author of Revelation, namely, the prophecies from Isaiah and Jeremiah announcing the fall of Babylon. The angelic announcement in Rev. 14.8 recalls similar statements in Isa. 21.9 and Jer. 51.8, suggesting their fulfillment and thus re-inscribing the authority of the prophetic statements. The idea of Babylon making the nations drunk, introduced in the second part of Rev. 14.8, also appears in Jeremiah 51, but there Babylon herself is presented as a cup (v. 7: 'Babylon was a golden cup in the Lord's hand') and the element of fornication is absent. The features of the (golden) cup, as well as making the 'inhabitants of the earth' drunk, reappear in Rev. 17.1–5 in the description of the whore, but it is in Revelation 18 where the focus shifts to the destruction of Babylon as city that the prophecies against Babylon from Jer. 50–51 play their most prominent role.[25]

---

23 Collins, 'Revelation 18', p. 200.

24 As Jan Fekkes points out, this text may have played a role in the formulation of Revelation 17.2a and 18.3b, 9b ('the kings of the earth have committed fornication with her') (*Isaiah and Prophetic Traditions in the Book of Revelation: Visionary Antecedents and their Development* [JSNTSup, 93; Sheffield: Sheffield Academic Press, 1994], pp. 211–12).

25 Elements of correspondence can be found between the following verses: Rev. 18.2 and Jer. 51.37, 43; Rev. 18.3 and Jer. 51.7; Rev. 18.4 and Jer. 50.8; 51.6, 45; Rev 18.5 and Jer. 51.9; Rev. 18.6 and Jer. 50.15, 29; Rev. 18.8 and Jer. 50.31.34.

More important for our purpose is Isaiah 47, where Babylon is presented as a woman, but not a whore.[26] Isa. 47.7–9 depicts Babylon as ruler/queen, an image represented in Rev. 18.7–8. In both cases Babylon is introduced as a speaking subject who self-confidently denies being a widow, a fate said to await her in the near future.[27] Isaiah 47 may also have played a role in the formulation of Rev. 17.16, as in both cases part of the punishment of the woman called Babylon involves her being stripped naked (cf. Isa. 47.3), a motif that also occurs in Ezek. 16.39; 23.10, 29; and Nah. 3.5. Is this to be taken as a form of public exposure or as a prelude to sexual violence and so part and parcel of the physical violence to which the women are subjected?[28] Most commentaries on Isaiah 47 seem to follow the strategy already noticed with Revelation 17: 'The easiest solution taken to the problem of this metaphor by many commentaries and studies is to ignore the fact of the rape or to play it down to such an extent that it virtually disappears.'[29]

Of the elements Rev. 17.16 uses to describe the fate of Babylon, one remarkable distinction from the earlier texts emerges: the prophetic texts offer no direct parallel for the image of devoured flesh.[30] And yet, this gruesome fate is not without its parallels in the Hebrew Bible either. In Gen. 40.19 Joseph interprets the dream of the chief baker, who saw birds eating the food out of the uppermost basket on his head, as a prediction that 'within three days Pharaoh will lift up your head – from you! – and hang you on a pole, and the birds will eat the flesh from you'. A similar fate awaits the people of the land in Jer. 34.20 because they transgressed the covenant. Ezekiel prophesies against Gog: 'I will give you to birds of prey of every kind and to the wild animals to be devoured' (39.4). The closest parallel to Rev. 17.16 is found in 1 Kgs 21.23, where being devoured is first predicted by Elijah, and later recalled by Jehu (2 Kgs 9.36–37), as the fate awaiting Jezebel. The Septuagint shows a clear correspondence with Rev. 17.16 as it uses the same expression, 'to eat someone's

---

26 The idea of fornication (πορνεία) is however not completely absent, insofar as it is explicitly mentioned in the LXX of Isa. 47.10 (καὶ ἡ πορνεία σου ἔσται σοι αἰσχύνη).

27 Other elements of correspondence exist between Isa. 47.9, 12 and Rev. 18.23, where reference is made to Babylon's sorcery (the LXX even has the same wording: ἐν τῇ φαρμακείᾳ σου) and between Isa. 47.14 and Rev. 18.8, insofar as both texts refer to being burned by fire.

28 Since the modern concept of 'rape' cannot simply be transposed to biblical texts, I prefer to use the term 'sexual violence' here. See further Brenner, *Intercourse of Knowledge*, pp. 136–38.

29 Majella Franzmann, 'The City as Woman: The Case of Babylon in Isaiah 47', *Australian Biblical Review* 43 (1995), pp. 1–19 (17). Franzmann also points out that the dethronement of rulers in the Hebrew Scriptures seems to be gender-differentiated, as sexual abuse only takes place in the case of the women in question (cf. Jer. 13.22, 26–27). That sexual violence is also taking place in the case of Rev. 17.16 has been acknowledged more recently by several commentators. So, e.g., Tina Pippin, *Apocalyptic Bodies: The Biblical End of the World in Text and Image* (London and New York: Routledge, 1999), pp. 92–97; Moore, *God's Beauty Parlor*, p. 183; Harry O. Maier, *Apocalypse Recalled: The Book of Revelation after Christendom* (Minneapolis, MN: Fortress Press, 2002), p. 165.

30 According to Ruiz (*Ezekiel in the Apocalypse*, p. 366), this image 'looks ahead to the use of Ezek 39,17–20 in Rev 19,17–8.21'. There are indeed verbal correspondences between these texts in so far as the expression 'to eat someone's flesh' is used. Massyngberde Ford (*Revelation*, p. 283) rather sees a connection with Lev. 26.27–33, because this text 'suggests that one should look for cannibalism'. However, she overlooks the difference in subject, because in Leviticus 26 the one punished (the people of Israel) will eat the flesh (namely, of their sons and daughters), while in Revelation the one punished will be eaten (namely, by the beast and its horns).

flesh'.[31] Other features that these women share serve as further evidence that the author of Revelation may have Jezebel in mind here. Notable is Jehu's reference in 2 Kings 9 to Jezebel's many whoredoms and sorceries. A similar accusation can be found in Rev. 2.20, where the woman prophet called Jezebel is accused of practicing fornication (πορνεία), a key element in Babylon's depiction as well.[32]

The link between Jezebel and Babylon is even more striking when one compares the portrait of Babylon in Revelation 17 with that of the woman prophet 'Jezebel' in Revelation 2. Duff argues that part of the author's rhetorical strategy is to identify in the mind of his readers his female rival with the whore.[33] The underlying story about Jezebel evoked in Revelation 2 and further used in chs 17–18 merges both pictures and thus facilitates the identification of the woman called 'Jezebel' with the whore called Babylon. The terms 'whore' and 'woman' used for Babylon in Revelation 17 are then used not just as metaphors, but are also meant to establish a link with a real person mentioned earlier in the book.

If the prophet Jezebel's death is left to the reader's imagination, Babylon's end is not. While 'Jezebel' will be 'thrown onto a bed' (Rev. 2.22), the description of Babylon's fate is far more explicit and graphic. The whore will be devoured by the beast and the ten horns, a reversal of similar scenes from Ezekiel, where the beast itself, representing Pharaoh/Egypt, is eaten (Ezek. 29.3–5; 32.2–8; 39.17–20);[34] her fate is a gory foreplay to the great supper of Rev. 19.17 even as it has echoes of the Last Supper. But while the body of Christ takes on salvific meaning, the body of the whore does not.[35] Reading for gender, therefore, reveals, as Pippin puts it, the 'apocalypse of women'[36] turning, in the case of Revelation 17, into a

31 The prediction in 2 Kgs 9.36 that the dogs 'shall eat the flesh of Jezebel' (καταφάγονται τὰς σάρκας Ιεζαβελ) corresponds with the one in Rev. 17.16 (τὰς σάρκας αὐτῆς φάγονται). The wording is the same, except that the Septuagint uses the compositum rather than the simplex form of the verb that appears in Rev. 17.16 and 19.18. Verbal correspondence also occurs between Rev. 19.2, where God is said to have avenged on Babylon the blood of his servants: (ἐξεδίκησεν τὸ αἷμα τῶν δούλων αὐτοῦ ἐκ χειρὸς αὐτῆς); and 2 Kgs 9.7b LXX: ἐκδικήσεις τὰ αἵματα τῶν δούλων μου καὶ τὰ αἵματα πάντων τῶν δούλων κυρίου ἐκ χειρὸς Ιεζαβελ, 'so that I may avenge on Jezebel the blood of my servants the prophets, and the blood of all the servants of the Lord'.

32 Further parallels may also be found in the way Babylon sees herself ruling as a queen in Rev. 18.7 and in the accusation of having deceived all nations by her sorcery (Rev. 18.23). Beale (*Revelation*, p. 884) lists 11 more parallels between Jezebel and Babylon, but not all of them are equally persuasive or to the point.

33 Paul Duff, *Who Rides the Beast? Prophetic Rivalry and the Rhetoric of Crisis in the Churches of the Apocalypse* (New York: Oxford University Press, 2001), pp. 89–92. A reading along the same lines is also offered by Maier, who observes that, as a result, the readers addressed in Revelation 2 find themselves recast in the roles of the whore's allies in Revelation 17 (*Apocalypse Recalled*, p. 84).

34 See also J. Priest, 'A Note on the Messianic Banquet', in J. H. Charlesworth (ed.), *The Messiah: Developments in Earliest Judaism and Christianity* (Minneapolis, MN: Fortress Press, 1992), pp. 222–38 (235).

35 The expression 'to eat one's flesh' is also used in John 6, where Jesus tells his audience that the bread he will give is his flesh and they wonder: 'How can this man give us his flesh to eat?' (v. 52). For the use of 'anti-eucharistic' language, see further Duff, *Who Rides the Beast?*, pp. 102–05. Another indication in that direction can be that the term used in Rev. 14.10, 16.19 and 17.4 for cup (ποτήριον) is also used in the accounts about the last supper (1 Cor. 11.25–26; Mark 14.23 and par.).

36 Tina Pippin, *Death and Desire: The Rhetoric of Gender in the Apocalypse of John* (Literary Currents in Biblical Interpretation; Louisville, KY: Westminster/John Knox Press, 1992), p. 47.

'pornoapocalypse'.[37] The whore represents the city of Rome under the cipher of Babylon; yet she is also more than that: she is a woman both within the text of Revelation (as Jezebel) and without in terms of the correspondence with female identity in the larger sociocultural world of the text's readers and in the biblical landscape of female imagery upon which the text draws.

Just a Metaphor?

The most important objection raised against such a reading in terms of gender is that the whore is a metaphor and so should not be taken as representing a 'real' woman. Objecting to Pippin's reading for gender, both Schüssler Fiorenza and Barr state that she absolutizes gender and does not do justice to the ambiguity of the image, since the whore is not just a woman but also a city. For Barr, 'admitting this ambiguity changes the moral equation that comes from the Whore's destruction'.[38]

This raises the question: to what extent is gender essential to the metaphor? Is it accidental that a city is represented as a woman? Could Babylon just as well have been represented by a male character? If, as Pippin claims, 'the "symbolism" of the evil empire would break down at this point',[39] why would that be? The answer to that question is that an image cannot be isolated from the sociocultural context in which it functions. In a patriarchal society, to compare the enemy to a woman is a means of ridiculing and denigrating him on the one hand, and of ascertaining one's own male superiority on the other.[40] What Exum and Brenner state for the prophetic texts under discussion holds true in this case as well. Inscribed in these metaphors are androcentric views on women, sexuality, and power in gender relations.[41] To use a woman as metaphor for a city is more than just a matter of grammar, as Schüssler Fiorenza suggests.[42] In the case of Babylon, the woman/city represents the other, viewed as alien territory to be conquered and eventually destroyed; the rhetoric thus presumes and affirms an analogy between military and sexual invasion, the colonizer

37 Pippin, *Apocalyptic Bodies*, p. 92.
38 David L. Barr, 'Towards an Ethical Reading of the Apocalypse: Reflections on John's Use of Power, Violence, and Misogyny', *SBLSP*, 36 (1997), pp. 358–73 (365); E. Schüssler Fiorenza, *Sharing Her Word: Feminist Biblical Interpretation in Context* (Boston, MA: Beacon Press, 1998), pp. 93–94.
39 Pippin, *Apocalyptic Bodies*, p. 94.
40 As Keller notes, to call him a whore is 'to vilify especially the enemy male, to feminize and abject, mock and reduce him (to ashes). But to claim that because the text does not intend misogyny it is innocent of its metaphoric subtext is to sweep *women*'s ashes under the carpet'. Catherine Keller, *Apocalypse Now and Then: A Feminist Guide to the End of the World* (Boston, MA: Beacon Press, 1996), p. 77.
41 J. Cheryl Exum, *Plotted, Shot, and Painted: Cultural Representations of Biblical Women* (JSOTSup, 215; Gender, Culture, Theory, 3; Sheffield: Sheffield Academic Press, 1996), pp. 120–21; Brenner, *Intercourse of Knowledge,* pp. 164–72.
42 'It must not be overlooked, however, that such female imagery for cities utilizes conventional language because then, as today, cities and countries were grammatically construed as feminine' (Elisabeth Schüssler Fiorenza, *Revelation: Vision of a Just World* [Edinburgh: T&T Clark, 1993], pp. 95–96).

presented as male, the colonized as female.[43] Gender, then, is also more than just a matter of convention; it plays a role in the message to be delivered. In his analysis of violence and the construction of gender in the Hebrew Bible, Harold Washington points to the intended effect of presenting divine judgment in terms of sexual assault: 'The shock value of these biblical texts derives from the feminine positioning of men, not from horror at violence against women. Indeed, it is the cultural appropriateness of raping women that generates the scandal of the prophetic threat addressed to men. The prophetic metaphor therefore co-opts and suppresses women's experience of sexual violence.'[44]

However, Babylon is depicted not only as a woman; she is further depicted as a whore (πόρνη). In the Hebrew Bible, this image is clearly gender-specific.[45] Moreover, as Brenner notes, most occurrences of both the verb and related nominal forms appear in the so-called pornoprophetic passages.[46] Revelation 17–19 calls only the woman a whore, not her male partners. They are described in terms of their male power status as kings, while others, such as 'the nations' or 'the inhabitants of the earth', are said to participate in '*her* fornication' (14.8; 17.2,4; 18.3; 19.2: πορνείας αὐτῆς). Moreover, the use of πόρνη/πορνεία and πορνεύω[47] is not merely descriptive; it also implies a moral judgment. In line with its use elsewhere in the New Testament, prostitution appears here in the first place as morally evil,[48] which also contributes to the negative image of the woman, who is held responsible for it.

The fact that the Great Whore is a metaphor does not make it less dangerous and harmful to 'real' women, because as metaphor it both reflects and reinscribes gender relations. On the one hand, such a metaphor can only be potent if it is rooted in existing views and practices that shape the lives of real people; on the other hand, its power and danger also lie in the fact that it confirms such views and practices and thus legitimizes them, which again affects the lives of real people. I agree with Stenström who states:

> an image as 'Babylon the Prostitute' speaks, on one, explicit, level about an earthly power which is not obedient to God. Still, on an implicit level, it reflects, expresses and reinforces views of female prostitutes, which are linked to views of women in general. Therefore, a

43 Jean K. Kim, '"Uncovering her Wickedness": An Inter(con)textual Reading of Revelation 17 from a Postcolonial Feminist Perspective', *JSNT* 73 (1999), pp. 61–81 (73). See also Mieke Bal, 'Metaphors He Lives By', *Semeia* 61 (1993), pp. 185–207 (203); and Collins, 'Feminine Symbolism', p. 31. As Moore observes: 'In the final analysis, John presents Christ, together with his Christians, as icons of masculinity, reserving feminine imagery for the enemy' (*God's Beauty Parlor*, p. 190).

44 Harold C. Washington, 'Violence and the Construction of Gender in the Hebrew Bible: A New Historicist Approach', *BibInt* 5 (1997), pp. 324–63 (356).

45 Phyllis Bird, '"To Play the Harlot": An Inquiry into an Old Testament Metaphor', in Peggy L. Day (ed.), *Gender and Difference in Ancient Israel* (Minneapolis, MN: Augsburg Fortress Press, 1989), pp. 75–94 (79): 'Prostitution shares with fornication, as defined in Israel, a fundamental female profile, despite the fact that both activities require active male participation and may involve male initiation (cf. Gen. 38:15–16)'. See also Exum, *Plotted, Shot, and Painted*, pp. 112–13.

46 Brenner, *Intercourse of Knowledge*, p. 148.

47 πόρνη: 17.1, 5, 15, 16; πορνεία: 17.2, 4; 18.3; 19.2; πορνεύω: 17.2; 18.3, 9.

48 See, e.g., its occurrence in lists of vices: Mk 7.21–22; Gal. 5.19–21; Col. 3.5.

feminist analysis of Revelation must be concerned with all the implicit assumptions about gender in the text.[49]

The view that the Great Whore is just a metaphor or image and therefore 'does not speak about a female person or refer to actual historical wo/men'[50] tends to obscure this relation between metaphor and reality. As Exum rightly observes: 'That metaphoric violence against women is not the same as real violence is true, but . . . it is nonetheless harmful to real women because it shapes perceptions of reality and of gender relations for men and for women.'[51]

Schüssler Fiorenza criticizes such interpretations, stating that 'reading simply in terms of gender reinscribes cultural femininity by naturalizing Revelation's symbolic figurative language'.[52] In my view, however, this critique is not justified, because these and related interpretations are not reading *simply* in terms of gender and they are not merely *re-inscribing* cultural femininity. It goes too far 'to imply (or, indeed, argue) that if an interpreter describes how something works, she or he is advocating for the maintenance of the practice'.[53]

Schüssler Fiorenza's own view is that 'although Babylon is figured as an elite woman, the rhetorical–symbolic discourse of Revelation clearly understands it as an imperial city and not as an actual woman'.[54] But, as I have stated, Rev. 17.16 resists such a reduction of the woman/whore to just a metaphor. The killing of the whore is too disturbing for that. It is like watching a horror movie and telling oneself that the blood is not real. It may well explain why this verse often gets so little attention in the discussion of these chapters or why the focus is placed solely on the destruction of Babylon as a city. But, as Keller notes: 'There is no veiling the way this vision of justice boils down to the burning and devouring of a woman's body.'[55]

It is therefore important to consider Babylon as Great City *and* Great Whore, as dominant, colonial power *and* prostitute. I agree with Schüssler Fiorenza that 'the "female" personifications of mother, virgin, or whore in Revelation must be problematized *not only* in terms of gender *but also* in terms of systemic structures of race, class and imperialist oppression'.[56] However, it is hard to understand then why she herself sets up an opposition between two reading strategies, namely a reading that focuses on gender and a rhetorical–political reading. The first reading is identified as the position of white Western feminist scholars and the second as that of feminist subaltern and postcolonial studies. I find this opposition dangerous,

---

49 Hanna Stenström, 'The Book of Revelation: A Vision of the Ultimate Liberation or the Ultimate Backlash? A Study in 20th Century Interpretations of Rev 14:1–5, with special emphasis on feminist exegesis' (PhD dissertation; Uppsala University, 1999), p. 53.

50 Schüssler Fiorenza, *The Book of Revelation: Justice and Judgment* (2nd edn, Minneapolis, MN: Fortress Press, 1998), p. 218.

51 Exum, *Plotted, Shot, and Painted*, p. 120 n. 55.

52 Schüssler Fiorenza, *Book of Revelation*, p. 218 (her comments are made with explicit reference to Pippin's work).

53 G. Aichele et al., *The Postmodern Bible* (The Bible and Culture Collective; New Haven, CT: Yale University Press, 1995), p. 262.

54 Schüssler Fiorenza, *Book of Revelation*, p. 219.

55 Keller, *Apocalypse Now and Then*, p. 76.

56 Schüssler Fiorenza, *Book of Revelation*, p. 218 (italics added).

because it suggests that gender research is apolitical. As Stenström states: 'feminist researchers must repeat basics: to speak about gender is to speak about a structure of power. To speak about power structures is to speak about something political. We must not allow that "gender" is taken from us and used as a code word for depoliticized research.'[57]

Moreover, I find the formulation of this opposition problematic. In the first case, 'being white' and 'Western' are used as seemingly unproblematic labels and the focus is then on individual scholars. The other position, however, is described as feminist subaltern and postcolonial *studies*. Here no reference is made to the scholars in question or to their color or cultural background. Thus the first category is presented as exclusively white and Western, while the second category seems to include all 'others'. As the analysis here demonstrates, issues of gender are much more complex and multi-layered in the ideologies of text and interpreters than simple dichotomization will allow. Indeed, such binary oppositions all too readily replicate the dualistic apocalypticizing discourse of Revelation, re-inscribing the power structures of the text.

Women as Subject and Object of Colonizing Discourse

In her postcolonial reading of Revelation 17, Kim observes how female readers of this text are placed in a double bind 'because we are forced to betray our sexual identity in order to share the perspective of the author/God; otherwise we have to identify ourselves with the female object in the text'.[58] Kim further argues that the whore not only refers to Rome as colonizing power, but also represents a colonized woman, exploited by the colonizers and abandoned by her own man. Thus 'sexually oppressed women are caught in a no-win situation between foreign and native men'.[59]

I find myself caught in another double bind here, because I share the critique of an oppressive and violent regime, while I resist the violence done to the whore. However, there is more. As a citizen of Belgium, a colonizing country,[60] I rather find myself identified with Babylon as locus of colonial power and oppression. Moreover, the red light district of Amsterdam with its prostitutes from all over the world is only one block away from where I work. The traffic in women is flourishing there. Since the 1980s the European sex-business has become big business. Women from Asia, Africa, South America and Eastern Europe are lured to Western Europe with false promises – and often, false passports too – and then forced into prostitution.[61] One

---

57 Stenström, 'Book of Revelation', pp. 284–85.
58 Kim, '"Uncovering her Wickedness"', p. 61.
59 Kim, '"Uncovering her Wickedness"', p. 63.
60 In 1884–85 Congo became the personal royal property of the Belgian king, Leopold II, and in 1908 the property of the Belgian state. It became independent in 1960.
61 According to the 'Trafficking in Persons Report' 2003 released by the U.S. Department of State, 'Belgium is a destination and transit country for trafficked persons, primarily young women from Sub-Saharan Africa, Central and Eastern Europe, and Asia, destined for Belgium's larger cities or other European countries for the purposes of sexual exploitation' (www.state.gov/g/tip/rls/tiprpt/2003/ [accessed 16 January 2009]).

famous luxury brothel in Hungary is actually called 'Villa Babylon'.[62] Soon enough, however, the women who arrive in Europe find out about the real nature of the jobs or the wealthy husbands they were promised.

The fate of Babylon described in Rev. 17.16 reminds me of the violence done to the women who refuse to prostitute themselves. Sometimes their passports are taken from them; sometimes they are guarded, locked up, intimidated and threatened, abused, raped and most often financially exploited. The death of the Great Whore reminds me of Nicolasa Duarte, a Dominican woman who worked in a striptease bar in Kortrijk, the city where I was born, and whose dead body was found packed in a suitcase thrown in the river in 1984. The pimp who was responsible for her death was arrested and even admitted to the murder, but he spent only three years in jail. Nicolasa had accepted a contract as *bailarina* in Europe to earn money for her poor family, but her life ended in this striptease bar.[63]

Reading Revelation 17 from this particular context as *Sitz im Tod* or 'black hole'[64] makes me aware of yet another aspect of the gender ideology embedded in the text, namely how the negative depiction of the whore obscures the social reality of prostitution. The focus of the text is on the character of the whore, and the strategy is to present her as morally evil. This is done in a number of ways. She is presented not only as a prostitute, but also as actively pursuing prostitution: 'She has made all nations drink of the wine of the wrath of her fornication' (14.8). This clearly puts the blame on her, since *she* made them drink and it is '*her* fornication'. Also contributing to her negative image is her presentation as being drunk with the blood of the saints and the blood of the witnesses to Jesus (17.6). As consumption of blood is explicitly forbidden in the Torah, this practice appears particularly repulsive. That she is presented as drunk makes her action even more excessive and demonstrates her lack of self-control (σωφροσύνη).[65] Both the woman prophet called Jezebel and Babylon transgress similar sexual boundaries and break food-related injunctions. In Revelation 2 the taboo is that of eating food sacrificed to idols (εἰδωλόθυτα); in Revelation 17 it is the consumption of blood. As Duff notes, the resultant picture in both cases is that of a woman who is out of control, thus tapping into cultural stereotypes regarding gender. Women operating independently in the public sphere should be shunned as potentially dangerous.[66] It can hardly be accidental that both Jezebel and Babylon lack male partners (and thus control) and that the only males

---

62 Chris de Stoop, *Ze zijn zo lief, meneer* (Antwerp: Kritak, 1992), p. 93.

63 de Stoop, *Ze zijn zo lief, meneer*, pp. 53–55.

64 The expression *Sitz im Tod* originally comes from Jon Sobrino, but it is adapted by Stenström to refer more specifically to the death context of women: 'By "death context of women", I understand the circumstances under which women die because they are women, and those where women do not die physically but are subjected to destructive powers which create a state of death during life' (Stenström, 'Book of Revelation', p. 23). Manuel Castells uses the cosmic metaphor 'black hole' for those regions of our society 'from which, statistically speaking, there is no escape from the pain and destruction inflicted on the human condition for those who, in one way or another, enter these social landscapes' (*End of Millennium* [The Information Age: Economy, Society, and Culture, III; Oxford: Blackwell, 1998], p. 162).

65 Duff, *Who Rides the Beast?*, p. 101.

66 Duff, *Who Rides the Beast?*, p. 108.

on the scene are presented as victims of these women, insofar as they have been deceived by them (2.20; 18.23).

Besides conveying negative elements in the description of the whore, the text also presents more explicit value judgments. Babylon is accused of blasphemy, impurity, abomination, iniquity, deceit and corruption,[67] and her sins are said to be 'heaped high as heaven' (Rev. 18.5). All these elements have this in common: the woman is pictured as morally reprehensible, which in turn makes her punishment look to be deserved. The text legitimizes as well as sanctions the measures taken against her by presenting them as being in accordance with God's will. The violence against her thus receives divine (i.e., absolute) justification in the constructed narrative context.

However, in order to reach this conclusion the Great Whore needs to be isolated and the social dimension of prostitution exposed. By social dimension I mean here prostitution as trade, and thus as a specific form of labor.[68] Albeit indirect, the only trace in the text that the whore is rewarded for her services is found in the description of her wealth. According to Rev. 17.4, 'the whore was clothed in purple and scarlet, and adorned with gold and jewels and pearls'. This description is repeated in 18.16 by the merchants who mourn for the destroyed city: 'Alas, alas, the great city, clothed in fine linen, in purple and scarlet, adorned with gold, with jewels, and with pearls!' Although in the previous context reference is made to the city's commercial activity, the source of her luxury is never made explicit.[69] The suggestion in the text seems to be that she is making profit from her lovers, one way or another. This connection may be fairly obvious as far as the wealth of Babylon as a colonial power is concerned,[70] and it could even hold true for a whore. Still, the social reality of prostitution remains out of sight. The cultural associations embedded in this discourse create a dynamic lens for characterizing the whore in purely negative terms, but the lens fails to engage the broader sociocultural contexts that engender prostitution in the ancient world and our own. In this sense, the righteous rhetoric of Revelation readily deconstructs itself, as the dualistic conceptual framework too easily allows for the colonized to play out a role reversal as colonizer, focused, sadly, on the dismemberment of the female body in text and history.

A trace of this observation may be left precisely in the gendered character of the metaphor itself, because the metaphor also reveals the 'gender-based division of

---

67 Βλασφημία: 17.3; ἀκάθαρτος: 17.4; 18.2; βδέλυγμα: 17.4, 5; ἀδίκημα: 18.5; πλανάω: 18.23; φθείρω: 19.2.

68 Reference to the situation of prostitutes in antiquity is made by Luzia Sutter Rehmann. According to her 'the waters' in 17.1, 15 can be seen as a realistic reference to the places where prostitutes were contacted ('Für Korinth ist es z.B. belegt, daß Sklavinnen in Bädern arbeiteten und dort, neben Handtuch und Seifenartikeln, den Gästen sexuelle Dienste anboten'. *Vom Mut, genau hinzusehen. Feministisch-befreiungstheologische Interpretationen zur Apokalyptik* [Lucerne: Edition Exodus, 1998], p. 97).

69 So also Sutter Rehmann: 'Es ist aber auffallend, daß wir nichts von einem Lohn erfahren, den sie von den Freiern erhalten würde' ('Die Offenbarung des Johannes: Inspirationen aus Patmos', in Luise Schottroff and Marie-Theres Wacker [eds], *Kompendium Feministische Bibelauslegung* [2nd edn, Gütersloh: Chr. Kaiser/Gütersloher Verlags,1999], pp. 725–41 [735]).

70 According to Duff, John's criticism is not directed at wealth as such (as the very similar description of Jerusalem demonstrates), but at the merchant class in Revelation 18 (Duff, *Who Rides the Beast?*, p. 63).

labor'. That the Great Whore is a woman has everything to do with economics and power. As Uy Eviota puts it: 'The intersection between economy, politics and gender is embodied in the sexual division of labour: the demarcation of those tasks which are paid and those not paid, differentials in pay, concentrations in occupations and job-levels within these occupations, and sexual servicing as the paid work of women.'[71] Gender ideology not only determines what sexual behavior is considered male or female and what sexual needs are 'natural' (including how one is supposed to fulfill them), but also the kind of work men or women are supposed to do. Economic and political forces play their role in the social and financial evaluation of this work as they determine if and what labor is being paid and how much. In his analysis of social global change in our own time, Castells points to the link between supply and demand 'made by the global criminal networks that control much prostitution throughout the world, and are always striving to find new, more profitable product lines and markets'.[72]

What is only a trace in the picture of the Great Whore is further substantiated in the examples I mentioned from my own context. They show, on the one hand, how the 'traffic in women' serves the sexual and economic needs of the still-colonial West, and how, on the other, these women are used and abused as slaves.[73] In my view, the ideology-critical power of Revelation falls short when it comes to gender ideology. The abuse of a whore as metaphor for a colonial power reveals this failure. As Kim states: 'the whore metaphor does not simply stand for the imperial city of Rome but also stands for women sexually involved in a colonizing context.'[74] The two cannot be separated, and the dramatic consequences of such metaphorization are exposed in the violence done to the whore. The reader is supposed to rejoice in her death, but not every reader does – at least not the resistant reader.

---

71 Elizabeth Uy Eviota, *The Political Economy of Gender: Women and the Sexual Division of Labour in the Philippines* (London/New Jersey: Zed, 1992), p. 9.

72 Castells, *End of Millennium*, p. 157.

73 As noted by Barr, a trace of the trafficking in human beings is present in Rev.18.13, where they are listed with other commodities for the colonial elite (Barr, 'Towards an Ethical Reading', p. 369).

74 Kim, '"Uncovering Her Wickedness"', p. 69.

FEMININE SYMBOLISM IN THE BOOK OF REVELATION*

ADELA YARBRO COLLINS

Feminine symbols are prominent in the second half of the book of Revelation, which extends from 12.1 to 22.5.[1] Symbols can be approached in a variety of ways. In the twentieth century a dominant mode of interpreting symbols among biblical scholars has been the history-of-religion approach. This method has sought to discover the origin and history of various symbols and to discern their meaning and function in one text by comparing it with other texts from the same historical context and culture.[2] This approach is very illuminating for the analysis of the three major feminine symbols in Revelation: the woman clothed with the sun in ch. 12, the prostitute of ch. 17 and the bride of the Lamb in chs 19 and 21. The vision of the woman clothed with the sun has a highlighted position as the opening account of the second half of the book.

The traditional Catholic interpretation of the woman clothed with the sun is that she is Mary, the mother of Jesus, since the child she brings forth is the Messiah. Most Protestant exegetes, and now many Catholic exegetes, have found that interpretation unlikely. Alternative interpretations are that she is personified Israel, Jerusalem, or the people of God. Such personifications are common in the prophetic traditions of Israel.[3]

A history-of-religion approach leads to the conclusion that the woman is presented as a goddess.[4] The vision is of a high goddess with astral attributes: the sun is her garment, the moon her footstool, stars her crown. The Greek word ἀστήρ could mean star or constellation, so it is likely that her crown is the circle of heaven, the zodiac.[5] These attributes suggest that she is a cosmic queen who has power over the rhythm of night and day and over human destiny, since the zodiac symbolizes fate.

Only a few goddesses in Hellenistic and early Roman times were depicted in such exalted fashion. These attributes, especially the sun and the zodiac, were usually associated with the male high-god, Zeus or his equivalent. Three goddesses who were so described were the Mother Goddess worshiped at Ephesus, who was identified with the Greek Artemis and the Roman Diana; the Syrian goddess Atargatis, whose

---

* First published in *Biblical Interpretation* 1.1 (1993). Reprinted with permission.

1 For an argument that the book of Revelation is structured into two main parts, see A. Yarbro Collins, *The Combat Myth in the Book of Revelation* (HDR, 9; Missoula, MT: Scholars Press, 1976), pp. 5–32.

2 An excellent commentary that emphasizes the history-of-religion approach to the book of Revelation is Wilhelm Bousset, *Die Offenbarung Johannis* (Göttingen: Vandenhoeck & Ruprecht, 1966; reprint of the 6th edn, 1906).

3 Hos. 1–3; Ezek. 16, 23; Isa. 54, 60, 62, 66; Mic. 4.9–10.

4 Collins, *The Combat Myth*, pp. 71–76.

5 Franz Boll, *Aus der Offenbarung Johannis: Hellenistische Studien zum Weltbild der Apokalypse* (Stoicheia, 1; Leipzig: Teubner, 1914), p. 99, n. 1.

name is a combination of Astarte and Anat; and Isis, the ancient Egyptian goddess who was worshiped in new forms all over the Mediterranean world in the Hellenistic and Roman periods.

The iconography of Isis seems to be the closest to the woman of Revelation 12. She was called 'female sun', 'second sun' and 'mistress of heaven' in temple inscriptions in Egypt in the late kingdom.[6] In a novel written during the second century CE, an appearance of Isis to a man named Lucius is described. He addresses her as 'Queen of Heaven'. She is called 'a very bright apparition'. On the midpoint of her forehead is a round disc like the moon. Her robe resembles the night sky: it is shining black and covered with stars; in the midst of the stars is the moon in mid-month.[7]

The plot of Revelation 12 involves an attack of a monster on a pregnant woman in order to destroy her and especially her child. Since the child is the one who will rule the nations, the implication is that the dragon wishes to prevent the child's kingship in order to be ruler himself. In Egyptian mythology, Set kills his brother Osiris in a struggle for kingship. Isis, who is their sister and also Osiris's wife, revives Osiris, who becomes king of the underworld. She conceives a child by the resuscitated Osiris, Horus, who, when he is grown, kills Set and becomes king. This complex of myths is similar in general outline to the plot of Revelation 12.[8]

A much closer parallel can be found in some versions of the story of Leto.[9] Leto is a very ancient Greek goddess, one of the Titans, children of Heaven and Earth, who ruled before the Olympian gods. She was one of the few Titans who had a cult in historical times, possibly because of the importance of her children, Apollo and Artemis. Homer and Hesiod simply say that she bore them and give no details. A later hymn in Homeric style, 'To Delian Apollo', says that Leto wandered far and wide seeking a place to bear Apollo and was refused time and again because each place feared to receive the mighty god. Finally Delos agreed, when Leto promised that Apollo would build his temple there and honor Delos over all his other cult sites. Leto is said to have labored for nine days and nights. All the chief goddesses were there supporting her except Hera and Eilithyia, the goddess of sore travail. Hera was envious of the faultless and strong son Leto was about to bear, so she stayed away and prevented Eilithyia from knowing of Leto's trouble. Finally, the other goddesses bring Eilithyia to Delos and Leto brings forth Apollo, holding on to a palm tree. In the third century BCE, Callimachus, an Alexandrian poet, wrote a hymn to Delos in which he tells a somewhat different version of the story of Apollo's birth. According to this version, Hera forbade any land to afford Leto refuge, but at last Delos ventured to disobey.

In Chapter 140 of a Latin translation of Greek myths attributed to Hyginus (second century CE), we find the version of Apollo's birth story which is closest to Revelation 12 (it is found in other primary sources as well):

---

6 Jan Bergman, *Ich bin Isis: Studien zum memphitischen Hintergrund der griechischen Isisaretalogien* (Uppsala: The University Press, 1968), p. 162.

7 Apuleius, *Metamorphoses* 11.

8 Collins, *The Combat Myth*, pp. 62–63.

9 Collins, *The Combat Myth*, pp. 63–65.

Fabulae 140. Python

Python, son of Earth, was a huge dragon. He was accustomed to giving oracles on Mount Parnassus before Apollo. He was informed by an oracle that he would be destroyed by the offspring of Leto. At that time Zeus was living with (*concubit*) Leto. When Hera learned of this, she caused it that Leto give birth where the sun does not reach. When Python perceived that Leto was pregnant by Zeus, he began to pursue (her) in order to kill her. But, by order of Zeus, the North Wind (*Aquilo*) lifted Leto up and carried her to Poseidon; Poseidon protected her, but in order not to rescind Hera's decree, he carried her to the island Ortygia and covered the island over with waves. When Python did not find Leto, he returned to Parnassus. But Poseidon returned the island Ortygia to the upper region, which island has been called Delos afterward. There, holding on to an olive tree, Leto gave birth to Apollo and Artemis, to whom (pl.) Haphaestus gave arrows as a gift. Four days after they were born, Apollo avenged his mother. He went to Parnassus and killed Python with arrows. (Therefore he is called Pythian.) He put his bones in a tripod and placed (the tripod) in his temple, and established funeral games for him, which are called Pythia.[10]

The narrative of Revelation 12 and the story from Hyginus share a basic plot, which is a mythic pattern of combat widespread in the ancient Near East and the Greco-Roman world.[11] The myths that share this pattern depict a struggle between two divine beings and their allies for universal kingship. One of the combatants is usually a monster, often a dragon. This conflict may reflect cultural and political changes and struggles in the regions in which these myths were formed, repeated and modified. The basic conflicts in human life and nature are also reflected in these myths. The monster is often associated with chaos, sterility and death, while his opponent is associated with order, fertility and life. Thus their conflict is presented as a cosmic battle whose outcome will constitute or abolish order in society and fertility in nature. The mythic pattern has the following elements:

A. The Dragon Pair: (1) husband and wife or (2) brother and sister or (3) mother and son
B. The Attack: to keep the chief god from coming to power or to remove him
C. The Champion's Death
D. The Dragon's Reign
E. The Recovery of the Champion: accomplished by his wife, sister, mother or son
F. Battle Renewed and Victory
G. Restoration and Confirmation of Order

The role of the woman in the plot of Revelation 12 is not that of the goddess ally, which belongs to the theme of the Recovery of the Champion or to the theme of Renewed Battle and Victory. Rather she is the threatened mother of the hero, a role that belongs to the theme of the Attack and to the theme of the Dragon's Reign. Like Leto, she is depicted as the mother of a heroic figure under attack by a dragon

---

10 For the Latin text, see H. J. Rose (ed.), *Hygini Fabulae* (2nd edn, Lugduni Batavorum: A.W. Sythoff, 1963), pp. 102–03.

11 Joseph Fontenrose, *Python: A Study of the Delphic Myth and Its Origins* (Berkeley: University of California Press, 1959); Neil Forsyth, *The Old Enemy: Satan and the Combat Myth* (Princeton, NJ: Princeton University Press, 1987).

because of the threat posed by her child. Nor does Revelation 12 come to a reso-
lution in the restoration of order. The victory of Michael and the angels over the
dragon and his angels is only partial: the dragon is defeated in heaven but reigns on
earth. The final defeat of the dragon is described in 20.7–10. The restoration of order
that follows this victory involves the creation of a new heaven and a new earth (21.1).
As in many other ancient texts, the establishment of order involves a sacred
marriage: the hero, the Lamb, is united with his bride, the new Jerusalem (21.2, 9).
The sacred marriage symbolizes new life with the ancient connotations of fertility.

It may seem strange that the author who condemned assimilation of Greco-
Roman culture in the messages to seven churches (Revelation 2–3) would adapt
Greco-Roman religious traditions in recounting his visions. John's use of the mythic
pattern described above shows that he shared the ancient mythic consciousness. It
also suggests that he was forced to come to terms with the feminine aspect of the
divine. Mother goddesses were very prominent in Asia Minor. The temple to Artemis
in Ephesus was one of the seven wonders of the world. Sardis was another major
center of the cult of the mother goddess.

The woman clothed with the sun is best understood as the Heavenly Israel; she is
portrayed as God's spouse, whom he protects, as mother of the messiah, and of all
believers (v. 17).[12] Like the symbol of the Lamb, the woman is characterized both by
power and by weakness. Her power is manifest in her description as a heavenly being,
as cosmic queen, and in her ability to bring forth a child who will be universal king.
Her weakness is evident in her vulnerability to the attacks of the dragon, her inability
to protect herself and her child, and her dependency on outside help for protection
and rescue.

Her story is a paradigm for the audience of the book. Like her, they have a
heavenly identity: they are God's kingdom in the world, God's priests (1.6); their
names are written in the book of life (3.5). But they are also vulnerable: some have
been arrested, some killed; their legal status in the Roman empire is precarious. The
rescue of the woman and her being nourished in the wilderness suggests to the
audience that God will deliver them as God delivered the people of Israel from
Egypt.

The feminine aspect of the divine is also manifest in the symbol of the Bride of the
Lamb. According to an inscription from the third century BCE, the sacred marriage
of Zeus and Leto took place in Didyma, near Ephesus, where there was a shrine of
Apollo at which oracles were given.[13] Statues of Zeus and Leto, together with their
twin offspring, were erected in the third century CE in Didyma, so their cult seems to
have endured.[14]

Traditional readings of Revelation have identified the Bride with the Church or
with the soul of the individual Christian that is united with Christ after death. A
history-of-religion approach would see the influence of the sacred marriage in the
formation of this symbol. The vision has also been shaped by Isaiah 54, in which
Jerusalem is depicted as God's wife. The construction of the new Jerusalem out of

---

12 Collins, *The Combat Myth*, pp. 134–35.

13 Albert Rehm, *Didyma*, part 2: *Die Inschriften* (gen. ed. Theodore Wiegand; ed. of this
vol. Richard Harder; Berlin: Mann, 1958), p. 116.

14 Rehm, *Didyma*, pp. 115–17, nn. 89–90.

precious metals and stones may have been suggested by Isa. 54.11–12: 'I will set your stones in antimony, and lay your foundations with sapphires. I will make your pinnacles agate, your gates of carbuncles, and your wall of precious stones.' This text was interpreted by the community at Qumran as an allegorical description of the 'Congregation of His Elect', namely, the community itself.[15] The Bride, the new Jerusalem, in Revelation symbolizes the community of the faithful at the time of their uniting with God and the Lamb in the new age.

The fulfillment of God's creation and God's interaction with humanity cannot be described in purely abstract terms or in metaphors that are only masculine. Both the masculine and the feminine are needed to express the richness, complexity and vitality of the created world in its fulfillment. This vision of the new creation as a wedding is a counterbalance to Rev. 14.1–5. Because of the present crisis, which John implied was about to intensify, the ideal was to renounce sexual relations and to prepare for the end.[16] At the same time, as one of the fundamental characteristics of God's good creation, sexuality is a symbol of the new creation, of wholeness, of the time of salvation.

Contrasted with the Bride, who is clothed in pure linen (19.8), is the Prostitute of Revelation 17. The contrasting parallel is quite deliberate as the literary structure shows. The vision of the Prostitute is an elaboration of the seventh bowl, as the vision of the Bride of the Lamb in ch. 21 is an elaboration of the seventh vision in the last series. Each of these visions is introduced in the same way. In each case, one of the angels who had the seven bowls comes to John and says, 'Come and I will show you . . . ' (cf. 17.1 with 21.9). Each time, what the angel describes is a female. In both passages, the angel carries John away in the spirit in order to show him the vision.

In ch. 17, the name written on the woman's forehead is Babylon the great. She symbolizes a city. The prophets of ancient Israel often personified cities as women, both Jerusalem and enemy cities. This metaphor may reflect an ancient Near Eastern understanding of goddesses as protectors of particular peoples or cities. This protective goddess, often called the Fortune of the city, was usually portrayed with a crown that looked like a city wall. The origin of these ideas cannot be determined, but the wall of the ancient city-fortress may have suggested the encircling comfort and security of the womb or a mother's arms.

The classical prophets also spoke of cities and nations as harlots. Nahum, in a triumphal ode celebrating the fall of the Assyrian empire, refers to Nineveh as a prostitute (Nah. 3.4). The image expresses the attraction other nations felt toward the center of power. The context suggests that Nineveh is maligned in large part because of its treacherous and deceitful dealings with other nations. In a late addition to the oracles against Tyre and Sidon in Isaiah 23, the restoration of Tyre is described as the return to favor of a forgotten prostitute. Prostitution here seems to express a way of life in which no scruples limit the quest for wealth.[17] Elsewhere (Isa. 1.21; Hosea 1–4; Jer. 3.6–10; Ezek. 16; 23.5–21), it is Jerusalem, Samaria, Israel

15 Geza Vermes, *The Dead Sea Scrolls in English* (2nd edn, New York: Penguin, 1975), pp. 228–29.
16 A. Yarbro Collins, *The Gospel and Women* (Orange, CA: Chapman College, 1988), p. 23–28.
17 Isa. 23.15–18; cf. Ezek. 28.16–18.

and Judah who are depicted by the prophets as prostitutes, with prostitution symbolizing unfaithfulness to Yahweh expressed in foreign alliances and the acknowledgment of other gods.

The frequency of the use of the prostitute as a symbol for Yahweh's people has led some to identify the prostitute of Revelation 17 with Jerusalem. The text suggests a different identification, however. The seven heads of the beasts are interpreted as seven hills (17.9), a detail that recalls the city of Rome. In the last verse, the woman is said to be the great city that has dominion over the whole earth (v. 18). These remarks make clear that the woman symbolizes the ancient city of Rome. Like Nineveh, Rome has seduced many nations into alliances because of its overwhelming and attractive power. Like those of Tyre, its commercial enterprises are widespread, enriching some and making the poverty of others harder to bear. Idolatry is a factor here as well, although the image has shifted. Rather than depicting the people of God as a prostitute, who has lusted after male gods and their human representatives instead of remaining faithful to Yahweh, Revelation presents the foreign god as female, as a prostitute who seduces the inhabitants of the earth.

The ancient Romans not only personified their city but allowed it to be worshiped in the cities of the empire as the goddess Roma. Roma was worshiped, sometimes alone, sometimes with one or more emperors, in many cities of western Asia Minor. From one point of view, Revelation 17 is anti-Roman propaganda. It is a parody of the honor given Roma: her supporters worship a prostitute, not a goddess! Besides idolatry, the qualities especially condemned in Rome are violence, oppression, arrogance and pride. According to Revelation 17–18, the imperial system involves bloodshed (17.6, 18.24), slavery (18.13), and a false, overblown sense of self-sufficiency and power (18.7).

The history-of-religion approach interprets the feminine symbols of Revelation in light of their origins and in terms of their meaning and function in the historical context in which the book was written. A quite different perspective on these symbols is opened up by placing them in the context of a psychological interpretation of symbols in the tradition of Carl Jung. My thinking along these lines has been stimulated by Erich Neumann's book *The Origins and History of Consciousness*.[18] The question immediately arises whether his study is, in effect, an analysis of the origins and history of *male* consciousness only, or whether his description of stages of consciousness applies to females as well. This question will be addressed at the appropriate points below.

According to Neumann, the first stage in the evolution of consciousness is the time when the ego is contained in the unconscious. The symbol of this stage is the uroboros, the circular snake, the primal dragon that begets, impregnates and slays itself. In terms of the history of consciousness, this stage has given rise to creation myths. With regard to the individual psyche, it is the stage of infancy and early childhood when the ego is not yet detached from 'the round', the surrounding world, the primordial mother, the uroboros. The notion that there is a time when the ego is contained within the unconscious seems to apply equally well to females as to males.

---

18 Erich Neumann, *The Origins and History of Consciousness* (German original: *Ursprungsgeschichte des Bewusstseins*; Zürich: Rascher Verlag, 1949; trans. R. F. C. Hull; New York: Pantheon Books, 1954).

The androgynous image of the uroboros is appropriate for both sexes. Further analysis, however, is needed of the creation myths associated with this stage of consciousness to see whether or not they represent the consciousness of both males and females. The Babylonian creation myth, *Enuma Elish*, for example, seems to represent a male point of view, since the mother of the gods, Tiamat, is killed by the emerging king of the gods, who creates the heaven and the earth from her body.

The next stage is one in which the ego has separated from the uroboros, but is still under its dominance. The symbol of this stage is the Great Mother. This great uroboric Mother Goddess has two sides: she is the good mother who nourishes and lavishes affection, and she is also the wicked mother who devours and destroys. The myths that relate to this stage or layer of consciousness focus on the earth and symbols of vegetation, on fertility and growth, on agriculture and the sphere of food. In terms of the individual psyche, this stage relates to the ego's establishment of a certain degree of autonomy in later childhood and adolescence. This stage is related to the Madonna image: the Mother Goddess with the Divine Child, a symbol that emphasizes the good, protective, side of the mother. It is also related to the myths of a Mother Goddess in her relationship to her son-love, the myths of Cybele and Attis, Aphrodite and Adonis, and Ishtar and Tammuz. These son-lovers are loved, slain, buried, and bewailed by the Mother, and then reborn through her. The masculine principle is differentiated from the feminine, but it is not yet strong enough to be an independent counterbalance to it. The maternal is still primary and dominant. Fear and a sense of death characterize this stage or layer.

In principle, this stage of consciousness could represent the experience of both males and females, since boys and girls may experience the mother as both loving and threatening. Neumann's elaboration of the basic insight, however, is clearly from a male point of view; the mother is perceived as lover in a sexual sense. In the development of most girls, such perceptions are oriented to the father. Further research could be done to see whether there is evidence of myths involving the Father God and his daughter-lover.

Subsequent stages involve the formation of the conscious, higher ego, the development of the independence of the ego and of consciousness by the rise of principles of analysis, distinction and the delimitation of opposites. The myths that relate to these stages or layers are the myth of the separation of the World Parents and the hero myths, especially the slaying of the dragon, the liberating of the female captive, and the acquisition of the dragon's treasure. The hero's fear of the dragon corresponds to the male's fear of the female in general. The dragon symbolizes the Great and Terrible Mother. Like the uroboros, the Great Mother is, in a sense, bisexual. She possesses masculine, but not paternal, features. Her aggressive and destructive features may be defined as masculine. These aggressive and destructive elements of the Great Mother can appear symbolically and ritually as separate figures detached from her, such as animals. The horrible sea monster is originally the Great Mother's dependent phallic consort. He is the dragon or bull who represents the destructive side of the uroboros. Later, however, when the patriarchate has succeeded to the Great Mother's sovereignty, the role of the Terrible Father is projected upon the masculine representatives of the destructive side of the Goddess. This is done especially when it is in the interests of patriarchal development to emphasize the figure of the 'good mother'.

The stages of the development of the individual psyche, as Neumann defines them, apply to both males and females. Females as well as males develop a conscious, higher ego, independence of the ego and consciousness by the use of analysis, distinction and the delimitation of opposites. Feminist analysis of culture, however, has questioned the heavy value placed on independence and dichotomous thinking. The myths that Neumann associated with these later stages clearly express the male point of view. The hero is male; the major threat is a negative female and the major prize is a positive female. The notion of the 'good mother' plays a role in social organization in which men are dominant.

In Neumann's terms, following Bachofen, the 'patriarchate' refers to a masculine world symbolized by spirit, sun, consciousness and ego. The matriarchate is a world dominated by the unconscious, by a preconscious, prelogical, pre-individual way of thinking. In the development of the myth of Athena, the old mother goddess is defeated by a new, feminine spiritual principle. Athena was not born of woman, but sprang from the head of Zeus; thus she is opposed to the earthy, unconscious feminine element. She is the companion and helper of the masculine hero. She has attributes of the old mother deity, but the maternal power is subdued. The limitations of the gender-specific symbolism are obvious. Such symbolism creates 'moods and motivations', to borrow Clifford Geertz's terms, that do not give men permission to draw upon the creativity of the unconscious of women to develop logical abilities.

Turning to the book of Revelation, we find manifestations of the Great Mother symbol. The great prostitute of ch. 17 is the Terrible Mother. Her character as a prostitute symbolizes the seductive and charming power of the Great Mother's lure toward self-dissolution in the unconscious sea of participation, of non-individuation. This aspect is brought out by her seat upon many waters (v. 1), a symbol of the feminine unconscious, and by the allusions to drunkenness, a path toward forgetfulness, toward impersonal ecstasy (v. 2). The beast upon which she rides is her phallic consort, showing her power over the animal world of fertility, birth, growth and decay. Her threatening, violent side is manifest in the remark that she drinks human blood (v. 6). The Terrible Mother must be appeased by blood and needs to be soaked with and nourished by blood in order to be fruitful. The Jungian perspective leads us to find in the representation of Rome as the Great Mother a reflection of the struggle of Christian faith as a religion of individuation and consciousness to free itself from Greco-Roman culture and religion, which were more rooted in the participation mystique.

A feminist perspective leads to the observation that this vision is an expression of a male imagination. Tina Pippin has argued that the vision of the prostitute in Revelation 17 is sadistic, erotic and pornographic.[19] 'Sadism' may be defined as delight taken in seeing someone else suffer. This definition is applicable to Rev. 17.1–19.10, but Pippin seems to imply that sadism always involves an erotic aspect.

---

19 Tina Pippin, 'The Reproduction of Power: Feminism, Marxism and the Ideology of Reading', unpublished paper given at the Annual Meeting of the Society of Biblical Literature in New Orleans, 1990. See now, Tina Pippin, *Death and Desire: The Rhetoric of Gender in the Apocalypse of John* (Literary Currents in Biblical Interpretation; Louisville, KY: Westminster/John Knox Press, 1992).

I find no evidence of sexual desire in these chapters. Revelation 17 is 'pornographic' in the etymological sense; it draws a picture (γράφειν) of a prostitute (πόρνη). 'Pornography' in general usage, however, means a text that expresses or seeks to evoke sexual excitement. The term should not be used more broadly for any linguistic expression that is offensive to us (as twenty-first-century people). The violence in Revelation 17 and the male perspective are due to the fact that war in the ancient world (and often in the modern world) involves violence against actual women and the use of female symbolism to express degradation.

The woman of ch. 12 is the Great Mother in her protective, good aspect. Motherhood is explicit in the depiction of a pregnant woman, her labor, and the mention of her giving birth to a son. The Madonna symbol is suggested. Her originally earthy nature is perhaps reflected in the fact that the earth is her ally in the struggle with the dragon (v. 16). But like Athena, she represents a new feminine principle that incorporates consciousness and supports the patriarchate. Although she is associated with the primordial feminine symbols of the earth and the moon, these symbols are overshadowed by the masculine symbols of the sun and the stars. Her association with the masculine world of spirit and thought is also symbolized by her being given the wings of the great eagle and by her flight into the desert (v. 14).

The threatening, destructive side of the Great Mother has been split off from the good mother and is represented by the dragon. The woman, along with her son, represents the spiritual masculine principle that is in danger of being swallowed by darkness, by the uroboric dragon that represents the maternal unconscious. The narrative of ch. 12 is a segment of a hero myth, with the male child cast as the hero who must slay the dragon. The conflict between the hero and the dragon is not fully resolved in ch. 12. The renewed battle and ultimate victory of the hero are described in chs 19–22.

Although the hero myth of Revelation does not involve a female captive being held by the dragon, the Bride of the Lamb has an analogous role. In the old fertility myths, the young hero king had to overcome a monster before being united with the Earth Mother in the sacred marriage, a union that restored the fertility of the year. In the hero myth of later stages of consciousness, the freeing of the captive expressed a new stage in the evolution of masculine consciousness, namely, the crystallization of the anima from the mother archetype. In other words, the hero kills only the terrible side of the female, and his own fear of the female, in order to set free the fruitful and joyous side with which she joins herself to him.

Rev. 14.1–5 represents the stage of the non-liberation of the captive, the continued dominance of the Great Mother under her deadly aspect. The final result of this dominance is alienation from the body and from the earth, hatred of life, and world negation. The destruction of the prostitute, the Terrible Mother, in chs 17 and 18, and the defeat of the dragon, in ch. 20, make possible the union of the Lamb with the Bride and he founds his kingdom with her.

In Neumann's interpretation of the developed hero myths, the hero's rescue of the captive corresponds to the discovery of a new psychic world. The kingdom that they found together is a new continent of cultural accomplishment that breaks away from the world of the First Parents. The kingdom of the Lamb in Revelation is ambiguous. It may be seen as the new Jerusalem, a new vision of human society on earth, or as a return to paradise, the annihilation of human creativity in a return to the womb. This ambiguity may be resolved in particular readings and applications of Revelation.

In the course of this exploratory Jungian interpretation, I have made some observations relating to a feminist analysis of the symbols of Revelation. A further observation of this type is that the symbolic use of prostitution is problematic. In the Hebrew Bible and in rabbinic literature, the word translated as 'prostitute' (*zonah*) has a wide range of meaning. It refers to any woman who transgresses the regulations surrounding her sexuality, not only to the ordinary prostitute, but also to the unmarried woman who has intercourse with anyone other than her betrothed, to the adulteress, and to the widow who has intercourse that does not fulfill the laws of levirate marriage. Reflection on the use of the term in a feminist context increases awareness of the sexual double standard. In a patriarchal system, it is essential that wives be faithful to their husbands for a variety of reasons, one being the need for legitimate, easily identifiable male heirs. The fidelity of men to their wives, however, is often considered inessential or even undesirable. In order to avoid a situation in which men fulfill their sexual desire with other men's wives or daughters, a special class of women is needed: prostitutes. The image of the prostitute is then used to define and enforce a strict code of female dress and behavior.

It is difficult today to use the prostitute as a simple, unambiguous negative symbol for other reasons too. In Greek and Roman society, many prostitutes came to be such because they were abandoned as infants or captured in war and made slaves. Today many prostitutes are women who were sexually abused as children or victims of violence or incest. Poverty, lack of self-esteem, and other factors beyond personal choice and control often lead women to become prostitutes. Behind the symbolic use of prostitution is the positive value of fidelity. The challenge is to resymbolize that value in a way that expresses mutuality between men and women and does not blame the victims of the sexual double standard and sexual exploitation.

Not just the symbol of the prostitute, but all the feminine symbols of Revelation are ambiguous when viewed from the point of view of the desirability of mutuality between men and women, and of flexibility in the definition of male and female roles. In comparison with exclusively abstract theological language or with texts that use only masculine symbols, Revelation makes a positive contribution by using both masculine and feminine symbols to describe the heavenly world, God's interaction with the earthly world, and salvation in the new age. The particular forms of the feminine symbols, however, are limited and limiting for women. The major symbols are mother, prostitute and bride. These are all relational terms with the male at the center. The normative person is male. The hero is male. Women are defined in terms of their sexual and reproductive roles. The Mother of Revelation 12 is good, but she is hardly even protector and nourisher any more. She herself must be protected and nourished. She is almost totally dependent on the male high God; she must be rescued. A positive value expressed in the notion of the 'bride' is the cooperative relationship between men and women, but the image of the 'bride' in our culture is overlaid with sentiment and consumerism. Furthermore, 'bride' and 'prostitute' are two sides of a binary opposition that arises from a male perspective. This character makes the retrieval of the symbol 'bride' undesirable. What is needed is a resymbolization of male and female partnership in the daily tasks of living, as well as in the larger challenges that face our society and culture.

Jezebel Speaks: Naming the Goddesses in the Book of Revelation

Mary Ann Beavis

I warn every one who hears the words of the prophecy of this book: if any one adds to them, God will add to them the plagues described in this book, and if any one takes away from the words of the book of this prophecy, God will take away their share in the tree of life and in the holy city, which are described in this book. (Rev. 22.18–19)[1]

The End of the Bible

As the last book in the Christian Bible draws to a close, the prophet John utters a solemn warning that anyone who tampers with the words of his book will be punished by plague and eternal death. My students sometimes remind me that these words are at 'the end of the Bible', and that to raise the question of adding to or subtracting from the canon (as I sometimes do in class) is forbidden and dangerous. In answer, I explain that from a historical–exegetical perspective, these are merely the final words of one biblical book, the Apocalypse, placed at the end of the Christian Testament after a centuries-long process of canonical formation. To at least some students, this explanation is not satisfying; surely, someone is bound to insist, not only the writing of the biblical books but also the process of canonization (whatever it was) was divinely inspired. The irony that the sacred scripture of Christianity ends with words tantamount to a curse (cf. Deut. 28.58–68) goes uncriticized.

The Apocalyptist's effort to prevent the addition of further visionary material to the book evidences the anger and jealousy against other Christian teachers and prophets expressed in Rev. 2–3: the false apostles of Ephesus (2.2); the hated Nicolaitans (2.6, 15); the 'synagogue of Satan' in Smyrna (2.9; cf. 3.9); the members of the church at Pergamum who 'hold to the teaching of Balaam' (2.13–14); the Thyatirans who tolerate the teaching of 'the woman Jezebel' (2.20); the 'dead' members of the church at Sardis (3.1); the 'lukewarm' Laodiceans whom Christ threatens to spit out of his mouth (3.16). One cannot help but wonder whether the members of these communities heeded the prophet's warnings, or whether they persisted in the activities for which they were so harshly censured.

Admittedly, it is not quite accurate to say that Revelation 'ends' with John's imprecation; it is followed by a promise that the Lord is coming soon and an invocation of grace on 'everyone' (Rev. 22.21). Nevertheless, as an interpreter with a fundamentalist Christian upbringing – a background shared with some of my students, who cherish vivid apocalyptic beliefs – I cannot help feeling slightly threatened by the prospect of tampering with the content of Revelation by offering an interpretation that would profoundly offend the author, John of Patmos: an

---

1 Unless otherwise indicated, biblical quotations are from the Revised Standard Version (RSV).

exercise that threatens both to 'add to' and to 'take away from' the words of the book. In fact, my chapter in this anthology (much like the other chapters), informed by historical–critical biblical scholarship and feminist thealogy, amounts to a kind of sequel to Revelation, in that it is 'a work that follows another work and can be complete in itself and seen in relation to the former and also what follows it'.[2] What could be more brazen than deliberately flaunting John's solemn warning? The Apocalyptist's maledictions on 'the woman Jezebel', the Christian leader of Thyatira whose prophecies and teachings prompt the prophet to wish dreadful punishments upon her and her followers (Rev. 2.20–23a), would, no doubt, also be heaped upon me, not just by John, but by those who view critical or thealogical interpretation as 'rewriting the Bible'. I therefore must stand in solidarity with 'Jezebel' and the other members of the seven churches castigated by John, and offer an interpretation of the Apocalypse that would drive its author to want to throw me, with 'Jezebel', on a 'sickbed' (Rev. 2.21, RSV), a threat that the prophet John and his enthusiasts attribute to divine inspiration. I do this in the conviction that John's harsh and vindictive utterances are false prophecies and that the charism of Rev. 22.21 is a more authentic expression of the best in Christianity.

All the Goddesses of Revelation

One of the sins attributed to 'Jezebel' – like 'Balaam', not the real name of the prophet, but a nickname citing a notorious biblical villain who came to a violent end (Rev. 2:14; cf. 2 Kgs 9.30–37; Num. 31.8) – is her teaching that Christians may conscientiously eat 'food sacrificed to idols' (Rev. 2.20) and, perhaps, participate in pagan religious festivals associated with trade guilds.[3] Apart from the observation that this was a practice that even the apostle Paul tolerated, with reservations, as having a legitimate theological rationale – since 'no idol in the world really exists' and believers are no better or worse off for eating or not eating such foods (1 Cor. 8.4, 8) – it illustrates the multiple religious influences and dilemmas that shaped the theologies and experiences of early Christians. The prophetess's offensive teaching may simply have been that since the pagan gods have no objective existence, feasting in 'an idol's temple' (cf. 1 Cor. 8.10) is no offense against Christian monotheism. More than that, Jezebel's advice might have been an attempt to secure the safety of the Christians by giving the illusion that they are supporting the state and its gods (cf. 1 Pet. 1.17; Mk 12.17; Mt. 22.21; Lk. 20.25); her 'beguilements to immorality' (Rev. 2.20, 21) may simply be a rejection of the Apocalyptist's strong emphasis on celibacy and his manifest suspicion of women, whom he regards as a possible source of defilement for virgin men (Rev. 14.4).

Much to John's disgust (and perhaps to hers), his female prophetic rival might also have recognized as disguised goddesses the larger-than-life female figures that erupt out of the prophet's visionary experience – the Woman Clothed with the Sun

2 Tina Pippin, *Apocalyptic Bodies: The Biblical End of the World in Text and Image* (London/New York: Routledge, 1999), p. 1.

3 See Elisabeth Schüssler Fiorenza, *Revelation: Vision of a Just World* (Proclamation Commentaries; Minneapolis, MN: Fortress Press, 1991), p. 56. I use the term 'pagan' without any pejorative sense, but rather to refer to devotees of non-monotheistic religions.

(Rev. 12.1), the Earth (12.16), the Whore (17.1–6), and the Bride (19.7; 21.2, 9; 22.17) – since she, like John, lived in a world permeated with belief in and imagery of multiple male and female deities.

Naming the Goddesses

Biblical scholars have identified many elements from ancient Mediterranean mythology and astrology that underlie the symbolism of the Apocalypse.[4] In a book that has been characterized as profoundly misogynistic by some feminist interpreters,[5] and that is so uncompromisingly monotheistic, it is surprising that the female 'signs' (σημεῖα) witnessed by John, both positive and negative, resemble goddesses who would have been familiar to anyone living in first-century CE Asia Minor. For example, Elisabeth Schüssler Fiorenza observes that the pregnant 'Woman Clothed with the Sun' in Rev. 12.1–17 conjures a familiar, first-century image:

> The myth of the queen of heaven with the divine child was internationally known at the time of John. Variations appear in Babylonia, Egypt, Greece, Asia Minor, and especially in texts about astral religion. Elements of this myth are: the goddess and the divine child, the great red dragon and his enmity to mother and child, and the motif of the protection of the mother and child. . . . As in other versions of the myth, the dragon seeks the child not yet born in order to devour and kill him. The dragon therefore pursues the pregnant woman for the child she carries. In other forms of the myth, the woman is either carried away to give birth in a protected place or she gives birth in a miraculous way and escapes the onslaught of the dragon together with the newborn. In Revelation 12 the child is exalted to heaven while the woman is carried to the desert for the sake of her own protection.[6]

Two specific mythic narratives that have been connected with Revelation 12 are the Leto–Apollo–Python and the Isis–Horus–Typhon legends. A. Yarbro Collins concludes that Apocalypse offers a synthesis of the two:

> In Revelation 12 we seem to have a fusing of Leto and Isis traditions: such a combination is not surprising since analogous birth stories were associated with the two goddesses. The narrative of ch. 12 reflects the pattern of these myths, particularly the pattern of the Leto myth. The description of the woman reflects the typical image of Isis.[7]

---

4 E.g., Hermann Gunkel, *Schöpfung und Chaos in Urzeit und Endzeit: Eine religionsgeschichtliche Untersuchung über Gen 1 und Ap Joh 12* (Göttingen: Vandenhoeck und Ruprecht, 1895); Wilhelm Bousset, *Die Offenbarung Johannis* (Göttingen: Vandenhoeck und Ruprecht, 1906); Franz Boll, *Aus der Offenbarung Johannis: Hellenistische Studien zum Weltbilt des Apokalypse* (Amsterdam: Hakkert, 1964 [1914]); A. Yarbro Collins, *The Combat Myth in the Book of Revelation* (HDR, 9; Missoula, MT: Scholars Press, 1976); Bruce J. Malina, *On the Genre and Message of Revelation: Star Visions and Sky Journeys* (Peabody, MA: Hendrickson, 1995); Jacques M. Chevalier, *A Postmodern Revelation: Signs of Astrology and the Apocalypse* (Toronto: University of Toronto Press, 1997).

5 E.g., Tina Pippin, *Death and Desire: The Rhetoric of Gender in the Apocalypse of John* (Literary Currents in Biblical Interpretation; Louisville, KY: Westminster/John Knox Press, 1992); Catherine Keller, *Apocalypse Now and Then: A Feminist Guide to the End of the World* (Boston, MA: Beacon Press, 1996).

6 Schüssler Fiorenza, *Vision of a Just World*, p. 80.

7 Collins, *Combat Myth*, pp. 75–76.

Leto is the mother of Apollo and Artemis,[8] pursued by the serpent-dragon Python (also known as Drakaina, Drakōn, Echidna and Serpens), eager to devour the newborn gods.[9] Leto's twins would have been well known to 'Jezebel's' people, the Thyatirans, as Artemis Boreitene was the patron of that city, and she shared a shrine with her brother-consort Apollo Tyrimnaeus; their images appeared on the local coinage (see Figure 1).

Figure 1. Coin with head of Artemis Boreitene, Thyatiria, c. 222–268 CE. Photo courtesy of the Fitzwilliam Museum, Cambridge.

Isis is the great Egyptian goddess whose jealous brother-in-law, the crocodilian Seth–Typhon, stalks her in order to prevent the birth of her son, Horus.[10] In all three versions of the myth, the pregnant divine woman is saved by a powerful male deity: Leto by Boreas,[11] Isis by Ra, the Woman by God, who translates her newborn son to his celestial throne and prepares a place in the desert where the Woman is 'nourished for 1,260 days' (Rev. 12.5–6).[12] The rescue of the Woman and her son is followed by a heavenly battle between Michael and his angels against the Dragon and his hosts, who are cast down to earth (12.7–9). The Apocalyptist makes it clear that the

---

8 Colin J. Hemer, *The Letters to the Seven Churches of Asia in Their Local Setting* (JSNTSup, 11; Sheffield: JSOT Press, 1986), p. 118.

9 Hemer, *Letters*, pp. 63–65. For ancient versions of this myth, see Pausanius, *Guide to Greece* 10.6.5; Hyginus, *Fabulae* 53, 140; Ovid, *Metamorphoses* 1.434; Seneca, *Hercules Furens* 453. The monster is portrayed as female in some texts and as male in others.

10 Hemer, *Letters*, pp. 62–63; cf. Chevalier, *A Postmodern Revelation*, pp. 330–31. On the identification of Seth and Typhon, see Plutarch, *On Isis and Osiris* 41, 49, 62. Plutarch's work contains the most complete Greek version of the myth.

11 The monster's attack on Leto is later punished by Apollo, who kills the beast at Delphi (for ancient references, see n. 9 above).

12 To this mix should be added the myth of Perseus's rescue of Andromeda from the many-headed serpentine Hydra; all of these figures are immortalized in constellations.

Dragon (ὁ δράκων) is also 'that ancient Serpent (ὁ ὄφις ὁ ἀρχαῖος) who is called the Devil and Satan, the deceiver of the whole world' (v. 9).

The apparition of the star-crowned, sun-clad, moon-treading woman 'in the heavens' (Rev. 12.1) might also have been associated by the ancients with the constellation Virgo, which, according to Malina, was identified with many goddesses in John's time: 'Aphrodite, Isis, Dike, Demeter, Magna Mater, Eileithyia, Tyche, Pax, Atargatis or Dea Syria, Iuno [Venus] coelestis of the Carthaginians', but especially with Isis in Egypt.[13] Manilius's first-century CE astrological poem *Astronomica* (2.31) identifies her as Erigone, the daughter of Icarius, who hanged herself in grief over the death of her father and who was exalted to the stars for her filial devotion. However, an alternative myth of Virgo is that she is Astraea (Justitia), who dwelt on earth to live with human beings in the Golden and Silver Ages, but who flew to heaven when the corrupt Age of Bronze arrived (Aratus, *Phaenomena* 96–136). Manilius conflates Erigone with Justitia (Lady Justice) and predicts that 'she will produce a man to direct the laws of the state and the sacred code, one who will tend with reverence the hallowed temples of the gods' (*Astronomica* 4.544–46). Virgo is traditionally depicted as a winged maiden carrying a sheaf of wheat.[14] The ancient heavens were also populated with starry giant snakes and dragons: Typhon, Hydra, Scorpio, Serpens, Draco.[15] Malina identifies Scorpio, adjacent to Virgo in the zodiac, as the serpent-dragon of Revelation 12.[16] The pattern of Virgo/Justitia, imagined as a winged celestial woman adjacent to Scorpio, roughly fits the scene depicted in Rev. 12.1–6, especially if the Woman (about to give birth to the messiah) is identified with Israel (characterized by the quality of Justice), and the Dragon is aligned with Rome, as Scorpio is with Italy by some ancient astrologers.[17]

In Revelation, the 'great red dragon with seven heads and ten horns and seven diadems upon his head' (12.3) is aggressively masculine; explicitly called 'that ancient serpent . . . the Devil and Satan' (12.9), he is identified with the wily snake of the

---

13 Malina, *Genre and Message*, p. 159; Malina does not cite the primary sources of these identifications but refers the reader to André Le Boeuffle, *Les noms latins d'astres et constellations* (Paris: Belles Lettres, 1977), pp. 212–15.

14 See G. P. Goold, 'Introduction', in Manilius, *Astronomica* (trans. G. P. Goold; Cambridge, MA: Harvard/London: William Heinemann, 1976), p. xxv, citing Ptolemy, *Syntaxis mathematica* 7.5.

15 Goold, 'Introduction,' pp. 159–62. The ancient signs of the zodiac and other constellations were very similar to those recognized today; see Lester Ness, 'Astrology and Judaism in Late Antiquity' (PhD dissertation; Oxford, OH: Miami University, 1990), ch. 2 (http://www.smoe.org/arcana/diss.html, accessed 21 January 2009); Tamsyn Barton, *Ancient Astrology* (London/New York: Routledge, 1994), pp. 18–63; see also the summary of Manilius's first-century CE astrological poem *Astronomica*, pp. xxiii–xxx. The ancient astronomer Ptolemy held that the prominence of serpent-like constellations made death by snake-bite more likely; see Barton, *Ancient Astrology*, p. 168, citing Ptolemy, *Tetrabiblos* 4.9.200.

16 Malina, *Genre and Message*, pp. 160–62. Scorpio is mentioned immediately after Virgo by Manilius (*Astronomica* 2.31). If the dragon/serpent/Satan/Devil is associated with Rome, the ancient association of Scorpio with Italy may be relevant here (see Malina, *Genre and Message*, p. 103, citing Franz Boll, *Aus der Offenbarung Johannis*). However, it should be noted that ancient correspondences between zodiacal signs and nations were not constant; Manilius has a different list, in which Italy corresponds to Libra (*Astronomica* 4.744–817; noted by Malina, *Genre and Message*, p. 103; see also Barton, *Ancient Astrology*, p. 182).

17 See note 16.

Garden of Eden (Gen. 3.1–15).[18] The serpent of Genesis, of course, is not Satan, although the conflation of the snake and Satan was known in early Christian interpretation (Rom. 16.20; cf. 2 Cor. 11.3, 14). Long before Genesis was written, the serpent was a symbol associated with goddesses, notably the Canaanite/Syrian goddess Qedeshet.[19] In Genesis, the ancient serpent is demoted to the status of a sly trickster;[20] in Revelation, the snake is demonized into the incarnation of ancient, cosmic evil (12.9; 20.2). Catherine Keller cites the opinion of many feminist theologians that the vilification of the serpent reflects a process that had started many centuries before in Ancient Middle Eastern mythology:

> At the end of time, the dragon in a cosmic tantrum knocks down the stars. But the dragon was there before the stars were up. It was resting in liquid latency, as the salty abyss, the *tehom*, out of which all things were made. In Genesis the dragon remains anonymous, masked as the 'face of the deep'. In Genesis 2 [*sic*], the noun *tehom* translates the Sumerian *tiamat* – the creator-mother-dragon of the *Enuma Elish*.[21]

The idea that the *Enuma Elish* portrays Tiamat as a dragon or serpent is contested by scholars of the Ancient Middle East. Many scholars of the early twentieth century, such as Friedrich Delitzsch, in his classic *Babel and Bible*, interpreted the Sumerian goddess Tiamat as a serpentine monster.[22] Alexander Heidel reflects a more recent consensus when he argues that simply because Tiamat is said to have given birth to monster-serpents (Tablet I.132–40), this does not mean she was envisioned as a serpent herself, since she bore good and benevolent gods as well as non-ophidian monsters.[23] Charles Penglase agrees that Tiamat is not portrayed as a serpent in the *Enuma Elish*, but he notes that monstrous serpents are closely associated with the goddess as a leading feature of Marduk's battle with her.[24] In support of the

---

18 For ancient Jewish identifications of the serpent of Eden with Satan, see J. Kugel, *The Bible As It Was* (Cambridge/London: Belknap Press, 1997), pp. 72–75; cf. *1 Enoch* 69.6; *4 Macc.* 18.7–8; *2 Enoch* 31.4–6.

19 See James M. Efird, 'Serpent', in Paul Achtemeier (gen. ed.), *Harper's Bible Dictionary* (San Francisco, CA: HarperSanFrancisco, 1985), p. 928; see also Robert M. Good, 'Asherah', *Harper's Bible Dictionary*, pp. 74–75; and Steve Wiggins, 'The Myth of Asherah: Lion Lady and Serpent Goddess', *Ugarit-Forschungen* 23 (1992), pp. 383–94 The serpent is not a uniformly positive symbol in antiquity, nor is it associated only with goddesses. Goddesses associated with serpents include: Athena, whose shield is decorated with them; Hygeia, who, like her father Asclepius, carries a serpent-entwined staff; the snaky-haired gorgon Medusa; the Punic Tanit ('She of the Serpent'); and several Egyptian goddesses (Renenutet, Meretseger, Wadjet). Most relevant to the discussion of Revelation, Python (*Pytho*), the great serpent who attacks Leto, is female and associated with divination. Male deities (e.g., Hermes, Asclepius, Seth–Typhon) are also associated with snakes or portrayed in serpentine form.

20 Susan Niditch, 'Genesis', in Carol A. Newsom and Sharon H. Ringe (eds), *The Women's Bible Commentary* (London: SPCK/Louisville: Westminster/John Knox Press, 1992), pp. 3–33 (14).

21 Keller, *Apocalypse Now and Then*, pp. 68–69. The noun *tehom* actually appears in Gen. 1.2.

22 Friedrich Delitzsch, *Babel and Bible* (Chicago, IL: University of Chicago Press, 1906), p. 159; Hermann Gunkel, *Genesis* (Göttingen: Vandenhoeck and Ruprecht, 1917), p. 126; L. W. King, *The Seven Tablets of Creation* (London: Luzak & Co., 1902), p. lxxi n. 1.

23 Alexander Heidel, *The Babylonian Genesis* (2nd edn, Chicago, IL/London: University of Chicago Press, 1951), p. 83.

24 Charles Penglase, *Greek Myths and Mesopotamia: Parallels and Influence in the Homeric Hymns and Hesiod* (London/New York: Routledge, 1994), p. 103.

identification of Tiamat as a serpent or dragon, *Enuma Elish* V. 59 relates that in the midst of the battle, Marduk 'twisted the tail' of the goddess, indicating, at least, that she was imagined theriomorphically.[25] Heidel suggests that like other Mesopotamian goddesses (Ishtar, Ningal, Ninlil and Ninsun), Tiamat was imagined as a wild cow.[26] However, it is plausible that a sea goddess (who gives birth to giant serpents, as well as to other monsters and deities) would be understood as a sea serpent or dragon, rather than as a land animal. Furthermore, in the Greek version of the Tiamat–Marduk myth, Apollo's defeat of Python (in Greek, the feminine *Pytho*), the monster is serpentine and (usually) female.[27] The Apocalyptist's recasting of the Greek version of the myth can be diagrammed as follows:

Leto	the Woman Clothed with the Sun
Apollo and Artemis	the royal son of the Woman
Pytho	the serpent-dragon-devil-Satan
Boreas (sent by Zeus)	Michael (sent by God)
Apollo defeats Python	the serpent-dragon is consigned to 'a lake of fire and sulfur', presumably at the command of Christ (Rev. 20.2, 10)

The female archetype of the serpent-dragon most proximate to Revelation, then, is not the mother-goddess Tiamat slaughtered by her son, the upstart warrior-god Marduk, but her Greek mythological counterpart, the monstrous Python, slain by Leto's son Apollo (sometimes aided by Artemis). Thus, although the identification of Tiamat as a serpentine goddess may be questionable, Keller's assertion that Revelation 12 marks a stage in the 'degradation of the goddess and the demonization of the serpent' that is present in Genesis 2–3 and that 'presupposes a widespread Middle Eastern revolt against cosmic mothers' has some validity.[28]

Tiamat, mother of serpents, becomes the Greek Python, who, like her Babylonian prototype, is slain by a male hero.[29] Unlike Marduk, Apollo kills to avenge his mother, a minor deity. In the Leto–Python–Apollo myth, the primal goddess is demoted to the role of damsel in distress, and Hera, the instigator of the attack on Leto, is the divine villain of the piece, a jealous wife easily foiled by Zeus and his solar son. Revelation, in turn, pits 'that ancient serpent', Python in satanic (and astrological) disguise, against the heavenly Woman, about to give birth to a male

25 See J. B. Geyer, 'Twisting Tiamat's Tail: A Mythological Interpretation of Isaiah XIII 5 and 8', *VT* 37 (1987), pp. 164–79.

26 Heidel, *Babylonian Genesis*, p. 86.

27 Penglase, *Greek Myths*, p. 83.

28 Keller, *Apocalypse Now and Then*, p. 69. For an account of the marginalization of goddesses in the Ancient Middle East by an Assyriologist/Sumerologist, see Tikva Frymer-Kensky, *In the Wake of the Goddesses* (New York: The Free Press, 1992), p. 70–89.

29 On the influence of Babylonian mythology on Greek myths, see Penglase, *Greek Myths*; on the knowledge of Babylonian creation myths in the Greek world, see Heidel, *Babylonian Genesis*, pp. 75–81.

child, who, like Marduk, Apollo and the son of Justitia, is destined to rule as a pre-eminent male deity (12.5). In Rev. 20.10, the prophet triumphs over the completion of the ancient matricide/deacide when the satanic serpent is thrown, with the beast and the 'false prophet' (cf. Rev. 2.20), into the sulfurous, fiery lake where s/he will suffer in torment 'day and night for ever and ever' (like her masculine counterpart, Seth–Typhon, banished to the Serbonian lake by Horus [Herodotus 2.144; 3.9]).

The next divine female to emerge in Revelation's kaleidoscopic and syncretic imagery is the Whore, Babylon, 'arrayed in purple and scarlet, and bedecked with gold and jewels and pearls, holding in her hand a golden cup full of abominations and the impurities of her fornication' (17.4). The Great Whore is seated upon 'many waters' and 'sitting on a scarlet beast which was full of blasphemous names, and it had seven heads and ten horns' (17.1, 3); the seven heads of the beast are 'seven mountains on which the woman is seated' (17.9). The voracious Babylon is a cipher for her younger sister Roma, a city goddess depicted on a sestertius minted during the reign of Vespasian as 'seated on Rome's seven hills, with the river Tiber running below'.[30] Henry S. Robinson describes the depiction of the goddess on the coin in more detail:

> The reverse represents Roma seated right upon a rocky mass divided into seven 'hills' which rise in part behind her; she wears Amazon costume (short tunic) with the right breast bared, and a crested helmet; her right elbow is supported on one of the high 'hills' at her back, her right hand touches the back of her head; in her left hand she holds a *parazonium* (or an eagle-crested scepter) which is supported upon her left knee; her right foot is thrust forward, the left drawn back; in front, toward the left, she-wolf and twins; at right, Tiber Pater, semi-recumbent, to left, in field, at left and right, S C; below, in exergue, ROMA.[31]

In Revelation, the Roman goddess becomes a monstrous mother, like Tiamat, associated with bestial offspring and violence: 'mother of harlots and of earth's abominations . . . drunk with the blood of the saints and the blood of the martyrs of Jesus' (Rev. 17:5–6). In the Hebrew Bible, even the nation of Israel can be personified as a prostitute or adulteress when 'she', like the human prophetess 'Jezebel', strays from her divine husband, YHWH, and follows other gods (Lev. 20.5; 17.7; Deut. 31.11; Judg. 2.17; 8.27, 33; Hos. 1–3; cf. Rev. 2.20).[32]

Unlike other Ancient Middle Eastern gods, the biblical YHWH has no real

---

30 Susan R. Garrett, 'Revelation', in Carol A. Newsom and Sharon H. Ringe (eds), *The Women's Bible Commentary* (Louisville, KY: Westminster/John Knox Press, 1992), pp. 377–82 (380); cf. Chevalier, *Postmodern Revelation*, pp. 164, 348. For a photo of the sestertius of Vespasian, see Henry S. Robinson, 'A Monument of Roma at Corinth', *Hesperia* 4 (1974), pp. 470–84 (p. 84, Plate 106a). Robinson's article describes the excavation of a monument at Corinth that he identifies as a statue of the goddess Roma seated on the seven hills of Rome.

31 Robinson, 'Monument', p. 482. An image of the coin can be viewed at: http://biblelight.net/vatican.htm (accessed 19 January 2009).

32 Phyllis Bird, '"To Play the Harlot": An Inquiry into an Old Testament Metaphor', in Peggy L. Day (ed.), *Gender and Difference in Ancient Israel* (Minneapolis, MN: Augsburg Fortress Press, 1989), pp. 75–94.

goddess-wife; his only female companionship (other than the figure of Wisdom [Prov. 8.22–31; Wis. 7.22–8]) is in the form of his metaphorical, and sometimes adulterous wife, Israel.[33] Here, the whorishness of Israel is projected onto Babylon/ Roma, and YHWH's wayward wife is born again as the imperial city's foil, the Heavenly Jerusalem, transformed, like the errant Gomer of Hosea, into a fitting bride, but not before she has been consigned to the wilderness by her husband, Christ the Lamb, a stand-in for the God of Israel (Hos. 2.3–13; Rev. 12.6, 14).

The Great Goddess Unearthed

The unnamed Woman Clothed with the Sun loses her heavenly status and falls to the earth once she has produced the divine heir, who is caught up to the throne of God for safekeeping (12.5). The woman flees to the wilderness, where she is nourished for 'a time, times and half a time' in a place prepared for her by God (12.6, 14). The identity of the Divine Woman is further unveiled; she is indeed YHWH's adulterous but now rehabilitated wife, Israel, once rescued from Egypt and Pharaoh 'on eagles' wings' (Exod. 19.4; Deut. 32.11), now given 'the two wings of the great eagle' (12.14) for her flight from the serpent.[34] In the seer's shifting, mythopoeic vision, she will re-emerge, transformed into 'the holy city the new Jerusalem', decked out 'like a bride' for her divine husband/son, the Lamb (21.2, 9). The polluted whore-goddess Babylon/Roma, whose destruction has been depicted in loving detail (17.16–18.24), is supplanted by another divine lady,[35] the bejewelled Bride, who is so pure that 'nothing unclean shall enter her, nor any one who practices abomination or falsehood, but only those who are written in the Lamb's book of life' (21.27).

But, as Pippin observes, the entry of the faithful into the Bride Jerusalem amounts to a mass penetration:

> The Bride is a beautiful virgin who marries the Lamb and becomes the heavenly city. The virginal 144,000 male followers, who represent the whole number of the pure and faithful, are allowed to enter the Bride. This scene is disturbing because the imagery is that of mass intercourse. After the holy war all the blessed (men) partake in a double ecstasy: killing the enemy woman and sharing the victor's spoils of war. Women in this narrative are not safe. They are killed or 'prepared as a bride adorned for her husband' (Rev. 21.2).[36]

33 See G. Baumann, 'Connected by Marriage, Adultery, and Violence: The Prophetic Marriage Metaphor in the Book of the Twelve and the Major Prophets', in *SBLSP* 38 (1999), pp. 552–69. On the pre-exilic worship of Asherah as consort of YHWH, see William G. Dever, *Did God Have a Wife? Archaeology and Folk Religion in Ancient Israel* (Grand Rapids, MI: Eerdmans, 2005).

34 Collins (*Combat Myth*, p. 66) interprets Rev. 12.14 as referring to the Woman's rescue by an eagle, but the wording of the verse (καὶ ἐδόθησαν τῇ γυναικὶ αἱ δύο πτέρυγες τοῦ ἀετοῦ τοῦ μεγάλου; 'and the woman was given the two wings of the great eagle') implies that *she* becomes winged.

35 Possibly, the image of Babylon/Rome as a prostitute echoes the Babylonian goddess Ishtar's patronage of prostitutes (cf. Herodotus 1.199).

36 Tina Pippin, 'The Revelation to John', in Elisabeth Schüssler Fiorenza (ed.), *Searching the Scriptures: A Feminist Introduction and Commentary* (2 vols; New York: Crossroad, 1994), vol. 2, pp. 109–30 (119).

No longer wearing her astral adornments (for there is no more need for lamplight or sun),[37] the Bride glows in the primeval light of God and the Lamb, enveloping the servants of God eternally (22.1–5).

Goddess feminists Monica Sjöö and Barbara Mor interpret city-building as a strategy of conquest over the archetypal goddess, the Great Mother:

> This worldwide attack and conquest of the cosmic serpent is called in patriarchal story the 'victory over the waters', through which emerged 'stable forms' and the 'organization of the world'. That is, the male political world. The Rock of Jerusalem reached deep into the subterranean waters (Tehom) it was said; the Jerusalem Temple is situated directly above her, its Holy Rock containing 'the Mouth of Tehom'. Babylon was built above the 'Gate of Apsu', the serpent waters before creation, Apsu the other half of Tiamat. Everywhere, this mythic rite of building the holy male city on the conquered body of the Mother-Serpent is enacted as the *origin* of patriarchy. The sun-worshipping pharaohs of later Egypt slay the dragon Apophys, Apollo slays Gaia's Python. The Greek hero Perseus slays the Amazonian Medusa – who is described as three-headed (the Triple Goddess) with snakes writhing from her three heads. St. George slays the dragon in England; even St. Patrick must drive the snake from the snakeless Ireland. And in Hebrew Genesis, the serpent is doomed by the War God Yahweh to be forever the enemy of the human race: to be crushed under our heels, and to give back to us only poison. In Christian prophecy, in Revelation 12–21.1, the final extinction of the dragon is promised with a king-messiah who kills the watery cosmic snake, and then takes over the world throne unchallenged: 'and there was no more sea'. This event is prefigured in Psalms 74.13: 'Thou breakest the heads of the dragons in the water.' The consistency of all these myths is commensurate with their reality.[38]

While this chain of associations is thealogical, not historical–critical, the ancient Babylonian myth of the defeat of the sea-goddess Tiamat, mother of the gods and of 'monster serpents sharp of tooth and not sparing the fang' (*Enuma Elish* II.20–21),[39] does reverberate through the Leto–Apollo–Python myth and its recasting in Revelation 12. However, even in the closing scenes of Revelation, the vanquished Goddess takes her place. The divine city (πόλις) is personified as female; within the boundaries of the Bride Jerusalem, even God and the Lamb, radiant and glorious though they may be, are forever enthroned (Rev. 22.1). Perhaps, as C. G. Jung intuited, she is Dame Wisdom, a manifestation of the 'Hebrew Goddess', *Chochmah/ Sophia*,[40] portrayed in Proverbs as a woman of the city (Prov. 8.1–9.6). Despite his best efforts, the seer cannot completely erase the idolatry that he so vigorously condemns: traces of the goddesses can be discerned. In the new creation, there is no sea (Rev. 21.1), the abode of Tiamat, goddess of the bitter waters, but the crystalline

---

37　Keller asserts that the verbal form of the word 'apocalypse' *(apokalyptein)* refers to 'the marital stripping of a veiled virgin' (Keller, *Apocalypse Now and Then*, p. 1), but she does not refer to the ancient source of this etymology. On the Jewish custom of the veiling and unveiling of brides, see Mendell Lewittes, *Jewish Marriage: Rabbinic Law, Legend, and Custom* (Northvale, NJ/London: Jason Aronson, 1994), p. 88 (cf. *Ketubot* 16b).

38　Monica Sjöö and Barbara Mor, *The Great Cosmic Mother: Rediscovering the Religion of the Earth* (San Francisco, CA: Harper & Row, 1987), pp. 250–51.

39　Translation in Heidel, *Babylonian Genesis*, p. 26.

40　C. J. Jung, *Answer to Job* (London: Routledge & Kegan Paul, 1954), p. 126. The phrase 'Hebrew Goddess' is from Raphael Patai, *The Hebrew Goddess* (New York: KTAV, 1967).

stream that gushes forth from beneath the throne of God and the Lamb recalls Tiamat's epithet Mother Huber ('Mother River'; *Enuma Elish* I.132).[41] The tree of life, famously associated with the goddess Asherah, grows on either side of the river, bearing medicinal leaves 'for the healing of the nations' (Rev. 22.2; cf. 2.7).[42] However, like the body of Tiamat, split apart by her son to create the cosmos,[43] the New Jerusalem, Bride of the Lamb, is dormant, encompassing the new creation of her Son (21.1–3).

Despite the prominence of divine females in Revelation (the Sun-Clad Woman, the demonized and masculinized Serpent, the Great Harlot Babylon/Roma, YHWH's cosmic Bride), their mythological sources are carefully suppressed; Isis–Leto, Tiamat and Roma are never named; even the heavenly Jerusalem is only 'like a bride' (Rev. 21.3). As Chevalier observes:

> In the case of Revelation, allegorical connections erected between spirits and stars are based on the principle of approximation, not of consubstantiation. While logocentrism can use astrological imageries to unfold its doctrine of history and spirituality, it cannot afford to be confused with astralism and the deification of visible rulers of heaven and the earth.[44]

Even the prophetess 'Jezebel' is not given her proper name; she is nicknamed after an infamous villain and enemy of the Israelite prophet Elijah (1 Kgs 16.31; 19.1–3), who is himself the typological counterpart of John of Patmos. Both Jezebels are unrepentant 'idolaters' cursed to destruction – along with their 'children' – by prophets (1 Kgs 21.23; 2 Kgs 9.30–37; 10.1–17; Rev. 2.22–23a). In fact, neither Jezebel is known by her true name, for as Karla Bohmbach points out, 'As vocalized in the MT the name can be read as either "islands of dung" or "no dung", generally recognized as parodies of the consonantal form meaning "no nobility" or "Where is the prince?"'[45]

Nonetheless, the prophet makes one slip and names the greatest and most ancient goddess in the Greek pantheon in what Jung calls 'the thoroughly pagan remark'

---

41 Penglase (*Greek Myths*, p. 103) notes that both Tiamat and Python have a riverine aspect; Tiamat in her guise as Mother Huber; Python with the River Pleistos at Delphi (Callimachus, *Hymn to Delos* 92).

42 On the association of Asherah with trees, see Good, 'Asherah', pp. 74–75. On trees as sites of popular worship in ancient Israel, see Deut. 12.2; 1 Kgs 14.23; 2 Kgs 16.4; 17.10; 2 Chron. 28.4; Isa. 57.5; Jer. 2.20; 3.6, 13; Ezek. 6.13. On the role of the sacred tree in the cult of Artemis at Ephesus, see Hemer, *Letters*, pp. 41–47. Hemer argues that the Apocalyptist deliberately used the biblical tree of life as a foil for the tree shrine of Artemis in Ephesus, described by Callimachus (*Hymn to Artemis* 237–39) and Dionysius Pereigetes (826–29); Hemer notes that D. G. Hogarth, who excavated the lowest levels of the Artemesium at Ephesus, found remains he identified with this tree shrine (p. 45). He further observes (p. 47) that 'the tree by which the goddess was born, an olive, survived there in the reign of Tiberius. The place continued sacred, and was still in Strabo's day the scene of an ancient festival. Its temples still contained ancient wooden images' (Tacitus, *Annals* 3.61; Strabo, *Geography* 14.1.20).

43 See Heidel, *Babylonian Genesis*, p. 9: Marduk 'divided the colossal body of Ti'âmat into two parts to create the universe'.

44 Chevalier, *Postmodern Revelation*, p. 362.

45 Karla G. Bohmbach, 'Jezebel', in David Noel Freedman (ed.), *Eerdmans Dictionary of the Bible* (Grand Rapids, MI: Eerdmans, 2000), pp. 713–14 (713). The latter was probably her real name.

of Rev. 12.16: 'And the Earth helped the woman'.[46] The word 'earth' (γῆ) occurs frequently in Revelation (77 times in all), most often in its secular meaning of the soil, the dry land, or the planet and its inhabitants – the opposite of heaven. But in Rev. 12.13–17, the ancient Mother Goddess (Γῆ, *Gaia*) comes to life and rescues the heavenly Woman, banished to the wilderness, from a flood sent by the Serpent, thrown down to the earth by Michael and his angels: 'But Γῆ came to the help of the woman, and Γῆ opened her mouth and swallowed the river which the Dragon had poured from his mouth' (Rev. 12.16).[47] The pagan roots of the prophet's vision are unmasked, and the Mother of all the gods and goddesses is inadvertently named by the militantly monotheistic seer. Seemingly oblivious to the heavenly battle waged by the masculine sky-gods, she becomes the savior of the beleaguered Mother of the Son.

The Prophet and the Prophetess

In *Answer to Job*, C. G. Jung offered a psychological explanation both for the violence of John's apocalyptic visions and for the mythological motifs that are so evocative of the paganism he despised. Working from the tradition that John of Patmos is also the author of the Johannine epistles, Jung interprets the hatred and vengefulness of the Apocalypse as the 'shadow side' of the theologian of love (1 John 4.7–21):

> The 'revelation' was experienced by an early Christian who, as a leading light of the community, presumably had to live an exemplary life and demonstrate to his flock the Christian virtues of true faith, humility, patience, devotion, selfless love, and denial of all worldly desires. In the long run this can become too much, even for the righteous. Irritability, bad moods, and outbursts of affect are the classical symptoms of chronic virtuousness.[48]

Jung's insight that the Apocalyptist's visions are sublimations of his fierce resentment of rival teachers and adamant rejection of paganism is compelling: 'Who hates the Nicolaitans? Who thirsts for vengeance and even wants to throw "the woman Jezebel" on a sickbed and strike her children dead? Who cannot have enough of bloodthirsty fantasies?'[49] However, Jung's conclusion that the 'brutal impact' of the prophet's visions does not indicate severe psychosis, but an authentic experience of the fearsome side of God,[50] is unsatisfying.

---

46 Jung, *Answer to Job*, p. 131; cf. Pippin, 'Revelation to John', p. 118; Chevalier, *Postmodern Revelation*, p. 354.

47 Chevalier notes: 'A similar story tells of the dragon [Python] raising the waters against Leto so that she could not bear Apollo, and then the earth rescuing the mother by letting the island of Delos rise above the flood' (*Postmodern Revelation*, p. 330). Chevalier, however, does not cite an ancient source for this story. In Hyginus's *Fabulae* 140, Neptune is said to have protected her from Python on the isle of Ortygia (Delos) by causing it to be covered with waves, while Latona (Leto), clinging to an olive tree, gave birth to her twins.

48 Jung, *Answer to Job*, p. 143.

49 Jung, *Answer to Job*, p. 144.

50 Jung, *Answer to Job*, p. 145.

In the letters to the seven churches, John's most vicious threats are reserved for 'Jezebel' and her followers; the word so discreetly translated as 'sickbed' (κλίνη) in several prominent translations of the Bible (e.g., RSV, NAB, ESV, NKJV), simply means bed,[51] and evokes an image of the rape of the 'adulteress', whose accursed 'children' are no doubt to be identified with her disciples.[52] In the ensuing visions, the prophet's obsession with the πορνεία (prostitution/fornication) of the woman Jezebel (2.20–21), closely associated with her idolatrous tendencies, takes on cosmic proportions, irrupting forth in the distorted and disguised images of divine women, mothers, virgins and whores. As Tina Pippin observes:

> In all of these metaphors of the religious body as female goddesses are captured and subdued and molded (or in Apoc. 12 exiled) to fit male fantasies of the ideal female. The Bride is adorned as counter to the stripping and burning of the Whore. The marriage of the Bride counters the death/funeral of the Whore. The ancient goddess in all her characteristic diversity of motherhood, erotic sexuality, virginity, and as warrior, justice giver, caretaker, creatrix of nature and arts, and destroyer is segmented into these binary oppositions of good and evil, whore and virgin mother.[53]

Much to John's disgust, the early Christian woman he so detested probably continued her ministry of teaching and preaching in Thyatira while he remained imprisoned on Patmos. Just as the Apocalyptist slips by writing the divine name Γῆ (12.16), he unconsciously expresses his intense resentment and jealousy of the 'woman/wife [γυναῖκα] Jezebel' – who, like Babylon/Rome and like YHWH's unfaithful spouse Israel, is a prostitute/adulteress and idolater – by projecting her divine archetypes onto the cosmos, casting them down and transforming them into tame feminine stereotypes of Mother (Revelation 12), Whore (Revelation 17) and chaste Bride (Revelation 21–22).

The Goddess and the New Millennium

Jung observed that the aptness of John's vision of a violent and turbulent future could not be denied in the light of the events of the second half of the twentieth century:

> The four sinister horsemen, the threatening tumult of trumpets, and the brimming vials of wrath are still waiting; already the atom bomb hangs over us like the sword of Damocles, and

---

51 Today's NIV has 'I will make her very sick', as does the WE; the NASB has 'bed of sickness'. Metzger notes that there are several textual variants intended to intensify Jezebel's punishment, including *astheneian* (1597 and cop[sa]) and 'several (Latin) manuscripts known to Primasius read *luctum* ("sorrow, affliction")' (Bruce M. Metzger, *A Textual Commentary on the Greek New Testament* [London/New York: United Bible Societies, 1971], p. 733). These obscure glosses do not account for the translators' choice of 'sickbed' in so many English versions, but perhaps they are early attempts to disguise the sexual connotations of the threat to the prophetess.

52 Josephine Massyngberde Ford observes that 'the Greek word here can mean a bed or sickbed' (*Revelation* [AB, 38; Garden City, NY: Doubleday, 1975], p. 403), but states her preference for Ramsay's translation of the term as 'dining couch' (W. M. Ramsay, *The Letters to the Seven Churches of Asia* [London: Hodder & Stoughton, 1904], p. 352).

53 Pippin, *Death and Desire*, p. 79.

behind that lurk the incomparably more terrible possibilities of chemical warfare, which would eclipse even the horrors described in the Apocalypse.[54]

In this third millennium, the added spectre of ecological disruption – so gleefully forecast in Rev. 8.6–9.21 – is one of the 'new narratives of world destruction' listed by Rosemary Radford Ruether in *Gaia and God*: overpopulation and poverty, shortages of food and energy, global climate change and pollution, species extinction, militarism and war.[55] Ironically, it is not the solitary sky father but the old Mother Goddess Γῆ/*Gaia* who is often invoked for inspiration in the face of these 'horrors'. Notably, the Gaia Hypothesis, an ecological perspective that conceptualizes Planet Earth as a self-regulatory living organism, has been adopted by both scientists and environmental activists.[56] But, as Ruether observes, God and Gaia, two metaphors for the divine, which she classifies as covenantal (God) and the sacramental (Gaia), *both* originate in nature:

> One speaks from the mountaintops in the thunderous masculine tones of 'thou shalt' and 'thou shalt not'. It is the voice of power and law, but speaking (at its most authentic) on behalf of the weak, as a mandate to protect the powerless and to restrain the power of the mighty. There is another voice, one that speaks from the intimate heart of matter. It has long been silenced by the masculine voice, but today is finding again her own voice. This is the voice of Gaia. Her voice does not translate into laws or intellectual knowledge, but beckons us into communion.[57]

It should be emphasized that Ruether, as a Christian theologian, seeks to integrate these two 'voices', which, she explains, 'are both our own', and are both necessary for the health of the planet:

> We need both of these holy voices. We cannot depend on volunteerism alone to save rain forests and endangered species, set limits to the exploitation of animals and sanction abusers. . . . But, without the second voice, our laws have no heart, no roots in compassion and fellow feeling. They fail to foster a motivating desire for biophilic living.[58]

---

54 Jung, *Answer to Job*, p. 146.

55 Rosemary Radford Ruether, *Gaia and God: An Ecofeminist Theology of Earth Healing* (San Francisco, CA: HarperSanFrancisco, 1992), pp. 86–114.

56 See James E. Lovelock, *Gaia: A New Look at Life on Earth* (Oxford/New York: Oxford University Press, 1979); idem, *The Ages of Gaia: A Biography of Our Living Earth* (New York: Norton, 1988); Allan Hunt Badiner, *Dharma Gaia: A Harvest of Essays in Buddhism and Ecology* (Berkeley, CA: Parallax, 1990); Allan S. Miller, *Gaia Connections: An Introduction to Ecology, Ecoethics, and Economics* (Savage, MD: Rowman and Littlefield, 1991); John R. Gribbin, *Hothouse Earth: The Greenhouse Effect and Gaia* (New York: Grove Weidenfeld, 1990); Stephen B. Scharper, 'The Gaia Hypothesis: Implications for a Christian Political Theology of the Environment', *Cross Currents* 2 (1994), pp. 207–21; Daniel T. Spencer, *Gay and Gaia: Ethics, Ecology and the Erotic* (Cleveland, OH: Pilgrim Press, 1996); Lynn Margulis and Dorion Sagan, *Slanted Truths: Essays on Gaia, Symbiosis, and Evolution* (New York: Copernicus, 1997); Tyler Volk, *Gaia's Body: Toward a Physiology of Earth* (New York: Copernicus, 1998); Grant H. Potts, 'Imagining Gaia: Perspectives and Prospects on Gaia, Science and Religion', *Ecotheology* 81 (2003), pp. 30–49; Stephen H. Schneider, *Scientists Debate Gaia: The Next Century* (Cambridge, MA: MIT Press, 2004); Anne Primavesi, *Gaia's Gift: Earth, Ourselves and God after Copernicus* (London: Routledge, 2004).

57 Ruether, *Gaia and God*, p. 254.

58 Ruether, *Gaia and God*, p. 255.

She also acknowledges that there are elements of both 'covenantal tradition' and 'sacramental tradition' grounded in the Jewish and Christian scriptures that are conducive to environmental healing.[59] The 'Goddess' she invokes is not simply the opposite of the 'God' of the western monotheistic traditions;[60] by Gaia, Ruether does not mean the primal deity of Greek mythology,[61] but the ecological metaphor formulated by James Lovelock and Lynn Margulis that envisions the earth as a living, interdependent system and that envisions evolution working for the good of all species.[62] However, the kind of reintegration of the 'masculine' and 'feminine' concepts of the sacred (and even of the monotheistic and pagan traditions) called for by many feminist ecotheologians is the kind of 'syncretism' so abhorred by John of Patmos.[63] Perhaps the prophetess of Thyatira, with her lenient attitude towards residual pagan practices among her disciples, would approve.

Postscript

Jezebel

slandered as heathen
reviled as whore
seen huddled in the night
long nails idly tapping
clicking against the pavement
crouched on the curb
cars and rain and snow and men
pass before you like a dream
splashing blood on your feet

away on the mountain top
where they plotted against you
away on the hills

59 Ruether, *Gaia and God*, pp. 204–53.

60 Ruether, *Gaia and God*, p. 247. As Elizabeth A. Johnson has shown (in *She Who Is: The Mystery of God in Feminist Theological Discourse* [New York: Crossroad, 1992], pp. 69, 136, 166, 183, 210), the involvement of the divine in creation, especially through the metaphor of Woman-Wisdom, is prominent in the biblical tradition, especially in the Jewish books of Proverbs, Sirach, Wisdom and Baruch, in which *Chochmah/Sophia* is imaged as both female and powerful: 'She reaches mightily from one end of the earth to the other, and she orders all things well' (Wis. 8.1).

61 Somewhat surprisingly, none of the Greek myths associated with Γῆ/Gaia is invoked in *Gaia and God*. The Greek creation story that Ruether cites (and rejects) is from Plato's *Timaeus* (pp. 22–26), noting its deleterious influence on Christianity (pp. 26–31). The Gaia of Greek mythology is a powerful primal goddess, mother of the Titans and Titanides, who in addition to her nurturing qualities (see the *Homeric Hymn to Earth*) is as powerful and tempestuous as her Mesopotamian counterpart Tiamat.

62 See Potts, 'Imagining Gaia', pp. 34, 38. Even the Neopagan Oberon Zell-Ravenheart does not conceptualize Gaia as 'an entity already possessing consciousness, as critical writers assume religious advocates of Gaia would argue, but rather an entity that has the potential for consciousness' (Potts, 'Imagining Gaia', p. 39, citing Oberon Zell-Ravenheart, 'Theagenesis: The Birth of the Goddess', *Green Egg* 30, 123 [July–August 1998], pp. 16–20 [20]).

63 E.g., Ruether, *Gaia and God*; Sallie McFague, *The Body of God: An Ecological Theology* (Minneapolis, MN: Fortress Press, 2004); Heather Eaton, *Introducing Ecofeminist Theologies* (London: T&T Clark, 2005).

where the sun is not hampered by moonlight
and trees are trees not lamp posts
where you reigned in your finery
where they hailed you as queen
all seems far away and long ago
there is no room for vengeance now
but the prick of the needle
sometimes reminds you of teeth

queen of the prostitutes
you whisper the words
taste them against your tongue
then spit them to the ground
they lie in puddles of white
but a moment
before they scale your legs
and sink beneath your skin

                                        Caryn Swark[64]

64 Caryn Swark, http://carynswark.blogspot.com/2007_08_13_archive.html (accessed 21 January 2009). Printed with permission of the author.

A Man's Choice: Wealth Imagery and the Two Cities of the Book of Revelation

Greg Carey

Revelation employs images of women to advance its agenda, a program that involves wealth and commerce. Female images, the Whore and the Bride, serve as primary vehicles through which Revelation contrasts wealth associated with the Beast over against wealth associated with the Lamb. While Babylon the Whore embodies the acquisitiveness and exploitation of Roman imperial commerce, the Bride descends, at once opulent and pure, as the New Jerusalem in which all may drink water from the river of life and eat fruit from the tree of life. In Barbara Rossing's terms, Revelation thus poses a 'choice between two cities'.[1] It demands that its audience flee Babylon for the New Jerusalem, that they exit the Whore and enter the Bride.

Both dimensions of this program, matters pertaining to wealth and to gender, have received intense attention over the past fifteen years. Nearly all interpreters acknowledge the basic dynamics of the program: Revelation concentrates its wealth agenda in its depiction of these two women. It acknowledges the wealth generated by the Whore, but it characterizes Babylon's commerce as murderous and corrupt. Revelation depicts the New Jerusalem as *even more opulent* than Babylon, but pure. How, precisely, do gender dynamics shape the rhetorical expression of Revelation's wealth program? The question requires a more specific level of analysis than simply the observation that Revelation pits one prototypically evil woman against her prototypically virtuous antitype. Exploring how Revelation's wealth imagery employs *rhetography*, the rhetoric of the senses, to dramatize the difference between one woman and another, this essay finds not simply that Revelation destroys Babylon with its wealth and then attributes wealth to the New Jerusalem; it finds also that the *kinds* of wealth – what can be seen, touched, tasted, sounded, and smelled – differ substantially.[2]

The differences reflect common gender conventions from Mediterranean antiquity. Despite diverse gender values throughout Roman culture, numerous sources characterize women as more influenced by their senses than their intellect and thus open to evil influence through external stimulation. In the same system, masculinity inclines toward the intellectual and the ideal. As a result, modesty in women becomes highly valued. To Babylon Revelation attributes vibrant colors, rich tastes, fragrant odors and melodic sounds, while the text restricts the New Jerusalem to white garments, 'pure' or 'clear' gold and precious stones, the tastes and

---

1 Barbara Rossing, *The Choice Between Two Cities: Whore, Bride, and Empire in the Apocalypse* (Harrisburg, PA: Trinity Press International, 1999).

2 See the developing work of Vernon K. Robbins, who characterizes rhetography as 'evoking pictures through pictorial expression' ('Conceptual Blending and Early Christian Imagination', http://www.helsinki.fi/collegium/events/Robbins.pdf [accessed 21 January 2009], p. 2).

smells of water and unspecified fruit, and a different array of sounds. In short, Revelation characterizes Babylon as a decadent, sensually coded woman and the New Jerusalem as a modest virgin prepared for her wedding day.

While the Whore and the Bride convey much of the freight with respect to Revelation's wealth program, they do participate in a larger whole. The Whore belongs to what I call the 'Beast Group', the Bride to the 'Lamb Group'. Careful attention to the distribution of wealth throughout the Apocalypse reveals a consistent pattern, an 'ascetic aesthetic'. The Beast Group participates in a fuller range of color, texture, taste, smell and sound than does the Lamb Group. The Lamb Group's wealth resides in intense light, 'white' or 'pure' color complemented by gold, music sometimes pleasant and sometimes harsh, unspecified tastes, and odors largely related to liturgical settings. Revelation's wealth program demonstrates an ascetic dimension that is reflected in its two most compelling feminine images.

Wealth and the Apocalypse

Interpreters agree that the Book of Revelation 'redistributes' wealth, largely through its sensory rhetoric or *rhetography*. The Apocalypse acknowledges that Rome accumulates and generates wealth but, through image and symbol, it eliminates wealth from the Dragon and its associates, most notably the Whore, while it assigns wealth to the Lamb and its followers. J. Nelson Kraybill describes the reversal in this way: 'Faithful believers now suffering poverty and powerlessness some day will enjoy wealth and safety in the New Jerusalem.'[3] More pointedly, Robert M. Royalty claims that Revelation 'parallels' and 'mimics' the relationship between wealth and status in Greco-Roman society, not redeeming it but attempting 'to replace it with a Christianized version of the same thing'.[4] The Lamb is worthy to receive wealth (5.12).

Interpreters differ, however, on the circumstances and motivations that lie beneath Revelation's wealth program. Some assert that Revelation opposes Rome *primarily* because the imperial system is exploitative.[5] Others emphasize that the Apocalypse condemns Rome for its idolatry, particularly the imperial cult, with its

---

3 Nelson Kraybill, *Imperial Cult and Commerce in John's Apocalypse* (JSNTSup, 132; Sheffield: Sheffield Academic Press, 1996), p. 25.

4 Robert M. Royalty, *The Streets of Heaven: The Ideology of Wealth in the Apocalypse of John* (Macon, GA: Mercer University Press, 1998), pp. 245–46.

5 Among those who emphasize the Apocalypse's economic dimensions, so it seems for Richard Bauckham, *The Theology of the Book of Revelation* (NTT; Cambridge, UK and New York: Cambridge University Press, 1993), pp. 35–39; *idem, The Climax of Prophecy: Studies in the Book of Revelation* (Edinburgh: T&T Clark, 1993), pp. 338–83; Harry O. Maier, *Apocalypse Recalled: The Book of Revelation after Christendom* (Minneapolis, MN: Fortress Press, 2002); Néstor Míguez, 'Apocalyptic and the Economy: A Reading of Revelation 18 from the Experience of Economic Exclusion', in Fernando F. Segovia and Mary Ann Tolbert (eds), *Reading from This Place.* Vol. 2: *Biblical Interpretation and Social Location in Global Perspective* (Minneapolis, MN: Fortress Press, 1995), pp. 250–62; Pablo Richard, *Apocalypse: A People's Commentary on the Book of Revelation* (The Bible and Liberation Series; Maryknoll, NY: Orbis Books, 1995); and Elisabeth Schüssler Fiorenza, 'Babylon the Great: A Rhetorical-Political Reading of Revelation 17–18', in David L. Barr (ed.), *The Reality of Apocalypse: Rhetoric and Politics in the Book of Revelation* (SBLSym, 39; Atlanta, GA: Society of Biblical Literature, 2006), pp. 243–69.

indictment of trade a more ancillary concern.[6] Still others perceive Revelation's real gravity in disputes related to the economic and social disparities among the seven churches.[7] Alternatively, one might refuse to elevate one concern above the others by asserting that worship, power and wealth are inextricably linked.[8]

For the purposes of this essay, we need not assume that we know how economic and political realities rank among Revelation's motivating concerns. Let us take a step back from such broad contextual questions to matters of detail. What kinds of wealth accrue to the Whore and the Beast Group, and what kinds to the Bride and the Lamb Group? In particular, we shall attend to the imagery of the senses – sight, sound, taste, texture and smell. While Revelation indicts the Whore for generating wealth for the merchants of the earth, the 'luxury' it ascribes to her as well as to all those identified with the Beast looks prettier, tastes better, feels nicer, and smells richer than do the items ascribed to the Lamb and its followers.[9] In short, Revelation promotes an ascetic aesthetic that favors the abstract and pure Bride over the more specific and sensual Whore.

Gendering Revelation's Wealth

Interpreters further agree on one of the devices Revelation employs to promote its wealth agenda, the 'choice' between Babylon and the New Jerusalem. On one side is Babylon the Whore – not only sexual but also excessive and acquisitive.[10] Revelation

---

6 Thus Kraybill, *Imperial Cult and Commerce*; Steven J. Friesen, *Imperial Cults and the Apocalypse of John: Reading Revelation in the Ruins* (Oxford and New York: Oxford University Press, 2001).

7 So Paul Duff, *Who Rides the Beast? Prophetic Rivalry and the Rhetoric of Crisis in the Churches of the Apocalypse* (New York: Oxford University Press, 2001); Royalty, *Streets of Heaven*.

8 James Chukwuma Okoye, 'Power and Worship: *Revelation* in African Perspective', in David Rhoads (ed.), *From Every People and Nation: The Book of Revelation in Intercultural Perspective* (Minneapolis, MN: Fortress Press, 2005), pp. 110–26. This represents my best understanding of A. Yarbro Collins's work, including *Crisis and Catharsis: The Power of the Apocalypse* (Philadelphia, PA: Westminster Press, 1984), pp. 84–140; see also her 'Insiders and Outsiders in the Book of Revelation and Its Social Context', in Jacob Neusner and Ernest S. Frerichs (eds), *'To See Ourselves as Others See Us': Christians, Jews, 'Others' in Late Antiquity* (Scholars Press Studies in the Humanities; Chico, CA: Scholars Press, 1985), pp. 187–218, and 'Revelation 18: Taunt Song or Dirge?', in J. Lambrecht (ed.), *L'Apocalypse johannique et l'Apocalyptique dans le Nouveau Testament* (BETL, 53; Gembloux: Leuven University Press, 1980), pp. 185–204 (203). Likewise for Wes Howard-Brook and Anthony Gwyther, *Unveiling Empire: Revelation Then and Now* (Maryknoll, NY: Orbis Books, 1999), p. 116; Barbara Rossing, 'City Visions, Feminine Figures, and Economic Critique: A Sapiential Topos in the Apocalypse', in Benjamin G. Wright III and Lawrence W. Wills (eds), *Conflicted Boundaries in Wisdom and Apocalypticism* (Atlanta, GA: Society of Biblical Literature, 2005), pp. 181–96; and Jean-Pierre Ruiz, 'Praise and Politics in Revelation 19.1–10', in Steve Moyise (ed.), *Studies in the Book of Revelation* (New York: T&T Clark, 2001), pp. 69–84.

9 In my view the NRSV translation of στρῆνος and στρηνιάω in terms of luxury (18.3, 7, 9), though followed by some commentators and potentially congenial to my argument, somewhat misses the point. The term may indicate inordinate desire, acted out aggressively, not necessarily its end result in luxury. In Rev. 18.3, 9 it is linked with *porneia*. Thus, the translations 'sensuality' or 'lived sensually' may better incorporate both the erotic and the material dimensions of the terms.

10 Rossing, *Choice Between Two Cities*.

calls its audience to 'come out' of her (18.4).[11] Opposed to Babylon the Great is the New Jerusalem, the Bride – not only virginal but also resplendent in wedding costume, decked out in gold and precious stones. Revelation invites the audience to 'come' in to her (22.17).[12] The conflicts depicted in the Apocalypse intensify until the book's end identifies this final choice. The opulence demonstrated by both women draws our attention, yet clearly Revelation favors one and condemns the other.

Revelation's gender imagery, particularly the symbols of the Whore and the Bride, presents the fulcrum for feminist ethical assessment.[13] Some interpreters, warning against Revelation, argue that it depicts women only in sexually identified terms. Its images – Jezebel the promiscuous prophet, the Woman Clothed with the Sun as Sky Mother, Babylon the Whore, and the New Jerusalem the Bride – are all determined by their sexualized, gender-coded identity.[14] Other interpreters note the danger inherent in such imagery but take a more ambivalent position. A. Yarbro Collins suggests that the Bride, through her marriage to the Lamb, discloses the feminine aspect of the divine and demonstrates that the new creation requires the 'richness, complexity, and vitality' of both male and female symbols.[15] Still others likewise acknowledge the problematic nature of Revelation's female imagery yet subordinate this problem to other concerns. Elisabeth Schüssler Fiorenza, for example, emphasizes the book's resistance to imperial oppression over against its reliance upon conventional images of virtuous and wicked women:

> Such a liberationist reading of Revelation's rhetoric subordinates the book's depiction of cosmic destruction and holy war to its desire for justice, which is repeated throughout the book. It puts in the foreground those rhetorical features of the text that aim at moving the audience to practical engagement in this struggle for God's qualitatively new world of salvation.[16]

11 For Revelation's apparently male audience, see Stephen D. Moore, 'Revolting Revelations', in Ingrid Rosa Kitzberger (ed.), *The Personal Voice in Biblical Interpretation* (New York: Routledge, 1999), pp. 183–200 (191). Rev. 14.1–5 has received a great deal of attention and commentary, with interpreters taking the 144,000 virgins who 'have not defiled themselves with women' as (a) a sign of sexual asceticism or preparation for holy war or (b) a more metaphorical image according to which their sexual purity indicates avoidance of imperial and idolatrous corruption.

12 Tina Pippin calls attention to the erotic imagery of coming out and coming in in *Death and Desire: The Rhetoric of Gender in the Apocalypse of John* (Literary Currents in Biblical Interpretation; Louisville, KY: Westminster/John Knox Press, 1992).

13 Alison Jack has contributed a survey of feminist interpretations of the Apocalypse that at several points coincides with some judgments here. See her 'Out of the Wilderness: Feminist Perspectives on the Book of Revelation', in Steve Moyise (ed.), *Studies in the Book of Revelation* (New York: Continuum, 2001), pp. 149–62.

14 Pippin represents the most clear and complete critique along these lines (*Death and Desire*). Jean K. Kim posits the Whore as a cipher for Rome but also as a victim, exploited by both foreign and native men ('"Uncovering Her Wickedness": An Inter[Con]textual Reading of Revelation 17 from a Postcolonial Feminist Perspective', *JSNT* 73 [1999], pp. 61–81).

15 'Feminine Symbolism in the Book of Revelation', *BibInt* 1 (1993), pp. 20–33 (24–25), see reprinted in this volume, pp. 121–30; cf. A. Yarbro Collins, 'The Book of Revelation', in John J. Collins (ed.), *The Encyclopedia of Apocalypticism* Vol. 1: *The Origins of Apocalypticism in Judaism and Christianity* (New York: Continuum, 1998), pp. 384–414 (408–09).

16 Elisabeth Schüssler Fiorenza, *Revelation: Vision of a Just World* (Proclamation Commentaries; Minneapolis, MN: Fortress Press, 1991), p. 122.

This essay stops short of assessing the ethical import of Revelation's feminine imagery. Instead, it engages a more particular question: how does Revelation's wealth rhetography relate to this imagery? Acknowledging that Revelation voices one ancient masculine perspective on both wealth and gender, and acknowledging as well that Revelation addresses its audience in masculine terms, what may we learn from *how* Revelation distributes and attributes wealth, and how might Revelation's wealth imagery bear upon questions of gender?[17]

Visual Bling

The cold and the hard dominate Revelation's wealth imagery. Gold and precious stones abound, as do the trappings of royalty such as thrones and crowns. These items are largely common to the Lamb and Beast Groups, and they are especially concentrated in descriptions of the Whore and the Bride.

Revelation distributes thrones and crowns widely within the Lamb Group. Not only does the Deity sit on a throne (especially 1.4; 4.2), so also do Christ (introduced 3.21; 22.1, 3), the heavenly elders (introduced 4.4), and faithful believers (3.21; 20.4). The river that flows through the New Jerusalem proceeds from the throne, where God and the Lamb reside in the city (22.1–3). Similarly, the Dragon and the Beast possess thrones (e.g., 2.13; 13.2), though with fewer references to their enthronement. As for crowns (στέφανοι) and diadems (διαδήματα), we find these associated with the Lamb (19.12) and Son of Man (14.14), the elders (introduced 4.4), the Woman Clothed with the Sun (12.1), and faithful believers (among other locations promised in 2.10 and 3.11). The rider of conquest (6.2) and the locust beasts (9.7) own crowns as well. The Dragon (12.3) and the Beast (13.1) wear diadems, though a semantic distinction between 'crowns' (good) and 'diadems' (bad) cannot be made since the Lamb wears 'many diadems' (19.12).

Gold and precious stones are omnipresent. The risen Christ is the source of gold for believers (3.18). Lampstands, crowns, bowls and censers in heaven are golden, as is the altar. The Heavenly City is made of gold and yet is 'clear' or 'pure' as glass (ἡ πόλις χρυσίον καθαρὸν ὅμοιον ὑάλῳ καθαρῷ, 21.18, cf. 21. 21)! Jewel imagery primarily attaches itself to the New Jerusalem. The city's very appearance is jewel-like, again 'clear' or 'pure' (κρυσταλλίζοντι, 21.11); jewels and pearls stand out in its foundation stones (21.19–21). This blending of opulence with purity may well be a carry-over from priestly discourse, a point supported by the facts that the city requires no temple and that the jewels in its foundation stones reflect the jewels from the ephod of the high priest.[18] Conversely, the Whore is decked out in gold, jewels and pearls, and she holds a golden cup (17.4). Gold, silver, precious stones and pearls

17 I am particularly indebted to my colleague Julia O'Brien, who guided me in framing this question.

18 David Aune provides a succinct discussion of the twelve precious stones (*Revelation 17–22* [WBC, 52C; Nashville, TN: Thomas Nelson Publishers, 1998], p. 1165).

are the first four items in the list of her cargo (18.12).[19] The inhabitants of the earth construct 'idols' from gold and silver as well as more common materials (9.20). In short, crowns and thrones, gold and jewels are associated with both Lamb and Beast Groups, though with far more frequency, perhaps even more intensity, with the former. The depictions of the Whore and the Bride both emphasize gold and jewels, though crowns and thrones apply more to the Bride and her inhabitants.

Revelation features another splendidly accessorized woman, the Woman of Chapter 12. She is clothed with the sun, she wears a crown with a dozen stars, and the moon is at her feet. Her depiction more resembles that of the risen Jesus than the Bride, yet it conforms to the Bride as well in its implied purity and naturalness and in its imagery marked by intensity rather than by color. The woman of Revelation 12 is dazzling, yet the contrast between Babylon and the New Jerusalem is so clear and so intense that the Whore and the Bride represent the primary choice Revelation poses to its audience.[20]

We might also consider the texture of these items associated with Bride and Whore: all of them are 'hard and cold'. However opulent, they bring pleasure to the eyes but not the other senses. Moreover, the images of 'clear' or 'pure' gold and stones participate in a broader trend of Revelation's ascetic wealth imagery. The Lamb Group, apart from gold and the New Jerusalem's jewels, is largely colorless; the Beast Group is marked by purple and scarlet.

(Dis)chord for the Ear

Compared to most biblical books, Revelation is full of sound: trumpets, harps, songs, shouts, lightning and thunder, earthquakes. In some cases, one gets the impression of harsh, violent noise. The trumpets of judgment seem that way, at least to me. While it is difficult to judge whether the heavenly songs that so punctuate Revelation are melodious, the harps held by the victorious believers who sing the Song of Moses suggest that they are (15.2-4). Even so, when the 144,000 sing their New Song, Revelation gives mixed messages. The collective heavenly voice sounds at once like many waters and loud thunder – and like the sound of harpists (14.2-3). Often Revelation mentions shouting from the heavenly realm, which includes both judgment and doxology. Prior to its judgment the Beast Group counters such sounds with a more pleasant variety. Along with acclamation to the Beast (13.4), the Beast Group enjoys an orchestra of musical instruments, far more diverse than the harps and trumpets of the Lamb Group. With these, Babylon heard the sound of labor and the rejoicing of wedding partners. She once enjoyed these pleasures, but

---

19 This may represent a standard critique of Roman luxury. Peter S. Perry points out that Dio Chrysostom also lists silver and gold at the beginning of a similar list, along with luxurious fabrics ('Critiquing the Excess of Empire: A *Synkrisis* of John of Patmos and Dio of Prusa', *JSNT* 29 [2007], pp. 473–96 [485, 489]). I thank Peter Perry for providing me with an electronic copy of his article prior to its publication.

20 Elisabeth Schüssler Fiorenza challenges the 'good woman/bad woman' opposition posed by Rossing and others by including the Woman Clothed with the Sun in the moral equation ('Babylon the Great', p. 264).

no more. The Whore's fall marks an end of music and indeed of culture: 'and the sound of harpists and minstrels and of flutists and trumpeters will be heard in you no more . . . and the voice of bridegroom and bride will be heard in you no more' (18.22–23).

In summary, the Beast Group seems to enjoy a richer auditory experience than does the Lamb Group. As for the Bride, her arrival is announced by proclamations from a loud voice and from the One who sits upon the throne. Otherwise, no music attends her. Moreover, the sound associated with the Lamb Group is ambiguous, ranging from the jarring to the potentially melodious.

Plush Texture

I have suggested that the presence of gold, precious stones, crowns and thrones in Revelation indicates opulence but not necessarily a pleasing texture. What else may we say about the tactile rhetography of the Lamb Group and the Beast Group? Perhaps the closest we can get to this topic is clothing. The Lamb Group is distinguished by its white robes, and we also learn a little about fabrics. Clean (or pure) shining linen (λίνον καθαρὸν λαμπρόν) with gold belts adorns the angels who bring the seven plagues (15.6), while the risen Christ also wears a gold belt (1.13). These images recollect both the Book of Exodus (28.39; 39.27–39), where priestly garments are in view, and the Book of Daniel (10.5), which describes the heavenly figure who mediates the seer's vision. We then learn that the Whore both wears and supplies 'fine linen' (βύσσινος, 18.12, 16), which also adorns the Bride (19.8) and the heavenly armies (19.14).

Our best evidence suggests that this 'fine linen', shared by both the Lamb and Beast Groups, represents a luxurious fabric, soft to the touch. It also could serve, unlike many other fabrics, to bandage wounds. The biblical tradition ordinarily presents βύσσινος (or βύσσος) in contexts depicting luxury as well as with respect to priestly affairs.[21]

Another possible allusion to softness occurs in Revelation's reference to Jezebel's bed (2.22). Whether this bed indicates luxury, promiscuity or illness remains unclear. The bed likely evokes multiple meanings, alluding at least both to Jezebel's *porneia* and to her cursed fate.

Despite the common fabrics, the Beast Group enjoys a far more colorful world than does the Lamb Group. Reflecting Revelation's emphasis on purity, the Lamb and its associates dress in white. Soiled garments indicate corruption (3.4), while clean garments identify faithful living (e.g., 3.5, 18; 6.11; 22.14). Their only ornamentations are crowns and golden belts. The risen Christ's head and hair are white; although his feet resemble bronze, the emphasis lies in their brilliance rather than their color (1.14–15). As we have seen, the gold and precious stones in the New Jerusalem are translucent. Even the Bride's wedding garments are 'bright and pure' (or 'clear') (λαμπρὸν καθαρόν, 19.8). Thus, Revelation emphasizes intense light that bleaches color from the experience of the Lamb and its followers. When Revelation

---

21 Luxury: see Gen. 41.42; 2 Chron. 2.13 (LXX); 3.14; Est. 1.6; 6.8; 8.15; Prov. 31.22; Isa. 3.23; 19.9; Ezek. 16.10, 13; 27.7; 1 Esd. 3.6; Lk. 16.19. Priestly affairs: see many references in Exodus; 1 Chron. 15.27; 2 Chron. 5.12. Also note the references to the heavenly intermediary in Dan. 10.5; 12.6–7.

also draws attention to the Bride's costume – 'like a bride adorned for her husband' – it withholds visual detail.[22]

One prominent set of items lends color to the New Jerusalem, if not to the personified Bride. 'Every sort of precious stone' decorates the foundations of the city wall: jasper, sapphire, agate, emerald, onyx, carnelian, chrysolite, beryl, topaz, chrysoprase, jacinth and amethyst. Likewise, twelve pearls adorn the twelve gates (21.18–21). Though these stones belong among the 'cold and hard' elements in which the Lamb Group excels, the assortment offers Revelation's richest color palette.

Luxurious scarlet and purple color the Beast Group, particularly the Whore. The dragon is fiery red (πυρρός, 12.3), while the Beast is scarlet (κόκκινος, 17.3). Dressed in purple and scarlet (17.4; 18.16), the Whore also trades in these precious dyes (18.12). Her garments contribute to her desirability.[23] While Revelation goes into great detail describing the New Jerusalem, the portrayal largely applies to topography and architecture, not to the personified Bride. In stark contrast, the detailed exposition of the Whore's appearance overwhelms her characterization as a great city. A woman 'adorned like a bride for her husband' scarcely captures attention like her intoxicated counterpart does: this sensuous woman rides a Beast, wears purple and scarlet, adorns herself with gold and jewels and pearls, holds a golden cup, and bears a mysterious name on her forehead.[24]

Revelation insists that Rome's apparent beauty, confirmed by her association with purple and scarlet, is transcended by the intense light that comes only from the heavenly realm. At one level, this pictorial argument provides another instance in which Revelation acknowledges Rome's attractions, even as it insists upon the Lamb's greater glory, for in all cases the comparisons involve an implicit critique of the Beast Group. For example, the Whore's colorful garments are stripped from her, while her opulence masks excessive desire and murderous revelry. Often overlooked, however, is the ascetic dimension of Revelation's palette. The Apocalypse accords color to Babylon's garments but not to those of the Bride. Revelation prefers intense, gleaming white to richly textured scarlet and purple.

Taste and Smell

Apart from the controversy over idol-food (2.14, 20), Revelation offers only a few references to taste and smell. Babylon's cargo list (18.12–13) includes several items that appeal to both senses. Cinnamon, spice, incense, myrrh and frankincense all represent luxury items, and it is possible that some among the rich drank myrrh.[25] The Whore also trades in wine, oil, fine flour and wheat. Among these only fine flour constitutes a luxury item, but all four items reflect Rome's dependence upon sea commerce.[26] The lament over Babylon calls attention specifically to the loss of fruit

---

22 Here I distinguish between the Bride's costume and the depiction of the new city, which includes many colorful stones.

23 See Pippin, *Death and Desire*, pp. 65–68.

24 For modesty and the adornment of brides, see Lynn R. Huber, *Like a Bride Adorned: Reading Metaphor in John's Apocalypse* (Emory Studies in Early Christianity; New York: T&T Clark, 2007), pp. 130–33.

25 Lucian, *Nigrinus* 31, though perhaps this is satirical. Cited in Royalty, *Streets of Heaven*, p. 208.

26 Bauckham, *Climax of Prophecy*, pp. 360–63.

(18.14). While livestock (cattle and sheep, mentioned in 18.13) served many purposes apart from food, the juxtaposition to flour and wheat suggests that the primary allusion is to meat, a luxury item far more accessible to the wealthy than to most people. Although brief, the list in Rev. 18.13 communicates Roman extravagance. It also evokes remarkably intense and clashing smells: 'cinnamon, spice, incense, myrrh, frankincense, wine . . . animals and sheep and horses . . . and bodies – and human souls' (καὶ κιννάμωμον καὶ ἄμωμον καὶ θυμιάματα καὶ μύρον καὶ λίβανον καὶ οἶνον . . . καὶ σῖτον καὶ κτήνη καὶ πρόβατα, καὶ ἵππων . . . καὶ σωμάτων, καὶ ψυχὰς ἀνθρώπων).

Revelation assigns other, repulsive, tastes to the Beast group. These include the Dragon's desire to eat human flesh (12.4), along with drinking blood (16.6; 17.6), *porneia* (14.8), wrath (14.10; 16.19), and the unspecified abominations and impurities the Whore imbibes (17.5–6). Moreover, the Beast Group experiences the smoke and sulfur of judgment (9.17–18; 14.10; 19.20; 20:10; 21:8). The tastes and smells associated with the Whore are particularly striking, in that they range from the aromatic and the delicious to the detestable.

Revelation assigns other smells and tastes to the Lamb Group. While the Beast Group trades in fragrances, the Lamb Group also smells incense and smoke (5.8; 8.3–4; 15.8). The Lamb Group appears to savor the smoke of Babylon's destruction: 'Once more they said, "Hallelujah! The smoke goes up from her forever and ever"' (19.3). Smoke appears in a range of other contexts, from liturgy (8.4; 15.8) to destruction (9.2–3, 17–18; 14.11; 18.9, 18; 19.3).

As for taste, the bitterness of the scroll John ingests (10.9–10) is not among the tastes experienced by or promised to the Lamb Group. The taste of the scroll itself is 'like honey': 'So I went to the angel and told him to give me the little scroll; and he said to me, "Take it, and eat; it will be bitter to your stomach, but sweet as honey in your mouth." So I took the little scroll from the hand of the angel and ate it; it was sweet as honey in my mouth, but when I had eaten it, my stomach was made bitter.' Revelation promises faithful believers two food items. Those who conquer in Pergamum may anticipate 'the hidden manna' (τοὺς μάννα τοὺς κεκρυμμένου, 2.17). Astride the river that bisects the New Jerusalem stands the tree of life, which produces a different fruit every month (22.2). While wine is the choice beverage for the Beast Group, the saints will receive the fresh, pure water of life that flows through the New Jerusalem (7.17; 21.6; 22.1, 17).[27]

Although potentially the most delectable of Revelation's tastes, the hidden manna and the tree's fruit suffer from a lack of specificity. Ancient rhetoricians spoke of creating a picture 'before the eyes of the audience'. Aristotle maintained that an orator should not leave the imaginative work to the audience (*Rhet.* 1410b). From the perspective of rhetography, Revelation's account of hidden manna and the New Jerusalem's varieties of fruit carry less gustatory punch than the evocation of fresh water, and far less than wine and cinnamon.

In summary, it is difficult to assess smell and taste for the Beast Group. The Beast Group receives the most explicit and the most delightful smells and tastes; it drinks wine and enjoys spices and fragrances. Conversely, the Beast Group also tastes blood

---

27 I am grateful to Amy-Jill Levine, who points out that Revelation does not explicitly indicate that the saints drink this water.

and human flesh; it lives with the smell of smoke and sulfur that indicate its own condemnation. All these tastes and smells occur with special intensity with respect to the Whore. The smells and tastes assigned to the Lamb Group are less specific, perhaps less evocative, even if the Apocalypse implies their superiority to those of the Beast Group. What does the hidden manna taste like? What kinds of fruit does the tree of life produce, and do they correspond to fruit familiar to mortals? The Bride's fresh, pure water would have been quite rare for ancient city dwellers, but it lacks the rich connotations of Babylon's wine.

Babylon the 'Strange Woman'

Revelation's appropriation of Scripture has drawn intense attention. Many inter-preters note that the polemic against the Whore draws upon Ezekiel's condemnation of Tyre and Sidon (Ezek. 26.1–28.26), as well as Isaiah's indictment of Tyre as a prostitute (Isa. 23.15–18). Yet generally ignored are the ways in which the Whore recalls the 'Strange Woman' of Proverbs 7. This woman dresses as a prostitute (Prov. 7.10), and she calls attention to the colored fabrics that cover her couch and her bed. Linen (אטון מצרים; the Greek reads 'tapestries', ἀμφιτάποις) from Egypt adorns her couch (7.16; see Ezek. 27.7); myrrh, aloes and cinnamon perfume her bed (אהלים וקנמון, 7.17; the Greek offers κρόκος, 'crocus' or 'saffron').[28] All these items – remarkable dress, textiles and fragrances – resound in the presentation of the Whore and the recitation of her cargo. Revelation introduces the woman as a Whore, then calls attention to her luxurious clothes and jewelry (Rev. 17.4). The Whore's cargo includes cinnamon and myrrh (18.13). One might argue that the Whore recalls Proverbs' Strange Woman just as clearly as she does the prophets' Tyre and Sidon.

Visual rhetoric associated with the Bride also echoes Ezekiel (especially chapters 40–48), yet little about her depiction recalls Woman Wisdom from Proverbs. The 'fruit better than gold and silver' of Prov. 8.19 may provide an intertext to Rev. 22.2: 'the tree of life with its twelve kinds of fruit, producing its fruit each month; and the leaves of the tree are for the healing of the nations.' Thus, while Revelation's Whore recalls the Strange Woman through particular fabrics and scents, the only possible link between the Bride and Woman Wisdom (and a tenuous one at that) lacks speci-ficity. Even in its appropriation of Scripture, the portrayal of the Whore far exceeds that of the Bride in both detail and texture.

Conclusions

This essay at once relies upon and advances the argument that Revelation reverses the ascription of wealth from Rome and its allies (the Beast Group) to faithful believers and their heavenly advocates (the Lamb Group). Yet it does so with a twist. Revelation does not transfer *all* the wealth assigned to the Beast Group. Instead, it largely eliminates things that provide pleasure to the touch, taste and smell. The bright and clear colors Revelation assigns to the Lamb Group all shine when they

---

28 While the Hebrew tradition suggests linen, the LXX does not indicate the nature of the fabric. If Revelation is drawing upon Proverbs 7, it would seem to rely upon a Hebrew text base.

reflect light, while the Beast Group enjoys richer, more light-absorbent colors. The Beast Group's auditory associations are richer than those of the Lamb Group. In these respects the Beast Group enjoys a richer sensory experience than does the Lamb Group, even as Revelation insists that the wealth accruing to the Lamb Group far surpasses that offered by the Beast and the Whore, and even as Revelation intimates that Beastly luxury is just a thin veneer for grotesque pleasures such as cannibalism.

The Lamb Group exceeds the Beast Group in matters related to precious metals and precious stones – things that signify opulence yet remain 'hard and cold'. As for sound, the Lamb group enjoys music and endures trumpet blasts, lightning flashes and the like, while Babylon's pleasant sounds exceed those of the Lamb Group in range if not in frequency of allusions. The Beast Group exceeds the Lamb Group in richness of color, taste and smell, even if some of the smells and tastes are noxious.

Revelation's two most compelling feminine images, the Whore and the Bride, express these tensions most intensely. Moreover, Revelation insists upon the Whore's destruction. The Beast Group's prosperity is coming to an end. Yet the overall luxury of the Beast Group attends to the senses with a richness and variety that far surpasses the 'hard and cold' opulence of the Lamb Group. As I once heard the Episcopal bishop Nathan Baxter say, 'Whoever said, "I'd rather be a doorkeeper in the house of the Lord than dwell in the tents of sinners" has never dwelt in the tents of sinners.' Revelation gives the impression that Babylon would be more pleasant than the New Jerusalem.

Yet we have found another side to Revelation's wealth imagery. Where the Beast Group enjoys sound, color, taste and smell, the Lamb Group is marked by intense light and translucent purity. In Revelation's world, bright, white and clear are more compelling than purple, red and scarlet, hidden manna more delectable than cinnamon, heavenly choruses more melodious than instrumental music and the rejoicing of newlyweds. Again, Revelation portrays this contrast most intensely with respect to the Whore and the Bride.

This aesthetic pattern supports an ascetic reading of Revelation. Interpreters agree that Revelation calls believers to abandon the social, cultural, commercial and religious systems of Roman imperial life. They further agree that Revelation's program calls its audience to significant, even severe, sacrifices. 'Coming out' from the city would prove especially onerous to believers who aspire to prosperity and regard commerce as a path up the social and economic ladders. Perhaps related to this ascetic aesthetic are Revelation's allusions to the wilderness (12.6, 14) and sexual abstinence (14.4). Do such passages promote a movement that abandons life in the cities for an austere wilderness experience? Do they encourage the sorts of rigorous asceticism that many perceive at Qumran, in the ministry of John the Baptist and in the *Ascension of Isaiah*? It seems to me that detailed speculations positing specific referents for desert dwelling and celibacy make too much of too little evidence, yet Revelation's wealth imagery would fit such a context admirably. The Lamb and its followers may surpass the wealth of the Beast, and the depiction of that wealth suits an ascetic disposition.

With respect to gender, Revelation's ascetic sensibilities are particularly suggestive. Clearly, Revelation encourages revulsion at the Whore's acquisitive desire. Nevertheless, the book's idealized woman offers nothing by way of tactile luxury. No specific color, taste or smell attends her. This stands in stark contrast to Revelation's evil woman, who abounds in specific color, taste and scent. In its evocation of Proverbs' Strange Woman, Revelation likewise emphasizes her tactile dimensions. In contrast, Revelation could have drawn upon the sensual dimensions associated with Woman Wisdom, but it ignores them almost entirely. Thus, Revelation rejects, even destroys, the more fully embodied sensuality presented by Babylon in favor of the New Jerusalem's idealized and abstract opulence.

Some primary sources assert self-control primarily as a masculine virtue, and 'self-indulgence of women' a female vice (Aristophanes, *Lys.* 387). Philo, for example, associated women with the senses and the desire to satisfy them, and he contrasted the feminine to the more rational masculine nature (*On the Creation* 165–66). The *Testament of Reuben* (5.1–6) develops the convention that women use their appearance to entice men to share their lewd behavior.[29] In this context modest appearance was a trait highly prized in women, sometimes appearing first in lists of women's virtues.[30] Exemplary here is Turia, an Augustan woman who avenged the murders of her parents, raised dowries for her female relatives, took care of her husband's business during his exile and helped to secure his return, and pursued those who had caused him misfortune. In her eulogy Turia's husband enumerates the following virtues: 'your modesty, deference, affability, your amiable disposition, your faithful attendance to the household duties, your enlightened religion, your unassuming elegance, the modest simplicity and refinement of your manners' (*CIL* 6.1527).[31]

Sure enough, some early Christian texts admonish women to dress modestly (e.g., 1 Tim. 2.9–10; 1 Pet. 3.1–5). The way in which Revelation employs female images to embody its ascetic aesthetic betrays an aversion to what Gail Corrington Streete names 'terrifying female power'.[32] The choice between two women pits the embodied, lustful and hardly modest Babylon, who dresses in purple and scarlet, against the idealized, passive and modest Bride, whose opulence consists of gold and jewels that are 'pure' or 'clear'. Revelation's choice between two cities implies men's choice between a woman of substance and agency and a woman reduced to a passive ideal.

29 See Bernard P. Prusak, 'Woman: Seductive Siren and Source of Sin? Pseudepigraphal Myth and Christian Origins', in Rosemary Radford Ruether (ed.), *Religion and Sexism: Images of Woman in Jewish and Christian Traditions* (New York: Simon and Schuster, 1974), pp. 89–116, esp. pp. 92–93.

30 For the citation of the *Lysistrata* see John J. Winkler, *The Constraints of Desire: The Anthropology of Sex and Gender in Ancient Greece* (New York: Routledge, 1990), p. 190. See also Mary Rose D'Angelo, '"Knowing How to Preside over His Own Household": Imperial Masculinity and Christian Asceticism in the Pastorals, Hermas, and Luke-Acts', in Stephen D. Moore and Janice Capel Anderson (eds), *New Testament Masculinities* (Semeia Studies; Atlanta, GA: Scholars Press, 2003), pp. 241–71, esp. pp. 265–71.

31 Elaine Fantham, Helene Peet Foley, Natalie Boymel Kampen, Sarah B. Pomeroy and H. Alan Shapiro, *Women in the Classical World* (New York: Oxford University Press, 1994), pp. 318–19.

32 Gail Corrington Streete, *The Strange Woman: Power and Sex in the Bible* (Louisville, KY: Westminster/John Knox Press, 1997), p. 158. See the discussion on pp. 152–58.

Unveiling the Bride: Revelation 19.1–8 and Roman Social Discourse*

Lynn R. Huber

The final book of the Christian canon, the Book of Revelation, begins with the Greek word ἀποκάλυψις ('apocalypse', or revelation). When Revelation was written, sometime during the late first century CE, ἀποκάλυψις described the act of lifting off a veil or, metaphorically, bringing something into sight. The term bears a linguistic similarity to ἀνακάλυψις, which was used to describe the lifting of a veil, such as the lifting of the bride's veil at the culmination of a wedding.[1] Perhaps not coincidentally, Revelation culminates with an announcement of the wedding of the Lamb (19.7) and the descent of the Lamb's bride (21.2, 9). In these verses, John mimics Roman nuptial–familial rhetoric as part of his overall critique of the Roman Empire. Although he places different actors within the stereotypical roles of Roman marriage, John offers no critique of these roles as such. Instead, he manipulates cultural assumptions about marriage, applying them to the Risen Christ and the community (envisioned as dwelling within and comprising a new Jerusalem), while simultaneously assuming an anti-familial ethos.

Contemporary Critical Interpretations of Revelation's Nuptial–Familial Imagery

Traditional historical–critical interpretations of Revelation's wedding imagery typically note the intertextual connections between this imagery and the Hebrew Bible prophetic traditions in which a personified Zion is metaphorically married to God (e.g., Ezekiel 16, Hosea 1–2, Isa. 61.10). Representative of this approach is George Caird's assertion that just as Israel or Jerusalem can be described as God's metaphorical wife or bride, so the Christian community or the Church can be described as Christ's wife or bride.[2] Caird's approach resembles a mathematical formula in which one term replaces another to determine the identity of Revelation's bride. This traditional approach continues in Gregory K. Beale's more recent commentary.[3] Beale uses prophetic antecedents to decode the meaning of the component parts of the nuptial imagery, especially the imagery of the bride's wedding clothes in Revelation 19. He argues, for example, that Revelation draws upon Isa. 61.10, in

---

* I owe a special word of thanks to A.-J. Levine for her helpful suggestions, although the essay's shortcomings are my own. This chapter reflects ideas more fully developed in Lynn R. Huber, *Like a Bride Adorned: Reading Metaphor in John's Apocalypse* (New York: T&T Clark, 2007).

1 See John H. Oakley, 'Nuptial Nuances: Wedding Images in Non-Wedding Scenes of Myth', in Ellen D. Reeder (ed.), *Pandora: Women in Classical Greece* (Princeton, NJ: Princeton University Press, 1995), pp. 63–72.

2 G. B. Caird, *The Revelation of St. John* (Black's New Testament Commentary, 19; Peabody, MA: Hendrickson, 1993), p. 234.

3 Gregory K. Beale, *The Book of Revelation: A Commentary on the Greek Text* (NIGTC; Grand Rapids, MI: Eerdmans, 1999).

which the personified Zion refers to God's clothing 'her', and that, in so doing, Revelation similarly employs adornment language to communicate 'God's sovereign provision'.[4] In this way, Beale, like Caird, uncovers the OT allusions behind Revelation's nuptial–familial imagery in order to identify its meaning. This approach tends to be atomistic in its reading of Revelation's imagery; it does not explore how, for instance, the image of the wedding of the Lamb functions in relation to the text's overall rhetorical strategy.

In response to the traditional historical–critical approach, feminist critic Elisabeth Schüssler Fiorenza argues for reading Revelation as 'visionary rhetoric'.[5] She maintains that Revelation's mythopoeic language functions to make sense of John's rhetorical situation and to provide John's audience with a symbolic universe that challenges the dominant rhetoric of the Roman Empire.[6] Revelation's alternative world view reflects the early Christians' experience of oppression within a context that belies their conviction that Christ inaugurated God's just reign over the earth.[7] Further, Revelation seeks to persuade its audience to act in manner in accord with the vision it presents.

In constructing this alternative symbolic universe, John draws upon traditional Jewish and Greco-Roman metaphors and myths. Although these reworked myths and metaphors can be understood as having limitless potential meanings, attention to how they evoke their rhetorical situations allows the interpreter to make sense of the text's imagistic language.[8] In particular, Revelation's wedding imagery reworks the depiction of Jerusalem and Israel as the wife or bride of God found in the Hebrew prophets, although understanding this imagery requires exploration of how it 'fits' its rhetorical situation.[9] Schüssler Fiorenza only gives limited attention to this imagery, addressing it primarily in relation to the issue of how to interpret Revelation's gendered imagery in general. On this latter point, she warns against approaching gendered language and imagery as a 'closed system' in which grammatical gender language is equated with actual gender.[10] Attention to Revelation's rhetorical situation suggests that this gendered imagery is not primarily about gender; rather, the imagery functions as part of John's indictment of the Roman Empire and as a call to Christian resistance within this context.[11] Schüssler Fiorenza acknowledges that Revelation's use of gendered language and sexual metaphor opens the text up to the possibility of de-politicized readings that substitute moralizing for political resistance; however, reading this imagery in light of Revelation's rhetorical context reinforces the argument that this text as a whole ultimately calls Christians to resist Roman injustice.[12]

---

4 Beale, *The Book of Revelation*, p. 938.

5 Elisabeth Schüssler Fiorenza, 'Visionary Rhetoric and Social-Political Situation', in *eadem*, *The Book of Revelation: Justice and Judgment* (2nd edn; Minneapolis, MN: Fortress Press, 1998), pp. 181–203.

6 Elisabeth Schüssler Fiorenza, *Revelation: Vision of a Just World* (Proclamation Commentaries; Minneapolis, MN: Fortress Press, 1991), p. 29.

7 Schüssler Fiorenza, *Vision of a Just World*, pp. 54–55.

8 Schüssler Fiorenza, 'Visionary Rhetoric and Social-Political Situation', p. 187.

9 Schüssler Fiorenza, *Vision of a Just World*, p. 102.

10 Schüssler Fiorenza, *Vision of a Just World*, p. 14. See also Elisabeth Schüssler Fiorenza, *Sharing Her Word: Feminist Biblical Interpretation in Context* (Boston, MA: Beacon Press, 1998), pp. 88–101.

11 Schüssler Fiorenza, *Vision of a Just World*, p. 111.

12 Schüssler Fiorenza, 'Visionary Rhetoric and Social-Political Situation', p. 203.

In *Death and Desire: The Rhetoric of Gender in the Apocalypse of John*, Tina Pippin challenges interpreters to examine 'the deep structures of the text', particularly the ways that Revelation constructs political and social relationships.[13] Pippin examines how Revelation employs the language and imagery of desire and gender as a means of pushing its audience to make a choice against the dominant social and political order.[14] Assuming its readers are heterosexual males, Revelation incorporates feminine imagery to arouse, figuratively and literally, the audience's interest in pursuing one goal – entering the heavenly city personified as a woman – over another – remaining within the personified city identified as Babylon.[15] Placed in contrast to a negatively construed image of feminine power (the great prostitute of ch. 17), Revelation's bride is the eroticized woman of male fantasy: she is undefiled, silent, and ready for her man.[16] Pippin argues that this image reflects male fantasies and completely discounts any inkling of feminine agency, thereby mitigating any liberating message Revelation may ideally communicate.[17]

While Schüssler Fiorenza and Pippin ultimately disagree over whether Revelation's gendered language and imagery subvert its liberative message, they both push feminist critics to move beyond the surface of the text to explore the structures through which it persuades its audience. In particular, Schüssler Fiorenza's description of Revelation as visionary rhetoric provides a helpful tool for imagining how its imagery functions to describe its context and to construct an alternative plausibility structure. In so doing, she provides a framework for thinking about how Revelation appropriates and shapes ideological assumptions within its rhetorical milieu.

One scholar who begins to think about the text's description of the wedding of the Lamb in a way consistent with Schüssler Fiorenza's understanding of Revelation as visionary rhetoric is Steven J. Friesen. In his *Imperial Cults and the Apocalypse of John*, Friesen goes far in exploring the means by which Revelation challenges Roman imperial discourse, including the Empire's claims to absolute power and authority.[18] He argues, in a way similar to that of Schüssler Fiorenza, that Revelation reinterprets its context as a tool for resisting the dominant society. However, following the observations of Leonard Thompson, Friesen argues that Revelation's open hostility toward Roman rule and discourse also serves to persuade and provoke the text's audience to accept its world view.[19] To this end Revelation assimilates traditional imagery to de-legitimate forms of Roman discourse. Almost in passing, Friesen suggests that Revelation's nuptial imagery appropriates traditional Roman gender conventions in order to pursue its own 'subversive religious goals'.[20]

---

13 Tina Pippin, *Death and Desire: The Rhetoric of Gender in the Apocalypse of John* (Literary Currents in Biblical Interpretation; Louisville, KY: Westminster/John Knox Press, 1992), p. 26.

14 Pippin, *Death and Desire*, pp. 22, 43.

15 Pippin, *Death and Desire*, p. 73.

16 Pippin, *Death and Desire*, pp. 73–77.

17 Pippin, *Death and Desire*, p. 92.

18 Steven J. Friesen, *Imperial Cults and the Apocalypse of John: Reading Revelation in the Ruins* (New York: Oxford University Press, 2001).

19 Friesen, *Imperial Cults*, p. 145. See also Leonard L. Thompson, *The Book of Revelation: Apocalypse and Empire* (New York: Oxford University Press, 1990).

20 Friesen, *Imperial Cults*, p. 178.

Such observations encourage us to investigate how Revelation's nuptial–familial imagery functions in relation to the dominant discourse of Revelation's milieu. Approaching Revelation as visionary rhetoric, this essay explores the ways in which Revelation's nuptial imagery might reflect and respond to the Roman Empire's dominant social discourse. In so doing, it contributes another chapter to the feminist project of uncovering assumptions about gender that undergird Revelation's nuptial imagery. Thus, it provides additional material for critical reflection about whether Revelation's vision seeks liberation from or maintenance of the status quo.

Unveiling the Social Context of Revelation and Roman 'Family Values'

Written during the reign of Domitian (81–96 CE), Revelation constructs an alternative world view to counter that of the Roman Empire. At the center of the Roman imperial world view was the assertion that the reign of Augustus (27 BCE–14 CE) restored a failing Republic to an earlier, pristine state and, consequently, bettered the world as a whole.[21] Imperial propaganda, spread throughout the Empire on coinage and in monumental art, lauds Augustus as 'savior'. Referring to this propaganda, Richard A. Horsley comments, 'Remarkable is the attribution of the very structure of societal life itself to Caesar as the divine Source of life and Savior of society . . . '[22] A Roman coin from 12 BCE visually communicates this attribution as it depicts Augustus lifting up a feminine personification of Rome who kneels before him.[23] In fact, Augustus was honored as savior of the Empire through the imperial cults popular in Asia Minor, the location of Revelation's audience.[24]

This salvific work included Augustus's efforts to restore the Republic and spread traditional Roman values, such as piety toward the gods and duty to the Empire, through a program of social and political rhetoric.[25] In the *Res Gestae Divi Augusti* (c.14 CE), an inscription on a temple in Ankara, Asia Minor, but found in other locations as well, Augustus proclaims, 'By the new laws, carried with me as [sponsor,] many model traditions of our ancestors that were falling out of use in our [generation] *I restored* and [handed on] as *models* of many things to be imitated by

---

21 Friesen, *Imperial Cults*, p. 123.

22 Richard A. Horsley, 'Religion and Other Products of Empire', *JAAR* 71 (2003), pp. 13–44. This article includes a translation of an inscription from Asia Minor, c.19 BCE, which characterizes Augustus as 'Savior'.

23 Paul Zanker, *The Power of Images in the Age of Augustus* (trans. Alan Shapiro; Ann Arbor: University of Michigan Press, 1988), p. 91.

24 The presence of the Roman imperial cults in Asia Minor receives much attention from Revelation scholars who debate whether participation in these cults was made mandatory by the Empire or by social pressure. Recent discussions of the imperial cult tend to favor the latter thesis, pointing out that the cults were especially popular in Asia Minor, in contrast to the West, as a means of demonstrating fidelity to the Empire. See S. R. F. Price, *Rituals and Power: The Roman Imperial Cult in Asia Minor* (Cambridge, UK: Cambridge University Press, 1984), as well as Friesen, *Imperial Cults*, pp. 145–51.

25 Zanker, *Power of Images*, pp. 101–02.

posterity.'[26] Couched in terms of returning to an earlier time marked by morality and virtue, the topics of family and marriage provided central elements of this imperial ideology. The Augustan moral vision highlighted the importance of the *domus* or the οἶκος (the household or home) in maintaining Roman peace and power.[27] Not only was the stability of the imperial household itself understood as crucial to the Pax Romana (e.g., Ovid, *Fast.* 1.709–22), the strength of individual families was also believed to be essential to maintaining civil order.[28] Since, as Cicero described, the family was the 'nursery' of the state, the Empire had a stake in encouraging product-ive families (*De officiis* 1.54). Furthermore, loyalty to the Empire could be measured by one's coherence to the imperial understanding of the household (Dio Cassius, *Roman History* 56.2).[29]

The Empire communicated its perspectives on the family through legislation,[30] coins, state-sponsored ceremonies, public art and monuments.[31] Such imperial discourse permeated the urban areas of Asia Minor, including the cities to which Revelation is addressed. The imagistic social propaganda was so pervasive that

26 Robert K. Sherk, 'The "Res Gestae" of Augustus', in *idem* (ed. and trans.), *The Roman Empire: Augustus to Hadrian* (Cambridge, UK: Cambridge University Press, 1988), pp. 41–51, l. 8.5. This inscription purports to be authored by Augustus himself. While the original inscription may have been on his tomb in Rome, fragments of the text have been discovered throughout the Mediterranean world; the Ankara inscription is the most complete. See also Suetonius, 'Augustus', *Lives of the Caesars* (trans. J. C. Rolfe; 2 vols; LCL; Cambridge, MA: Harvard University Press, 1913), l. 34, and Tacitus, *The Annals* (trans. John Jackson; 2 vols; LCL; Cambridge, MA: Harvard University Press, 1937), l. 3.25.

27 The question of how Romans understood the concepts of *domus* and *familia* continues to be debated, reflecting the ambiguity inherent within the primary sources. See Dale B. Martin, 'The Construction of the Ancient Family: Methodological Considerations', *JRS* 86 (1996), pp. 40–60; Carolyn Osiek and David L. Balch, *Families in the New Testament World: Households and House Churches* (Louisville, KY: Westminster John Knox Press, 1997); Beryl Rawson, 'The Roman Family', in *eadem* (ed.), *The Family in Ancient Rome: New Perspectives* (Ithaca, NY: Cornell University Press, 1986), pp. 1–57; Richard P. Saller and Brent D. Shaw, 'Tombstones and Roman Family Relations in the Principate: Civilians, Soldiers, and Slaves', *JRS* 74 (1984), pp. 124–56.

28 Mark D. Fullerton, 'The *Domus Augusti* in Imperial Iconography of 13–12 B.C.', *AJA* 89 (1985), pp. 473–83.

29 Eva Cantarella, 'Marriage and Sexuality in Republican Rome: A Roman Conjugal Love Story', in Martha C. Nussbaum and Julia Sihvola (eds), *The Sleep of Reason: Erotic Experience and Sexual Ethics in Ancient Greece and Rome* (Chicago, IL: University of Chicago Press, 2002), pp. 269–82.

30 Augustan legislation included the *Lex Julia de maritandis ordinibus* (18 BCE) and the *Lex Papia Poppaea* (9 CE), both of which promoted marriage and childbearing and discouraged adultery among citizens (e.g., Dio Cassius, *Roman History* 56.1–10; Plutarch, *Caes.* 15). Legal incentives, including freedom from male legal guardianship, were offered to citizen women who bore multiple children. While this legislation applied only to citizens within the Empire, it is indicative of Roman attempts at promoting its vision of 'the family'. It was not until 320 CE that the Emperor Constantine repealed Augustan penalties against the unmarried. Suzanne Dixon, *The Roman Family* (Baltimore, MD: The Johns Hopkins University Press, 1992), pp. 61–97; Judith Evans Grubbs, *Law and Family in Late Antiquity: The Emperor Constantine's Marriage Legislation* (Oxford: Oxford University Press, 1995), pp. 103–12 and *eadem, Women and the Law in the Roman Empire: A Sourcebook on Marriage, Divorce, and Widowhood* (London: Routledge, 2002), pp. 83–85; Susan Treggiari, *Roman Marriage: Iusti Coniuges from the Time of Cicero to the Time of Ulpian* (Oxford: Clarendon Press, 1991), pp. 60–80.

31 Zanker, *Power of Images*, p. 3.

'people could not have been oblivious to it, and it must have influenced their per-ceptions'.[32] One can see how the views of the Empire touched 'the rich and the powerful, and everyone, slave and free . . . ' (Rev. 6.15). This is not to say that all the people accepted Rome's views; rather, the point is that imperial discourse pro-vided the prevailing backdrop for other forms of discourse, including that of Christians.

Those rulers who succeeded Augustus, including Domitian, generally supported the social discourse that he initiated, including his emphasis on restoring the traditional understanding of the household. Until recently, Revelation scholars relied heavily upon the portrayal of Domitian in Suetonius's biography, which describes the emperor as a philanderer and adulterer.[33] Brian W. Jones, however, argues that Suetonius's depiction of such sexual misbehavior is standard vituperation designed to arouse public loyalty to Domitian's successor, Trajan.[34] Indeed, Suetonius acknowledges that Domitian sought to correct 'public morals' and enforced laws on adultery, in spite of committing adultery himself (*Dom.* 8). Even Domitian embraced (at least publicly) and promoted the Augustan moral vision. Martial comments in one of his infamous epigrams, 'It used to be a game to betray the sacred marriage torch and a game to castrate innocent males. You forbid both, Caesar, and come to the aid of future generations; for by your order their birth is made safe. Under your rule no man shall be either eunuch or adulterer. Formerly (alas for our morals!) even a eunuch was an adulterer' (6.2).[35] Likewise, Domitian's devotion to the goddess Minerva, who was associated with the domestic arts of spinning and weaving as well as the art of war, reflected his commitment to maintain-ing the values of the *domus* and its traditional gender roles.[36] Domitian's furtherance of Augustan moral ideals indicates that the dominant discourse of Revelation's milieu embraces the imperial vision of the family or household initiated by Augustus.

An important aspect of Roman social discourse about the *domus* involved pre-senting the imperial family as *the* ideal family,[37] the ultimate example of which was the Arc Pacis in Rome. This monument depicts the imperial family, including unprecedented images of the imperial women and young children,[38] in a religious

32 Beryl Rawson, 'From "Daily Life" to "Demography"', in Richard Hawley and Barbara Levick (eds), *Women in Antiquity: New Assessments* (London: Routledge, 1995), pp. 1–20 (16).

33 Suetonius, *Lives of the Caesars*. For a discussion of problems associated with the use of Sueto-nius to construct a portrait of Domitian and to uncover Revelation's milieu see Thompson, *Book of Revelation*, pp. 95–109.

34 Brian W. Jones, *The Emperor Domitian* (London and New York: Routledge, 1992), p. 39.

35 Martial, *Epigrams* (trans. Walter C. A. Ker; 2 vols; rev. edn, LCL; Cambridge, MA: Harvard University Press, 1978–79).

36 Eve D'Ambra, *Private Lives, Imperial Virtues: The Frieze of the Forum Transitorium in Rome* (Princeton, NJ: Princeton University Press, 1993), p. 11.

37 Fullerton, *Domus Augusti*, pp. 473–83. See also Susan Fischler, 'Social Stereotypes and Histor-ical Analysis: The Case of Imperial Woman at Rome', in Léonie J. Archer, Susan Fischler and Maria Wyke (eds), *Women in Ancient Societies: An Illusion of the Night* (London: Macmillan, 1994), pp. 115–33.

38 A photograph appears in Elaine Fantham et al. (eds), *Women in the Classical World: Image and Text* (New York: Oxford University Press, 1994), p. 295.

procession.[39] Coinage minted throughout the Empire, bearing likenesses of the imperial family, served to present them as an ideal to be emulated. For example, Domitian and Domitia Longina are depicted as physically similar, thereby communicating their supposed marital harmony, even though Domitia was exiled for a short time for committing adultery.[40] The imitation of imperial portraits on Roman funerary art suggests that citizens and freed-people to some extent understood images of the members of the imperial family as visual models and, quite likely, as models of behavior.[41]

Depictions and descriptions of the imperial family could even take on divine overtones. Scholars debate whether the Roman emperors, including Domitian, required others to refer to them with divine epitaphs;[42] however, imperial rhetoric clearly depicts the emperors and their family members as divine and as part of the *domus divina* (divine household).[43] Iconography on coins that circulated throughout the Empire portrays the imperial family in the guise of gods and goddesses. In coinage from Asia Minor, for example, Domitia Longina appears as Venus, holding a helmet and spear, suggesting she embodies the same characteristics as the goddess, while elsewhere she appears as Ceres or Juno.[44] This iconography communicates coherence among divine will, the imperial family and imperial visions of family, as well as implicitly suggesting divine approval of those who similarly embraced the imperial vision.

The Idealized Roman Woman: Bride, Wife and Mother

The imperial vision of the *domus* demanded a specific understanding of feminine gender. The Empire's emphasis on productive families necessitated maintaining traditional Greco-Roman views about women's ideal traits and roles.[45] Dio, writing in the third century CE, encapsulates this view of idealized feminine gender in a speech he attributes to Augustus: 'For is there anything better than a wife who is chaste (σωφροσύνη), domestic, a good housekeeper, a rearer of children; one to gladden you in health, to tend you in sickness; to be your partner in good fortune, to console you in misfortune; to restrain the mad passion of youth and to temper the unseasonable harshness of old age?' (*Roman History* 56.3.3).[46]

---

39 Visual propaganda was not limited to Augustan Rome. A relief of Septimus Severus and his family located in Libya (c. 206 CE) hints at the geographical and temporal scope of such art. See Fantham et al., *Women in the Classical World*, p. 359.

40 Eric R. Varner, 'Domitia Longina and the Politics of Portraiture', *AJA* 99 (1995), pp. 187–206.

41 Eve D'Ambra, 'The Cult of Virtues and the Funerary Relief of Ulpia Epigone', in *eadem* (ed.), *Roman Art in Context: An Anthology* (Upper Saddle River, NJ: Prentice Hall, 1993), pp. 104–14.

42 Thompson, *Book of Revelation*, pp. 104–107.

43 Maureen B. Flory, 'The Deification of Roman Women', *The Ancient History Bulletin* 9.3–4 (1995), pp. 127–34 (134). See also Fullerton, 'The *Domus Augusti*', pp. 473–83.

44 Varner, 'Domitia Longina', pp. 200–202.

45 Although competing views of gender did exist within the Empire, most of the ancient texts that were preserved and circulated, and which consequently are still in existence, reflect the views of the dominant culture. The dominant view, while not completely static, exhibits a great deal of consistency in how ideal feminine gender was depicted. See Suzanne Dixon, *Reading Roman Women: Sources, Genres and Real Life* (London: Duckworth, 2001), pp. 32–36.

46 Dio Cassius, *Roman History* (trans. Earnest Cary; 9 vols; LCL; Cambridge, MA: Harvard University Press, 1914).

As with the imperial view of the *domus*, the traits of the ideal Roman woman were communicated through a variety of means, including wedding imagery and rituals.

One of the central roles associated with the feminine gender was that of wife, and it was assumed that all females, with few exceptions, would or should marry. (This assumption is particularly evident in the Greek-speaking parts of the Empire.) Roman wedding traditions both emphasized the importance of the role of wife and effectively communicated the nature of this gender role. The numerous depictions of weddings in funerary art, including images of couples grasping hands before Juno and scenes depicting mythological weddings, point to the event's cultural importance.[47]

In the Greco-Roman milieu the role of 'bride' (*nova nupta*, νύμφη) marked a shift in the female's social identity from virgin[48] to wife and so her entrance into the role for which she was born.[49] This transition was suggested by the main element of the traditional Roman wedding, the *deductio*, which began at the home of the bride, the home of her *pater familias*, and ended at her new home, that of the bridegroom (Catullus 61.30; see also Plutarch, *Quaest. rom.* 29–30).[50] In Latin, the procession was described as *ducere uxorem*, which means literally 'to lead a wife', suggesting that the wedding was understood as a transition for the female and not the male. In fact the groom need not be present at the wedding for it to be official.[51]

Wedding rites and traditions, including the bride's costume, further emphasized the transition of the bride into the role of wife. Just prior to her wedding the bride changed from a child's tunic, worn by both girls and boys, to the tunic worn exclusively by women.[52] By changing out of the androgynous garment of childhood into a garment specifically associated with women, the bride adopts her appropriate gendered role. (This also implies that in the dominant discourse becoming a wife equalled becoming a woman.) The bride-to-be wove her own garment, the *tunica recta*, indicating her preparedness for adopting her new role, which ideally included

---

47 Susan Wood, 'Alcestis on Roman Sarcophagi', *AJA* 82 (1978), pp. 499–510.

48 For a discussion of the age of Roman girls at marriage, including a description of some of the difficulties involved in determining this, see Brent D. Shaw, 'The Age of Roman Girls at Marriage: Some Reconsiderations', *JRS* 77 (1987), pp. 30–46.

49 The importance of this event in the social understanding of feminine gender is evident in Pliny's heartfelt lament at the death of a young girl: 'Hers is a truly tragic and untimely end – death itself was not so cruel as the moment of its coming. She was already engaged to marry a distinguished young man, the day for the wedding was fixed, and we had received our invitations. Such joy, and now such sorrow!' (Pliny, 'To Aefulanus Marcellinus', in *Pliny: Letters* [trans. William Melmoth; 2 vols.; LCL; Cambridge, MA: Harvard University Press, 1915], V.xvi.6).

50 Catullus: *Catullus, Tibullus and Pervigilium Veneris* (trans. Francis Warre Cornish; LCL; Cambridge, MA: Harvard University Press, 1962); Plutarch: *Quaestiones Romanae* in *Moralia* vol. iv (trans. Frank C. Babbitt; LCL; Cambridge, MA: Harvard University Press, 1936).

51 'A woman can, it is agreed, marry a man who is absent either by means of a letter from him or by means of a messenger, *if she is led to his house*. But a woman who is absent cannot be married by a husband either through a letter or by a messenger from her. For *deductio* is necessary to the house of the husband, not the wife, for the former is the domicile of the marriage', Pomponius, *Dig.* 23.2.5, translated in Treggiari, *Roman Marriage*, p. 167.

52 Treggiari, *Roman Marriage*, p. 163.

cloth production and weaving (Xenophon, *Oec.* 5–6).[53] Similarly, during the wedding procession the bride and/or her attendants carried implements associated with wool-working and weaving, such as spindles and distaffs (Plutarch, *Quaest. rom.* 30).[54] The presence of the tools of cloth production implied that the bride was skilled in household management,[55] which was often metonymically indicated through references to a woman's wool-working, spinning and weaving.[56] The ideal wife produced clothing not only for herself but also for those within her home. According to Suetonius, the Emperor Augustus bragged that he wore only cloth spun by the women of his family, rather than cloth that was purchased (*Aug.* 73). Reflecting this idealized view of feminine gender, references to women's wool-working appear frequently in funerary epitaphs. For example, the tomb of a certain Murdia, who lived during the time of Augustus, proclaims that she 'was like other good women in her modesty, decency, chastity, obedience, *wool-work* . . .'[57] Some funerary monuments depict women with wool-working implements, such as a ball of yarn or baskets for wool, visually indicating their proficiency in maintaining the household and their coherence to the societal vision of a 'good woman'.[58] Like the adoption of the *tunica recta*, allusions to textile production in the context of Roman wedding rites point to the bride's shift into her role as wife, a central element of which was caring for the household.

A bride's ability to weave represented her readiness to assume the role of her husband's partner in supporting the household economy. The two had corresponding roles in maintaining the household, although the wife's sphere of influence was primarily within the *domus* and the husband's was primarily outside it. The legal definition of marriage, which applied only to citizens,[60] implied that the husband and wife ideally functioned as a partnership. Modestinus explains, 'Marriage is the *coniunctio*, the joining together of a man and woman and the sharing of their entire life, the joint participation in rights human and divine.'[59] The fact that Roman marriages were predicated upon the mutual assent of the parties involved – described as *affectio maritalis* (a marital attitude) – and not upon a legal contract likewise reflected the assumption that marriage was a partnership.[61] The almost ubiquitous

53 Xenophon, *Oeconomicus* (trans. E. C. Marchant; LCL; Cambridge, MA: Harvard University Press, 1923).

54 Dixon, *Reading Roman Women*, pp. 117–18.

55 In the essays 'That Women Too Should Study Philosophy' and 'Should Daughters Receive the Same Education as Sons?', Musonius Rufus (first century CE) pinpoints household management as the most important job of a wife. The essays are translated by Cora E. Lutz, 'Musonius Rufus: The Roman Socrates', *Yale Classical Studies* 10 (1947), pp. 3–147.

56 For instance, a tombstone from Phrygia groups together female symbols, including wool-working implements, a mirror and shoes, in contrast to symbols of masculine gender, such as tools and construction materials. See Fantham et al., *Women in the Classical World*, p. 371.

57 Translated by Natalie Kampen in Fantham et al., *Women in the Classical World*, p. 318.

58 E.g., Dixon, *Reading Roman Women*, plate 15; D'Ambra, 'Cult of Virtues', p. 109.

59 *Dig* 23.2.1, as quoted in Jane Gardner, *Women in Roman Law and Society* (London: Croom Helm, 1986), p. 47.

60 'Roman citizens have *conubium* [the capacity to marry] with Roman citizens, but with Latins and foreigners only if the privilege was granted. There is no *conubium* with slaves.' *Tituli Ulpiani* 5.3–5 as quoted in Treggiari, *Roman Marriage*, p. 43.

61 Ulpian, *Dig* 24.1.32.13; Quintillian, *Institutio* 5.11.32; Treggiari, *Roman Marriage*, pp. 54–57.

image of a married couple grasping hands (sometimes in the context of a wedding) depicted upon funerary monuments points to the popularity of the concept of marital harmony.[62] This handclasp, the *dextrarum iunctio*,[63] visually and metonymically communicates the values of partnership (*societas*/κοινωνία) and agreement (*concordia*).

The ideal of marital harmony did not typically imply an equal partnership,[64] but a partnership that involved the wife's conforming to the views, needs and desires of her husband. Plutarch suggests that a wife should be like a mirror that reflects the true likeness of the husband, even his character (*Advice* 14).[65] Diogenes Laertius, writing in the third century CE, illustrates this ideal in his description of the female philosopher Hipparchia, who fell in love with and married the notorious Cynic Crates. Despite the pleas of her parents and even warnings issued by Crates himself, Hipparchia adopts her husband's unconventional lifestyle, including his itinerant ways and his mode of clothing (*Lives of the Philosophers* VI.2–3). As her husband's partner, the ideal Roman wife modelled her life in relation to that of her husband. While it is mistaken to assume that the ideals of the dominant rhetoric reflect reality, numerous funerary inscriptions suggest that the population generally accepted that this ideal of marital partnership or *concordia* was how things 'should be'. Epitaphs throughout the Empire and from a wide range of social classes laud the values of partnership and marital harmony.[66] One tomb inscription reads, 'We lived harmonious and with equal character',[67] and another (possibly from the second century CE)

62 Because the handshake motif occurs also between same-sex couples, Davies argues that the handclasp is not indicative of a marriage-type of relationship. See Glenys Davies, 'The Significance of the Handshake Motif in Classical Funerary Art', *AJA* 89 (1985), pp. 627–40. Other scholars interpret this same evidence to mean that some ancient same-sex partners lived as married couples (whether legally or not), much like today. See Bernadette J. Brooten, *Love Between Women: Early Christian Responses to Female Homoeroticism* (Chicago, IL: University of Chicago Press, 1996), pp. 59–60.

63 The handshake motif also appears in the context of political relationships. See Louis Reekmans, 'La "dextrarum iunctio" dans l'iconographie romaine et paléochrétienne', *Bulletin de l'Institut historique Belge à Rome* 31 (1958), pp. 23–95.

64 Roman law, including laws concerning marriage and women's issues, assumed that women were incapable of making their own decisions. Consequently, free women were almost always under some form of guardianship or male legal authority. While in classical Roman law women were often married with *manus*, meaning that upon marriage they became legal subordinates to their husbands, this practice was losing favor during the first century. Even when women were not legally subordinate to their husbands, they were still required to be under the authority of a male guardian (*tutor*). The guardian, appointed by the woman's *paterfamilias*, was usually not her husband, although this may have been more common in the Eastern provinces. Furthermore, even if a woman's legal guardian were someone other than her husband, the ideal Roman wife was still expected to live in harmony with her husband; otherwise the marriage was dissolved. For a clear discussion of the complexities surrounding Roman laws on marriage and tutelage, see Grubbs, *Women and the Law*, pp. 21–22, 81–83.

65 Plutarch, *Advice to the Bride and Groom* in *Plutarch's Advice to the Bride and Groom and A Consolation to His Wife: English Translations, Commentary, Interpretive Essays, and Bibliography* (trans. Donald Russell; ed. Sarah B. Pomeroy; New York: Oxford University Press, 1999), pp. 5–13.

66 Treggiari, *Roman Marriage*, pp. 249–53; Suzanne Dixon, 'The Sentimental Ideal of the Roman Family', in Beryl Rawson (ed.), *Marriage, Divorce, and Children in Ancient Rome* (Oxford: Clarendon Press, 1991), pp. 99–113.

67 Translated from the *CIL* by Treggiari, *Roman Marriage*, p. 245.

describes the ideal of harmony indirectly by praising a wife who was married to her husband for thirty years without a quarrel![68]

In addition to representing the bride's ability to serve as her husband's partner, the presence of spinning and weaving tools within the context of wedding rites also served as a metaphorical indicator of the bride's supposed morality. In the Roman world a woman's moral character consisted primarily of her chastity or sexual self-control (σωφροσύνη).[69] A woman who worked wool remained within the *domus* and was not, according to the logic of this discourse, outside looking for sexual adventures. A second century BCE funeral monument from Smyrna visually represents the connection between textile work and staying within the home: its relief depicts the interior of a home, including columns and a window, where a female subject receives a spindle from a servant.[70]

The metaphorical connection between chastity and spinning and weaving played an important part in Roman myth, including myths describing Rome's foundation. For example, Livy (first century CE) recounts the story of Lucretia, whose chastity is tested by her husband, one of the first consuls of the Roman Republic, and his friends. Lucretia is proven chaste when she is found working her wool late at night, rather than engaging in adulterous affairs as her husband's friends had expected.[71] Ovid's version of the myth highlights the connection between Lucretia's sexual fidelity and her spinning, as he notes that around Lucretia's bed were baskets of wool and not, by implication, lovers (*Fasti* 2.740).[72] Despite, or perhaps on account of Lucretia's fidelity, one of her husband's companions rapes her. Distraught, Lucretia takes her own life so that her loss of chastity might not set a negative example for other women (Livy I.58.7–8). Livy comments that outrage over Lucretia's death led to the expulsion of the ruling dynasty and so the establishment of the Republic. Thus Rome, according to the dominant discourse, was founded through avenging a woman's chastity, and the Empire's continued strength resided in its continued vigilance in maintaining this feminine virtue.[73]

In *Spinning Fantasies: Rabbis, Gender, and History*, Miriam Peskowitz describes the connection between Roman depictions of 'women's work' and maintaining the ideological vision of the dominant discourse:

> Femininity and sexuality were not just important for individual women, for families and local communities. They were enmeshed in larger notions of Empire. Wool-working women were familiar metaphors for building one's society and renewing its culture.[74]

---

68 Translated from the *CIL* by Natalie Kampen in Fantham et al., *Women in the Classical World*, pp. 369–70.

69 D'Ambra, 'Cult of Virtues', pp. 109–10.

70 See Fantham et al., *Women in the Classical World*, p. 158.

71 *Livy* (trans. B. O. Foster; 14 vols; LCL; Cambridge, MA: Harvard University Press, 1919).

72 Ovid, *Fasti* (trans. James George Frazer; 2nd rev. edn, ed. G. P. Goold; LCL; Cambridge, MA: Harvard University Press, 1989).

73 Hans-Friedrich Mueller, '*Vita, Pudicitia, Libertas*: Juno, Gender, and Religious Politics in Valerius Maximus', in *Transactions of the American Philological Association* 128 (1998), pp. 221–63 (228). Conversely, a major component of Roman social discourse entailed lamenting female licentiousness as a sign of the decline of the Empire. See Dixon, *Reading Roman Women*, pp. 56–65.

74 Miriam Peskowitz, *Spinning Fantasies: Rabbis, Gender, and History* (Berkeley, CA: University of California Press, 1997), p. 71.

By incorporating items associated with spinning and weaving, Roman weddings reflected and consequently furthered Roman views of gender and the family. This is not to say that individual women embraced the claims of the dominant culture; rather, it points to how traditions transmit views that support the dominant ideology. Appropriation of these traditions, whether in practice or through imagery, necessarily perpetuated the ideas of gender and the family embedded within the traditions themselves.

Finally, although Roman law assumed that couples who married possessed affection toward one another, described as a 'marital attitude', Roman law and social discourse emphasized that the aim of marriage was ultimately procreation. Under Roman law women were rewarded for fulfilling this ideal[75] (although these efforts were not necessarily successful in encouraging marriage and childbearing; Tacitus, *Annals* III.25).[76] Images of the imperial family celebrated the presence of imperial children. Indicative of this ideology is a coin, minted a number of years after Revelation, bearing an image of Faustina the Younger with her six children. While imperial rhetoric would hold Faustina as an ideal, her large family was exceptional. Domitia Longina, Domitian's second wife, bore the emperor a daughter and a son, both of whom died in infancy and before Domitian ascended to power. Despite this, Domitia's role as mother to Domitian's son was lauded in imperial coinage (including coins depicting the infant son divinized and sitting upon a globe) minted during her husband's reign.[77] Pointing to the public's general acceptance of the ideal of bearing children is the eulogy for Turia (c. 12–8 BCE). Turia's husband describes how they longed for a child, although they never had one. He recalls, 'Disconsolate to see me without children you wished to put an end to my chagrin by proposing to me a divorce, offering to yield the place to another spouse more fertile ... '.[78] Turia's epitaph reflects the dominant societal assumption that marriage was intended to yield children and provides a glimpse into the reality of Roman families that were childless. Although Turia and her husband apparently remained childless, the failure to bear children was a failure to live out the ideal promoted through imperial discourse.

The dominant rhetoric of the Roman Empire, the prevailing discourse within Revelation's milieu, extolled the virtues of the *domus* and marital harmony. Communicated through a variety of means, the imperial vision of the ideal household was related to a very specific view of feminine gender. In fact, various elements of the Roman wedding marked the traits and roles of the ideal Roman woman. Moreover, the importance of the *domus* within Roman imperial rhetoric, including the propaganda produced during Domitian's reign and the popularity of this theme

75 In Roman law women required guardianship by a male. Free-born women could escape guardianship by bearing three children, while freed-women could receive the same privilege by bearing four. Bearing children also provided women with privileges when it came to inheriting from their husbands (Treggiari, *Roman Marriage*, pp. 69–73).

76 A second-century dowry document located in Egypt points to the continued applicability of this legislation, describing the marriage between two Roman citizens as complying 'with the Julian law concerning marriage which was passed for the purpose of procreating children' (Reprinted by Jane Rowlandson [ed.], *Women and Society in Greek and Roman Egypt: A Sourcebook* [Cambridge, UK: Cambridge University Press, 1998], p. 182). See also *Dig.* 24.3.1 and Catullus 61.205.

77 Varner, 'Domitia Longina', p. 188.

78 Cantarella, 'Marriage and Sexuality in Republican Rome', p. 278.

among citizens and freed-people living within the Empire, suggests that Revelation's use of familial–nuptial imagery reflects and/or responds to the presentation of these themes.

Reading Revelation's Familial–Nuptial Imagery: 19.1–8

John recounts the events of earth and heaven as they appear, and so as they 'really are', from his vantage point in the heavenly throne room (Rev. 4.1). Through the use of vision language, including imperatives to 'See!' (e.g., 4.1, 6.2), John prompts his audience to envision and experience the events and entities that he describes. As Schüssler Fiorenza explains, John encourages his audience to re-vision the world around them, including the Roman Empire and its political and social rhetoric.[79] The hymn in Rev. 19.1–8 functions as part of this re-visioning:

[1]After these things I heard something like the great sound of a multitude in heaven saying, 'Alleluia! Salvation and glory and power to our God! [2]For true and just are his judgments, since he has judged the great prostitute who corrupted the earth with her prostitution . . . [3]and the smoke from her goes up for ever and ever!'[6] And I heard something like the voice of a great crowd . . . saying, 'Alleluia! For the Lord our God, the Almighty, has begun to reign! [7]Let us rejoice and exult and give glory to him; since (ὅτι) the wedding of the Lamb (ὁ γάμος τοῦ ἀρνίου) has come and his wife has prepared herself (ἡ γυνὴ αὐτοῦ ἡτοίμασεν ἑαυτήν). [8]And it has been given to her that she be clothed in fine linen, shining and clean. For the fine linen is the just works of the saints'.

In this short hymn John constructs an image that counters Roman imperial claims about the nature of the *domus* and reapplies traditional Roman rhetoric about the family to the Lamb (the Risen Christ) and the Christian community. Revelation accomplishes this by manipulating traditional views of gender and marriage, including elements associated with the Roman wedding, to prompt the audience to envision a new image of the *domus*.

Echoing traditions that personify cities and communities as women, the hymn begins with a celebration of the destruction of the personified 'Babylon' – the great prostitute (τὴν πόρνην τὴν μεγάλην; 19.2). Revelation's depiction of Babylon as a prostitute (ch. 17) echoes the Hebrew Bible's prophetic depictions of cities, including Jerusalem, as women. In these traditions feminine imagery often serves as a tool for critiquing cities and communities perceived to have been 'unfaithful' to God (e.g., Ezekiel 16, 23).[80] The tradition of personifying cities as women existed within

---

79 For a discussion of how Revelation uses rhetorical cues to encourage its audience to envision an alternative world, see David Barr, 'Blessed Are Those Who Hear: John's Apocalypse as Present Experience', in Linda Bennett Elder, David L. Barr and Elizabeth Struthers Malbon (eds), *Biblical and Humane: A Festschrift for John Priest* (Atlanta, GA: Scholars Press, 1996), pp. 87–103.

80 See Jean-Pierre Ruiz, *Ezekiel in the Apocalypse: The Transformation of Prophetic Language in Revelation 16,17–19,10* (European University Studies Series, XXIII. Theology Vol. 376; Frankfurt am Main: Peter Lang, 1989) and Jan Fekkes, *Isaiah and Prophetic Traditions in the Book of Revelation: Visionary Antecedents and their Development* (JSNTSup, 93; Sheffield: Sheffield Academic Press, 1994). For a discussion of Ezekiel's use of feminine imagery to depict Jerusalem, see Julie Galambush, *Jerusalem in the Book of Ezekiel: The City as Yahweh's Wife* (SBLDS, 130; Atlanta, GA: Scholars Press, 1992) and Fokkelien van Dijk-Hemmes, 'The Metaphorization of Woman in Prophetic Speech: An Analysis of Ezekiel XXIII,' *VT* 43 (1993), pp. 162–70.

Roman political and social rhetoric as well. While depictions of the city of Rome as the goddess Roma are probably the most well known,[81] the custom was even more widespread.[82] Roman visual rhetoric used the female figure to depict various nations and peoples, including those conquered by the Empire. For example, at the temple of the imperial cult in Aphrodisias, Asia Minor, relief images of women represented defeated nations, such as Britain.[83] Following the convention of depicting cities and peoples as women, John personifies the city of Babylon as a prostitute in Rev. 17.1–18. Interpreters generally agree that this description of 'the great city (ἡ πόλις ἡ μεγάλη) that has authority over the kings of the earth' (17.18) evokes the character of the city of Rome.[84] Further, this prostitute sits upon seven mountains (17.9), just as the city of Rome sat upon 'seven hills' (e.g., Pliny, *Natural History* 3.5.66–67).[85]

In depicting the city of Rome as a prostitute John effectively extends Revelation's anti-Roman perspective, heretofore directed at political, economic and religious elements of the Empire, to Roman social discourse as well. His depiction of Rome as a sexually promiscuous woman and the 'mother of prostitutes' (17.5) implies that the Empire is far from the ideal it promotes. As described above, Roman social discourse highlighted the importance of a woman's chastity and her role within the home, even linking these traits to the foundation of the Empire in the story of Lucretia. Depicting Rome as a prostitute challenges imperial claims of restoring the traditional view of the *domus*. Further, by textually destroying Rome's personification, John creates the possibility of establishing a counter-image to the prostitute and to Roman views of the ideal *domus*.

The celebration of the prostitute's demise and the announcement of the Lamb's wedding are united within the context of a hymn lauding God's reign: 'For the Lord our God, the Almighty, has begun to reign! Let us rejoice and exult and give glory to him; *since* the wedding of the Lamb has come' (19.6–7). Announcing the wedding of the Lamb within a political context echoes Roman social discourse, which similarly united political and familial imagery. Often this union involved depicting the imperial family in divinized terms that linked them to the gods. The depiction of the wedding of the Lamb in the context of a hymn celebrating God's reign can be understood as serving a similar function, while simultaneously challenging the legitimacy of the imperial vision. Revelation's wedding imagery connects the Lamb and, by extension, his wife to God. The connection is implied by the suggestion in Rev. 19.7 that the wedding of the Lamb serves as the rationale for heavenly rejoicing over God's reign, as indicated through the conjunction ὅτι ('since' or 'for'). In

---

81 For an example of Rome depicted as the goddess Roma during the time of Domitian, see the images of the Cancelleria reliefs in Diana E. E. Kleiner, *Roman Sculpture* (New Haven, CT: Yale University Press, 1992), p. 190. For a discussion of the goddess Roma see Ronald Mellor, 'The Goddess Roma', *ANRW* 17.2, pp. 950–1030.

82 Kleiner, *Roman Sculpture*, pp. 224–26.

83 R. R. R. Smith, '*Simulacra Gentium:* The Ethne from the Sebasteion at Aphrodisias', *JRS* 78 (1988), pp. 50–77.

84 For a discussion of reasons for reading Babylon as a critique of Rome see Friesen, *Imperial Cults*, pp. 138–40.

85 Pliny, *Natural History* (trans. H. Rackham; 10 vols; LCL; Cambridge, MA: Harvard University Press, 1971–1989).

contrast to the Roman image of the imperial *domus divina*, John presents an image of the Lamb and his wife, within the context of God's reign. Instead of the divinized images of Domitian and Domitia Longina, John presents a different royal family, which for him is the only family connected to the divine.

Creating this familial image counters the Empire's view of the *domus*, especially since the hymn proclaims that the wedding has already begun.[86] The wedding of the Risen Christ, the Lamb, is not a future event: the use of the aorist verb translated 'has come' indicates that it has been initiated (19.7); the marriage between the Lamb and his wife is a present reality and not only a future event. The family that Revelation depicts as a challenge to the imperial vision exists for John within the present, even if it may appear differently to John's audience.

The hymnic wedding announcement describes the Lamb's partner not as his bride (νύμφη) but as his woman or wife (γυνή). Some ancient manuscripts replace νύμφη with γυνή, assimilating 19.7 to 21.2 and 21.9, which describe the New Jerusalem descending like a bride (νύμφη).[87] The use of γυνή in 19.7, instead of νύμφη, actually coheres to Roman marriage and wedding traditions, in which the bride takes on the symbols of her role as wife. Using the term 'wife' within the context of the wedding of the Lamb, Revelation encourages the audience to envision the woman in the transitional state of the wedding, the time in which she anticipates her future role or identity. While the wedding of the Lamb 'has come', John fails to mention an explicit conclusion to this wedding. Chapter 21 describes the bride again as she 'descends' from heaven, using a present participle καταβαίνουσαν (21.2, 10).[88] In some sense, Revelation encourages the audience to envision the wife of the Lamb, his bride, in a state of perpetual *deductio*. The bride of the Lamb exists entirely as a transitional or liminal figure.

The use of the possessive pronoun in the phrase 'his wife', ἡ γυνὴ αὐτοῦ, depicts the bride solely in relationship to her husband: the bride or woman is defined by her relationship to her husband. Such identification was typical in Revelation's social context, as the Roman woman was often referred to as her husband's wife.[89] Like her Roman counterparts, the wife of the Lamb is defined by her relationship to her husband. Yet, Revelation's wedding imagery serves to characterize the Lamb's wife and not her groom or husband. Even though the heavenly throng describes this event as the 'wedding of the Lamb' (ὁ γάμος τοῦ ἀρνίου), the hymnic stanza focuses

---

86 Revelation's use of the aorist verbs ἐβασίλευσεν (v. 6) and ἦλθεν (v. 7) to describe these respective events creates some translation difficulties. Many commentators treat these as inceptive aorists, describing action that has begun. See David E. Aune, *Revelation 17–22* (WBC, 52C; Nashville, TN, Thomas Nelson Publishers, 1997–98), p. 1016.

87 Aune, *Revelation 17–22*, p. 1017. Likewise, some modern English translations render γυνή as 'bride' (e.g. NIV, NIB, NASB).

88 Augustine's reading of Rev. 21.2 exploits this sense of continuing action, as he writes, 'This City has been coming down from heaven since its beginning' (Augustine, *Civ.* xx.17). Augustine, *The City of God Against the Pagans* (trans. William Chase Greene; 7 vols; LCL. Cambridge: Harvard University Press, 1960).

89 The Roman woman's name was typically a feminized version of her father's clan name (*nomen*). She could be referred to also through reference to her father's *cognomen*. At marriage, she might be referred to through her husband's *cognomen*. See Harold Whetstone Johnston, *The Private Life of the Romans* (rev. Mary Johnston; Chicago, IL: Scott, Foresman and Company, 1932), §58.

upon the wife's character. This focus remains consistent with the fact that Roman weddings typically served to mark the female's (and not the male's) transition into a new gender role.

The announcement of the wedding of the Lamb in Rev. 19.7 begs the question of the bride or wife's identity. The answer is not made clear until 21.2: 'And I saw the holy city, a new Jerusalem descending out of heaven from God prepared as a bride (νύμφη) adorned for her husband' (cf. 21.10).[90] The Lamb's bride is, like the prostitute of ch. 17, a city – a new Jerusalem. John again draws upon the tradition of depicting cities and nations as women. Thus, Revelation depicts the new Jerusalem, which is both dwelling place (city) and community of people, as a woman. The Lamb's bride is that city in which God dwells with humanity, ἡ σκηνὴ τοῦ θεοῦ μετὰ τῶν ἀνθρώπων (21.3): the new Jerusalem describes both the place and the people of God.[91]

Some scholars argue that the characterization of the new Jerusalem, the bride of the Lamb, functions solely as an image of a place and not specifically as an image of community. Notable is Barbara Rossing, who counters the community imagery in *The Choice Between Two Cities: Whore, Bride, and Empire in the Apocalypse*.[92] Rossing notes that Revelation's personification of cities functions as part of a rhetorical topos found in Jewish wisdom and Greco-Roman literary traditions. This topos uses contrasting images of two places or two women to represent two distinct ethical options. This 'two women' topos persuades an audience to align itself with the woman characterized, through references to her appearance and behavior, as desirable, rather than with the woman characterized as undesirable. John encourages his audience to associate itself with the bride, but not to envision itself as the bride. As evidence for this claim, Rossing cites Rev. 19.9, which immediately follows the hymn announcing the wedding of the Lamb: 'Blessed are those who are invited to the wedding banquet (τὸ δεῖπνον τοῦ γάμου) of the Lamb.' Rossing challenges, 'In light of the macarism of Rev. 19.9, scholars who argue that the bride is the church in this text are faced with the task of explaining how readers can be both bride and guests in the same scene.'[93] The blessing formula, she maintains, prompts the audience to read itself as the wedding guests, which for her precludes the possibility of the audience reading the bride of the Lamb also as a community image.

. While the blessing formula in Rev. 19.9 encourages the audience to identify with those invited to the wedding banquet, those receiving the blessing, this does not rule out reading the wife of the Lamb in 19.7–8 as a community image as well. Revelation's extremely fluid language is prone to moving from one image to the next based upon linguistic similarities and metaphorical connections. Commenting upon

---

90 Revelation 21 offers parallel visions of the descent of the new Jerusalem. Scholars often attribute this 'duplication' to an editorial error or mindless repetition. See, for instance, Aune, *Revelation 17–22*, 3, p. 1115.

91 Robert H. Gundry, 'The New Jerusalem: People as Place, Not Place for People', *NovT* 29 (1987), pp. 254–64.

92 Barbara Rossing, *The Choice Between Two Cities: Whore, Bride, and Empire in the Apocalypse* (Harrisburg, PA: Trinity Press International, 1999), p. 137.

93 Rossing, *Choice Between Two Cities*, p. 140.

the shift of imagery in Rev. 19.8–9, George Caird points out that a similar transition occurs in Rev. 7.17 in which 'the Lamb is also the shepherd. . . .'[94] Likewise, Babylon, a woman who is a city, sits upon a beast with seven heads that are seven mountains and seven kings (17.9–10). In other words, Revelation's visionary language resists the rules of linear logic, such as would disallow the community from identifying itself with the bride and with those present at the wedding banquet.

Revelation is not addressed to individual believers, but to Church communities, specifically 'the seven churches in Asia' (1.4), and John offers these churches a number of images through which to envision the identity of the Christian community as a whole. Among these is the image of a new Israel and, subsequently, a new Jerusalem. In Revelation 7 John depicts the 'servants of our God', those with whom the audience would presumably identify, as a reconstituted twelve tribes of Israel numbering 144,000 individuals (7.4–8). John later describes these 144,000 as those who remain faithful to the Lamb (14.1–5), again encouraging the audience to envision itself through the image of Israel. John further prompts his audience to envision itself as Israel by leading it through a series of plagues that recall the plagues leading up to Israel's exodus from Egypt (16.1–21).[95] By encouraging the audience to envision itself as Israel, which the Hebrew Bible prophets depict, metonymically, as Zion or Jerusalem (Ezekiel 16),[96] John also prepares his readers to envision the Christian community as the new Jerusalem. Revelation's explicit depiction of the Christian community as a new Israel invites the audience to envision itself in terms of the new Jerusalem as well.

While the explicit connection between the bride and the new Jerusalem does not occur until Revelation 21, the description of the woman's garment in 19.8 alludes to the connection between the bride and the community. The bride's garment, described as fine linen (βύσσινος),[97] is comprised of the righteous or just deeds of the 'saints' (τὰ δικαιώματα τῶν ἁγίων [19.8]). This suggests that the community as a whole, the community of saints (or those who aspire to become saints), is embodied in the image of the Lamb's wife. As noted earlier, the ideal Roman bride wove her own bridal costume, including the *tunica recta*, to demonstrate her ability to fulfill the role of a wife, her primary gender role. Just as the ideal Roman bride actively constructed a garment indicative of her new identity, so the community of the saints, which will become the new Jerusalem, creates its own bridal garment. The language of the saints creating the bride's garment prompts the audience, which John calls to be saints, to envision itself as the Lamb's bride. In addition, the imagery encourages the audience to envision itself as transitioning into its role in relation to the Lamb.

94 Caird, *Revelation of St. John,* p. 234.
95 Schüssler Fiorenza, *Vision of a Just World*, pp. 92–102.
96 Moshe Greenberg, *Ezekiel 1–20* (AB, 22; Garden City, NY: Doubleday, 1983), p. 301. Joseph Blenkinsopp likewise reads the reference to Jerusalem as a metonym for Israel in general (*Ezekiel* [Louisville, KY: John Knox, 1990], p. 76).
97 The LXX translation of Ezekiel 16, which describes Jerusalem as God's wayward wife, also uses the relatively unusual adjective βύσσινος. In so doing, this text depicts *God clothing* the city-woman: 'I clothed you with embroidered cloth . . . I bound you in fine linen and covered you with rich fabric' (Ezek. 16.10).

In spite of Schüssler Fiorenza's observation that Revelation's gendered images are not specifically about gender, some feminist interpreters fault John's depiction of the bride as relatively passive.[98] The image of the bride constructing her own garment belies this reading, as does the hymn's earlier proclamation that the bride 'has prepared herself' (ἡτοίμασεν ἑαυτήν). The active verb ἡτοίμασεν and the reflexive pronoun ἑαυτήν assume the woman's agency in preparing for her new role. Through this language Revelation's hymn encourages the audience to envision the community actively adorning itself just as a bride prepared herself for her wedding. As a Roman bride adopted a costume indicating her new role, so this community takes on a costume indicative of its new role. In this way, John draws upon traditional elements of Roman weddings, which typically functioned in support of the dominant view of the *domus*, even though his image of the bride serves as part of his critique of Roman social discourse.

As in Roman social discourse, Revelation's wedding imagery communicates the characteristics that the ideal 'woman' should embody, although in this case the woman is metaphorical. The characteristics John wishes upon the community, through his description of the bridal garment, reflect traditional Roman views of brides and wives. The bride's 'shining' (λαμπρός) garment complements Revelation's characterization of both God and the Lamb (the risen Christ) in terms of 'light' (e.g., 1.12–16; 22.5). Anything or anyone near the divine throne reflects God's light, including the face of Christ (2.6). The image of shining garments, therefore, suggests that the bride is near the divine and/or the Lamb. The suggestion that the bride reflects the light of the Lamb or God recalls the ideal of partnership in Roman discourse about marriage and weddings. As Plutarch suggested, the ideal wife serves as a mirror of her husband, reflecting his true nature.

Revelation encourages the audience to envision the bridal garment as clean or pure (καθαρός). Given the metaphorical connection between cloth production and chastity in Roman social discourse, the reference to the purity of the bridal garment implies that the Lamb's bride is sexually pure. The bride of the Lamb thus resembles Livy's characterization of the chaste Lucretia, who spins wool and avoids adultery. In contrast to the uncleanness of the great prostitute, who holds a cup full of the impurities of her fornications (τὰ ἀκάθαρτα τῆς πορνείας αὐτῆς [Rev. 17.4]), the purity of the bride's garment signals her fidelity to the Lamb. Ideally, the community's affection and allegiance are with the Lamb alone. Thus, John communicates that it is the Christian community and not Rome or members of the imperial family that embody the values of the ideal Roman woman. The community is called to become the ideal woman within the *domus divina*.

Since the connection between the bride and the community, the new Jerusalem, becomes explicit primarily in ch. 21, the image of purity in Rev. 19.8 can also be read as a call to individual moral purity. Images of the imperial family in Roman social discourse often served to represent ideals for emulation, and it is possible to imagine Revelation's image of the Lamb's bride being read in a similar fashion. Earlier, John had encouraged the audience of Revelation to envision itself as a virginal multitude.

98 Pippin, *Death and Desire*, p. 72. Marla Selvidge also characterizes the bridal image as one of passivity in 'Powerful and Powerless Women in the Apocalypse', *NeoT* 26 (1992), pp. 157–67.

The 144,000 identified with the twelve tribes of Israel in Revelation 7 are also characterized as 144,000 male virgins (παρθένοι) who have not 'stained' themselves with women (οἳ μετὰ γυναικῶν οὐκ ἐμολύνθησαν [Rev. 14.1–5]).[99] Not only does this imagery reveal that Revelation assumes a metaphorical connection between sexual activity and cleanliness, but it also implies that Revelation assumes celibacy as an ideal. Schüssler Fiorenza argues that these references to virginity and sexual purity describe 'cultic purity': the followers of the Lamb do not 'defile' themselves by worshiping the gods (including the divinized members of the imperial cult) of the Roman Empire.[100] In light of the politicized nature of family in the Roman world, it seems more than likely that a critique of the Empire can be understood as advocating not just metaphorical 'abstinence', but literal abstinence as well. Whether or not John understands celibacy to be an attainable state, Revelation depicts virginity and celibacy positively and as a characteristic of those who 'follow the Lamb' (14.4). Consequently, the celebration of the bride's 'pure' garment can be interpreted as a call to emulate the sexual purity of the Lamb's wife.

In Roman social discourse celibacy is decidedly anti-family and anti-Empire. As noted above, legal incentives were offered to citizen women who bore multiple children, and freed-people were encouraged bear children as well. Eva Cantarella observes that the pressure to bear children was so strong that citizens and freed-people sometimes divorced so that a wife could marry another man to bear his children. This was the case with the Roman politician Cato and his wife Martia,[101] and it was the basis for Turia's proposed solution to her childless marriage. For Revelation to suggest celibacy as an ideal, therefore, explicitly counters the Augustan moral vision expressed throughout Roman social discourse.

Furthermore, the vision of the 144,000 'male virgins' reveals Revelation's assumption of an audience in terms of masculine gender. While it is not clear if John envisions the Christian community as exclusively male or whether he uses masculine gender as normative, the image of the male virgins points to the fact that Revelation's vision of the bride, a feminine gender role, requires males to imagine themselves and their community in feminine terms. The text, as Joanna Dewey notes, 'subsumes all the faithful, women and men, into the image of a female'.[102] Since the community is comprised not only of women, but also of men (and perhaps exclusively of men), the image of the bride involves a certain degree of

99 The apparent reference to male virgins is unusual. The term παρθένοι typically describes young women who have not married (see Aune, *Revelation 6–16*, p. 811). Virginity in men was not necessarily valued within the Greco-Roman milieu. See Peter Brown, *The Body and Society: Men, Women, and Sexual Renunciation in Early Christianity* (New York: Columbia University Press, 1988), p. 28. For a full discussion of the 144,000 virgins in relation to Roman social discourse, see Lynn R. Huber, 'Sexually Explicit? Re-reading Revelation's 144,000 Virgins as a Response to Roman Social Discourses', *Journal of Men, Masculinities and Spirituality* 2.1 (2008), pp. 3–28 (http://www.jmmsweb. org/issues/volume2/number1/pp3–28).

100 Schüssler Fiorenza, 'Visionary Rhetoric and Social-Political Situation', p. 190.

101 Cantarella examines the case of Cato and Martia, in which Cato allows Martia to marry his friend Hortensius so that the latter could conform to the legal and social rules concerning procreation. Cantarella notes that this practice was not restricted to elite families, but juridical sources suggest it was practiced in a variety of class contexts. Cantarella, 'Marriage and Sexuality in Republican Rome', pp. 269–82.

102 Joanna Dewey, 'Response: Fantasy and the New Testament', *Semeia* 60 (1992), pp. 83–89.

gender-bending. As we saw in our analysis of Roman social discourse, the bride embodied the characteristics of idealized feminine gender; by encouraging the audience to envision itself as a bride Revelation encourages the audience, male and female, to envision itself in the terms of feminine gender and as embodying the characteristics of the ideal wife in relation to the Lamb. This vision demands that the men and women within Revelation's communities consider what it means for the Christian community as a whole to be defined solely in relation to the Lamb and to live in anticipation of maintaining the 'household of the Lamb'. The text remains silent on what this household might look like, leaving the bride in a perpetual state of *deductio*, and thereby providing subsequent interpreters a place to imagine implications of Revelation's vision.[103]

Conclusion

The nuptial–familial imagery introduced in Rev. 19.1–8 challenges and counters the claims of Roman social discourse, specifically claims of restoring the ideal *domus* and propaganda depicting the imperial family as the *domus divina*. However, in constructing an image to counter the Roman moral vision, Revelation appropriates the Roman view of idealized feminine gender. It manipulates this view of gender, especially as embodied in Roman wedding traditions, in its vision of the bride of the Lamb. In particular, Revelation encourages its audience to envision the Lamb's wife as embodying the transitional role of the Roman bride, who anticipates her role as wife by weaving her own wedding garment. The description of the bride's garment, moreover, prompts the audience to envision itself as a bride who actively prepares to take on the role of faithful wife. Revelation creates for the community a vision of itself transitioning into the role for which it is destined, a role that demands fidelity to the Lamb, the Risen Christ.

Even though Revelation appropriates the characteristics of idealized feminine gender in its depiction of the bride, it arguably subverts the dominant view of the household and its corresponding gender ideals. It does this not by criticizing the traditional views of gender as such, but by applying traditional gender expectations to the Christian community as a whole. John calls the Christian community, described primarily in masculine terms, to envision itself as the bride who will become the wife of the Lamb. This invites us to reflect further on the interplay between an audience's gender identity and the gendered identities envisioned by the text. For instance, might prompting a masculine-identified audience to envision itself as embodied within the feminine gender encourage that audience to rethink the categories of 'masculine' and 'feminine', especially as they relate to communities?

Even though Revelation challenges Roman discourse about the family, including its view of feminine gender which emphasized the woman's role in the home and her significance primarily as a mother, contemporary readers, especially feminist readers, may still find Revelation's bridal imagery unpalatable. This is particularly true if the imagery functions as a call to celibacy, since the text then qualifies the importance of

---

103 For instance, in her visions Hildegard of Bingen echoes Revelation's image of the new Jerusalem, describing the Christian community as a woman who bears children. Hildegard, *Scivias* (trans. Columba Hart and Jane Bishop; Mahwah, NJ: Paulist Press, 1990), II.3.

something many contemporary interpreters find important to the individual self – sexuality. While one might argue that Revelation's vision of the Lamb's wife does not serve to shape individual behavior – rather it serves to shape communal identity – one cannot avoid the fact that the imagery implicitly suggests emulation. In the Roman milieu, images of the imperial family provided models for individual behavior. By echoing this imagery John arguably sets up the Lamb and his wife as similar models for behavior. Thus, even though Revelation's nuptial–familial imagery challenges the claims of the dominant social rhetoric, the text's views on gender fall short of being subversive, let alone liberative.

Hypermasculinity and Divinity*

Stephen D. Moore

In *The Vision of God*, an extraordinarily erudite tome first published in 1931, Kenneth E. Kirk, Bishop of Oxford, set out to demonstrate that the dictum 'the end of life is the vision of God', which he takes to be a New Testament doctrine, has, through the ages, 'been interpreted by Christian thought at its best as implying in practice that the highest prerogative of the Christian in this life as well as hereafter, is the activity of *worship*. . . . '[1] And Kirk does succeed admirably in showing that elite Christian theologians, at least until the Reformation, tended overwhelmingly to view the vision of God as being indissolubly bound up with the worship of God.

But what is the New Testament basis for the belief that the end of life is the vision of God? Having disposed of various 'Old Testament anticipations' of the dictum, along with sundry pagan anticipations of it, Kirk proceeds to survey the New Testament at some length,[2] before turning to the daunting expanse of post-biblical Christian theology and following selected currents upstream to his own time. But although he devotes stretches of text to the Synoptic Gospels and the Fourth Gospel, the letters of Paul and the Letter to the Hebrews, and even the Letter of James, he scarcely mentions the Book of Revelation except in passing – a curious omission indeed, for in what other New Testament text are the vision and worship of God so fully fused? Celestial life, according to Revelation, is the beholding of God, and the beholding of God irresistibly elicits the unending worship of God (4.8–11; 5.13–14; 7.9–12, 15; 8.3–4; 11.15–18; 14.1–3; 15.2–4; 19.1–18; 21.22–23; 22.3–5).[3]

---

* This essay is excerpted, by permission of the publisher, from my book *God's Gym: Divine Male Bodies of the Bible* (New York and London: Routledge, 1996). In the decade or so that has elapsed since that work appeared, the stream of books and shorter studies on Revelation, the Roman imperial cult, the contemporary cult of bodybuilding, and other topics germane to the essay has, of course, continued unabated. I considered feeding these disparate developments into the essay for the purposes of this reprint, but abandoned the idea once it became clear that doing so would not alter my basic arguments. Instead I have crafted an 'afterword', impelled by a barrage of searching questions put to the essay by series editor Amy-Jill Levine. Adequate answers to even half of her questions, however, would have resulted in an afterword several times longer than the essay to which it is appended. A more ample response to her thought-provoking questions will have to await another venue. I am also indebted to my PhD student Grant Gieseke for stimulating conversation on the roles of the gaze in Revelation.

1 Kenneth E. Kirk, *The Vision of God: The Christian Doctrine of the* Summum Bonum (London: Longmans, Green & Co., 1931), p. ix, his emphasis. The phrase 'the end of life is the vision of God' is adapted from Irenaeus, *Haer*. 4.20.

2 A more restricted perusal of the vision of God in the New Testament, confined mainly to the Synoptic Gospels (and frequently critical of Kirk), can be found in A. Raymond George, *Communion with God in the New Testament* (London: Epworth Press, 1953), pp. 93–122.

3 Cf. 5.8–12; 12.10–12; 14.7; 16.5–7; 19.10; 22.8–9. Unending worship is a frequent feature of apocalyptic depictions of heaven (see, e.g., *1 En.* 39.12–14; 40.2; 71.7; *2 En.* 21.1; *T.Levi* 3.8).

Heaven Can Be Hell

And the throne of God and of the Lamb shall be in it, and his slaves shall serve him. . . .
(Rev. 22.3)

What does it mean to worship God? The essence of divine worship, for Kirk, is an overwhelming sense of one's own smallness, a profound sense of one's own insignificance, a painful sense of one's own imperfection, relative to the immensity, power and perfection of the deity. Gazing at God, the worshiper 'sees himself to be nothing . . . Worship tells us much good of God, but little good of ourselves . . . For that we may praise Him, but it leaves us nothing upon which to pride ourselves'.[4]

A more recent book by Richard Bauckham returns repeatedly to the topic of worship in Revelation.[5] Bauckham's understanding of worship echoes that of Kirk (and innumerable other theologians). Commenting on the vision of the heavenly throne room in Revelation 4, for example,[6] Bauckham remarks:

> Especially prominent in the vision is the continuous worship by the four living creatures and the twenty-four elders. It is a scene of worship into which the reader who shares John's faith in God is almost inevitably drawn. We are thereby reminded that true knowledge of who God is is inseparable from worship of God. The song of the four living creatures and the hymn of the twenty-four elders express the two most primary forms of awareness of God: the awed perception of his numinous holiness (4.8; cf. Isa. 6.3), and the consciousness of utter dependence on God for existence itself that is the nature of all created things (4.11). These most elemental forms of perception of God not only require expression in worship; they cannot be truly experienced except as worship.[7]

There was a time when I myself would have endorsed such sentiments enthusiastically, indeed gambled heavily on their veracity. For what does the Pentecostal prayer meeting, with its ecstatic cacophony of tongues, or the Cistercian cloister, with its ethereal chorus of plainsong, purport to be, if not antechambers to the celestial throne room, and I have lingered long in both waiting rooms. But I must confess that my reactions to such sentiments have since been refashioned by a series of texts

---

4 Kirk, *The Vision of God*, p. 448.

5 Richard Bauckham, *The Theology of the Book of Revelation* (NTT; Cambridge, UK and New York: Cambridge University Press, 1993). This slim book is a companion to Bauckham's bulkier *The Climax of Prophecy: Studies on the Book of Revelation* (Edinburgh: T&T Clark, 1993). The former is distinguished from the latter by a strong apologetic thrust. It attempts to argue the relevance of Revelation for the current theological scene, one frequently inimical to it.

6 A scene that Jürgen Roloff has rightly described as 'the theological center of the book' (*The Revelation of John* [trans. John E. Alsup; Continental Commentaries; Minneapolis, MN: Fortress Press, 1993], p. 68).

7 Bauckham, *Theology of Revelation*, pp. 32–33. Revelation's heavenly liturgy, frequently seen as a projection of early Christian liturgy, has been a recurrent focus of scholarly attention; see, e.g., Lucetta Mowry, 'Revelation 4–5 and Early Christian Liturgical Usage', *JBL* 71 (1952), pp. 75–84; M. H. Shepherd, *The Paschal Liturgy and the Apocalypse* (London: Lutterworth, 1960); Erik Peterson, *The Angels and the Liturgy* (trans. Ronald Walls; New York: Herder & Herder, 1964), pp. 1–13; Leonard L. Thompson, *The Book of Revelation: Apocalypse and Empire* (New York: Oxford University Press, 1990), pp. 53–73.

(what can one do in a waiting room but read?), subtle philosophical texts and not-so-subtle psychoanalytic texts, texts as ingenious and insidious as Derrida's 'Différance', or as crude and rude as Freud's *The Future of an Illusion*.[8] I must be a simple fellow, for the latter in particular spoke to me powerfully, or rather roared in my ear. Hurriedly honing a blunted blade that had once belonged to Feuerbach, Freud argues that the worshiper in his or her relationship to the divine parent faithfully mirrors the child's relationship to its own all-too-human parents – its pervasive sense of its own smallness relative to the towering stature of its parents, its painful sense of its own powerlessness relative to the apparent omnipotence of its parents, its profound sense of its own dependence on its parents for its day-to-day survival, indeed for its very existence.[9] If God has so often been regarded as a father in our culture, Freud slyly implies, it is because the father has so often been regarded as a god in our homes. Issuing from such a domestic shrine myself, this line of argument proved extremely seductive to me.

Bauckham may come from a happier home. Dubiously he cites the tendency of some recent theologians, feminist theologians in particular, to castigate traditional images of the sovereignty of God as projections of patriarchal domination.[10] For Bauckham, Revelation is entirely innocent of such charges:

> Revelation, by avoiding anthropomorphism, suggests the incomparability of God's sovereignty. In effect, the image of sovereignty is being used to express an aspect of the relation between God and his creatures which is unique, rather than one which provides a model for relationships between humans. Of course, the image of the throne derives from the human world, but it is so used as to highlight the difference, more than the similarity, between divine sovereignty and human sovereignty. In other words, it is used to express transcendence. Much of the modern criticism of images of this kind seems unable to understand real transcendence. It supposes that the relation between God and the world must be in every respect comparable with relations between creatures and that all images of God must

8 See Jacques Derrida, 'Différance', in *idem, Margins of Philosophy* (trans. Alan Bass; Chicago, IL: University of Chicago Press, 1982), pp. 1–27; Sigmund Freud, *The Future of an Illusion*, in James Strachey et al. (eds and trans.), *The Standard Edition of the Complete Psychological Works of Sigmund Freud* (London: Hogarth Press and the Institute of Psycho-Analysis, 1953–74 [hereafter referred to as *SE*]), XXI, pp. 5–56.

9 Freud, *Future of an Illusion*, pp. 17–30, an argument anticipated in *Leonardo da Vinci and a Memory of his Childhood*, *SE*, XI, p. 123, and a 1910 letter to Jung (William McGuire [ed.], *The Freud/Jung Letters: The Correspondence between Sigmund Freud and C. G. Jung* [trans. Ralph Manheim and R. F. C. Hull; Princeton, NJ: Princeton University Press, 1974], pp. 183–84), and re-echoed in *New Introductory Letters in Psycho-Analysis*, *SE*, XXII, p. 168. The 'illusion' of the title alludes to Feuerbach's famous claim that the relation of reason to religion 'amounts only to the destruction of an *illusion*' (*Das Wesen des Christentums* [Leipzig: O. Wigand, 1841], p. 408, his emphasis). In later years Freud recanted, suggesting that this theory of Jewish and Christian religion as the infantile projection of omnipotence onto a divine Father had been ill-founded ('Postscript' to *An Autobiographical Study*, *SE*, XX, p. 72). But here Freud is merely preparing the way for his own deeply personal and largely positive revaluation of Judaism in *Moses and Monotheism*, *SE*, XXIII, pp. 1–137; see the exegesis of the latter presented in The Bible and Culture Collective, G. Aichele et al., *The Postmodern Bible* (The Bible and Culture Collective; New Haven, CT: Yale University Press, 1995), esp. pp. 192–94.

10 He singles out Daphne Hampson, *Theology and Feminism* (Oxford: Basil Blackwell, 1990), pp. 151–53, and Sallie McFague, *Models of God: Theology for an Ecological, Nuclear Age* (Philadelphia, PA: Fortress Press, 1987), pp. 63–69.

function as models for human behavior. It is critical of images of transcendence, such as sovereignty, but *it takes transcendence to mean that God is some kind of superhuman being alongside other beings*. Real transcendence, of course, means that God transcends all creaturely existence. As the source, ground and goal of all creaturely existence, the infinite mystery on which all finite being depends, his relation to us is unique.[11]

And yet my suspicions persist. What if at the core of all these subtle scholastic formulations there were nothing but a superhuman being after all – an embarrassingly muscular being, insatiably hungry for adulation, but subjected to a stringent diet throughout centuries of (unsuccessful) Christian apologetics aimed at stripping away its all-too-robust flesh? The God of Revelation might be just such a being, just such a creature, just such a projection.

To begin with, Revelation is not as free of anthropomorphism as Bauckham suggests. After all, the being seated on the throne *is* human in form: 'Then I saw in the right hand (ἐπὶ τὴν δεξιάν) of the one seated on the throne a scroll . . . ' (5.1; cf. 5.7).[12] 'Revelation 5.1 is closely modeled on Ezek. 2.9–10', as Bauckham himself observes.[13] The latter passage begins: 'I looked, and a hand [יד; LXX: χείρ] was stretched out to me, and a written scroll was in it'. What is more, 'John's account of his vision of God [Revelation 4] is considerably indebted to Ezekiel's vision of the divine throne (Ezek. 1)'.[14] What are we then to conclude? That the enthroned figure that John 'saw' in his vision was one and the same as the enthroned figure that Ezekiel 'saw' in his? Isn't that what John would want us to conclude?[15] And what Ezekiel saw, seated upon the throne, was דמות כמראה אדם (lit. 'a likeness like the appearance of a man', 1.26).[16]

In fairness to Bauckham, however, it must be admitted that John does refrain from attempting to describe the divine physique, preferring to focus attention instead on the adulation and self-abasement of the celestial audience eternally privileged to behold it (4.8–11). Among contemporary cultural and subcultural spectacles, it is the bodybuilding posing routine that best encapsulates the surrealistic scenario that

11 Bauckham, *Theology of Revelation*, pp. 44–45, emphasis added.

12 R. H. Charles, having twice noted how John 'avoids anthropomorphic details' (*A Critical and Exegetical Commentary on the Revelation to St John* [ICC; 2 vols.; Edinburgh: T&T Clark, 1920], I, p. 113; cf. p. 115), ironically goes on to elucidate ἐπὶ τὴν δεξιάν in the following terms: 'The book-roll lies on the open palm of the right hand, not in the hand' (p. 136).

13 Bauckham, *Climax of Prophecy*, p. 246; cf. pp. 248–49.

14 Bauckham, *Climax of Prophecy*, p. 246. For a more detailed discussion of the relationship between Ezekiel 1 and Revelation 4, see Christopher Rowland, *The Open Heaven: A Study of Apocalyptic in Judaism and Early Christianity* (New York: Crossroad, 1982), pp. 222–26.

15 Cf. Rowland, *Open Heaven*, pp. 226–27.

16 Which LXX renders as ὁμοίωμα ὡς εἶδος ἀνθρώπου. M. Eugene Boring offers a different, but not unrelated, interpretation of 'the one seated on the throne': 'John intentionally withholds any description of the central figure on the throne, leaving a blank center in the picture to be filled in by the figure of the Lamb – yet another means of affirming that God is the one who defines himself by Christ' (*Revelation* [Interpretation: A Bible Commentary for Teaching and Preaching; Louisville, KY: John Knox Press, 1989], p. 103). By implication, then, the dimly described figure on the throne points us back, not only to Ezekiel 1, but also to Rev. 1.13–16, the dazzlingly described figure of the 'one like a Son of Man'.

Revelation sets before us.[17] Note, for example, the static quality of the figure who is the principal focus of worship in Revelation.[18] From his first to his last appearance in the book, he sits immobile and almost aphasic on his throne (he speaks only in 1.8 and 21.5–8).[19] Alan M. Klein has remarked on the 'static, statuesque nature of bodybuilders in competition . . . '.[20] The typical posing routine is less a spectacle of motion than a succession of stills; the bodybuilder hits and holds a pose, wringing every last drop from it, massive muscles straining, face frozen in a grimace posing as a smile, before proceeding to the next pose. The God of Revelation is similarly engaging in a posing exhibition. He is the static, statuesque embodiment of absolute power, and his celestial audience cannot get enough of him. Indeed, seen in this (heavenly) light, he looks very much like an idol (a matinee idol?), despite the author's iconophobic attempts to prevent this very thing from happening.

God's silence further accentuates both his statuesque demeanor and his likeness to the bodybuilder. 'Like the cartoon without a caption, the hypermuscular body . . .

17 For practical reasons, my remarks on bodybuilders will be confined to the male of the species. At present, the criteria governing women's competitive bodybuilding are ambiguous in the extreme. For male competitors, the invariable formula for success is muscle mass, symmetry and 'definition' (i.e., clear visibility of the detailed musculature produced by the relative absence of subcutaneous fat). A competitor cannot have too much mass provided it is symmetrical and defined. But for female competitors there is an intangible fourth ingredient – femininity – that sets strict limits on the amount of muscle that can be amassed. *Flex*, the premier hardcore 'musclemag', now regularly features centerfolds of female bodybuilders posing nude. The shots are prefaced by the following statement, which says it all:

> Women bodybuilders are many things, among them symmetrical, strong, sensuous and stunning. When photographed in competition shape, repping and grimacing or squeezing out shots, they appear shredded, vascular and hard, and they can be perceived as threatening. Offseason they carry more bodyfat, presenting themselves in a much more naturally attractive condition. To exhibit this real, natural side of women bodybuilders, *Flex* has been presenting pictorials of female competitors in softer condition. We hope this approach dispels the myth of female-bodybuilder masculinity and proves what role models they truly are.

For an incisive analysis of this glaring double standard, see Anne Bolin, 'Vandalized Vanity: Feminine Physiques Betrayed and Portrayed', in Frances E. Mascia-Lees and Patricia Sharpe (eds), *Tattoo, Torture, Mutilation, and Adornment: The Denaturalization of the Body in Culture and Text* (SUNY Series on the Body in Culture, History, and Religion; Albany: State University of New York Press, 1992), pp. 79–99.

18 Jesus is the secondary focus of legitimate worship in the book (see esp. 5.8–14). See further Bauckham, *Theology of Revelation*, pp. 58–63, and *Climax of Prophecy*, pp. 118–49, esp. p. 139.

19 Unless the anonymous interjections in Rev. 11.12 ('Come up here!') and 16.17 ('It is done!') also be attributed to God.

20 Alan M. Klein, *Little Big Men: Bodybuilding Subculture and Gender Construction* (SUNY Series on Sport, Culture, and Social Relations; Albany: State University of New York Press, 1993), p. 257. It is not for nothing that the (Caucasian) bodybuilder's tan-in-a-bottle is known as 'bronzer', for the bodybuilder is a bronze statue (see Samuel Wilson Fussell, 'Bodybuilder Americanus', in Laurence Goldstein [ed.], *The Male Body: Features, Destinies, Exposures* [Ann Arbor: University of Michigan Press, 1994], pp. 42–60 [45]). Cf. Rev. 1.15 where the awesome figure of the risen Christ has 'feet like burnished bronze [χαλκολίβανος]'. The original model for the statue that Jesus has become, namely, the angel of Dan. 10.4–6, is said to have 'arms and legs like the gleam of burnished bronze [נחשת קלל; LXX: χαλκοῦ στίλβοντος]' (cf. Dan. 2.32; Ezek. 1.7).

is supposed to communicate without an act; its presence is its text'.[21] Klein quotes an unnamed bodybuilder who confides, 'I wanna be the biggest thing. I wanna walk on stage . . . without even posing, and people would just – (opens eyes in wonder) . . . I won't even have to pose, I'll be so awesome.'[22] Presumably the one seated on the great white throne (20.11) is himself beyond posing, although he would have ample room to strut and flex should he choose to. In the East, as Josephine Massyngberde Ford reminds us, 'the absolute ruler sat on an ornate throne. Archaeological discoveries show such thrones with a high back, a base decorated with pictures of conquered peoples and several steps leading up to it . . . '.[23] As such, Revelation's representation of the deity anticipates the publicity poster for the 1984 sword-and-sandal epic, *Conan the Barbarian*, which showed a brooding Arnold Schwarzenegger slumped on a massive throne, his equally massive bulk artfully draped over its contours.[24] Certainly, Schwarzenegger was not stretched in the role. 'My relationship to power and authority', confessed the off-screen colossus, with disconcerting candor, 'is that I'm all for it . . . Ninety-five percent of the people in the world need to be told what to do and how to behave'[25] – by the remaining five per cent, presumably.

'It's Dorian's world; we're just visiting it', reads the caption to a recent article in *Flex* magazine.[26] Dorian Yates, who has dominated professional bodybuilding in the 1990s much as Arnold dominated it in the 1970s, has also deployed the image of the throne to represent the (made-in-heaven?) marriage of absolute power and utter submission. 'The evening's entertainment highlight at the 1995 Night of Champions in New York was the guest appearance of a near 300-pound Dorian Yates', the article begins.[27] The curtain drew back to reveal Dorian pensively perched on an ornate throne, and resplendent in an ermine-trimmed crown and robe. Other

---

21 Klein, *Little Big Men*, p. 274. 'No inane comments, only total majestic silence' is Gerhard Krodel's admiring remark on the taciturn figure on the throne (*Revelation* [Augsburg Commentary on the New Testament; Minneapolis, MN: Augsburg, 1989], p. 155).

22 Klein, *Little Big Men*, p. 273.

23 Josephine Massyngberde Ford, *The Revelation of St. John* (AB, 38; Garden City, NY: Doubleday, 1975), p. 70. From ch. 4 on, the throne is ubiquitous in Revelation (e.g., 5.6; 7.9; 8.3; 12.5; 14.3; 16.7; 19.5; 20.11; 21.3; 22.1, 3). G. B. Caird comments, 'The final reality which will still be standing when heaven and earth have disappeared is the great white throne (xx. 11)' (*The Revelation of Saint John* [Black's New Testament Commentary, 19; London: A. & C. Black, 1966], p. 62).

24 Arnold's early action movies, along with those of Sylvester Stallone, portrayed the male bodybuilder as the ultimate warrior. 'The more exaggerated the musculature, the more it had to explain itself in mounds of dead bodies' (Mark Simpson, *Male Impersonators: Men Performing Masculinity* [New York: Routledge, 1994], p. 24; cf. Yvonne Tasker, *Spectacular Bodies: Gender, Genre and the Action Cinema* [New York: Routledge, 1993], pp. 77–83; 118–23; William Warner, 'Spectacular Action: Rambo and the Popular Pleasures of Pain', in Lawrence Grossberg, Cary Nelson and Paula A. Treichler [eds], *Cultural Studies* [New York: Routledge, 1992], pp. 672–88). Compare the mountains of dead bodies that litter the landscape of Revelation (6.4, 8; 8.9, 11; 9.15, 18; 11.13; 14.19–20; 15.2–10; 16.18–21; 19.11–21; 20.9, 15; 21.8; cf. 6.15–17; 8.4–6; 11.18; 14.9–11; 18.8, 19, 21; 19.2–3; 22.18), irrefutable proofs that the exaggerated majesty of the one seated on the throne is warranted: he can kill at will without lifting a finger – or moving a muscle.

25 Quoted in George Butler, *Arnold Schwarzenegger: A Portrait* (New York: Simon & Schuster, 1990), p. 34.

26 Peter McGough, 'At the Court of King Dorian', *Flex* (September 1995), pp. 197–98 (the caption occurs in the issue's table of contents).

27 McGough, 'At the Court of King Dorian', p. 197.

accessories included a pair of angelic attendants who abased themselves at Dorian's feet. 'The girls then divested the three-time Mr. Olympia of his imperial accouterments, as a prelude to Dorian's posing before a raucous 3000 strong standing-room-only crowd'.[28] Hardly the 'myriads of myriads and thousands of thousands' of which Revelation speaks (5.11), but then Dorian does not (yet) claim to be God.

For Klein, there is something profoundly disturbing, indeed fascist, about the spectacle of the bodybuilder on the posing dais. 'Bodybuilding leads in various sociocultural directions', he writes, 'but none is quite so disturbing or dramatic as its connection to fascist aesthetics and cultural politics. The fetishism for spectacle, worship of power, grandiose fantasies ... dominance and submission in social relations are all essential characteristics shared by bodybuilding and fascism ... '.[29] But these are also the essential characteristics of Revelation (if 'dominance and submission in social relations' is extended to embrace divine–human relations), each so ubiquitous as to beggar documentation.

The avoidance of anachronism is not, perhaps, my strongest suit as an exegete. Indeed, I frequently employ anachronism deliberately as an exegetical tactic (taking my cue from the fact that anachronism is what biblical scholars fear most, that fear is but the obverse of fascination, and that the fascinating merits pursuit more than flight).[30] And yet my description of Revelation as fascist is not intended altogether anachronistically. We should not presume on too narrow a definition of this singularly useful term. The *New Webster's Dictionary*, for example, having outlined the historical roots of the term ('the ideological outlook and its extremist manifestations in Mussolini's Italian counterrevolutionary movement ... and in his dictatorship'), goes on to define it more generally as 'any political or social ideology ... which relies on a combination of pseudo-religious attitudes and the brutal use of force for getting and keeping power'. It may, of course, be objected that if this profile were to fit any political or social ideology of the first century CE it would surely be that of the Roman state and not that of the fledgling Christian communities squirming under its sandal – such as those from which Revelation itself emerged, and to which it is addressed.[31] And yet the theology or ideology of Revela-

---

28 McGough, 'At the Court of King Dorian', pp. 197–98. Bodybuilder Bev Francis remarks on an earlier appearance of Yates: 'At the show, I had goose pimples as I announced Dorian, 'cos backstage I'd seen what he looked like – nobody has ever carried that much muscle. When he walked onstage there was such a collective intake of breath from the 1,000 or so crowd that all the oxygen left the auditorium' (quoted in Peter McGough, 'Hard Times', *Flex* [January 1994], p. 114). Yates's 5-foot, 10-inch frame carries around 295 lbs in the off-season, which is when the epiphany in question occurred.

29 Klein, *Little Big Men*, p. 254; cf. pp. 253–67 *passim*; also Kenneth R. Dutton, *The Perfectible Body: The Western Ideal of Male Physical Development* (New York: Continuum, 1995), pp. 206–09.

30 See especially my *Mark and Luke in Poststructuralist Perspectives: Jesus Begins to Write* (New Haven, CT: Yale University Press, 1992).

31 The degree of persecution with which John's target audience was faced, and the general situation in which it found itself, has long been a matter of debate. Recent contributions include J. P. M. Sweet, *Revelation* (Westminster Pelican Commentaries; Philadelphia, PA: Westminster Press, 1979), pp. 27–35; David E. Aune, 'The Social Matrix of the Apocalypse of John', *Papers of the Chicago Society of Biblical Research* 26 (1981), pp. 16–32; A. Yarbro Collins, *Crisis and Catharsis: The Power of the Apocalypse* (Philadelphia, PA: Westminster Press, 1984), pp. 84–110; Boring, *Revelation*, pp. 9–23; and Thompson, *Book of Revelation*, esp. pp. 15–17, 171–97, 202–10.

tion is anything but simple inversion, reversal or renunciation of the political and social ideology of imperial Rome. Instead it represents the apotheosis of this imperial ideology, its ascension to a transhistorical site.

This conclusion is implicit in much of what critical commentators write on Revelation, although some work hard to circumvent it. M. Eugene Boring, for example, claims that the repeated accolade, 'Worthy are thou [ἄξιος εἶ]' (4.11; 5.9; cf. 5.12), directed to God and the Lamb, 'reflects the acclamation used to greet the [Roman] emperor during his triumphal entrance', while the title 'our Lord and God' [ὁ κύριος καὶ ὁ θεὸς ἡμῶν] (4.11; cf. 4.8; 11.17; 15.3; 16.7; 19.6) 'is paralleled by Domitian's insistence that he be addressed by this title'.[32] David E. Aune, for his part, claims that the detail of the twenty-four elders casting their crowns before the divine throne (4.10) 'has no parallels in Israelite-Jewish literature', but is comprehensible only in light of the custom of presenting crowns to a sovereign, which was 'inherited by the Romans from the traditions of Hellenistic kingship'.[33] And Boring cites Tacitus's description of how the Parthian King Tiridates laid his diadem at the feet of Nero's seated effigy in order to offer suitably obsequious homage to the Roman emperor.[34]

What of the number twenty-four itself? Aune has an intriguing suggestion to make. 'Roman magistrates were permitted to be accompanied by the number of lictors bearing fasces which corresponded to the degree of imperium which they had been granted', he begins. (As it happens, the fasces, a bundle of rods bound together

32 Boring, *Revelation*, p. 103; cf. p. 21. Although Boring does not mention it, the argument that the 'Worthy art thou' acclamation was used in the imperial cult goes back at least to Erik Peterson, *Heis Theos: Epigraphische, formgeschichtliche, und religionsgeschichtliche Untersuchungen* (FRLANT, 41; Göttingen: Vandenhoeck & Ruprecht, 1926), pp. 176–80. Like the majority of New Testament scholars, Boring believes that Revelation was written during the latter years of Domitian's reign (more on this below). Did Domitian really insist on being addressed as 'Lord and God', as commentators on Revelation routinely claim? (The only exceptions that I am aware of are Collins, *Crisis and Catharsis*, pp. 71–72; Krodel, *Revelation*, pp. 36–37; Thompson, *Book of Revelation*, pp. 104–107; and Wilfred J. Harrington, *Revelation* [Sacra Pagina; Collegeville, MN: Liturgical Press, 1993], pp. 9–10). Probably not, as we shall see, although the title does seem to have been applied to him nonetheless.

33 David E. Aune, 'The Influence of Roman Imperial Court Ceremonial on the Apocalypse of John', *Papers of the Chicago Society of Biblical Research* 28 (1983), pp. 5–29 (12–13). See further Theodor Klausner, 'Aurum Coronarium', in Ernst Dassmann (ed.), *Gesammelte Arbeiten zur Liturgiegeschichte, Kirchengeschichte und christlichen Archäeologie* (Münster: Aschendorff, 1974), pp. 292–309; Fergus Millar, *The Emperor in the Roman World (31 BC–AD 337)* (Ithaca, NY: Cornell University Press, 1977), pp. 140–43.

34 Boring, *Revelation*, p. 103, adducing Tacitus, *Ann.* 15.28. Similar lists of parallels are frequent in the scholarly literature on Revelation; see, e.g., Charles, *Critical and Exegetical Commentary*, I, p. 133; Dominique Cuss, *Imperial Cult and Honorary Terms in the New Testament* (Paradosis, 23; Fribourg: Fribourg University Press, 1974), pp. 62–63; Colin J. Hemer, *The Letters to the Seven Churches of Asia in Their Local Setting* (JSNTSup, 11; Sheffield: JSOT Press, 1986), pp. 86–87; Eduard Lohse, *Die Offenbarung des Johannes* (NTD, 11; Göttingen: Vandenhoeck & Ruprecht, 1979), p. 36; Roloff, *Revelation of John*, p. 72; Elisabeth Schüssler Fiorenza, *Invitation to the Book of Revelation: A Commentary on the Apocalypse with Complete Text from the Jerusalem Bible* (Garden City, NY: Image Books, 1981), p. 76; Thompson, *Book of Revelation*, p. 58; and esp. Ethelbert Stauffer, *Christ and the Caesars* (trans. K. Gregor Smith and R. Gregor Smith; London: SCM Press, 1955), pp. 166ff.

with the blade of an axe projecting, later gave Italian *Fascismo*, which adopted it as an insignia, its name.)

> Consuls were permitted twelve lictors. Augustus apparently had twelve lictors from Actium . . . though it is possible that he had twenty-four lictors until 27 BCE. At any rate the standard number of twelve lictors, indicative of the degree of imperium, was doubled by Domitian to twenty four. These lictors, of course, were not crowned, nor did they wear white robes. They did, however, constitute part of the official crowd of public servants which constantly surrounded the emperor.[35]

Self-abasing celestial officials, the twenty-four elders prostrate themselves repeatedly before the divine throne (4.10; 5.8; 7.11; 11.16; 19.4). 'The practice of the ritual of *proskynesis* before the early Roman emperors is incontrovertible', adds Aune, and he goes on to substantiate his claim.[36]

Distantly related to Domitian's double allotment of lictors were Nero's Augustiani, an elite corps of presentable young men whose principal function was to lead the applause whenever the emperor deigned to make an appearance – an imperial cheerleading squad, if you will. Suetonius estimates the size of this squad at 'more than five thousand'.[37] Dominique Cuss has argued that the acclamations led by the Augustiani were designed to 'underline the imperial claims to divinity'.[38] Paraphrasing Tacitus, she states: 'Day and night, the applause and acclamations of these young men echoed around the palace, using such extravagant terms while describing the beauty and voice of the emperor, that they could have been applied to the gods.'[39] Or to God. Compare Rev. 4.8–11: 'Day and night without ceasing [ἀνάπαυσιν οὐκ ἔχουσιν ἡμέρας καὶ νυκτός] they sing . . . ' – and the words of the song follow, the singers in question being the 'four living creatures' supported by the twenty-four elders. Together they drum up a chorus that swells until it encompasses every voice in the heavenly throne room (5.8–12), and then every voice in the universe (5.13), acclamation after acclamation washing over 'the one seated on the throne', and his *Divi Filius*, 'the Lamb'.[40]

35　Aune, 'Roman Imperial Court Ceremonial', p. 13; cf. Millar, *The Emperor in the Roman World*, p. 67. The primary source is Dio Cassius, *Hist.* 67.4.3.

36　Aune, 'Roman Imperial Court Ceremonial', pp. 13–14.

37　Suetonius, *Nero* 20.3. The Augustiani are also mentioned in *Nero* 25.1; Tacitus, *Ann.* 14.15; Dio Cassius, *Hist.* 61.20.4–5; cf. 63.8.2–3; 63.15.2; 63.18.3. Nero is a brooding presence in Revelation, as has long been recognized, serving to epitomize the evil that its author sees embodied in Rome. See further Cuss, *Imperial Cult and Honorary Terms*, pp. 88–95; A. Yarbro Collins, *The Combat Myth in the Book of Revelation* (HDR, 9; Missoula, MT: Scholars Press, 1976), pp. 176–83; Ulrich B. Müller, *Die Offenbarung des Johannes* (Gütersloh: Gerd Mohn; Würzburg: Echter Verlag, 1984), pp. 297–300.

38　Cuss, *Imperial Cult and Honorary Terms*, p. 77; cf. Aune, 'Roman Imperial Court Ceremonial', p. 16.

39　Cuss, *Imperial Cult and Honorary Terms*, p. 78. The sentence from Tacitus begins: 'Days and nights they thundered applause [*Ii dies ac noctes plausibus personare*], bestowed the epithets reserved for deity upon the imperial form and voice . . . ' (*Ann.* 14.15; LCL trans.).

40　Strangely, Cuss does not appear to have Revelation 4–5 in mind as she paraphrases Tacitus. Instead she is in the midst of a lengthy gloss on the 'blasphemous names' on the head of the beast from the sea (13.1; cf. 17.3). Aune, however, does connect the Augustiani with the perpetual adorers of Revelation 4–5 ('Roman Imperial Court Ceremonial', pp. 16–18).

Such parallels could be multiplied; we have not yet emerged from Revelation 4–5, much less examined the extent to which the heavenly throne room in Revelation as a whole (in which it functions as the principal setting) mirrors the Roman imperial court.[41] What do the scholars themselves make of these parallels? Cuss is utterly noncommittal in her conclusions. Aune is less tight-lipped, although also relatively noncommittal:

> John's depiction of the ceremonial in the heavenly throne room has been significantly influenced in its conceptualization by popular images of Roman imperial court ceremonial. For the most part, the individual constituents of that ceremonial used by John in his depiction of the heavenly ceremonial have been heightened, expanded and given even greater cosmic significance. The result is that the sovereignty of God and the Lamb have been elevated so far above all pretensions and claims of earthly rulers that the latter, upon comparison, become only pale, even diabolical imitations of the transcendent majesty of the King of kings and Lord of lords.[42]

Is this Aune's own view of the matter, or merely his rendition of John's view? Aune leaves us guessing. Considerably less guesswork is required in the case of Boring. He states,

> The correlation of imagery from the imperial cult with that used to express faith in the sole sovereignty of God simply shows that all earthly claims to sovereignty are only pale imitations and parodies of the One who sits upon the one throne. Christians dare not give this homage to another.[43]

Boring's summation does echo Aune's. The difference, however, is that Boring's popularly pitched but splendidly competent commentary on Revelation is everywhere punctuated by professions of faith, generally implicit but frequently explicit, so that Boring's theological viewpoint seems to blend completely with that of John. Boring stands staunchly by John's shoulder throughout, not only as his interpreter, faithfully translating even his most alien sentences and sentiments into contemporary theological idiom, but also as his disciple. Boring everywhere apologizes for John, and nowhere criticizes him.[44]

---

41 Nor is the imperial court the only place to look for such parallels. A recent paper by Ernest P. Janzen argues that Revelation usurped the innovative imagery of Domitian's coinage in order to represent Jesus. 'Domitian and Jesus not only shared roles as the divine mediator figures for the Empire and the Christians of Asia Minor, they also shared the wardrobe of empowerment' ('The Jesus of the Apocalypse Wears the Emperor's Clothes', in *SBLSP* 33 [1994], p. 370).

42 Aune, 'Roman Imperial Court Ceremonial', p. 22; cf. p. 5.

43 Boring, *Revelation*, p. 103; cf. pp. 185, 187, 192–93, 211, 214–15.

44 The other pole of current scholarship on Revelation, that which subjects its ideology to stringent critique, is best represented by Tina Pippin; see, e.g., her *Death and Desire: The Rhetoric of Gender in the Apocalypse of John* (Literary Currents in Biblical Interpretation; Louisville, KY: Westminster/ John Knox Press, 1992); 'Eros and the End: Reading for Gender in the Apocalypse of John', *Semeia* 59 (1992), pp. 193–210; 'The Heroine and the Whore: Fantasy and the Female in the Apocalypse of John', *Semeia* 60 (1992), pp. 67–82; 'Peering into the Abyss: A Postmodern Reading of the Bottomless Pit', in Edgar V. McKnight and Elizabeth Struthers Malbon (eds), *The New Literary Criticism and the New Testament* (JSNTSup, 109; Sheffield: Sheffield Academic Press, 1994), pp. 251–68; 'The

The same is true of Bauckham, at any rate, in his *Theology of the Book of Revelation*. He refrains from attempting to connect the protocol of the divine throne room with imperial court ceremonial. Nevertheless, his view of the relationship between the two thrones – the two empires – matches that of Aune and especially that of Boring:

> The Roman Empire, like most political powers in the ancient world, represented and propagated its power in religious terms. Its state religion, featuring the worship both of the deified emperors and of the traditional gods of Rome, expressed political loyalty through religious worship. In this way it absolutized its power, claiming for itself the ultimate divine sovereignty over the world. And so in effect it contested on earth the divine sovereignty which John sees acknowledged in heaven in chapter 4. The coming of God's kingdom on earth must therefore be the replacement of Rome's pretended divine sovereignty by the true divine sovereignty of the One who sits on the heavenly throne.[45]

What do these parallel claims amount to, these accusations of pretention, these assertions that Roman imperial power is but a parody or pale imitation of divine power? What are Aune, Boring and Bauckham actually saying? Simply that God's imperial splendor far exceeds that of the Roman emperor, just as the emperor's splendor far exceeds that of any of his 600 senators, and just as the senator's splendor far exceeds that of any provincial plebeian, and so on down the patriarchal line to the most subdued splendor of the feeblest father of the humblest household? If so, the difference between Roman sovereignty and divine sovereignty would be quantitative rather than qualitative in Revelation.

Bauckham himself is not unaware of the problem. '[I]t would subvert the whole purpose of John's prophecy', he admits, 'if his depiction of the divine sovereignty appeared to be a projection into heaven of the absolute power claimed by human rulers on earth.' But this danger 'is averted by a kind of apophaticism in the imagery', he claims, 'which purges it of anthropomorphism and suggests the incomparability of God's sovereignty'.[46] Apophaticism is 'negative theology', he explains, and it 'radically distinguishes God from all creaturely beings by conceiving him in negative terms: he is *not* what creatures are'.[47]

How does Revelation rate as negative theology? Encumbered by the exaggerated masculinity of its deity, it limps awkwardly indeed beside the consummately restrained and exquisitely delicate theological probings of a Pseudo-Dionysius, a Meister Eckhart, or other Christian thinkers more commonly termed apophatic.[48]

Revelation to John', in Elisabeth Schüssler Fiorenza (ed.), *Searching the Scriptures: A Feminist Introduction and Commentary* (2 vols; New York: Crossroad, 1993, 1994), vol. 2, pp. 109–30.

45 Bauckham, *Theology of Revelation*, p. 34; cf. pp. 39, 43, 44–45, 59, 143, 159–60, 162–63.

46 Bauckham, *Theology of Revelation*, p. 43.

47 Bauckham, *Theology of Revelation*, p. 43 n. 8, his emphasis. Boring makes a parallel claim, arguing that Revelation has recourse to 'that philosophical tradition which claims that, while we cannot say what the transcendent word of God is, we can to some extent truly represent it by saying what it is not. John thus sprinkles his "description" of the new Jerusalem with affirmations of what will not be there' (*Revelation*, p. 216, his emphasis, introducing a section entitled 'Via Negativa').

48 Further on negative theology, see Stephen D. Moore, *Poststructuralism and the New Testament: Derrida and Foucault at the Foot of the Cross* (Minneapolis, MN: Fortress Press, 1994), esp. pp. 23–24.

Has John really succeeded in 'purging' his text, as Bauckham claims? Has he really evacuated it, voided it of whatever modern theological sensibilities might deem unseemly or unsightly, specifically the glorification of absolute power? Has his apophatic purgative not been too mild for that? Has he not merely broken wind at best?

For power of an alarmingly pure kind is what God's reign in Revelation boils down to. Here is Bauckham's (accurate) account of the life awaiting the blessed in the heavenly city (Rev. 21.1–22.5):

> As for the image of God's rule in the eschatological kingdom, what is most notable is the fact that all the implication of distance between 'the One who sits on the throne' and the world over which he rules has disappeared. His kingdom turns out to be quite unlike the beast's. It finds its fulfillment not in the subjugation of God's 'servants' (22.3)[49] to his rule, but in their reigning with him (22.5). The point is not that they reign over anyone: the point is that God's rule over them is for them a participation in his rule. The image expresses the eschatological reconciliation of God's rule and human freedom, which is also expressed in the paradox that God's service is perfect freedom (cf. 1 Pet. 2.16). Because God's will is the moral truth of our own being as his creatures, we shall find our fulfillment only when, through our free obedience, his will becomes also the spontaneous desire of our hearts. Therefore in the perfection of God's kingdom theonomy (God's rule) and human autonomy (self-determination) will fully coincide.[50]

A Foucauldian nightmare, this vision of heaven (but whose?) represents the absolute displacement of outward subjection, tangible coercion, by inner self-policing, which is now so deeply implanted in the believer as to be altogether indistinguishable from freedom. Revelation does present the individual with an option, of course – to be 'tortured [βασανισθῆναι] with fire and sulfur' instead 'in the presence of the holy angels and in the presence of the Lamb', 'the smoke of [one's] torment' ascending 'for ever and ever' (14.10–11; cf. 9.5; 20.15; 21.8).[51] We are deep within the dystopian netherworld of Foucault's *Discipline and Punish*:[52] on one side, the absolute monarch publicly exacting frightful physical punishment on all who oppose his will; on the

---

49 God's slaves (δοῦλοι), actually. Bauer remarks on this rendering of δοῦλος: '"servant" for "slave" is largely confined to Biblical transl. and early American times' (W. Bauer, W. F. Arndt, F. W. Gingrich and F. W. Danker, *Greek–English Lexicon of the New Testament and Other Early Christian Literature* [3rd edn, Chicago, IL: University of Chicago Press, 2000], s.v. δοῦλος).

50 Bauckham, *Theology of Revelation*, pp. 142–43; cf. p. 164.

51 An option stated even more baldly in *4 Ezra* 7.36–38: 'Then the pit of torment shall appear, and opposite it shall be the place of rest; and the furnace of Hell shall be disclosed, and opposite it the Paradise of delight. Then the Most High will say to the nations that have been raised from the dead, "Look now, and understand whom you have denied, whom you have not served, whose commandments you have despised! Look on this side and on that; here are delight and rest, and there are fire and torments!"' (B. M. Metzger, 'The Fourth Book of Ezra', in J. H. Charlesworth [ed.], *The Old Testament Pseudepigrapha* [2 vols.; New York: Doubleday, 1983], vol. 1, pp. 517–60 [538]; cf. Mt. 25.31–46).

52 Michel Foucault, *Discipline and Punish: The Birth of the Prison* (trans. Alan Sheridan; New York: Pantheon Books, 1977). This is not the place for a general introduction to Foucault. Among the innumerable introductions available, at least three relate his work to biblical studies; Aichele et al., *The Postmodern Bible*, pp. 138–44; Elizabeth Castelli, *Imitating Paul: A Discourse of Power* (Literary Currents in Biblical Interpretation; Louisville, KY: Westminster/John Knox Press, 1991), pp. 35–58; Moore, *Poststructuralism and the New Testament*, pp. 85–94.

other side, a more 'benign' realm in which the rack, the stake and the scaffold have been rendered obsolete – but only because the ruler's subjects are no longer capable of distinguishing his will from their own.[53]

For Foucault, the modern 'disciplinary societies', with their insidious strategies of coercion and control,[54] have succeeded and surpassed the pre-modern 'societies of the spectacle', with their rituals of dismemberment, disembowelment and immolation enacted in the public squares. Both these regimes coexist, however, in Revelation's 'new heaven and new earth' (21.1; cf. 20.11) – not unexpectedly, since the two regimes represent the two faces of power, one scowling, the other smiling, and Revelation's climactic vision (21.1–22.5) is a vision (a projective fantasy?) of power absolutized. On the one hand we read, 'Blessed are those who wash their robes, so that they will have the right to the tree of life and may enter the city by the gates' (22.14). Bauckham has told us what awaits them inside. On the other hand we read, 'Outside [ἔξω] are the dogs [οἱ κύνες] and sorcerers and fornicators and murderers and idolaters, and everyone who loves and practises falsehood' (22.15; cf. 21.27).[55] What will be their fate as outsiders? John has already told us that: 'But as for the cowardly, the unbelieving [ἀπίστοις], the polluted, the murderers, the fornicators, the sorcerers, the idolaters, and all liars, their place will be in the lake that burns with fire and sulfur [ἐν τῇ λίμνῃ τῇ καιομένῃ πυρὶ καὶ θείῳ], which is the second death' (21.8; cf. 19.20b; 20.14–15; Gen. 19.24).

The Beatific Vision

. . . on him, on him alone, had I leisure avidly to gaze. . . .

(Statius, *Silvae* 4.2.40, on Domitian)

Who, then, is the God of Revelation? As I have been implying, he is revealed not through Jesus Christ so much as through the Roman emperor. For many of the emperors, the temptations of the flesh assumed a unique form: the temptation to become divinized flesh. To be or not to be a god?[56] Tiberius sternly rejected the divine

---

53 Cf. Krodel's telling remarks on the 'four living creatures' (4.6–8): 'They are God's pets within the heavenly court . . . Readers of this commentary should not be upset that I speak of God's pets. They should remember their own faithful dogs and cats whose joy it is to live in their presence, to please them and adore them. Worship ought to be just that . . . God's pets in John's vision are the symbol of harmony and worship yet to come, when God shall dwell among his people (21.1–22.5)' (*Revelation*, pp. 156–57).

54 The supreme example of such a strategy would be television, although this is a 'disciplinary technology' that Foucault himself never examined, preferring to focus instead on such phenomena as modern medicine (especially psychiatry), modern prisons and modern sexuality.

55 Who are these 'dogs'? 'The term "dog" is used in Scripture for various kinds of impure and malicious persons', contends Robert H. Mounce. He appeals in particular to Deut. 23.17–18, in which 'the term designates a male cult prostitute' (*The Book of Revelation* [NICNT; Grand Rapids, MI: Eerdmans, 1977], p. 394). A more extensive examination of these miserable mutts can be found in Heinrich Kraft, *Die Offenbarung des Johannes* (HNT; Tübingen: Mohr [Siebeck], 1974), pp. 279–80.

56 On the inception of the Roman imperial cult, see Lily Ross Taylor, *The Divinity of the Roman Emperor* (Middletown, CT: American Philological Association, 1931) (she limits herself to Julius Caesar and Augustus); Stefan Weinstock, *Divus Julius* (Oxford: Clarendon Press, 1971); Duncan Fishwick, *The Imperial Cult in the Latin West: Studies in the Ruler Cult of the Western Provinces of the Roman Empire* (Etudes préliminaires aux religions orientales dans l'Empire romaine, 108; 4 vols; Leiden: Brill, 1987–92), I, pp. 46–72. Shorter treatments include Cuss, *Imperial Cult and Honorary Terms*, pp. 27–35; Müller, *Die Offenbarung des Johannes*, pp. 257–60.

honors dangled enticingly before him. So did Augustus (less energetically, to be sure), Claudius and Vespasian, although all three were deified after death, as was Titus. Caligula greedily seized the opportunity to become a god, wallowing in divinity. So did Julius Caesar, to a lesser extent, as well as Nero, and possibly Domitian.[57]

Domitian's exploits and excesses are of perennial interest to scholars of Revelation, most of whom date the book to the latter years of his reign, which began inauspiciously in 81 CE and ended ignominiously in 96.[58] Did Domitian, ravenous for adulation, gluttonous for deification, really gorge on forbidden fruit, appropriating for himself the title 'Lord and God', as his biographer Suetonius claims? In the *Lives of the Caesars*, we read:

> With . . . arrogance he began as follows in issuing a circular letter in the name of his procurators, 'Our Lord and God bids that this be done [*Dominus et deus noster hoc fieri iubet*]'. And so the custom arose of henceforth addressing him in no other way even in writing or in conversation.[59]

This would have been a bold self-designation indeed, even by the standards of the imperial court, for a deified emperor, or *divus*, did not a *deus* make. 'The best an emperor could expect after death was to be declared a *divus*, never a *deus*', explains a more recent biographer of Domitian, Brian W. Jones, and 'a living one had to make do with even less'. And if Domitian could so overcome his natural modesty, 'why should he hesitate to proclaim it publicly (and epigraphically)?'[60] But the title has yet to turn up in any inscription, coin or official document. It does seem to have been applied to Domitian nevertheless; his contemporary, Martial, does so, for one, and clearly implies that others did so as well.[61] Dio Cassius, too, tells of a certain

---

57 See further Donald L. Jones, 'Christianity and the Roman Imperial Cult', *ANRW* II, 23.1024–35 (Tiberius to Domitian; altogether, the article spans Tiberius to Constantine).

58 Here, for once, critical scholarship is in step with church tradition. Irenaeus claimed that John had his visions 'toward the end of the reign of Domitian' (*Haer.* 3.50.3; cf. Eusebius, *Hist. Eccl.* 3.18.1; Victorinus, *Comm. Apoc.* 10.11). For concise reviews of the (mainly internal) evidence relevant to establishing the date of composition, see Hemer, *Letters to the Seven Churches*, pp. 1–12; Mounce, *Book of Revelation*, pp. 31–36; Sweet, *Revelation*, pp. 21–27; and for a more searching review, see Collins, *Crisis and Catharsis*, pp. 54–83. The latter in particular builds a highly compelling case for the Domitianic date. I realize, of course, that the hypothesis is not unassailable (see esp. J. A. T. Robinson, *Redating the New Testament* [Philadelphia, PA: Westminster Press, 1976], pp. 221–53; Rowland, *Open Heaven*, pp. 403–13; Kenneth L. Gentry, Jr., *Before Jerusalem Fell: Dating the Book of Revelation: An Exegetical and Historical Argument for a Pre-AD 70 Composition* [Tyler, TX: Institute for Christian Economics, 1989]), but I would prefer to avoid staging yet another rehearsal of a convoluted debate, and so will proceed to construct a reading based upon the majority opinion.

59 Suetonius, *Dom.*13.2 (LCL trans., with slight modifications). Similar claims concerning Domitian occur in Pliny, *Pan.* 2.33.4; 78.2; Dio Chrysostom, *Disc.* 45.1; Dio Cassius, *Hist.* 67.4.7; 67.13.4; Aurelius Victor, *On the Caesars* 11.2.

60 Brian W. Jones, *The Emperor Domitian* (London and New York: Routledge, 1992), p. 108.

61 Martial, *Epi.*, esp. 5.8; 7.34; 8.2; 9.66; 10.72; cf. 5.5; 7.2, 5; 8.82; 9.28. Does *Epi.* 5.8 lend support to Suetonius's claim that Domitian began an official letter with the self-designation 'Lord and God'? The passage reads: 'As Phasis in the theater the other day . . . was praising the edict of our Lord and God (*edictum domini deique nostri*), whereby the benches are more strictly assigned . . .' (LCL trans.).

Juventius Celsus, who, accused of conspiring against Domitian, saved his skin by prostrating himself before the emperor and addressing him 'as "Lord and God", names by which he was already being called by others'.[62] Domitian 'obviously knew that he was not a God', claims Jones, but 'whilst he did not ask or demand to be addressed as one, he did not actively discourage the few flatterers who did'.[63]

Of course, the *adulatio* lavished on Domitian by his most fervent flatterers was by no means limited to the hyperbole *Dominus et Deus*. Witness, for example, the laudatory immoderation of Martial and his fellow court poet, Statius, as reported by Kenneth Scott:

> Statius calls him *sacratissimus imperator, sacrosanctus, sacer*, and *verendus*. His home is described as *divina*. Indeed all that pertained to the monarch is named sacred ... The emperor's person is sacred, his side, breast, ear [Martial], and feet [Statius], and the rebellion of Saturninus against him is sacrilegious [Martial]. His name is *sacer* [Martial], as are his secrets [Statius]. His banquet is 'sacred' or 'most sacred'; the golden wreath which he bestows as prize in the Alban contest is 'sacred'; the day on which he feasts the people is *sacer*; his fish are 'sacred' [Martial]; his treasures are *sanctae*, and the nectar which he drinks is *verendum* [Statius].[64]

The devoted duo also insist that Domitian is a *deus praesens* – a Jupiter *praesens*, what is more – proximate, tangible and approachable, as distinct from the distant Olympian.[65] But it was not only in poetry that Domitian was hailed as Jupiter. The compliment occurs in epigraphic finds also, notably an Attic inscription that bestows the title Zeus Eleutherios on the emperor.[66] Numerous coins, too, struck by Domitian, depict him enthroned as 'father of the gods'.[67]

What of Roman Asia, that region to which Revelation is addressed (1.4; cf. 1.11; 2.1–3.22)? The province had two temples dedicated to Domitian, one at Ephesus, the other at Laodicea. A massive marble statue of the emperor erected in the Ephesian temple became a focal point of the imperial cult in Asia Minor.[68] 'Some impression

---

62 Dio Cassius, *Hist.* 67.13.4.

63 Jones, *Emperor Domitian*, p. 109.

64 Kenneth Scott, *The Imperial Cult under the Flavians* (New York: Arno Press, 1975), p. 100; see further Franz Sauter, *Der römische Kaiserkult bei Martial und Statius* (Tübinger Beiträge zum Altertumswissenschaft, 21; Stuttgart: Kohlhammer, 1934), esp. pp. 105–16.

65 See Sauter, *Der römische Kaiserkult*, pp. 51–54; Scott, *Imperial Cult under the Flavians*, pp. 107–08, 137–38.

66 Scott, *Imperial Cult under the Flavians*, p. 139.

67 Stauffer, *Christ and the Caesars*, pp. 167, 173; Jones, 'Christianity and the Roman Imperial Cult', p. 1033. See further Aline L. Abaecherli, 'Imperial Symbols on Certain Flavian Coins', *Classical Philology* 30 (1935), pp. 131–40 (136–39).

68 Although the cult's official center was Pergamum, with its temple dedicated to Roma and Augustus. Is the latter the cryptic 'throne of Satan' referred to in Rev. 2.13? Many have thought so (e.g., Elisabeth Schüssler Fiorenza, *The Book of Revelation: Justice and Judgment* [Philadelphia, PA: Fortress Press, 1985], p. 193; Müller, *Die Offenbarung des Johannes*, p. 110), although others have suggested that Satan's throne is instead the great altar of Zeus Soter that also stood at Pergamum (e.g., Ernst Lohmeyer, *Die Offenbarung des Johannes* [HNT; Tübingen: Mohr [Siebeck], 3rd edn, 1970], p. 25, drawing on Adolf Deissmann, *Licht vom Osten* [Tübingen: Mohr, 4th edn, 1923], p. 238), or even the city itself (e.g., Hemer, *Letters to the Seven Churches*, pp. 84–87; Roloff, *Revelation of John*, p. 51).

of the scale [of the statue] is given by the fact that the lower part of an arm is the height of a man', observes S. R. F. Price. 'The height of the whole, to the top of the spear which the standing figure was probably holding, was some seven to eight metres' – on the same scale, that is to say, as cult statues of the gods.[69] Statues of Apollo, Artemis and Leto, for example, each of them seven to eight meters tall, stood in Apollo's temple at Claros, a scant few miles from Ephesus; while Josephus tells of 'a colossal statue [κολοσσός] of the emperor [Augustus], no smaller than Zeus at Olympia, which served as its model', which dominated the temple of Roma and Augustus at Caesarea.[70] Tacitus, for his part, tells how the Senate, following a minor military victory, resolved to present Nero 'with a statue of the same size as that of Mars the Avenger, and in the same temple'.[71] Of Domitian's Ephesian colossus Price remarks, 'This is the most extreme form of the modeling of the emperor on the gods, no doubt with awesome impact on the population.'[72]

A colossal hard body – Greco-Roman culture and contemporary bodybuilding subculture converge strikingly in their respective conceptions of the godlike physique. A recent advertisement in the muscle magazines for GIANT MEGA MASS 4000, a weight-gaining product, features a 'hard and massive' Dorian Yates flexing alongside the caption, 'The Giant That Won This Year's Mr. Olympia' (Mr. Olympia currently being the most prestigious title in professional bodybuilding). Further into the four-page advertisement another elite bodybuilder, Gary Strydom, is labeled 'A Rock-Solid 260 lbs.', the giant container of GIANT MEGA MASS 4000 that he holds triumphantly aloft suggesting that he owes his statuesque condition to the miraculous product.[73] And what of the Mr. Olympia contest itself? 'In 1965 I created the Mr. Olympia contest,' explains Joe Weider, *princeps* of the bodybuilding empire. 'The name seemed appropriate. The time had come to enter the hallowed ground of the ancient Greek gods with incarnate image. We live among them.'[74] And in the

69 S. R. F. Price, *Rituals and Power: The Roman Imperial Cult in Asia Minor* (Cambridge, UK: Cambridge University Press, 1984), p. 187; cf. p. 255.

70 Josephus, *War* 1.21.7 § 414 (my trans.); cf. *Ant.* 15.9.6 § 339.

71 Tacitus, *Ann.* 13.8 (LCL trans.).

72 Price, *Rituals and Power*, p. 188. Price, a classicist, suggests that 'the establishment of the provincial cult of Domitian at Ephesus, with its colossal cult statue', looms behind Rev. 13.11–15, so that the beast from the land would be 'the priesthood of the imperial cult, particularly . . . in the province of Asia' (p. 197). Many New Testament scholars would concur with Price's identification of this beast; see, e.g., Lohse, *Die Offenbarung des Johannes*, p. 72; Cuss, *Imperial Cult and Honorary Terms*, pp. 96ff.; Müller, *Die Offenbarung des Johannes*, pp. 253ff.; Steven J. Scherrer, 'Signs and Wonders in the Imperial Cult: A New Look at a Roman Religious Institution in Light of Rev. 13.13–15', *JBL* 103 (1984): 599–610. Others would take a different view, e.g., Kraft, *Die Offenbarung des Johannes*, pp. 180ff.; Roloff, *The Revelation of John*, p. 161.

73 Reflecting on his own statuesque physique, Arnold Schwarzenegger remarks: 'You don't really see a muscle as part of you . . . You look at it as a thing and you say well this thing has to be built a little longer . . . or the tricep has to be thicker here in the elbow area . . . You form it. Just like sculpture' (quoted in Charles Gaines and George Butler, *Pumping Iron: The Art and Sport of Bodybuilding* [London: Sphere Books, 1974], p. 52; cf. pp. 106, 108; also Dutton, *Perfectible Body*, pp. 312–15).

74 Quoted in Klein, *Little Big Men*, p. 258. Klein also quotes Weider as saying, 'The modern bodybuilder has followed in the footsteps of the Greek Olympian gods. Obsessed with heroic proportions as they were, how far would the Greeks have taken physical development had they our knowledge of weight training?' (p. 259; cf. Dutton, *Perfectible Body*, p. 21).

course of a somewhat surreal exchange between former Mr. Olympia, Frank Zane, and Michael Murphy, founder of Esalen Institute in Big Sur, California, and 'a leader in the human potential movement', the latter enthuses, 'One of the things I've admired about your attitude, Frank, is your experimentation with somatic mutability, which has enabled you to change your body at will. The further reaches of training point to glimpses of divination of the body, a new kind of flesh.'[75]

Of course, the flesh in question is penile flesh; for what does it mean to say that size and hardness are the *sine qua non* of the bodybuilding physique except that the bodybuilder is an outsized penis in the state of permanent erection?[76] 'He hones his hard body (to be soft is anathema)', as one commentator remarks.[77] His body is '"pumped up", "rock hard" and "tight"', observes another.[78] And the current rage for 'vascularity' in competitive bodybuilding, calling for minimal subcutaneous fat, means that 'the road map of veins is clearly visible, standing out from the flesh in a fashion alarmingly reminiscent of an erect penis'.[79] On stage, the bodybuilder is 'turgid', 'constantly at attention, ready to explode', his entire body engorged like an enormous organ.[80] Arnold tells of the 'pump' that he gets when the blood is flooding his muscles: 'They become really tight with blood. Like the skin is going to explode any minute.'[81] Indeed, former Mr. Universe Steve Michalik entertained a fantasy that he would someday literally explode on stage, showering the worshipers with the viscous contents of his phallic physique.[82]

Domitian's cult too was preposterously phallic; how else should we interpret the massive marble-hard image of his power erected at Ephesus, to cite one of the more Priapean pillars of his cult? Unfortunately for Domitian, his splendid cult did not survive his assassination but swiftly wilted, the Senate according him a *damnatio memoriae* and having his statues – glorious statues, if his biographers are to be believed[83] – destroyed or rededicated. It appears that the Ephesian colossus was allowed to stand until late antiquity, however, although the temple housing it was rededicated to Vespasian and the statue itself passed off as a representation of the latter, the Flavian paterfamilias strapping the monstrous monument onto his own withered loins.[84] Indeed, were it not for the author of Revelation, Domitian's divinity might have died with him.

75　In Frank Zane, 'Train with Zane: Bodybuilding in Future-World', *Muscle & Fitness* (June 1994), p. 247.

76　Cf. Klein, *Little Big Men*, p. 247: 'The fear of size loss . . . is the converse of the bodybuilder's search for size and hardness . . .'.

77　Fussell, 'Bodybuilder Americanus', p. 46.

78　Simpson, *Male Impersonators*, p. 33.

79　Simpson, *Male Impersonators*, p. 33.

80　Fussell, 'Bodybuilder Americanus', pp. 46–47; cf. Dutton, *Perfectible Body*, p. 43; Rosalind Miles, *The Rites of Man: Love, Sex and Death in the Making of the Male* (London: Grafton Books, 1991), p. 111; Simpson, *Male Impersonators*, p. 22

81　Quoted in Butler, *Arnold Schwarzenegger*, p. 124. Hence Arnold's famous dictum, 'A good pump is better than coming' (see Gaines and Butler, *Pumping Iron*, p. 48).

82　Recounted in Fussell, 'Bodybuilder Americanus', p. 50.

83　Suetonius, *Dom.* 13.2; Dio Cassius, *Hist.* 67.8.1; cf. Pliny, *Pan.* 52.3.

84　See Scott, *Imperial Cult under the Flavians*, p. 97; Price, *Rituals and Power*, pp. 178, 255.

For in and through Revelation, the emperor ascends into heaven and becomes a god, and the god he becomes is none other than the Father of Jesus Christ. John's attempt to counter the magnificent imperial cult with the image of a yet more magnificent heavenly cult (the latter modelled in part upon the former) has resulted in a fascinating (con)fusion of figures, the Roman emperor coalescing into the Christian God. And so Domitian is assumed into heaven, together with all his court. He is decked out for battle, for Revelation is a military epic.[85] But his body armor or cuirass, sculpted to simulate a heavily muscled male torso, in the Roman manner, has vanished.[86] In its place is divinized flesh, the unimaginably muscular and exquisitely sculpted physique of the God of Israel,[87] whose appearance is of precious stones: 'And the one seated there looks like jasper [ἴασπις] and carnelian [σάρδιον]' (Rev. 4.3).

Why precious stones? Because precious stones are hard, and (phallic?) hardness is the *sine qua non* of a godlike physique, as we have seen. But why these precious stones in particular? G. R. Beasley-Murray explains,

> The appearance of God was as jasper and carnelian. The former could vary in appearance from a dull yellow or red or green, or even translucent like glass (as apparently in 21.11). In view of the later passage we may take the last to be in view. Carnelian, or sardius (originating from Sardis), was red. The divine appearance, therefore, was as it were transparent 'white' and red.[88]

The divine physique is characterized both by transparence and redness, meaning that the raw musculature of the deity is entirely visible through the skin. '[T]hin as Bible paper', the latter is 'so translucent one can visibly see raw tissue and striated muscle swimming in a bowl of veins beneath.'[89] The Heavenly Bodybuilder is thus the mythological – and myological – figure, the ambulatory anatomy chart, that all earthly bodybuilders aspire to be. 'When you hit a most-muscular pose', Arnold advises the bodybuilding neonate, '[you] should look like an anatomy chart – every area developed, defined, separated, and striated.'[90]

'He was tall of stature,' Suetonius writes of Domitian, 'handsome and graceful too [*praeterea pulcher ac decens*], especially when a young man,' although 'in later

---

85 'A Christian war scroll' is how Bauckham describes it (*Climax of Prophesy*, pp. 210–37).

86 'It is highly likely that the statue of Domitian at Ephesus, of which numerous fragments survive, was cuirassed' (Price, *Rituals and Power*, p. 182). Cuirassed statues of the Roman emperors were extremely common (cf. Taylor, *Divinity of the Roman Emperor*, pp. 179–80; Dutton, *Perfectible Body*, p. 49). Nude statues of the emperors were also common – fat-free, needless to say, and with excellent muscle tone, symmetry and definition – evoking more overtly than cuirassed statues the traditional representations of the gods (cf. Price, *Rituals and Power*, p. 183).

87 On which see Moore, *God's Gym*, pp. 86–102.

88 George R. Beasley-Murray, *Revelation* (2nd edn, NCBC; Grand Rapids, MI: Eerdmans, 1978), p. 113.

89 Fussell, 'Bodybuilder Americanus', p. 49.

90 Arnold Schwarzenegger and Bill Dobbins, *Encyclopedia of Modern Bodybuilding* (New York: Simon & Schuster, 1985), p. 291. In the 'most-muscular' pose, the bodybuilder leans forward, brings his or her clenched fists together in front of his or her crotch, bares his or her teeth, and flexes every muscle group simultaneously.

life he had . . . a protruding belly, and spindling legs . . . thin from a long illness'.[91] Yet the deified Domitian could hardly have been astonished at the physical metamorphosis that came with his apotheosis. After all, in the temple to Hercules that he had erected on the Appian Way, the cult statue of the massively muscled god had been fashioned with the facial features of the emperor himself.[92] And prescient Martial, noting how Hercules had ascended to the 'starry heaven' by virtue of the punishment he had inflicted 'on the wrestler of the Libyan palaestra, and by the throwing of ponderous Eryx in the Sicilian dust', had exclaimed how insignificant such feats appear when measured against Domitian's own prodigious prowess: 'How many weights heavier than the Nemean monster fall! How many Maenalian boars does your spear lay low!'[93] For these and other heroic deeds – 'three times he shattered the treacherous horns of Sarmatian Hister; he three times bathed his sweating steed in Gethic snow' – Domitian shows himself to be a *maior Alcides* (a 'greater Hercules') far outstripping the *minor Alcides*,[94] and deigning to supplement the latter's brutish physique with his own effulgent features.

A mighty warrior needs a mighty weapon. 'Around the throne is a rainbow [ἶρις]' (4.3; cf. Ezek. 1.28), we read, and this turns out to be Domitian's weapon. As numerous commentators have noted, this rainbow evokes that of Gen. 9.13: 'I have set my bow [קשת] in the clouds, and it shall be a sign of the covenant between me and the earth.'[95] A common interpretation of the latter passage, in turn, suggests that the bow set in the clouds after the Flood represents the war bow (also קשת) with which Yahweh wages his battles (cf. Deut. 32.23, 42; 2 Sam. 22.15; Pss. 7.12; 18.15 [14]; 77.18; 144.6; Lam. 2.4; 3.12; Hab. 3.9–11; Zech. 9.14), so that his placing it in the clouds would signify the cessation of his warlike hostilities against humanity.[96]

---

91 Suetonius, *Dom.* 18.1 (LCL trans.).

92 Scott, *Imperial Cult under the Flavians*, p. 143.

93 Martial, *Epi.* 5.65; cf. *idem, Spec.* 6B, 15, 27. Here and in what follows I am quoting Scott's translation of the *Epigrams* (*The Imperial Cult under the Flavians*, pp. 142ff.), which often reads better than Bailey's LCL translation.

94 Martial, *Epi.* 9.101; cf. 9.64. Statius, too, casts Domitian in the role of a *maior Alcides* (*Silv.* 4.2.50ff.). See further Sauter, *Der römische Kaiserkult bei Martial und Statius*, pp. 78–85.

95 See, e.g., Caird, *Revelation of St. John*, p. 63; Beasley-Murray, *Revelation*, p. 113; Ford, *Revelation*, p. 71; Mounce, *Book of Revelation*, p. 135; Sweet, *Revelation*, pp. 117–18; Boring, *Revelation*, p. 105; Robert W. Wall, *Revelation* (NIBCNT, 18; Peabody, MA: Hendrickson, 1991), p. 92. Oddly enough, although this connection is routinely noted in almost all the recent English-language commentaries on Revelation, one is hard-pressed to find a single German commentary that notes it.

96 Again, almost all the major commentaries on Genesis routinely note this interpretation, although not all of them accept it. Those that do include Gerhard von Rad, *Genesis: A Commentary* (trans. J. H. Marks; OTL; Philadelphia, PA: Westminster Press, 1972), p. 134; Umberto Cassuto, *A Commentary on the Book of Genesis* (4 vols; trans. Israel Abrahams; Jerusalem: Magnes Press, 1961–64), II, pp. 136–37 (more tentatively); Nahum M. Sarna, *Genesis* (The JPS Torah Commentary; Philadelphia: Jewish Publication Society, 1989), p. 63; and see, in addition, George E. Mendenhall, *The Tenth Generation: The Origins of the Biblical Tradition* (Baltimore, MD: The Johns Hopkins University Press, 1973), pp. 45–48; Moshe Weinfeld, *Deuteronomy and the Deuteronomic School* (Oxford: Clarendon Press, 1972), pp. 205–06. The interpretation is by no means a modern one, however: it also occurs in the Midrashim (see Cassuto, *Genesis*, II, p. 137, for details) and in Rambam (see Nehama Leibowitz, *Studies in Bereshit in the Context of Ancient and Modern Bible Commentary* [ed. and trans. Aryeh Newman; Jerusalem: World Zionist Organization Department for Torah Education and Culture, 4th edn, 1981], p. 86).

Thus it is that the deified Domitian suddenly finds himself in possession of Yahweh's awesome weapon. Now, the bow also happened to be the mortal Domitian's weapon of choice, according to Suetonius:

> He was . . . particularly devoted to archery [*sagittarum . . . praecipuo studio tenebatur*]. There are many who have more than once seen him slay a hundred wild beasts of different kinds on his Alban estate, and purposely kill some of them with two successive shots in such a way that the arrows gave the effect of horns. Sometimes he would have a slave stand at a distance and hold out the palm of his right hand for a mark, with the fingers spread; then he directed his arrows with such accuracy that they passed harmlessly between the fingers.[97]

Now divinized, Domitian's aim is still more deadly – and so are his intentions, as it happens. The rainbow in Rev. 4.3, far from representing the cessation of the deity's warlike hostilities against humanity, signifies instead their resumption, as the ensuing annihilation of the earth and its inhabitants testifies.[98]

All in all, then, the God of Revelation is a hypermasculine God. But masculinity in excess tends to teeter over inexorably into its opposite. Towering on stage, engorged muscles ready to explode through his taut skin, the male bodybuilder seems a veritable caricature of the ultra-virile male. In all probability, however, as ex-bodybuilder Sam Fussell discloses, 'he's pumped so full of steroids that he's literally impotent'.[99] 'But not only is he less of a man at his moment of majesty,' continues Fussell, 'he's actually more of a woman. Faced with a flood of surplus testosterone, the body reacts by temporarily shrinking the testicles (with a resultant sperm count drop) and releasing an estrogen counterbalance', which, over time, can engender a pair of pubescent breasts (the condition known as gynaecomastia, or 'bitch tits' in gym vernacular).[100] As Mark Simpson sagely observes, hardcore bodybuilding frequently epitomizes the inherent instability, the ambiguity, the flux of masculinity 'right at the moment it is meant to solidify it in a display of exaggerated biological masculine attributes'.[101]

---

97 Suetonius, *Dom.* 19 (LCL trans.). Domitian apparently inherited his father's prowess with the bow (cf. *idem, Tit.* 5.2).

98 I find Caird's caveat unconvincing: the rainbow 'warns us not to interpret the visions of disaster that follow as though God had forgotten his promise to Noah' (*Revelation of St. John*, p. 63), a sentiment echoed by all the other commentators listed in n. 95 above, with the exception of Ford.

99 Fussell, 'Bodybuilder Americanus', p. 52.

100 Fussell, 'Bodybuilder Americanus', p. 52; cf. Samuel Wilson Fussell, *Muscle: Confessions of an Unlikely Bodybuilder* (New York: Avon Books, 1991), pp. 110, 120.

101 Simpson, *Male Impersonators*, p. 30. For reasons such as this, there is at present a mounting interest in bodybuilding evident among cultural critics. In addition to the studies already cited (Bolin, 'Vandalized Vanity'; Dutton, *Perfectible Body*; Fussell, 'Bodybuilder Americanus'; Klein, *Little Big Men*; Simpson, *Male Impersonators*), see Anne Honer, 'Beschreibung einer Lebenswelt: Zur Empirie des Bodybuilding', *Zeitschrift für Soziologie* 14 (1985), pp. 131–39; Alphonso Lingis, *Foreign Bodies* (New York: Routledge, 1994), pp. 29–44; Camille Paglia, 'Alice in Muscle Land', in *eadem, Sex, Art, and American Culture: Essays* (New York: Vintage Books, 1992), pp. 79–82; W. E. Thompson and J. H. Bair, 'A Sociological Analysis of Pumping Iron', *Free Inquiry in Creative Sociology* 10 (1982), pp. 192–96; Margaret Walters, *The Nude Male: A New Perspective* (New York: Paddington Press, 1978), pp. 293ff.

Somewhat to his surprise, therefore, the emperor finds that he has also acquired a pair of female breasts in the course of his apocalyptic apotheosis. Well might he now accept the offer effusively extended to him by extravagant Martial in the seventh book of the *Epigrams*: 'Accept the rough breastplate [*crudum thoraca*] of the warrior Minerva, O you whom even the wrathful locks of Medusa fear.'[102] Domitian's ample Minervan bosom does prohibit him from exhibiting himself topless, but otherwise it does not affect the eternal posing routine that his life has now, blessedly, become. Certainly, it does not deter his audience. His raiment has been artfully cut to display his torso, arms and thighs to maximum advantage. His accessories include a rainbow, as we have seen, but its purpose is cosmetic as well as military. The rainbow 'looks like σμάραγδος,' we are told (4.3). Σμάραγδος (emerald?) 'varied in color from green to a colorless state', as Beasley-Murray notes. 'John may wish to indicate that about the Lord on the throne was a halo, green in color, which served alike to suggest and conceal his glory from his creatures.'[103]

The beholding even of his partially clothed, partially clouded, but altogether Priapean form elicits utter adulation, indeed outright adoration, in the vast audience (the myriad of Martials, the slew of Statiuses) that eternally throngs the heavenly temple.[104] For just as the temple is, or might as well be, a temple to the divine physique, a Go(l)d's Gym, the worship that resounds within it is, or might as well be, hero worship.[105] And that is precisely what the God of Revelation craves. Indeed, this vast audience of idolizers – nameless, faceless, countless (cf.5.11–13; 7.9–10; 19.1–8) – is actually nothing more than an infinite row of mirrors lining the interior walls of the heavenly city, which turns out to be a perfect cube some 12,000 stadia (approximately 1,500 miles) high, broad and long (21.16; cf. 1 Kgs 6.20). And the sole purpose of this vast mirrored enclosure is eternally to reflect the divine perfection back to the divinity himself. The emperor has become his own love object.

---

102 Martial, *Epi*. 7.1.

103 Beasley-Murray, *Revelation*, p. 113; cf. Roloff, *Revelation of John*, p. 69. The three gems that feature in his vision – jasper, carnelian, and emerald (?) – are also found on yet another breastplate, that of the high priest in Exod. 28.17–20; 39.8–21; cf. Rev. 21.18–21 (Ford, *Revelation*, p. 71).

104 The throne room in Revelation doubles as a temple (see esp. 14, 15, 17). In the East, palace and temple were often closely connected (see Peterson, *Angels and the Liturgy*, p. 54 n. 14).

105 Or better, superhero worship. Jesus, in particular, is a superhero throughout the New Testament. 'The Hulk, Superman, and their counterparts are definitely embodiments of hegemonic masculinity' (Klein, *Little Big Men*, p. 267; cf. Dutton, *Perfectible Body*, p. 154). As such, they can be regarded as contemporary incarnations of *the* incarnation, Jesus, who himself possesses hyper-masculine traits. Not only do superheroes have superhuman powers, as does Jesus, they are 'stoic in the face of pain, unemotional' (Klein, *Little Big Men*, p. 267). Note how Jesus tends to shed his emotions as we move from the 'low' Christology of Mark to the 'high' (heroic) Christology of the Fourth Gospel. 'What makes [these superheroes] even more masculine are their alter egos, all of whom are ordinary' (Klein, *Little Big Men*, p. 267; cf. Simpson, *Male Impersonators*, pp. 25–26). Mild-mannered Clark Kent is secretly Superman, for example, while egghead Bruce Banner is secretly the Hulk, and the carpenter from Nazareth is secretly the Son of God (especially in Mark). The recent death and resurrection of the Man of Steel (*Superman* nos. 75, 76) only serves to put a cap on the resemblance.

Afterword: Revelation's Big Reveal

When I saw her I was greatly amazed. (Rev. 17.6)

It was the unquestioned conjoining of worship and the gaze that initially caught my eye as I brushed off Bishop Kirk's *The Vision of God: The Christian Doctrine of the Summum Bonum*, the dusty tome that set the preceding essay in motion, while rummaging aimlessly in the university library one day. But Kirk's study sparks at least one further question for me not directly addressed in the essay. Those elite theologians whom Kirk eulogizes, and who wrote so rhapsodically on the Beatific Vision, were all, to a man, men. Apart from the Beatific Vision, it is in the sphere of male sexuality, arguably, that the gaze is linked most intimately with bliss. The question then arises: what might the relationship be between the Beatific Vision and the voyeuristic vision?

The male voyeuristic gaze can be said to shuttle between two poles and two goals: it can abject its object or exalt it. In the case of the Beatific Vision, the object seen elicits – or, better, exacts – worship; exaltation, not abjection, is thus the dominant register (in contrast, say, to Rev. 17.1–6, in which Rome, misogynistically decked out in drag, becomes the object of an abjecting gaze: 'Come and I will show you the comeuppance of the great whore . . . '). In male voyeurism, the worshipful mode finds its stereotypical expression in the following scenario: a boy or man, himself unseen, feasts his fevered eyes on the spectacle of an unsuspecting woman in a state of undress – a woman who, moreover, meets his own personal criteria for archetypal, awe-inspiring womanhood – and he climaxes in an ecstasy of worship. This scenario, however, is not the canonical one; for the object of the gaze in the Book of Revelation, and in the theological tradition of the Beatific Vision more generally, is male. An awe-inspiring male, then, and an altogether queerer vision.

But have I, perhaps, been overhasty in suggesting that the vision of God in Revelation, and in the Beatific Vision at large, is essentially voyeuristic? For if voyeurism classically entails an *unseen* observer, then the deity in Revelation is never the object of a voyeuristic gaze on the part of those who unceasingly abject themselves before him. It is only the reader of Revelation who, strictly speaking, is placed in the position of a voyeur – and irrespective of her or his extratextual gender, or sexual proclivities. John, the 'seer' of Revelation (as he is so aptly named), holds the heavenly door open for us ('I looked, and lo, in heaven an open door!' – 4.1) and implicitly invites us to peek over his shoulder at the secret spectacle unfolding within. For those already inside the throne room, however, 'the myriads of myriads and thousands of thousands' assembled around the throne (5.11), the looking is open and unabashed. Not voyeurism, then, technically speaking. Yet occupying a stance, nonetheless, that is uncomfortably intimate with that of the voyeur. For the act of looking, watching, staring, gazing, gaping, gawking, gawping, ogling . . . eternally transmuted into an act of enraptured worship, defines the audience of the heavenly throne room no less than the stereotypical voyeur, crouched behind a bush and transfixed by his own Beatific Vision. The worshipful gaze in Revelation, it is tempting to conclude, is thus a gendered gaze. More precisely, it is a masculine gaze, to the degree that voyeurism is commonly coded as masculine. (It cannot unequivocally or absolutely be coded as masculine, of course; otherwise *Playgirl* magazine would exist entirely outside the realm of the explicable and thus enjoy the status of a numinous object and sacred text.)

In pondering the visual agency of the heavenly audience of Revelation, I am playing a variation on the ending of my essay, which focused the heavenly throne room and heavenly city through the eyes of the enigmatic character at their center, 'the one seated on the throne'. I suggested that the innumerable throng of worshipers constitutes a vast mirrored enclosure the sole purpose of which is to reflect the divine perfection back to the deity, who thereby becomes his own eternal love object. But perhaps it is less a case of a single reflecting surface than of two mirrored surfaces facing and reflecting each other. For is not the deity also a mirror? (A mirror whose frame is anthropomorphism and before which theological 'reflection' – also aptly named – is endlessly enacted. Dismantle this frame and what remains of 'the biblical God'? Rather than resist the anthropomorphic lure, Christian theology has traditionally swallowed it hook, line and sinker: 'man' becomes 'God' in the very moment that 'God' becomes 'man'.) This divine mirror reflects me, the Christian worshiper, back to myself. But the me I see in this celestial mirror cannot merely be the mundane me. This me has undergone metanoia ('Repent then' – Rev. 2.16; cf. 2.5, 22; 3.3, 19; etc.), and, in consequence, metamorphosis (cf. 7.13–14: 'Who are these clothed in white robes . . . ?'). Or to translate all of this into a more contemporary idiom – and my sole interest in what remains of this afterword will be in (further) relating Revelation to contemporary popular culture – this supramundane me has undergone a *makeover*. Yet the marvels of the makeover in Revelation pale in relation to reality, as we are about to discover.

In contemporary U.S. culture, 'reality' has recently become the name for a rather unreal TV genre. The makeover, long a familiar feature of the Oprahesque talk show, has assumed the proportions of a veritable theophany within the reality genre. I have in mind particularly the recent reality series *The Swan*, together with its less lyrically titled twin *Extreme Makeovers*. (Unseemly, I realize, for a fifty-something professor of New Testament to squander his TV-viewing time on such fluff, especially when he could be deepening his knowledge of his field by watching *Mysteries of the Bible*-style documentaries instead, spilling his beer in excitement every time an old friend, now become talking head, appears on the screen. My sole excuse – a feeble one, no doubt – is that I'm a U.S. immigrant, and even after twenty-or-so years in this country I still occasionally feel like Alice in Wonderland, or even like John of Patmos as he plummets down his own, still more unreal, rabbit hole.)

'I consider that these present sufferings are not worth comparing with the glory that is to be revealed', the Apostle has attested (Rom. 8.18); and that verse might well be embroidered and framed above the beds of the weekly martyrs undergoing these extreme makeovers. So mummified in bandages are they that their brutalized faces are barely visible within the cocoon, following the torturous series of flesh-slicing, bone-breaking and fat-sucking 'procedures' to which they have been subjected before the prime-time audience in the operating theater become amphitheater: the liposuction, the tummy tuck, the breast augmentation; the eye lift, the brow lift, the facelift; the rhinoplasty, the otoplasty; the jaw surgery, the chin surgery, the cheekbone surgery, the oral surgery; and so on. Afterwards they are in more pain than Christ on his cross. And to what end?

Here we veer from Paul of Tarsus back to John of Patmos. For the vindicating moment of glory for these prime-time martyrs to the cult of youth and beauty is what the makeover reality show terms 'the Reveal'. On the night of her 'Big Reveal', the Revealee, whose transfigured face we have not yet been permitted to behold, is filmed from behind in slow motion and soft focus as she glides into the sacred space in which the Reveal will be consummated – an ample space lined with spectators whose expectant faces instantly light up with unfeigned awe as the Revealee makes her grand entrance. The indispensable instrument of the Big Reveal, however, is the outsized mirror on the other side of the room, veiled for now by a curtain. At a signal from the trembling Revealee – who, like us, has been denied the vision of her face all the while she has been in the tomb – the veil is ceremoniously raised. The Revealee's verbal response to the image in the mirror never varies; it is as predictable as any verbal response in any liturgical celebration. And it is intoned over and again as though for absolute emphasis: 'Omigod! Omigodomigodomigod! Oh. My. God.' And as she turns and faces the room, ecstatic tears coursing down her resculpted cheeks, the audience now takes up the awed refrain: 'Omigod!'

It is tempting to view this ritualistic scene as the quintessential moment of theophany in contemporary U.S. culture: theophany as self-revelation, the Beatific Vision as the Beautific Vision. For it is in this moment of utter physical transform-ation, seemingly, that the metaphysical is most unequivocally revealed (at least in TV-land – but is not that, as much as anything, now the American homeland?), eliciting instinctive, spontaneous acknowledgment of that fact in the ritual's participants. The comforting distance between 'My Lord and my God' (Jn 20.28; cf. Rev. 4.11) and 'Omigod!' all but vanishes at such moments. God may, among many other things, be Absolute Goodness, but beauty is the privileged symbol of goodness, or virtue if you prefer, in contemporary U.S. culture – not that contem-porary U.S. culture is original or unique in that regard, except in one way. The virtues most deafeningly and most incessantly trumpeted in the U.S. popular media, and, as such, the cardinal virtues of U.S. popular culture, are not four, as in Greco-Roman antiquity, but merely two: dieting and exercise.

Revelation's Big Reveal – or Biggest Reveal, rather, for it is merely one of many – occurs, appropriately enough, in the climactic chapter of the book and is announced with an admirable economy of words: 'they shall see his face' (22.4; cf. Exod. 33.18–23). The singling out of the deity's *face* for this climactic act of seeing (the text could, after all, just as easily announce 'they shall see his power', or 'they shall see his truth', or 'they shall see his justice') implies, arguably at least, that it is the *beauty* of the godhead that is in view (cf. Ps. 27.4; Isa. 28.5; 33.17) – not that beauty is altogether separable, of course, from power, truth, justice and all the other sterling attributes of Revelation's deity. But the foregrounding of God's face in this climactic instance seems to evoke the concept of God's beauty, just as the foregrounding of God's arm would evoke God's power or deliverance, or the foregrounding of God's eyes omniscience. This beauty, then, is no ananthropomorphic abstraction, no anemic Platonic idea. Rather, it is an embodied beauty, a gendered beauty, a *male* beauty, the eternal beholding of which is the quintessence of bliss within Revelation's world, or rather its heaven. The Bea(u)tific Vision in Revelation would thus seem – yet again, to echo the original conclusion of the essay – a narcissistic male fantasy enacted in a claustrophobic mirrored enclosure. Of the essence here is the hyper-idealized male image – absolute power residing in a body all but undescribed, but nevertheless coded as male, and beautiful enough, apparently, to merit an eternal, worshipful gaze. Everything else – the celestial city, the celestial throne, the celestial audience – is there merely to provide assorted pedestals for this image, and also to provide the illusion of transcendence. But there is no room for real transcendence (even assuming that real transcendence is ever possible) in the constricted space between the quasi-voyeuristic, implicitly male gaze and the reflected male image. Yet there is at least one element of truth in this celestial hall of reciprocally reflecting mirrors. The thunderous clamor of the heavenly chorus, its eternally reiterated ejaculation, does perfectly encapsulate the essence of this narcissistic transaction: 'Omigod! Omigodomigodomigod! Oh. My. God.'

Ms.Calculating the Endtimes: Additions and Conversation*

Catherine Keller

I am the first and the last.
I am the honored one and the scorned one.
I am the whore and the holy one.

Thunder: Perfect Mind, Nag Hammadi Codex

What does sex have to do with apocalypse – with a mythic war between a sword-tongued Messiah who in the End lives happily ever after with his bejewelled Virgin, and a majestic urban Whore with her beastly paramours? More or less everything, at the level of the dream. But then again, not much, at the level of its intentions – the marks of gender and the revelations of sex in the Book of Revelation are symbolic of more or less everything *but* sex.

> AJL: *How so? Might 'sex' be 'sex' when 'the whore' is involved but something other when 'good characters' are present? Might those 'virgins' be 'virgins' in terms of sexual practice as opposed to 'those who have not defiled themselves' spiritually with 'the goddess' or the Roman cult? That is, how do we know when sex is 'not sex'?*
> CK: *Yes, there might be more 'more' than 'less' in the 'everything but' of sex! The lascivious whore, distinctly embodying the imaginary of aggressive feminine lust, symbolizes the power of Rome – the dominant enactment of masculinity in the ancient world. If 'she' is a Drag Queen, John thereby mocks the manly rule of Rome with the most satisfying of epithets – 'You whore!' The Jewish or early Christian manhood thus striking back at the rival of its own terribly, indeed terrifyingly, masculine Messiah projects the whore as the symbol of a male power. Yet the symbol sets loose a whole force-field of sex/gender metonyms: of good masculine virginity vs a promiscuous and so ultimately feminized, decadent and doomed style of masculinity. So while the sexually charged images are not about sex, and the gender inflections do not intend gender teachings, the 'everything but sex' is soaked with sex, and the mythic genders do not allegorize away the question of gender within the uncomfortably close community of early Christians. . . .*

As the energies of sex and gender surge through the entire network of our most private and most collective lives, so they also pulse through the texts and the traditions of the religious imagination. This essay attempts to transcode the apocalyptic form of gender symbolism – that is, it tries at once to make conscious the binary codes of gender carried by the apocalyptic tradition and to interrupt them. It

---

* The original essay, 'Ms.Calculating the Endtimes: Gender Styles of Apocalypse', appears as Chapter 4 in Catherine Keller, *God and Power: Counter-Apocalyptic Journeys* (Minneapolis, MN: Fortress Press, 2005), pp. 53–65 (reprinted by permission). The present essay includes, along with the conversation with the editor, additional selections from *God and Power*.

brings a feminist lens to our theopolitical investigations. Or, rather, it makes explicit and central the feminist perspective that has from the start motivated a counter-apocalypse.

Apocalyptic movements emanate from a marginal, readily underestimated power, a powder keg of language ever ready to explode into practice. These movements are radical whether revolutionary or reactionary, and they are often – though pointedly not always – aggressively misogynist. They represent a wide swathe of 'subjugated discourses', popular or arcane, in Foucault's sense (though he did not investigate millennialisms).[1] The last will be first, will finally have their chance. The Second Coming signals a second chance for the losers of history, victims of oppression or of dissipation. And in the more bitter and usually sexist variants, true to the original, their enemies (those whores, those fornicating beasts, those sons of *bitches*) will get their comeuppance.

Of course the defiant rage is often defanged. The repetitive replays of endtime expectations, disappointments and displacements have lent the whole drama an aura of kitsch, like the soft-porn graphics – indispensable to dispensationalist pamphlets – of the whore of Babylon clad scantily in red, astride her many-headed beast.

Reflecting on another scene of apocalyptic stereotypes, Jeff MacGregor described *WrestleMania* as 'the end of the world as we know it'. Reading the 'seemingly inexplicable resurgence of professional wrestling' as the harbinger of doom, he quipped that 'the apocalypse will be televised'. And he was aware of the hypertrophy of pertinent scholarship: '1990's red-hot growth sector for media analysis: apocalypse theory'.[2] He neglected, however, to comment on the gender regression embodied in these bizarre heroes of postmodern hulkdom. Perhaps it seemed obvious. But sometimes signs of the times are so obvious, so in our face, that we miss their meaning. Costumed in comic-book melodrama, the most cartoonish exaggeration of bang-pow masculinity was 'coming again'.

MacGregor couldn't have known how *prophetic* his bit of pop culture analysis would prove. On the other side of the millennium divide, we have seen a second bodybuilder elected as the governor of a state. Surrounded with the oscillating messianic/demonic images of the nuclear Armageddon movies, the 'Terminator' who came to office was also known as 'the Grope'. He combined apocalyptic and sexist fantasy with Hollywood hyperproduction. Thus is the ancient holy warrior come (again) as a clownish, muscle-bound boaster, bulking up for the 'New American Century', the neocon era of pre-emptive hyperpower and unprovoked invasion. The millennial machismo threw itself upon the planet. The profits for its corporations have been, well, orgiastic, almost miraculous – they can't stop *coming*.

What Lee Quinby calls 'apocalyptic masculinity' may be good for big business. However, it does not bode well for the peaceable kingdom. In the face of such

---

1 Michel Foucault, '7 January 1976', in *idem*, *Society Must Be Defended: Lectures at the College de France, 1975–76* (trans. David Macey; New York: St. Martin's Press, 2003), pp. 1–22.

2 Jeff MacGregor, 'The New Pop Hero: A Mirage of Muscle and Men?', *The New York Times*, 28 March 1999, Arts and Leisure, pp. 1ff. MacGregor's account of this ludicrously masculinized version of the end of the world should be read in tandem with Stephen D. Moore's *God's Gym: Divine Male Bodies of the Bible* (New York and London: Routledge, 1996), a lucid exposé of the voracity and bulk of the apocalyptic God Himself (and see Moore's essay in this *Feminist Companion*).

monstrous masculinities, feminists may repudiate the whole range of covert and overt apocalypse, from those who with pious passion calculate dispensationalist endtimes to those who cold-bloodedly calculate corporate profits. No wonder Quinby has declared a feminist 'anti-apocalypse'![3] She unveils very precise archaeologies of the good/evil and male/female dualisms at play in North American Christian and political life. But without her sort of specific exploration of the apocalyptic tradition, feminism may fall into an anti-apocalyptic dissociation from the biblical prophetic paradigm. Without an engaged critique, anti-apocalypse may be tempted by a self-deceptive ms.calculation.

At a certain historical angle, the apocalyptic Other turns out to be inseparable from the feminist self. Disinterested distance collapses, for instance, in an analysis of the origins of the women's movement. Nineteenth-century millennialist themes permeate, indeed in part produce, the hope and the rhetoric of the 'New Woman'. This feminist apocalypse is itself readily pushed to the margins of the movement and forgotten. But then it returns (like a woman scorned) with a vengeance. I find it more promising to read the dreams than to repress them. We must then recognize in the feminist vision – which has after all done as much as any movement in history to reshape the world and even the church – a peculiar apocalyptic mirror-play. Perhaps a few keep it in play; the mirroring is liberated into parody, into the sort of ironic mimesis practiced by the French feminist theorist Luce Irigaray – to whose messianic movement/motion we turn in the end.

Femme du Siècle

Early in my work on apocalypse – as master text and historicized context of all western theopolitics. . . .

AJL: *What about 'eastern' theopolitics? Is this apocalyptic problem a uniquely western one? Does 'western' mean 'Christian'?*

CK: *'Western' is 'Christian' in the way that it is 'white' – by the power of dominative homogenization, a power not exclusive to the Christian west but energized by a distinctively righteous aggression. The peculiar apocalyptic, good vs evil, dynamism of the western monotheisms – in contrast to but not incommensurable with the Indian, Chinese and Japanese empires, in which Islam has played a role, but in which no singular God has dominated the imagination of world conquest – cannot be abstracted from the imperial objectifications of messianism. While the messiah is a*

---

3 I developed the concept of 'anti-apocalypse' in *Apocalypse Now and Then: A Feminist Guide to the End of the World* (Boston, MA: Beacon Press, 1996), before encountering Lee Quinby's delightful *Antiapocalypse: Exercises in Genealogical Criticism* (Minneapolis: University of Minnesota Press, 1994), which I was able to write into my book rather late, but as a pointed illustration of the persuasive force of this position. She has followed it up with *Millennial Seduction: A Skeptic Confronts Apocalyptic Culture* (Ithaca, NY: Cornell University Press, 1999). Here she performs insightful genealogies of the 'apocalyptic gender panic' of the Promise Keepers and of 'programmed perfection' through bioengineering. Tina Pippin's *Death and Desire: The Rhetoric of Gender in the Apocalypse of John* (Literary Currents in Biblical Interpretation; Louisville, KY: Westminster/John Knox Press, 1992) provides the collegial analog of a feminist deconstruction of Revelation within New Testament studies proper.

child of Judaism, it was Christian supersessionism that turned 'him' oedipally against the Jews. The triumphalist strand of Christianity, merging apocalyptic hope with imperial unification, permitted the global deployment of the apocalyptic warrior deity – against the Jews within, on the way, as in the Crusades, to the Infidel without.

I had intended a rather straightforward exposé of the self-fulfilling apocalypse prevalent in the nuclear/ecological/gender politics of the 1980s. But soon I recognized a strange logic at work. The more strident the opposition to Christian apocalyptic ideology – as in such paradigmatic cases as the Marxist metanarrative and, more to the present point, the work of philosopher Mary Daly – the more irresistibly the discourse takes on the demonizing dualism of apocalypse itself: the hope against every other calculable hope, the righteous rage for justice, the purity of a community of martyrs, the impatient hope for a qualitatively and materially transformed future, soon and very soon. Blasting the so-called First Coming of Christian theology 'as an absolutizing of men', Daly proposed an anti-apocalyptic 'overcoming of dichotomous sex stereotyping, which is the source of the absolutizing process itself'. This is surely in part the case. But note the apocalyptic terms of this overcoming: 'This event, still on its way, will mean the end of phallic morality. Should it not occur, we may witness the end of the human species on this planet.' That may also be.

Yet her prediction takes the form of a precise anti-apocalypse: 'Seen from this perspective the Antichrist and the Second Coming of women are synonymous.'[4] Her own perspective mirrors in reverse the binarism of the apocalypse, yet it was deliberate, parodic in its 'reversal of the reversals'. This is early second-wave feminism, its satiric anti-absolutes now commanding, after the *fin de millennium* drive to purge feminism of essentialism (of which Daly is the usual suspect), little loyalty. Daly stands in a long – and richly apocalyptic – tradition of her 'revolting hags'. She might not appreciate such a genealogy. Yet I think it allows us to resist any dismissal of her work and that of other irascibly indispensable prophets.

As though anticipating Daly's discourse over a century earlier, a young French proletarian activist named Claire Demar wrote, 'The word of THE WOMAN REDEEMER WILL BE A SUPREMELY REVOLTING WORD' [her upper case]. It will be 'the broadest, and consequently the most satisfying to every [sexual] nature, to every humor.' Demar evoked 'the Mother with her thousand voices' embodied in all women as a principle of resistance to masculine repression'.[5] Demar and the proletarian women's journal, the fledgling *Tribune*, had appeared in the margins of the Saint-Simonian community, a millennialist movement led by the charismatic Enfantin. Such utopian movements, like the Oneida community or Winstanley's earlier Diggers, prepared the way for Marxist socialism. Far from atheistic, how-

---

4 Mary Daly, *Beyond God the Father: Toward a Philosophy of Women's Liberation* (Boston, MA: Beacon Press, 1973), pp. 96–97. Daly amplifies her vision of the apocalypse as it transcends (absolutely) Christianity itself in *Gyn/Ecology: The Metaethics of Radical Feminism* (Boston, MA: Beacon Press, 1978).

5 Cited in Leslie Wahl Rabine, 'Essentialism and its Contexts: Saint-Simonian and Poststructuralist Feminisms', in Naomi Schor and Elizabeth Weed (eds), *The Essential Difference* (Books from Differences; Bloomington: Indiana University Press, 1994), pp. 130–50 (135).

ever, they were apocalyptic millennialists, unfolding the utopian prophecies of the eleventh-century visionary Joachim of Fiore. They envisioned a gender egalitarianism far-fetched for their time, encoded in the 'Woman Clothed with the Sun' of Revelation 12 loosely fused with the New Jerusalem. As Demar soon learned, however, the male leaders preferred their own fantasy of 'the Mother' or 'Lady Wisdom' to the work of the journal and of its living women.[6]

AJL: *What was the view of 'sexuality' Demar et al. held? Was procreation to stop? Was the body to be denied (as part of the problem) or celebrated (as part of the redemption)?*

CK: *Demar and her sister writers for the* Tribune *celebrate the redemptive female body indeed, drawing especially on the maternal potential as a power. Thus the seamstress Jeanne-Desiree Veret wrote: 'The banner of women is universal, for . . . are they not all united by the same bond, that of MATERNITY.'[7] The Saint-Simoniennes assume, as Leslie Wahl Rabine writes, comparing them to Hélène Cixous and the écriture féminine, 'the risk of essentialism in order to alter a hierarchical power relation with male theorists'.[8] Yet the echo of 'every nature' signals the non-traditional character of this appeal in its context, in which a socially recognizable female power was courageously mobilized against the not-yet-recognized power of the 'thousand voices' of women, and particularly working-class women.*

It took female-led utopias to resist – from *within* the codes of apocalypse – the tug of apocalyptic masculinity.

AJL: *Perhaps that is what we have now with feminist science fiction and fantasy: classically Sherry Tepper, Suzette Hayden-Elgin, Marge Piercy, etc., or the dystopic warnings of Margaret Atwood's* The Handmaid's Tale.

For instance, the apocalyptic millennialist movement of the Shakers, led by Ann Lee, who herself became identified by her followers as the Wisdom figure of Revelation 12, maintained a fascinating hybrid of gender egalitarianism and apocalyptic revolt. For the Trinitarian pattern of Joachite third-age millennialism it had substituted the radical concept of the Divine Couple, 'the Mother/Father God'. An extraordinary Shaker ditty identifies the age of the Antichrist, extending from the onset of orthodox imperial Christendom to her time, with the trinitarian hegemony:

> The monstrous beast, and bloody whore
> Reign'd thirteen hundred years and more;
> and under foot the truth was trod,
> By their mysterious threefold God:
> But while they placed in the *He*

---

6 'All that is a preparation for the public work of woman, but it is not a work of woman,' opined Enfantin of the work of the *Tribune.* 'It is we who give birth in pain to woman.' See also Keller, *Apocalypse Now and Then,* p. 228.

7 Cited in Rabine, 'Essentialism and its Contexts', p. 132.

8 Rabine, 'Essentialism and its Contexts', p. 135.

> Their sacred co-eternal *Three*,
> A righteous persecuted few
> Ador'd the everlasting *Two*.[9]

Thus is already lampooned what Daly would eventually mock as the cosmic Boys' Club, the ultimate symbol of male bonding. The apocalypse code is deployed freely, with the prophetic authority of a community of women prepared, if not to be martyred, to narrate their persecution and risk witness against the arch patriarchy of the church – and of course of the canonical apocalypse.

One can then follow rather precisely the increasing political force of feminist millennialist rhetoric. The Methodist Frances Willard, one of the most prominent public female voices of the late nineteenth century, announced 'the coming reign of God and of woman'.

> AJL: *Did Methodists have an 'apocalyptic rhetoric'? What did Wesley say about Revelation?*
>
> CK: *On the whole Methodists reflect the Enlightenment amillennialism of the Wesleys themselves, with an emphasis on present salvation, both individual and communal, rather than an imminent and exterior rupture of history. Cf. Methodist and Radical*[10]. . . . *Yet the peaceable millennialism of U.S. progressive movements carries a strong Wesleyan-holiness charge.*

The theopolitics of this eschatology is manifest: 'She will come into government and purify it, into politics and cleanse [it] . . . for woman will make home-like every place she enters, and she will enter every place on this round earth.'[11] Essentialist indeed – let she who is without essences cast the first stone! Even as such prophecy finds no secure religious home, it remained a politically effectual spiritual discourse. In 1881 Matilda Joslyn Gage wrote that 'the male element has thus far held high carnival, crushing out all the divine elements of human nature. . . . The recent disorganization of society warns us that in the disenfranchisement of women we have let loose the reins of violence and ruin which she only has the power to avert. . . . *All writers recognize women as the great harmonizing element of this "new era"*'.[12] A melodramatic moment of this spreading enthusiasm was recorded as a toast at the Illinois Women's Press Association, a bastion of New Womanhood, in 1891:

> Pealing! The clock of Time has struck the woman's hour,
> We hear it on our knees.
> All crimes shall cease, and ancient wrongs shall fail;
> Justice returning lifts aloft her scales,

---

9 Poem concluding Benjamin Young's *Testimony of Christ's Second Appearing* (1816), cited in Linda Mercadente, *Gender, Doctrine, and God: The Shakers and Contemporary Theology* (Nashville, TN: Abingdon, 1990), p. 13.

10 Joerg Rieger and John Vincent (eds), *Methodist and Radical: Rejuvenating a Tradition* (Nashville, TN: Kingswood Books, 2004).

11 Cited in Beryl Satter, *Each Mind a Kingdom: American Women, Sexual Purity, and the New Thought Movement, 1875–1920* (Berkeley: University of California Press, 1999), p. 112.

12 Satter, *Each Mind a Kingdom*, p. 112, emphasis added.

Peace o'er the world her olive wants extends,
And white-robed Innocence from Heaven descends.[13]

The New Jerusalem here descending as an enlightening 'Innocence' suggests the virginal (and of course white) purity of an apocalyptic essentialism to which the woman's movement remains indelibly indebted.

AJL: *Does Jesus play any role in these nineteenth-century women's scenarios?*

CK: *They appeal frequently to Jesus' relationships with women, and to his dependence upon 'certain women', like Joanna and Susanna, for support.*

Feminism may, through the challenge of its internal diversities and of a relativizing postmodernism, have outgrown its heritage of all-or-nothing utopian absolutes. But how would it do so – absolutely? Feminist anti-essentialism – with its sister oppositionalism, anti-apocalypse – remains an academic privilege earned by these pitched apocalyptic struggles.

AJL: *Is it a 'white western' privilege, given the strategic use of 'essentialist' rhetoric among 'feminists' (who might not, for various reasons, claim this designation) in the 'two-thirds world'?*

CK: *Gayatri Chakravorti Spivak, who had coined the phrase 'strategic essentialism', certainly suggests in* Critique of Postcolonial Reason[14] *that white women are often blind to the ethnocentrism of their criticisms of third-world women's essentialist arguments for feminism. For the latter often, as with the Saint-Simoniennes noted above, appeal to women's biology and maternity for traction against local patriarchies.*

But it only lurches toward dishonesty when we forget the mother of all oppositionalisms, the apocalyptic heritage fuelling our own righteous rhetoric.

AJL: *Who is this 'we'? All humanity? Christians? Feminists?*

CK: *Always a fair question. My strategically essentializing 'we' here seems to have meant: anyone reading this sentence, and their friends! That apocalyptic heritage endlessly escapes Christian or feminist supervision; yet it does not characterize the human as such.*

Women inside Apocalypse

Given the strong contribution of a feminist anti-apocalypse, I have needed to reveal a bit of the apocalypse hidden in feminism.

AJL: *What do you see as 'feminist anti-apocalypse'?*

CK: *In* Apocalypse Now and Then *I developed the categories of*

---

13 Satter, *Each Mind a Kingdom*, pp. 44-45.
14 Gayatri Chakravorti Spivak, *A Critique of Postcolonial Reason: Toward a History of the Vanishing Present* (Cambridge, MA: Harvard University Press, 1999).

retro-apocalypse (an uncritical, fundamentalizing return to Revelation's imminent apocalypse); neo-apocalypse (the affirmative but historically and critically contextualized use of Revelation by liberation theologians as a cry for justice); anti-apocalypse (a specifically feminist reaction against both the Christian text and the effects of its morally dualist, world-annihilating and misogynist desire); and counter-apocalypse (as the sign of my own strategic ambivalence, hoping to counteract the dualism without losing the justice).

The mirror-play of course does not cease just because it is seen. Perhaps it permits a wider refraction, a concave mirror like Irigaray's epistemic speculum, belying any easy distinction between (apocalyptic) other and (anti-apocalyptic) self. Indeed Quinby – the author of *Anti-Apocalypse* – staged her *Millennial Seductions* as 'skeptical revelations of an American feminist on Patmos' – thus herself embracing a deconstructive mirror-play, beyond mere opposition.

If the opposition of feminism to apocalypticism seems at first absolute, it's not because we unconditionally oppose a biblical text as such.

> AJL: *How did you/we get from opposition to 'apocalypticism' to opposition to a 'biblical text'? Why would the two be associated in the first place?*
> CK: *In my friend Lee Quinby's work, for example, which comes from cultural studies rather than from biblical or theological specialization, apocalypticism is often conflated with Biblicism in general, indeed with Christianity. And of course my 'we' there shares much of the anti-apocalyptic engagement, while ultimately countering its own, well, apocalyptic overgeneralizations.*

But our culture still deploys those devastating dualisms . . .

> AJL: *Yes, but is 'dualism' the same thing as 'apocalypticism'?*
> CK: *Dualism is a much wider category: mind/body dualism is characteristically Hellenistic, and lacks any apocalyptic gesture; apocalypticism is an intensification of a binary of good/evil active from Zoroaster and the Hebrew prophets on, that occasionally becomes absolute in the form of a moral dualism.*

that merge any excessive female desire with the demonic figure – all-consuming, all-consumed – of the Great Whore.

> AJL: *What of excessive 'male' desire?*
> CK: *Excessive male desire doesn't seem to attract demonization so much as a good scolding among apocalyptic believers today.*

John of Patmos's hysterical denunciation of his female competitor as 'Jezebel' may have been harmless enough in its context.

> AJL: *How would we know?*
> CK: *I guess if one believes Elisabeth Schüssler Fiorenza that the trope of 'Jezebel' was more directed against a community and a style of Christian assimilation to pagan society than against actual women, one might at least hope that it did*

little actual harm. But of course it may have contributed directly to the stifling of women's leadership. We don't know.

But due to the success of his letter to the churches, its sexist rhetoric has provided an indelible template for his fans. They have practiced such various readings as the polygamous and gynocidal terror of Jan Bockelson's sixteenth-century 'New Jerusalem' community,[15] fundamentalism's founding inscription of the New Woman as 'silly women of the last days',

> AJL: *Yet those women in Revelation are anything but 'silly' – John does not castigate them as stupid – and why not, given that 'silly woman' or 'foolish woman' was conventional polemic?*
> CK: *See my* Apocalypse Now and Then, *p. 244. It has a rather nice paragraph quoting fundamentalist sources . . . and justifying that name for my Chapter 6.*[16]

and David Koresh's harem. One is struck by the utility of sexism as an engine of empowerment for socially marginalized male believers.

> AJL: *Why should 'we' [i.e., 'one'] be? It is also a 'sign of empowerment' for the socially elite: the trophy wife, the 'conquests', the import of the 'potent' boss, the resistance to women penetrating that 'glass ceiling' . . .*
> CK: *But precisely the social disadvantages, felt or real, of fundamentalist males may contribute to their sense of emasculation by modern women and so to the intensification of male supremacism through a sense of Christian endtime urgency.*

Apocalypse has promoted an ascetic, heroic and dominating masculinity . . .

> AJL: *How so 'ascetic' given the immediately prior reference to Koresh's 'harem'?*
> CK: *Koresh may be the sort of exception who proves the rule – as it did in his community, where the other males had to practice ascetic self-restraint, even celibacy, while he blessed their women with his attention! Of course the strong moralism of fundamentalist views on sexual self-control and modesty do not signify any statistically more continent male population, let alone a lower than average rate of divorces.*

that energizes resistance to a perceived (and often real) oppression and that fuels revolutionary flames. It can declare the New Woman, or feminism, or for that matter any opponent (popes, enemy empires, Manhattan) the Whore of Babylon, and it can do so with a purity of rage unavailable to the compromised Christian mainstream.

In Revelation itself, amid a much wider and more interesting array of masculine types (sheep, warrior, male as part of the quartet with eagle, ox and lion, the male virgin, the prophets, the two beasts, the armies, the angels, etc.), women are offered

---

15 See Norman Cohn, *The Pursuit of the Millennium: Revolutionary Millenarians and Mystical Anarchists of the Middle Ages* (New York: Oxford University Press, 1970).
16 Catherine Keller, 'Silly Women of the Last Days', in *eadem, Apocalypse Now and Then*, p. 244.

three representational options: whore, mother, virgin. There is the *whore in power*, who has a human manifestation in Jezebel, the infamous name John lends his apparent female competitor – perhaps a prophetic leader – in the community of Thyatira (Rev. 2.20–23), and who has the dramatic allegorical form of Babylon the Great, the Great Whore – 'for all the nations have drunk of the wine of the wrath of her fornication' (Rev. 18.3). There is the *mother in agony* of Revelation 12, the 'woman clothed in the sun' who gives birth in torment, only to have her son whisked direct from the womb up to the Father for safekeeping, while her cosmic radiance fades fast to desert exile.

> AJL: *Or where she escapes the whole male scenario? Is she still out there? Does the 'son' ever show up again? Does the 'son' ever become a 'man'?*
>
> CK: *I've speculated in* Apocalypse Now and Then *on her return as the feminist movement! Most just say she's 'the church'. As to him: the usual Christian convention saying 'didn't you know he is Jesus?!' has of course no textual attestation. But the text does not weave its dreamlike fragments into a meta-narrative.*

And of course there is the *virgin in the end*, bride of the Lamb, the New Jerusalem herself, as perfect urban anti-type to the wickedness of Rome/Babylon.

> AJL: *Although she, like the whore, is continually penetrated. Are they mirrors? On the other hand, does Rome let everyone in whereas the New Jerusalem is a gated community?*
>
> CK: *Yes, in the New Jerusalem's 'open gate' lies the dis/closure within a dangerously closed symbolism! She's gated, but entered!*

A theopolitical paradox kicks in there, in the binary of the two feminized cities. For the Whore of Babylon symbolizes in its context imperial injustice, with its transnational market of luxury goods for Rome and its elite intermediaries. So liberation and third-world Christians have found in this text a stunning prophetic solidarity with the plight of the oppressed.[17] For instance, liberation theologian Nestor Miguez's exegesis of the Whore of Babylon deploys the rhetorical power of apocalypse to expose the empire of late capitalist global economics.[18]

> AJL: *Is 'late capitalist global economics' completely evil? Is it 'evil' because 'liberation theologians' say so? If it is completely evil, what should be put in its place?*
>
> CK: *The bigger question is whether liberation theology, and perhaps I in accompanying it on this point, apocalyptically demonize the global economy. It*

---

17 In Allan A. Boesak's brilliant commentary, *Comfort and Protest: Reflections on the Apocalypse of John of Patmos* (Philadelphia, PA: Westminster Press, 1987), much of which was written from a South African prison cell, he describes not a vengeful or violent but certainly a radical and militant vision of resistance to the apartheid systems, as client of the current superpower and its Babylonian system of power and commerce.

18 Nestor Miguez, 'Apocalyptic and the Economy: A Reading of Revelation 18 from the Experience of Economic Exclusion', in Fernando F. Segovia and Mary Ann Tolbert (eds), *Reading from This Place*, vol. 2: *Social Location and Biblical Interpretation in Global Perspective* (Minneapolis, MN: Fortress Press, 1995), pp. 250–62.

certainly is tempting! But, for instance, John Cobb's multiple attempts to disclose the destructive effects on community and ecology of unconstrained, unregulated transnational corporations, while distinguishing them from other meanings of capitalism and entrepreneurial local economies, belong to the counter-apocalypse more than the neo-apocalypse. Also, Marion Grau's 'trickster' reading of global capitalism, in which we work with our complicity rather than feigning a liberated innocence, is beautiful: Of Divine Economy.[19]

In Revelation the global trade in luxury items is portrayed as obscene. Hence the detailed diatribe against the merchants and the sea captains, by which Roman trade and rule extended throughout the known world: 'since no one buys their cargo any more, cargo of gold, silver, jewels and pearls, fine linen, purple, silk and scarlet, all kinds of scented wood, all articles of ivory, all articles of costly wood, bronze, iron and marble, cinnamon, spice, incense, myrrh, frankincense, wine, olive oil, choice flour and wheat . . . ' etc., down to slaves (Rev. 18.11–13). Such an economic hermeneutics as that of Miguez seems fitting and effective.[20] 'Babylon', he writes, 'stands for whatever system enthrones the marketplace . . . for whatever turns the human body and soul into merchandise for trade. Within such a system the only need that exists is the need of those who have the ability to pay; consequently the basic needs of all human beings yield to the luxury markets of the great merchants and traders.'[21]

The risk of martyrdom through protest advocated by John then can be read not as a sadomasochistic addiction to the phantasmagoria of violence, but as an inevitable consequence of subversion. 'As in the case of John, the system condemns those who expose the fetishistic nature of the marketplace.'[22]

> AJL: *Although John is not a martyr – and nor is he silenced. Indeed, is he not marketing – and does the canon not continue to market – his own fetishized views?*
>
> CK: *And yet despite the complicities, patriarchies and power drives of John and his ilk, Christianity at least does the hermeneutic of liberation theology a serious reading – even as we may enjoy Marcella Althaus Reid's* Indecent Theology, *with its deconstruction of the sexist and heterosexist pieties of the Latin American liberation fathers.*[23]

The 'apocalyptic hermeneutic' stands in intertextual fidelity to the western

19 Marion Grau, *Of Divine Economy: Refinancing Redemption* (London: T&T Clark, 2004).

20 Miguez argues 'that the mythopoetic language of apocalyptic and revelatory polysemy of Scripture make it possible to read this text from the perspective of the victims of the neoliberal capitalist marketplace and its imposed instrumental logic' ('Apocalyptic and the Economy', p. 260). This is no naive identity politics, no simplistic liberation polemic.

21 Miguez, 'Apocalyptic and the Economy', p. 261.

22 Its constant presentation of the Gross National Product (GNP) orthodoxy/free-market reform as the only way and 'its conviction that another alternative is bound to fail . . . also form part of this logic of death. In the end, such logic also includes self-destruction' (Miguez, 'Apocalyptic and the Economy', p. 262). Miguez straightforwardly names his hermeneutic apocalyptic: 'Apocalyptic literature stands out as the place par excellence for the expression of such a perspective' (p. 253).

23 Marcella Althaus Reid, *Indecent Theology: Theological Perversions in Sex, Gender, and Politics* (London: Routledge, 2001).

revolutionary tradition. As Ernst Bloch has argued in *The Principle of Hope*, this tradition derives its radical futurity, its utopia in hope for the fullness of justice for the poor, from the revived medieval apocalyptic tradition that runs from Joachim of Fiore through the Radical Franciscans to the Radical Reformation.[24] Thus, some feminist scholars, seeking (as feminism surely needs to do) to strengthen the bonds of solidarity with liberation movements based on economic, class and race analysis, defend it fiercely.

> AJL: *Concerning this 'economic/class/race' alliance: does 'religion' (an admittedly difficult category, occasionally artificial, and often overlapping with 'ethnicity') drop out? Does 'feminism' have a problem with 'religion'? Here I wonder about feminist-liberationist readings of Revelation that conclude that the violence is the rhetoric of 'Jewish apocalyptic' – with the implication that if the 'Jewish' could be removed, the text would be less violent, or 'more Christian'?*
>
> CK: *It remains a perennial Celsian temptation for feminists to save the good non-violent gospel from Jewish wrath and violence. But ironically the Apocalypses among the Jewish Pseudepigrapha, whether the* Books of Enoch *or the* Secrets of Enoch, *the* Sibyllines *or* 2 Baruch, *entertain far less violent visions than this Christian Apocalypse!*

The feminist advocates of apocalypticism mirror its righteousness assertively, as part of what I have called the liberation *neo-apocalypse*. Elisabeth Schüssler Fiorenza especially has called feminists to task for their dismissals of John's Apocalypse; she designates it the sole book of the New Testament wholly devoted to justice.[25]

> AJL: *Does this move – or the counter that argues for the dismissal of John on 'feminist' principles – seek to divide 'good feminists' from 'bad feminists'? How is this division different than John's castigation of 'Jezebel' (i.e., someone still within the 'Christian' system), for feminists in the academy who do not find Revelation helpful may well still be 'feminists' or 'feminist Christians'?*
>
> CK: *Excellent, if rhetorical, questions. I hope the counter-apocalypse proposed below answers them.*

Of course the simplistic oppositionalism of the apocalyptic rhetoric threatens to take possession of every such liberation neo-apocalypse, thus re-inscribing the absolutism that funds sexism (and as Daly absolutely insists, vice versa[26]).

Indeed, from the liberation point of view, which focuses on the power of 'comfort and protest' this text affords the oppressed, it is surprising that the Book of Revelation made it into the canon.

> AJL: *Would you talk about how the text provides 'the oppressed' 'comfort and power'? Is there a possible disjunction between what academic readers claim (often*

---

24 Ernst Bloch, *The Principle of Hope* (Studies in Contemporary German Social Thought; Cambridge, MA: The MIT Press, 1995).

25 Elisabeth Schüssler Fiorenza, *The Book of Revelation: Justice and Judgment* (2nd edn, Minneapolis, MN: Fortress Press, 1998).

26 Daly, *Beyond God the Father*, p. 133.

after reading in postcolonial theory, or feminism, other studies that locate systemic oppressions) and what those outside the academy find in the text.

CK: *I've tried to gather some of the sources beyond those cited here for the reality of that exegetical comfort and empowerment among Christian communities in Latin America and Africa in* Apocalypse Now and Then *and* God and Power. *Yet the retro-apocalyptic, fundamentalist and anti-liberationist uses of apocalypticism have flourished much more among communities of the poor here and abroad, under the often U.S.-guided tutelage of the religious right. At any rate the distance you name will remain irreducible; and the growing forms of tricontinental Christianity may be more characterized in this millennium – and just as troublingly so – by the 'gospel of prosperity'.*

Augustine of Hippo, ensconced as a bishop within the new Christian empire of the fourth century, accepted Revelation as canonical but warned in elitist tones against those chiliasts who read it literally. Yet he seemed less concerned with heading off a proto-fundamentalism than defusing its disorderly, indeed, revolutionary implications for history. His insistence that the millennium had already come with the triumph of the church in the newly Christianized Roman empire meant for him that there could be nothing qualitatively better within history. This triumphalism (without Augustine's own critical reserve) would be solidified as the basis for all orthodox Christian eschatology and the basis for the constitutive *anti-apocalypse* of the western mainstream.[27]

But the imperial center has turned systematically toward its apocalyptic margin nonetheless, seducing the combustible mythos toward anti-revolutionary ends. It has emulated Augustine's emphasis upon the final judgment and a hell for the disobedient (he argues in exquisite detail for the miraculous new creation of bodies capable of burning eternally in torment). Thus mainstream Christianity, for all its anti-apocalyptic defenses, strengthened itself with the vision, so foreign to most of the Hebrew and Christian Scriptures, of a holy messianic masculinity ennobling itself before the spectacle of the stripped whore and all her lovers burning in naked agony.

AJL: *Might this be a good thing, in that it restricts 'vengeance' or 'justice' to the deity and so takes humanity out of the role of master-punisher or arbitrary judge? I ask this as someone who spends most Monday evenings at Riverbend Maximum Security Institute, where Tennessee's Death Row is located, and where in the 'criminal (in)justice system' vengeance and arbitrary judgments sometimes play leading roles.*

CK: *It doesn't seem to have worked this way in Christian history! It seems like if we equate divine judgment with vengeance we go on –* imitatio dei – *proleptically acting it out. The non-violent or pacifist Christians in history have also downplayed final vengeance. Groups like the Quakers and Shakers disarm apocalypse and develop*

---

27 I developed this interpretation of Augustine's 'anti-apocalypse' in *Apocalypse Now and Then* as a way of accounting for the supernaturalist eschatology that saved the Church Triumphant from responsibility to challenge Christian empires; it has attracted some interest among historians of early Christianity such as Virginia Burrus.

> a non-violent millennialism. The Revelation-and-vengeance-loving Christians form
> the core of the Religious Right, who clamor for more executions. And I'd think we
> would want to leave final judgment to God, but precisely not justice. Working for
> justice now – including for the growing percentage of the incarcerated in this country
> [the U.S.A.] – might mean shifting 'vengeance is mine' out of its popular associations
> with the eternal pit of torture! To the 'new creation' in which only that which lives
> from justice and love lives . . .

In other words, the conservative anti-apocalypse of classical Christianity has
supported an apocalyptic underside, a hell-belly. It has reflected and absorbed the
apocalypse in ways Euro-American feminist scholars and other de-apocalypticizing
critics may find themselves mirroring: damning the damners, demonizing the
demonizers, excluding the excluders.[28]

Hegemonic secular modernity has repeatedly renewed itself by reabsorbing
apocalypse, as well, and indeed from its own originative 'new world'. Take for
example the surprising testimony of Christopher Columbus as to his own apocalyptic self-identity: 'Of the New Heaven and Earth which our Lord made, as St. John
writes in the Apocalypse, after He had spoken it by the mouth of Isaiah. He made
me the messenger thereof and showed me where to go.'[29] I have elsewhere excavated
the gendered morphology with which he envisioned this paradise as *breast*.[30] An old
tradition of the lost Eden, merging terrestrial paradise with apocalyptic hope, was
sucked at this critical moment in history into a new and aggressive literalism. The
fruits of his inspiration literally funded and founded the *otra mondo* – the 'other
world', later dubbed 'new world'. 'Revelation' from above became 'discovery' from
afar.

The apocalyptic realization of crusader warrior masculinity is now consolidated
under the banners of early modernity: cross, commerce and conquest. The dark
Other, defeated or else damned, would henceforth serve as the apocalyptic teat of a
series of western empires, manfully sucking the planet dry.

> AJL: *Does it surprise you that 'breast' imagery is absent in Revelation (contrast
> the* Odes of Solomon)? *The woman in Revelation 12 is a mother, but she does not
> nurse, and who nurses her son remains unexplored. Paradise appears to be a place of
> water, but not wine and not milk.*
>
> CK: *Interesting contrast – it puts me in mind of El Shaddai – the breasted one!
> And Genesis 49.25, 'Blessing of the breasts and of the womb'. As followers of Jesus
> became more alienated from their Judaism and more drawn into ideals of celibacy,
> they began to repress or displace the mammary imagery! So the aggressive reclam-
> ation of the 'breast of paradise' through conquest may be the return of the repressed.*

Characteristic of liberation theologians, Miguez, Boesak, González and even
Elisabeth Schüssler Fiorenza do not worry about the violence of the vision itself,

---

28 Keller, *Apocalypse Now and Then*, p. 159.
29 Letter to Torres, *Journals.* Cited in Keller, *Apocalypse Now and Then*, p. 159.
30 Catherine Keller, 'The Breast, the Apocalypse, and the Colonial Journey', in Charles B. Strozier
and Michael Flynn (eds), *The Year 2000* (New York: New York University Press, 1997), pp. 42–58.

apparently justified – at least as symbol – by the prior violence of empire. Thus they do not criticize the radical misogyny of apocalypse and its heirs. They do not question the spiritual machismo energizing itself from the cunning icon of the Great Whore's titillating demise.

> AJL: *Or, might one see the text as itself making detumescent that 'machismo' with the dominant image of the 'slain lamb'?*
> CK: *Ah, but he roars 'like a lion'!*

Certainly feminist perspectives can smite traditional left politics with an especially distracting case of cross-eyes. Out of a laudable if doctrinaire interest in keeping 'the eye on the prize', that is, focusing Christian energy on the single goal of struggle for social justice, it avoids interpretive ambiguity and ambivalence. It does not, for instance, consider the problem of 'colonial mimicry',[31] the re-inscription of the structures of power in the very act of resistance. It does not problematize the mutual mirroring of 'whore' and YHWH, both on their thrones. Feminist readings – prone to our own monofocal gaze, of course – constitute only one means of exposing the oppressive patriarchal models operative within the revolutionary vision.

So then on the other side we have those feminists and deconstructivists chilled by the bloody misogynist martyr's cult of apocalyptic lords and warriors. The title of Lee Quinby's feminist analysis of American culture as ridden with apocalyptic masculinity, *Anti-Apocalypse*, well summarizes this position, further elaborated in *Millennial Seductions*. Tina Pippin offers her own conclusions about John's Apocalypse: 'What remains is the misogyny and exclusion by a powerful, wrathful deity. In the Apocalypse, the Kingdom of God is the kingdom of perversity.'[32]

Unknowingly, such gendered deconstructions follow the lead of the feminist whom feminist poststructuralists love to dismiss as 'essentialist' – Mary Daly, who satirically decried the apocalyptic return of the Lord: 'This "Word" is doublespeak . . . preparing the way for a phallo-technic Second Coming. It is the announcement of the ultimate Armageddon, where armies of cloned Jesus Freaks (christian and/or nonchristian) will range themselves against Hags/Crones, attempting the Final Solution to the "problem" of Female Force.'[33] Daly, the most radical feminist apocalypse of anti-apocalypse, messianically declares her own final Armageddon: 'The ultimate contest was wrongly described in the Book of Revelation. . . . The author in his vision failed to note the Holy War waged by Wholly Haggard Whores casting off the bonds of whoredom.'[34]

While I may have been more swayed than these feminists by the largely non-white voices of the liberation tradition who read Revelation sympathetically, I too cast my lot with John's Jezebel. A rival Christian prophet, she provokes in John a misogynist

---

31 Homi K. Bhabha's term; see Chapter 3 in Keller, *God and Power*, p. 39.

32 Tina Pippin, *Apocalyptic Bodies: The Biblical End of the World in Text and Image* (London/New York: Routledge, 1999), p. 125; see also Tina Pippin, *Death and Desire*.

33 Daly, *Gyn/Ecology*, p. 88.

34 Daly, *Gyn/Ecology*, p. 105.

tantrum: 'Beware, I am throwing her on a bed, and those who commit adultery with her I am throwing into great distress, unless they repent. . . . I will strike her children dead' (2.22–23). The poetics of power, of conquest, of swords and iron rods pitted against female bodies, none too subtly symbolized as 'earthen pots' (2.27), penetrates the significatory field of the Apocalypse. A feminist ethic surely cannot in the long run re-veil the misogyny of its revelation.[35]

Whether essentialist or anti-essentialist, however, the repudiations of apocalypse tend to ignore the powerful religious, countercultural, and then secular millennialism stimulating progressive social movements, in particular the nineteenth-century women's movement and each stage of its further development.[36] To the extent that such postmodern feminisms do not take seriously the liberation hermeneutic, which can be dismissed as an essentialist knock-off of the Marxist metanarrative, to that extent they do not account for the economic, ethnic and coalitional implications of their own indignant anti-apocalypse.

Babylonian Bite

Attention to the varying standpoints *within* the story of apocalypse – standpoints that we as readers might experimentally occupy – might not damn us to the endless replay of apocalypse. It might rather allow us to question the power that apocalypse exercises, and the power that it condemns. Indeed such attention allows us to study and so to interrupt the 'apocalypse habit'. The point would not be to purify our discourse of all apocalyptic elements. For every purge reinscribes apocalypse – even the attempt to purge apocalypticism. The point would be instead (in something like Vipassana Buddhist style) to watch them arise, to pay attention to the habit. In any crisis of cultural or personal conflict, we may notice an operative code of victimized righteousness versus absolute evil begin to constellate.

> AJL: *Does this division allow 'us' to see ourselves as ethically pure? Do 'we' need an 'absolute evil' (ugly, bloated . . .) so that we can see ourselves as absolutely good?*
> CK: *'We' may seek scapegoats to allay the sense of meaninglessness and loss, and cling to the delusion of our innocence just when our guiding values come under threat.*

And behind the good/evil code lurks the fascinated expectation of total destruction on the one hand, by which we secretly collude with the evil; and the yearning for a utopia that is no possible place, by which we attempt to imagine the good nonetheless: a vicious cycle of habits, mostly unconscious. Might we practice a kind of *eschatological attentiveness* ('wake, for it comes like a thief in the night'), attention *to and through* apocalypse? Would this allow us to make the necessary discernments of right and wrong – while avoiding final judgments and disrupting the grim gaze of a warrior-judge upon ourselves or any others?

---

35 Despite even a great feminist New Testament scholar's (Elisabeth Schüssler Fiorenza) love of this text as the primary New Testament text of justice.

36 See Keller, *Apocalypse Now and Then*, which documents this theme extensively in the chapter on gender, 'Silly Women of the Last Days'.

AJL: *Or do we leave the 'final judgment' up to a distinct power and so disarm ourselves?*

CK: *As long as we can also abstain from final judgments about what an ultimate divine judgment might look like!*

Might the irony of a *counter-apocalypse* de-center the pattern in its religious and secular, sexist and feminist forms?

Parody may lend a lightening touch. Such humor has surfaced, for instance, in the satiric feminism of Susan Smith Nash's *Channel-Surfing the Apocalypse*, inspired by the endtime experience close to her home, in Oklahoma City. The terror had been inspired by a telling blend of white supremacist millennialism, the gun cult, a pilgrimage to Waco, and the frustration of Timothy McVeigh – a veteran of the Gulf War – that Bush Sr. had not gone after Saddam Hussein. (Too bad McVeigh couldn't hold on until the like-minded Jr. was elected.) Baghdad/Babylon has beckoned across the millennia. 'The bombing. A warning sign that something is wrong'.

AJL: *I wonder how a family member or loved one of someone killed by McVeigh might react to such 'parody'? When do we have 'parody' and when 'colonial mimicry'? Is parody perhaps the home of the distanced academic or artist whose audience is comprised of other academics and artists, and not of those who 'suffer' or 'are oppressed' (save for the oppression of not getting grants)? How do we know if/ when parody is 'political'? Does the funding source matter? The reception? The intent?*

CK: *All the folds of signification matter. But which trumps the others? Parody is not consolation. The satiric commentary operates at a remove from the narrative it mocks – or rather creates that remove. The Whore is already a parody of Roman power. As Bakhtin noted, it is difficult to tell where reverence ends and ridicule begins.*[37]

'Which myth do you prefer in the quest to explain it? Apocalyptic? Utopian? Evolutionary? Historical? Chaos theory?'[38] In a vignette called 'Signs That the End is Near (If Anyone Still Cares . . .)' she fantasizes shopping in a mall, where she sees a mannequin dressed in a seductive gypsy costume:

> You do not realize that it is a statue of 'The Great Harlot' who sits on a seven-headed scarlet-colored beast, and you do not see what is tattooed on her forehead: MYSTERY, BABYLON THE GREAT, THE MOTHER OF HARLOTS AND ABOMINATIONS OF THE EARTH. You like the ensemble, so you try it on. It's a purple and scarlet dress, bedecked with gold and precious stones. . . . As you try on the dress you feel a strange transformation.[39]

A man on the escalator comes on to her offensively. She grows fangs. I'll leave to the reader's imagination what happens to the offender. In her, uh, biting parody of lurid

---

37 Mikhail Bakhtin, *The Dialogic Imagination* (Austin: University of Texas Press, 1981), p. 77.
38 Susan Smith Nash, *Channel Surfing the Apocalypse: A Day in the Life of the Fin-de-Millennium Mind* (Penngrove, CA: Avec, 1996), p. 29.
39 Nash, *Channel Surfing the Apocalypse*, p. 37.

fundamentalist depictions of the Great Whore, Nash temporarily defangs the grim misogyny of the book.

> AJL: *How does she defang rather than reinforce? Is the preference that the 'whore' 'wins'? Is a vote for 'any woman' – regardless of platform – a vote for 'defanging misogyny'? And what might a Sinti or Roma reaction to the Whore's accessorizing and thus allure be?*
>
> CK: *Parody intensifies what it resists. And it may be that women – if we comprise a gender, or a genre – must try on that undecidable zone between 'whore' and 'holy', if only to resist the binary itself. Nash's manoeuvre may fail; but it initiates a risky and redemptive laughter.*

She inhabits a local geography in which the text of Revelation is never silent. Perhaps all of us in the United States do.

With less bite and more chew, I too have 'tried on' the feminine apocalyptic personae. I found myself writing little stories about the woman trapped within the man-made Great Whore. I found in her a fleshy powerflirt, Babs, who by the end of the second Christian millennium had entered into a conspiracy (a 'breathing together') with Jeri (alias New Jerusalem) and Sophia, the long-suffering sun-woman of Revelation 12, who had gained considerable earth-centered wisdom during her desert retreat.[40]

> AJL: *Did this 'trying on' get you anywhere? What were the receptions of the parables? Is 'earth-centred wisdom' a re-inscription of the old 'earth goddess good/ sky god bad' model?*
>
> CK: *My little parables, inserted between chapters of* Apocalypse Now and Then, *were intended to reopen possibilities rather than reinscribe dichotomies. Their success is as uncertain as Nash's. Did they get me anywhere? Just through that difficult book, with enough humor and humility to face the seriousness of a still self-fulfilling prophecy of doom, still threatening the human and all our earth-humus.*

The Incalculable Present

Luce Irigaray wrote, 'These prophets feel that, if something divine can still come to us, it will do so when we abandon all calculation. . . . These predecessors have no future – they come from it. Within them, it is already present. But who hears it? Obscurely their song waters the world. Of today, of yesterday, of tomorrow.'[41] Can something divine still come to us?

> AJL: *Does it come from the outside?*
>
> CK: *Not for her, for whom, fortunately the envelope between inside and out is sensitive, permeable. But then the divine is not simply from 'within' either.*

---

40 I refer the interested reader to the parables between the chapters of *Apocalypse Now and Then*.
41 Luce Irigaray, *Sexes and Genealogies* (trans. Gillian C. Gill; New York: Columbia University Press, 1993), p. 53.

Without that 'coming', our theopolitics devolves into mere ideology.

AJL: *Is that a bad thing? Does having a 'theo' make ideology kosher?*

CK: *That might make it truly poisonous! My point is just that without openness to that which still may come – our theism or our atheism reduces the future to predictability.*

Shall we follow Irigaray's admonition to 'abandon all calculation'? Can we cut free of every endtime calculus, every deadline, every deadening prediction of the end of the world, every profitable calculation of outcomes? Chaos theory does indeed suggest a non-linear temporality, not a circularity without newness, but the new that cannot be predicted.

AJL: *Is the new necessarily 'good' or is it just 'new'?*

CK: *The new can be the monster, the beasts, Armageddon . . . nonetheless the genius of the Hebrew trajectory lies very close to the articulation of the 'new' as valuable: 'Behold I do a new thing'; 'Sing a new song to the lord'. Are these verses improved by substituting 'good' for 'new'?*

Yet this invitation to abandon calculation, to leap beyond the safety nets of certainty, does not leap beyond the apocalypse. Like Derrida's 'messianicity without a messiah', irrupting from outside of Christian intention, it trembles in Irigaray with apocalyptic codes.[42] Does this song of the incalculable echo the purity of the masculinist messianism?

AJL: *Is 'purity' a problem (as it is for much of 'historical Jesus' research, wherein 'purity codes' are seen as promoting oppression, or wherein Jesus is seen as replacing the system of purity with a system of compassion)? Why is the term you use for 'masculinist messianism' 'purity'?*

CK: *'Purity' here is a synonym for a transcendent or untouched absoluteness; the Jewish purity codes signify embodied practices for integrating material life into divine relation – precisely not a dualistic path, though hardly 'pure' of patriarchy. The divinity I call upon has never been untouched, homogenous, merely transcendent.*

Is this prophetic *novum* another closeted feminist absolute? If so, we would no longer want it, need it, or believe it.

Yet it is Irigaray from whom feminist theory has learned the strategy of a mimetic parody, by way of assertion of gender difference in the face of the sexist Same.

AJL: *Does 'same/different' put us back into bifurcation? Does it necessarily essentialize both categories?*

CK: *It might. Yet I have never fought dualism with a monistic or pluralistic refusal of binaries and bifurcations, which form part of how creatures are structured and grow – it is only the tendency of binaries to harden (essentialize) into bounded*

42 Jacques Derrida, *Specters of Marx: The State of the Debt, The Work of Mourning & the New International* (London: Routledge, 2006), *passim.*

opposites that is apocalypse-prone. The 'same' is here another term for homogeniza-tion, by which difference becomes absolute and is defeated. But the problematic of post-structuralist difference/différance will take us too far afield, here.

So perhaps we may read Irigaray's eschatological oracles as parodic mimicry of the Christian apocalypse that helps us to unhinge it from its bitter misogyny and its terminal justice, while refreshing again the wilder, wider hope of the world with the dream of living waters, water free and pure for all – melodic, laughing waters. Quite consonant with Jürgen Moltmann's theology of hope, she announces a possibility that does not follow the line that can be extrapolated from the present but rather comes from the future, comes even now.

> AJL: *Is the search for something 'transcendent' something 'outside us'? Would you call what she does 'theo-politics'? And is there any biblical grounding for it, or does the Bible (the past) get erased in this 'future' or 'new' focus?*
>
> CK: *Her work has, one might say, theopolitical resonances. She is not a theo-logian or scholar of religion. But to many who are, her echoes of biblical themes seem revelatory, when refracted through such indirection.*

Does this eschatology not echo the New Testament promise of *ho erchomenos*, 'The One Who Comes'?

> AJL: *Does he not 'come' in the same way as your masculinist folks did above? Why is 'coming' desirable? Plus, this 'ho' in ho erchomenos is not a neuter 'the one' but 'he' (and surely not female, despite the English homophone).*
>
> CK: *Still, despite all the spurting masculinity of the metaphors of 'coming', would we want to leave coming to the guys and their gods? And would we want to erase the messianic lure of the possible? The criterion is this: if coming is opposed to becoming, it comes in the irruptive violence of the apocalypse. If it is an invitation to our endless becoming, our genesis, it keeps the world open and breathing.*

Indeed, as though instinctively, with no commentary and no reference to the history of apocalypticism, even biblical, she grasps the thousand-year-old Joachite vision of the third aeon, giving it a feminist face: she announces the opening of 'the third era' of 'the couple', 'the Spirit and the Bride'. This is a reference to Rev. 21.17: 'The Spirit and the Bride say, "Come"'.

Irigaray may have been thinking in terms of the dyad of her 'ethic of sexual difference'.[43] The Spirit is no groom, however. The Spirit blows where it will – into any or no sex, with any and all partners. The Bride of the Spirit suggests an open female subjectivity, a disclosing subjectivity. She comes from the future and

---

43 See Schor and Weed (eds), *The Essential Difference*. Questions concerning the heterosexism or essentialism of Irigaray's couple imagery are addressed constructively in Carolyn Burke, Naomi Schor and Margaret Whitford (eds), *Engaging with Irigaray: Feminist Philosophy and Modern Euro-pean Thought* (Gender and Culture; New York: Columbia University Press, 1994).

transforms the shame of the past into tensive paradoxes. She has always been coming. The open signifying field of her gender, her sex, does not make her any less female. The problems of history, the terrors of empire – her advent will not solve them. But they will not be solved without her.

> AJL: *Why then is she needed, or is the point that she's coming regardless? Why is she needed, if she reinscribes gender codes? Is the 'spirit' needed as well? And, if we have bride and spirit, do we do away with, e.g., Jesus, or the church?*
>
> CK: *Won't any use of the word 'woman' (for instance) reinscribe even as it transcribes? Do we expect to erase any of these gender codes? Or rather to transcode them, to shift and open and recode them, never pretending to the violence of an absolute novelty? The abusive coming of some new, even feminist, even postfeminist, supersessionism?*

As for the apocalyptic *Viens*, it will keep coming. Even Luce Irigaray, no later than Derrida, was waiting for what is to 'come'. There in the early 1980s she also, and just as startlingly, just as irreducibly, had recourse to the apocalypse: 'Waiting for parousia would require keeping all one's senses alert. Not destroyed, not covered, not "dirtied", our senses would be open.'[44] Without her we might not find the *body* of deconstruction. Why does it take a woman to recall us to our senses? This lost body is not female only, but it is nobody without the female. The opening of the senses requires more than the opening of a text – even as her text opens into the senses. But here virtually alone among post-structuralist Parisians, she invokes pneumatology, the study of spirit and spiritual things: 'Keeping the senses alert means being attentive in flesh and spirit.' That is an intensively theological proposition, no mere opening, but the opening by and in which I unveil myself as woman, by which my senses and even perhaps again, my eyes open. To wit: 'If God and the other are to be unveiled', she continues, full throttle apocalyptic, 'I too must unveil myself (I should not expect God to do this for me. Not this time . . .).'[45]

> AJL: *Why is 'unveiling' good or desirable? Do these apocalyptic visions eliminate mystery?*
>
> CK: *Unveiling might in its apocalyptic register mean a stripping bare, down to naked truth, total transparency; or – and this is how I hear her – it might mean the unveiling of that which is infinitely mysterious as precisely infinitely exceeding our vision. Or as Elliot Wolfson puts it kabbalistically: 'If, however, language is the veil through which the veil must be unveiled, then the unveiling itself is a form of veiling that will be veiled in the unveiling'.*[46]

Irigaray's startling allusion to Joachim of Fiore and this third epoch, 'the third era

---

44 Luce Irigaray, *An Ethics of Sexual Difference* (trans. Carolyn Burke and Gillian C. Gill; Ithaca, NY: Cornell University Press, 1991 [1984]), p. 148.

45 Irigaray, *An Ethics of Sexual Difference*, p. 148.

46 Elliot Wolfson, *Language, Eros, Being: Kabbalistic Hermeneutics and Poetic Imagination* (Bronx, NY: Fordham University Press, 2005).

of the West might, at last, be the era of the couple: of the spirit and the bride',[47] is evidence of her turning like Derrida to the end of the book of the end of the Book (Rev. 20.17). The great feminist prophet of the 'lips', the body parable of a subjectivity that is 'neither one nor two', but multiple,

> AJL: *Again, why is multiplicity to be valued? Is the desire for 'multiplicity without rank'? Is multiplicity ontologically or epistemological better than singularity, or 'one-ness'? Is the point perhaps to eschew 'monotheism'?*
>
> CK: *Irigaray, like all post-structuralists, has great interest in pluralism and its multiplicities. My own theological view is close to Laurel Schneider's* Beyond Monotheism: A Theology of Multiplicity,[48] *premised on the fact that 'monotheism' is a modern Christian concept, younger than the seventeenth-century term 'polytheism'. Her critique of 'the logic of the One' applies more to Greek ontotheology than to the complex and elusive emergence of the one God by way of the Hebrew trajectory. I have elsewhere suggested terms like 'the Manyone' to solicit the way in which a name like Elohim refuses a simple One vs Many ontology. But the short answer is yes, the multiplicity – the very diversity of life that is in Genesis 1 declared good and very good – is greatly to be valued. I would with Deleuze distinguish 'multiplicity' from 'plurality', as the latter lacks the internal 'pli', or fold. But that is a future book.*

has unexpectedly unveiled an apoca/liptic orifice for French feminism. Not short-changing the Joachite heritage, she states apodictically, 'The spirit and the bride invite beyond genealogical destiny to the era of the wedding and the festival of the world.

> AJL: *Should we still be talking about 'weddings'? How about 'holy unions'?*
>
> CK: *Indeed. Yet perhaps we want again to multiply rather than erase metaphors.*

To the time of a theology of the breath in its horizontal and vertical becoming, with no murders.'[49]

This is no coy literary device. Irigaray has joined the choir of feminist theologians.[50] She seeks not an apophatic nothingness, but a sensuous incarnation of God as female. The aim would be unlimited incarnation, not the single incarnation of a son, not even the dyadic one of a couple, but of all that is 'drawn into the mystery of a word that seeks its incarnation'.[51]

---

47 Irigaray, *An Ethics of Sexual Difference*, p. 146.

48 Laurel Schneider, *Beyond Monotheism: A Theology of Multiplicity* (London: Routledge, 2007).

49 Irigaray, *An Ethics of Sexual Difference*, p. 149.

50 Most of her later works confirm this constructive theological interest, especially, and most powerfully, the concluding Christological construction of *The Marine Lover of Friedrich Nietzsche* (trans. Gillian C. Gill; New York: Columbia University Press, 1991); also, *Sexes and Genealogies* and most readably *I Love to You: Sketch for a Felicity within History* (trans. Alison Martin; New York: Routledge, 1996).

51 Luce Irigaray, *The Forgetting of Air in Martin Heidegger* (trans. Mary Beth Mader; Austin: University of Texas Press, 1999), p. 178.

AJL: *This sounds like a perpetual pregnancy/parturition, which is beastly.*

CK: *Unlimited incarnation suggests for me that God did not become embodied just one time, the One and Only, the Once for all revelation, but is – as infinite – involved in all flesh (again, no pure Outside, which is a bad infinite after all, a bounded infinite). Perpetual parturition would be painful indeed! But enfleshment is not reducible to birth, nor the incarnation to the baby Jesus. Or the man. I mean by pancarnation a resistance to the triumphalist exceptionalism of the one incarnation. But birth is not erased but indeed metaphorically redistributed, as in Spinoza's natura naturans, echoed in 'natality', to use the trope that Hannah Arendt works out of Augustine's sense of creation – of fresh and flesh beginnings.[52] I wouldn't think either the one incarnation or its infinite multiplication reduces to the moment of pregnancy – though it is advent as I write and I do not want to erase the tired, old womb of Mary, only release her to her human past!*

I pray that her pneumatology of the couple, because it chooses the gender-ambiguous Spirit rather than the couple actually celebrated in John's pericope, the Lamb and the New Jerusalem, his Bride, may not serve the displaced cause of heterosexist renewal. Certainly it sidesteps the slaughterhouse atonement. Still, here too we need to keep our eyes open. Apocalyptic imagination always runs the risk of the binaries of the absolute purity of a purged future, from which we will always need an opening – a gap, an apophasis. Before it comes to murder. Before it comes.

Whatever comes, matters. It materializes. It makes a *difference.*

*   *   *

In a two-thousand-year-old wisdom papyrus, some anonymous prophet gathered together the shards and voices of women into a great 'I AM'. This wisdom figure – resembling the Chochmah of Proverbs and Solomon, but female beyond what the canon could tolerate – sings right to us. From her past the future still comes, the subject of an incalculable present tense. It relativizes absolute beginnings and endings; it disrupts the contradictories that structure feminine stereotypes. This self-revealing 'I' – whose veiled mystery is only deepened with each unveiling, multiplying its singularity – is a mimicry and a metamorphosis of every once-for-all, one-and-only word, every final apocalypse:

> I am the first and the last.
> I am the honored one and the scorned one.
> I am the whore and the holy one. I am the wife and the virgin.
> I am the mother and the daughter.
> I am the voice, whose sound is manifold
> and the word whose appearance is multiple.[53]

---

52 Hannah Arendt, *Love and Saint Augustine* (eds Joanna Vecchiarelli Scott and Judith Chelius Stark; Chicago, IL: University of Chicago Press, 1996).

53 A wisdom text usually considered Gnostic Christian, from the first three centuries CE, 'Thunder: Perfect Mind', 6.2, in James Robinson (ed.), *The Nag Hammadi Library* (San Francisco: Harper & Row, 1977), p. 271.

Abaecherli, A.L., 'Imperial Symbols on Certain Flavian Coins', *Classical Philology* 30 (1935), pp. 131–40.

Abley, M., *Spoken Here: Travels among Threatened Languages* (London: Heinemann, 2003).

Ackroyd, P.R., 'Goddesses, Women, and Jezebel', in Averil Cameron and Amélie Kuhrt (eds), *Images of Women in Antiquity* (Detroit, MI: Wayne State University Press, 1983), pp. 245–59.

Adorno, T.W., 'On the Use of Foreign Words', in R. Tiedemann (ed.), *Notes to Literature* (trans. S.W. Nicholson; 2 vols; New York: Columbia University Press, 1991), vol. 2, pp. 286–91.

Aichele, G. et al., *The Postmodern Bible* (The Bible and Culture Collective; New Haven, CT: Yale University Press, 1995).

Alföldi, A., 'Hasta-Summa Imperii: The Spear as Embodiment of Sovereignty in Rome', *AJA* 63 (1959), pp. 1–27.

Almås, E. and Espen Esther Pirelli Benestad, *Kjønn i bevegelse* (Oslo: Universitets-forlaget, 2001).

Angelopoulos, T., 'Το 'μετέωρο βήμα του πελαργού' ('The Suspended Step of the Stork'; Athens, Greece: Greek Film Center, 1991).

Appler, D.A., 'From Queen to Cuisine: Food Imagery in the Jezebel Narrative', *Semeia* 86 (1999), pp. 55–73.

Archer, L., 'The "Evil Women" in Apocryphal and Pseudepigraphical Writings', in *Proceedings of the Ninth World Congress of Jewish Studies. Division A: The Period of the Bible* (Jerusalem: World Union of Jewish Studies, 1986), pp. 239–46.

Arendt, H., *Love and Saint Augustine* (eds Joanna Vecchiarelli Scott and Judith Chelius Stark; Chicago, IL: University of Chicago Press, 1996).

Aspegren, K., *The Male Woman. A Feminine Ideal in the Early Church* (ed. René Kieffer; *Uppsala Women's Studies, Women in Religion*, 4; Acta Universitatis Upsaliensis [University Publications from Uppsala]: Stockholm and Uppsala: Almqvist & Wiksell, 1990).

Aune, D.E., 'The Apocalypse of John and the Problem of Genre', *Semeia 36* (1986), pp. 65–96.

— 'The Influence of Roman Imperial Court Ceremonial on the Apocalypse of John', *Papers of the Chicago Society of Biblical Research* 28 (1983), pp. 5–29.

— 'Intertextuality and the Genre of the Apocalypse', *SBLSP* 30 (1991), pp. 142–60.

— *Revelation 1–5* (WBC; 52A; Nashville, TN: Thomas Nelson Publishers, 1998).

— *Revelation 6–16* (WBC, 52B; Nashville, TN: Thomas Nelson Publishers, 1998).

— *Revelation 17–22* (WBC, 52C; Nashville, TN: Thomas Nelson Publishers, 1998).

— 'The Social Matrix of the Apocalypse of John', *Papers of the Chicago Society of Biblical Research* 26 (1981), pp. 16–32.

Badiner, A.H., *Dharma Gaia: A Harvest of Essays in Buddhism and Ecology* (Berkeley, CA: Parallax, 1990).

Bakhtin, M., *The Dialogic Imagination* (Austin: University of Texas Press, 1981).

Bal, M., 'Metaphors He Lives By', *Semeia* 61 (1993), pp. 185–207.

Barclay, J.M.G., *Jews in the Mediterranean Diaspora: From Alexander to Trajan* (Edinburgh: T&T Clark, 1996).

Barr, D.L., 'Beyond Genre: The Expectations of Apocalypse,' in *idem* (ed.), *The Reality of Apocalypse: Rhetoric and Politics in the Book of Revelation* (SBLSym, 39; Atlanta, GA: Society of Biblical Literature, 2006), pp. 71–90.

— 'Blessed Are Those Who Hear: John's Apocalypse as Present Experience', in Linda Bennett Elder, David L. Barr and Elizabeth Struthers Malbon (eds), *Biblical and Humane: A Festschrift for John Priest* (Atlanta, GA: Scholars Press, 1996), pp. 87–103.

— 'Elephants and Holograms: From Metaphor to Methodology in the Study of John's Apocalypse', *SBLSP* 25 (1986), pp. 400–411.

— 'Jezebel's Skinny Legs: (De)Constructing the Four Queens of the Apocalypse', http://www.wright.edu/~dbarr/jezebel.htm (accessed 21 January 2009).

— *Tales of the End: A Narrative Commentary on the Book of Revelation* (Santa Rosa, CA: Polebridge Press, 1998).

— 'Towards an Ethical Reading of the Apocalypse: Reflections on John's Use of Power, Violence, and Misogyny', *SBLSP* 36 (1997), pp. 358–73.

Barton, T., *Ancient Astrology* (London/New York: Routledge, 1994).

Bauckham, R., *The Climax of Prophecy: Studies in the Book of Revelation* (Edinburgh: T&T Clark, 1993).

— 'The Economic Critique of Rome in Revelation 18', in L. Alexander (ed.), *Images of Empire* (Sheffield: Sheffield Academic Press, 1991), pp. 47–90.

— *The Theology of the Book of Revelation* (NTT; Cambridge, UK and New York: Cambridge University Press, 1993).

Bauer, W., W.F. Arndt, F.W. Gingrich and F.W. Danker, *Greek–English Lexicon of the New Testament and Other Early Christian Literature* (3rd edn, Chicago, IL: University of Chicago Press, 2000).

Baumann, G., 'Connected by Marriage, Adultery, and Violence: The Prophetic Marriage Metaphor in the Book of the Twelve and the Major Prophets', *SBLSP* 38 (1999), pp. 552–69.

Beach, E.F., *The Jezebel Letters: Religion and Politics in Ninth-Century Israel* (Minneapolis, MN: Augsburg Fortress Press, 2005).

Beagley, A.J., *The 'Sitz Im Leben' of the Apocalypse with Particular Reference to the Role of the Church's Enemies* (BZNW, 50; Berlin: de Gruyter, 1987).

Beale, G.K., *The Book of Revelation: A Commentary on the Greek Text* (NIGTC; Grand Rapids, MI/Cambridge, UK: Eerdmans; Carlisle: Paternoster, 1999).

Beasley-Murray, G.R., *Revelation* (2nd edn, NCBC; Grand Rapids, MI: Eerdmans, 1978).

Bergman, J., *Ich bin Isis: Studien zum memphitischen Hintergrund der griechischen Isisaretalogien* (Uppsala: The University Press, 1968).

Bhabha, H.K., 'Signs Taken for Wonders: Questions of Ambivalence and Authority under a Tree Outside Delhi, May 1817', in *idem, The Location of Culture* (London: Routledge, 1994), pp. 102–22.

Bird, P., '"To Play the Harlot": An Inquiry into an Old Testament Metaphor', in Peggy L. Day (ed.), *Gender and Difference in Ancient Israel* (Minneapolis, MN: Augsburg Fortress Press, 1989), pp. 75–94.

Blenkinsopp, J., *Ezekiel* (Louisville, KY: John Knox, 1990).

Bloch, E., *The Principle of Hope* (Studies in Contemporary German Social Thought; Cambridge, MA: The MIT Press, 1995).

Blumstein, A.K., *Misogyny and Idealization in the Courtly Romance* (Studien zur Germanistik, Anglistik und Komparatistik; Bonn, Bouvier, 1977).

Böcher, O., *Die Johannesapokalypse* (ErtFor, 41; Darmstadt: Wissenschaftliche Gesellschaft, 1975), pp. 56–63.

Boesak, A.A., *Comfort and Protest: Reflections on the Apocalypse of John of Patmos* (Philadelphia, PA: Westminster Press, 1987).

Bohmbach, K.G., 'Jezebel', in David Noel Freedman (ed.), *Eerdmans Dictionary of the Bible* (Grand Rapids, MI: Eerdmans, 2000), pp. 713–14.

Bolin, A., 'Vandalized Vanity: Feminine Physiques Betrayed and Portrayed', in Frances E. Mascia-Lees and Patricia Sharpe (eds), *Tattoo, Torture, Mutilation, and Adornment: The Denaturalization of the Body in Culture and Text* (SUNY Series on the Body in Culture, History, and Religion; Albany: State University of New York Press, 1992), pp. 79–99.

Boll, F., *Aus der Offenbarung Johannis: Hellenistische Studien zum Weltbild der Apokalypse* (Stoicheia, 1; Leipzig: Teubner, 1914; 2nd edn, Amsterdam: Hakkert, 1964).

Bolman, L.G. and Terrence E. Deal, *Reframing Organizations: Artistry, Choice, and Leadership* (2nd edn, San Francisco, CA: Jossey-Bass, 1997).

Boring, M.E., *Revelation* (Interpretation: A Bible Commentary for Teaching and Preaching; Louisville, KY: John Knox Press, 1989).

Børresen, K., 'Patristic "Feminism": The Case of Augustine', in Ø. Norderval and K.L. Ore (eds), *From Patristics to Matristics: Selected Articles on Christian Gender Models by Kari E. Børresen* (Rome: Herder, 2002), pp. 33–47.

Bousset, W., *Die Offenbarung Johannis* (Göttingen: Vandenhoeck & Ruprecht, 1966; reprint of the 6th edn, 1906).

Boyarin, D., *Carnal Israel: Reading Sex in Talmudic Culture* (Berkeley and Los Angeles: University of California Press, 1993).

Brenner, A., *The Intercourse of Knowledge: On Gendering Desire and 'Sexuality' in the Hebrew Bible* (BibInt, 26; Leiden: Brill, 1997).

— (ed.), *A Feminist Companion to the Latter Prophets* (FCB, 8; Sheffield; Sheffield Academic Press, 1995).

— (ed.), *The Israelite Woman: Social Role and Literary Type in Biblical Narrative* (Sheffield: Sheffield Academic Press, 1985).

Brook-Rose, C., 'Woman as Semiotic Object', in Susan R. Suleiman (ed.), *The Female Body in Western Culture* (Cambridge, MA: Harvard University Press, 1986), pp. 305–16.

Brooten, B., *Love between Women: Early Christian Responses to Female Homoeroticism* (Chicago, IL: University of Chicago Press, 1996).

Brown, P., *The Body and Society: Men, Women, and Sexual Renunciation in Early Christianity* (New York: Columbia University Press, 1988).

Burke, C., Naomi Schor and Margaret Whitford (eds), *Engaging with Irigaray:*

Feminist Philosophy and Modern European Thought (Gender and Culture; New York: Columbia University Press, 1994).

Burns, J.E., 'Contrasted Women of Apocalypse 12 and 17', *CBQ* 26 (1964), pp. 459–63.

Butler, G., *Arnold Schwarzenegger: A Portrait* (New York: Simon & Schuster, 1990).

Caird, G.B., *The Revelation of St. John* (Black's New Testament Commentary, 19; London: A. & C. Black, 1966; New York: Harper & Row, 1987; Peabody, MA: Hendrison, 1993).

Camp, C.V., 'What is So Strange about the Strange Woman?', in David Jobling, Peggy L. Day and Gerald T. Shephard (eds), *The Bible and the Politics of Exegesis* (Cleveland, OH: Pilgrim Press, 1988), pp. 17–31.

Cantarella, E., 'Marriage and Sexuality in Republican Rome: A Roman Conjugal Love Story', in Martha C. Nussbaum and Julia Sihvola (eds), *The Sleep of Reason: Erotic Experience and Sexual Ethics in Ancient Greece and Rome* (Chicago, IL: University of Chicago Press, 2002), pp. 269–82.

Carey, G., *Elusive Apocalypse: Reading Authority in the Revelation to John* (Macon, GA: Mercer University Press, 1999).

Carpenter, M.W., 'Representing Apocalypse: Sexual Politics and the Violence of Revelation', in Richard Dellamora (ed.), *Postmodern Apocalypse: Theory and Cultural Practice at the End* (Philadelphia: University of Pennsylvania Press, 1995), pp. 107–35.

Carson, A., 'Putting Her in Her Place: Women, Dirt, and Desire', in D.M. Halperin, J.T. Winkler and F.I. Zeitlin (eds), *Before Sexuality: The Construction of Erotic Experience in the Ancient Greek World* (Princeton, NJ: Princeton University Press, 1990), pp. 135–70.

Cassuto, U., *A Commentary on the Book of Genesis* (4 vols.; trans. Israel Abrahams; Jerusalem: Magnes Press, 1961–64).

Castán, C. and Carlos Fuster, *La moneda imperial romana: Julio César, 100 a. C.–Rómulo Augusto, 476 d. C.* (Madrid: Graficinco, 1996).

Castelli, E.A., *Imitating Paul: A Discourse of Power* (Literary Currents in Biblical Interpretation; Louisville, KY: Westminster/John Knox Press, 1991).

— 'Romans', in Elisabeth Schüssler Fiorenza (ed.) *Searching the Scriptures: A Feminist Introduction and Commentary* (2 vols; New York: Crossroad, 1993, 1994), vol. 2, pp. 272–300.

Castells, M., *End of Millennium* (The Information Age: Economy, Society, and Culture, III; Oxford: Blackwell, 1998).

Charles, R.H., *A Critical and Exegetical Commentary on the Revelation of St John* (ICC; 2 vols; Edinburgh: T&T Clark, 1920).

Charlesworth, J.H. (ed.), *The Old Testament Pseudepigrapha* (2 vols; New York: Doubleday, 1983).

Cheng, S., '*Fremdwörter* as "The Jews of Language" and Adorno's Politics of Exile', in M. O'Neill (ed.), *Adorno, Culture and Feminism* (London: Sage, 1999), pp. 75–103.

Cheung, A.T., *Idol Food in Corinth: Jewish Background and Pauline Legacy* (JSNTSup, 176; Sheffield: Sheffield Academic Press, 1999).

Chevalier, J.M., *A Postmodern Revelation: Signs of Astrology and the Apocalypse* (Toronto: University of Toronto Press, 1997).

Cixous, H., *Coming to Writing and Other Essays* (eds D. Jenson, S.R. Suleiman and S. Cornell; trans. A. Liddle and S. Sellers; Cambridge, MA: Harvard University Press, 1992).

Cohn, N., *The Pursuit of the Millennium: Revolutionary Millenarians and Mystical Anarchists of the Middle Ages* (New York: Oxford University Press, 1970).

Collins, A.Y., *The Apocalypse* (New Testament Message, 22; Wilmington, DE: Michael Glazier, 1979).

— 'Apocalypse (The Revelation of John)', *NJBC*, pp. 996–1016.

— 'The Book of Revelation', in John J. Collins (ed.), *The Encyclopedia of Apocalypticism* Vol. 1: *The Origins of Apocalypticism in Judaism and Christianity* (New York: Continuum, 1998), pp. 384–414.

— *Crisis and Catharsis: The Power of the Apocalypse* (Philadelphia, PA: Westminster Press, 1984).

— *The Combat Myth in the Book of Revelation* (HDR, 9; Chico, CA: Scholars Press, 1976).

— 'Feminine Symbolism in the Book of Revelation', *BibInt* 1 (1993), pp. 20–33.

— *The Gospel and Women* (Orange, CA: Chapman College, 1988).

— 'Insiders and Outsiders in the Book of Revelation and Its Social Context', in Jacob Neusner and Ernest S. Frerichs (eds), *'To See Ourselves as Others See Us': Christians, Jews, 'Others' in Late Antiquity* (Scholars Press Studies in the Humanities; Chico, CA: Scholars Press, 1985), pp. 187–218.

— 'Reading the Book of Revelation in the Twentieth Century', *Interpretation* 40.3 (1986), pp. 229–42.

— 'Revelation 18: Taunt-Song or Dirge?', in Jan Lambrecht (ed.), *L'Apocalypse johannique et l'Apocalyptique dans le Nouveau Testament* (BETL, 53; Leuven/ Gembloux: University Press/Duculot, 1980), pp. 185–204.

— 'Women's History and the Book of Revelation', *SBLSP* 26 (1987), pp. 80–91.

Collins, J.J., *The Apocalyptic Imagination* (New York; Crossroad Continuum, 1984).

— 'The Genre Apocalypse in Hellenistic Judaism', in David Hellholm (ed.), *Apocalypticism in the Mediterranean World and the Near East* (Tübingen: Mohr Siebeck, 1989), pp. 531–48.

— 'Introduction: Towards the Morphology of a Genre', *Semeia* 14 (1979), pp. 1–20.

Cooper, K., *The Virgin and the Bride: Idealized Womanhood in Late Antiquity* (Cambridge, MA: Harvard University Press, 1996).

Counihan, C.M., *The Anthropology of Food and Body: Gender, Meaning, and Power* (New York: Routledge, 1999).

Cuss, D., *Imperial Cults and Honorary Terms in the New Testament* (*Paradosis*, 23; Fribourg: Fribourg University Press, 1974).

Daly, M., *Beyond God the Father: Toward a Philosophy of Women's Liberation* (Boston, MA: Beacon Press, 1973).

— *Gyn/Ecology: The Metaethics of Radical Feminism* (Boston, MA: Beacon Press, 1978).

D'Ambra, E., 'The Cult of Virtues and the Funerary Relief of Ulpia Epigone', in *eadem* (ed.), *Roman Art in Context: An Anthology* (Upper Saddle River, NJ: Prentice Hall, 1993), pp. 102–14.

— *Private Lives, Imperial Virtues: The Frieze of the Forum Transitorium in Rome* (Princeton, NJ: Princeton University Press, 1993).

D'Angelo, M.R., '"Knowing How to Preside over His Own Household": Imperial Masculinity and Christian Asceticism in the Pastorals, Hermas, and Luke-Acts', in Stephen D. Moore and Janice Capel Anderson (eds), *New Testament Masculinities* (Semeia Studies; Atlanta, GA: Scholars Press, 2003), pp. 241–71.

Davies, G., 'The Significance of the Handshake Motif in Classical Funerary Art', *AJA* 89 (1985), pp. 627–40.

de Man, P., 'The Return to Philology', in *idem, The Resistance to Theory* (Minneapolis: University of Minnesota Press, 1986), pp. 21–26.

de Stoop, C., *Ze zijn zo lief, meneer* (Antwerp: Kritak, 1992).

de Troyer, K., 'Septuagint and Gender Studies: The Very Beginning of a Promising Liaison', in A. Brenner and C. Fontaine (eds), *A Feminist Companion to Reading the Bible: Approaches, Methods and Strategies* (Sheffield: Sheffield Academic Press, 1997), pp. 326–43.

Deissmann, A., *Licht vom Osten* (Tübingen: Mohr, 4th edn, 1923).

Delitzsch, F., *Babel and Bible* (Chicago, IL: University of Chicago Press, 1906).

Delling, G., 'παρθένος', *TDNT* 5, pp. 826–37.

Derrida, J., 'Différance', in *idem, Margins of Philosophy* (trans. A. Bass; Chicago, IL: University of Chicago Press, 1982), pp. 1–27.

— *Specters of Marx: The State of the Debt, The Work of Mourning & the New International* (London: Routledge, 2006).

Deutsch, C., 'Transformation of Symbols: The New Jerusalem in Rv 21,1–22,5', *ZNW* 78 (1987), pp. 106–26.

Dever, W.G., *Did God Have a Wife? Archaeology and Folk Religion in Ancient Israel* (Grand Rapids, MI: Eerdmans, 2005).

Dewey, J., 'Response: Fantasy and the New Testament', *Semeia* 60 (1992), pp. 83–89.

Dixon, S., *Reading Roman Women: Sources, Genres and Real Life* (London: Duckworth, 2001).

— *The Roman Family* (Baltimore, MD: The Johns Hopkins University Press, 1992).

— 'The Sentimental Ideal of the Roman Family', in Beryl Rawson (ed.), *Marriage, Divorce, and Children in Ancient Rome* (Oxford: Clarendon Press, 1991), pp. 99–113.

Dougherty, C., *The Poetics of Colonization: From City to Text in Archaic Greece* (Oxford: Oxford University Press, 1993).

Douglas, M., 'Critique and Commentary', in Jacob Neusner (ed.), *The Idea of Purity In Ancient Judaism*: (SJLA, 1; Leiden: E.J. Brill, 1973), pp. 137–42.

— 'Deciphering a Meal', in *eadem, Implicit Meanings: Selected Essays in Anthropology* (2nd edn, New York: Routledge, 1999), pp. 249–75.

— *In the Wilderness: The Doctrine of Defilement in the Book of Numbers* (JSOTSup, 158; Sheffield: Sheffield Academic Press, 1993).

— *Purity and Danger: An Analysis of the Concepts of Pollution and Taboo* (London: Routledge & Kegan Paul, 1966).

Dube, M.W., *Postcolonial Feminist Interpretation of the Bible* (St. Louis, MO: Chalice Press, 2000).

Duff, P., *Who Rides the Beast? Prophetic Rivalry and the Rhetoric of Crisis in the Churches of the Apocalypse* (New York: Oxford University Press, 2001).

Dutton, K.R., *The Perfectible Body: The Western Ideal of Male Physical Development* (New York: Continuum, 1995).

Eaton, H., *Introducing Ecofeminist Theologies* (London: T&T Clark, 2005).

Efird, J.M., 'Serpent', in Paul Achtemeier (gen. ed.), *Harper's Bible Dictionary* (San Francisco, CA: HarperSanFrancisco, 1985), p. 928.

Eviota, E.U., *The Political Economy of Gender: Women and the Sexual Division of Labour in the Philippines* (London/New Jersey: Zed, 1992).

Exum, J.C., *Plotted, Shot, and Painted: Cultural Representations of Biblical Women* (JSOTSup, 215; Gender, Culture, Theory, 3; Sheffield: Sheffield Academic Press, 1996).

Fanon, F., *The Wretched of the Earth* (trans. Constance Farrington; New York: Grove Press, 1968).

Fantham, E., et al. (eds), *Women in the Classical World: Image and Text* (New York: Oxford University Press, 1994).

Fausto-Sterling, A., *Sexing the Body: Gender Politics and the Construction of Sexuality* (New York: Basic Books, 2000).

Fekkes, J., *Isaiah and Prophetic Traditions in the Book of Revelation: Visionary Antecedents and their Development* (JSNTSup, 93; Sheffield: Sheffield Academic Press, 1994).

Feuerbach, L., *Das Wesen des Christentums* (Leipzig: O. Wigand, 1841).

Fischler, S., 'Social Stereotypes and Historical Analysis: The Case of Imperial Woman at Rome', in Léonie J. Archer, Susan Fischler and Maria Wyke (eds), *Women in Ancient Societies: An Illusion of the Night* (London: Macmillan, 1994), pp. 115–33.

Fishwick, D., *The Imperial Cult in the Latin West: Studies in the Ruler Cult of the Western Provinces of the Roman Empire* (4 vols.; Etudes préliminaires aux religions orientales dans l'Empire romaine, 108; Leiden: Brill, 1987–92).

Flory, M.B., 'The Deification of Roman Women', *The Ancient History Bulletin* 9.3–4 (1995), pp. 127–34.

Fontenrose, J., *Python: A Study of the Delphic Myth and Its Origins* (Berkeley: University of California Press, 1959).

Ford, J.M., *Revelation* (AB, 38; Garden City, NY: Doubleday, 1975).

Forsyth, N., *The Old Enemy: Satan and the Combat Myth* (Princeton, NJ: Princeton University Press, 1987).

Fotopolous, J., *Food Offered to Idols in Roman Corinth: A Socio-Rhetorical Reconsideration of 1 Cor 8:1–11:1* (Tübigen: Mohr Siebeck, 2003).

Foucault, M., *Discipline and Punish: The Birth of the Prison* (trans. Alan Sheridan; New York: Pantheon Books, 1977).

— '7 January 1976', in *idem, Society Must Be Defended: Lectures at the College de France, 1975–76* (trans. David Macey; New York: St. Martin's Press, 2003), pp. 1–22.

Frankfurter, D., 'Jews or Not? Reconstructing the "Other" in Rev 2:9 and 3:9', *HTR* 94 (2001), pp. 403–25.

Franzmann, M., 'The City as Woman: The Case of Babylon in Isaiah 47', *Australian Biblical Review* 43 (1995), pp. 1–19.

Freud, S., *The Future of an Illusion*, in James Strachey et al. (eds and trans.), *The Standard Edition of the Complete Psychological Works of Sigmund Freud* (London: Hogarth Press and the Institute of Psycho-Analysis, 1953–74), XXI, pp. 5–56.

— *Totem and Taboo* (trans. A.A. Brill; New York: Vintage, 1918).

Friesen, S.J., *Imperial Cults and the Apocalypse of John: Reading Revelation in the Ruins* (New York: Oxford University Press, 2001).

Frymer-Kensky, T., *In the Wake of the Goddesses* (New York: The Free Press, 1992).

Fullerton, M.D., 'The *Domus Augusti* in Imperial Iconography of 13–12 B.C.', *AJA* 89 (1985), pp. 473–83.

Fussell, S.W., 'Bodybuilder Americanus', in Laurence Goldstein (ed.), *The Male Body: Features, Destinies, Exposures* (Ann Arbor: University of Michigan Press, 1994), pp. 42–60.

— *Muscle: Confessions of an Unlikely Bodybuilder* (New York: Avon Books, 1991).

Gaines, C. and George Butler, *Pumping Iron: The Art and Sport of Bodybuilding* (London: Sphere Books, 1974).

Galambush, J., *Jerusalem in the Book of Ezekiel: The City as Yahweh's Wife* (SBLDS, 130; Atlanta, GA: Scholars Press, 1992).

Gandhi, L., *Postcolonial Theory: A Critical Introduction* (New York: Columbia University Press, 1998).

García Martínez, F., *The Dead Sea Scrolls Translated: The Qumran Texts in English* (trans. W.G.E. Watson; 2nd edn, Grand Rapids, MI: Eerdmans, 1996).

Gardner, J., *Women in Roman Law and Society* (London: Croom Helm, 1986).

Garrett, S.R., 'Revelation', in Carol A. Newsom and Sharon H. Ringe (eds), *The Women's Bible Commentary* (Louisville, KY: Westminster/John Knox Press, 1992), pp. 377–82.

Gentry, Jr., K.L., *Before Jerusalem Fell: Dating the Book of Revelation: An Exegetical and Historical Argument for a Pre-AD 70 Composition* (Tyler, TX: Institute for Christian Economics, 1989).

George, A.R., *Communion with God in the New Testament* (London: Epworth Press, 1953).

Geyer, J.B., 'Twisting Tiamat's Tail: A Mythological Interpretation of Isaiah XIII 5 and 8', *VT* 37 (1987), pp. 164–79.

Giblin, C.H., *The Book of Revelation: The Open Book of Prophecy* (GNS, 34, Collegeville, MN: Liturgical Press, 1991).

Giblin, M.J., 'Dualism', in Letty M. Russell and J. Shannon Clarkson (eds), *Dictionary of Feminist Theologies* (Louisville, KY: Westminster/John Knox Press, 1996), p. 74.

Glenn, C., *Rhetoric Retold: Regendering the Tradition from Antiquity through the Renaissance* (Carbondale: Southern Illinois University Press, 1997).

Gooch, P.D., *Dangerous Food: 1 Corinthians 8–10 in Its Context* (Studies in Judaism and Christianity, 5; Waterloo, ON: Canadian Corporation for Studies in Religion, 1993).

Good, R.M., 'Asherah', in Paul Achtemeier (gen. ed.), *Harper's Bible Dictionary* (San Francisco, CA: HarperSanFrancisco, 1985), pp. 74–75.

Goold, G.P., 'Introduction,' in Manilius, *Astronomica* (trans. G.P. Goold; Cambridge, MA: Harvard/London: William Heinemann, 1976), pp. i–cxii.

Graham, E.L., *Making the Difference: Gender, Personhood and Theology* (London: Mowbray, 1995).

Grau, M., *Of Divine Economy: Refinancing Redemption* (London: T&T Clark, 2004).

Greenberg, M., *Ezekiel 1–20* (AB, 22; Garden City, NY: Doubleday, 1983).

Gribbin, J.R., *Hothouse Earth: The Greenhouse Effect and Gaia* (New York: Grove Weidenfeld, 1990).

Grosz, E., 'Bodies-Cities', in B. Colomina (ed.), *Sexuality and Space* (Princeton Papers on Architecture; Princeton, NJ: Princeton Architectural Press, 1992), pp. 241–53.

Grubbs, J.E., *Law and Family in Late Antiquity: The Emperor Constantine's Marriage Legislation* (Oxford: Oxford University Press, 1995).

— *Women and the Law in the Roman Empire: A Sourcebook on Marriage, Divorce, and Widowhood* (London: Routledge, 2002).

Gruen, E.S., *Diaspora: Jews Amidst Greeks and Romans* (Cambridge, MA: Harvard University Press, 2002).

Gundry, R.H., 'The New Jerusalem: People as Place, Not Place for People', *NovT* 29 (1987), pp. 254–64.

Gunkel, H., *Genesis* (Göttingen: Vandenhoeck and Ruprecht, 1917).

— *Schöpfung und Chaos in Urzeit und Endzeit: Eine religionsgeschichtliche Untersuchung über Gen 1 und Ap Joh 12* (Göttingen: Vandenhoeck und Ruprecht, 1895).

Hallissy, M., *Venomous Woman: Fear of the Female in Literature* (New York: Greenwood Press, 1987).

Hampson, D., *Theology and Feminism* (Oxford: Basil Blackwell, 1990).

Hanson, P.D., *The Dawn of Apocalyptic: The Historical and Sociological Roots of Jewish Apocalyptic Eschatology* (rev. edn, Philadelphia, PA: Fortress Press, 1979).

Harland, P.A., 'Honouring the Emperor or Assailing the Beast: Participation in Civic Life among Associations (Jewish, Christian and Other) in Asia Minor and the Apocalypse of John', *JSNT* 77 (2000), pp. 99–121.

Harrington, W.J., *Revelation* (Sacra Pagina; Collegeville, MN: Liturgical Press, 1993).

Hartman, L., 'Survey of the Problem of the Apocalyptic Genre', in David Hellholm (ed.), *Apocalypticism in the Mediterranean World and the Near East* (Tübingen: Mohr Siebeck, 1989), pp. 329–43.

Heidel, A., *The Babylonian Genesis* (2nd edn, Chicago, IL/London: University of Chicago Press, 1951).

Hellholm, D. (ed.), The Problem of Apocalyptic Genre and the Apocalypse of John', *Semeia* 36 (1986), pp. 13–64.

— *Apocalypticism in the Mediterranean World and the Near East* (Tübingen: Mohr Siebeck, 1989).

Hemer, C.J., *The Letters to the Seven Churches of Asia in Their Local Setting* (JSNTSup, 11; Sheffield: JSOT Press, 1986).

Hirdman, Y., 'Genussystemet – reflexioner kring kvinnors sociala underordning', *Kvinnovetenskaplig tidskrift* 3 (1988), pp. 49–63.

Hirschfield, J., 'Poetry and Uncertainty', *American Poetry Review* 34.6 (November/ December 2005), pp. 63–72.

Honer, A., 'Beschreibung einer Lebenswelt: Zur Empirie des Bodybuilding', *Zeitschrift für Soziologie* 14 (1985), pp. 131–39.

Hooke, S.H., 'The Myth and Ritual Pattern in Jewish and Christian Apocalyptic', in idem, *The Labyrinth: Further Studies on the Relationship Between Myth and Ritual in the Ancient World* (New York: Macmillan, 1935), pp. 213–32.

Horsley, R.A., 'Religion and Other Products of Empire', *JAAR* 71 (2003), pp. 13–44.

Howard-Brook, W. and Anthony Gwyther, *Unveiling Empire: Revelation Then and Now* (Maryknoll, NY: Orbis Books, 1999).

Huber, L.R., *Like a Bride Adorned: Reading Metaphor in John's Apocalypse* (Emory Studies in Early Christianity; New York: T&T Clark, 2007).

— 'Sexually Explicit? Re-reading Revelation's 144,000 Virgins as a Response to Roman Social Discourses', *Journal of Men, Masculinities and Spirituality* 2.1 (2008), pp. 3–28 (http://www.jmmsweb.org/issues/volume2/number1/pp3–28).

Humphrey, E.M., *The Ladies and the Cities: Transformation and Apocalyptic Identity in Joseph and Aseneth, 4 Ezra, The Apocalypse, and the Shepherd of Hermas* (Sheffield: Sheffield Academic Press, 1995).

Irigaray, L., *Ce Sexe qui n'en est pas un* (Paris: Minuit, 1977).

— *An Ethics of Sexual Difference*, trans. Carolyn Burke and Gillian C. Gill (Ithaca, NY: Cornell University Press, 1991 [1984]).

— *The Forgetting of Air in Martin Heidegger* (trans. Mary Beth Mader; Austin: University of Texas Press, 1999).

— *I Love to You: Sketch for a Felicity within History* (trans. Alison Martin; New York: Routledge, 1996).

— *The Marine Lover of Friedrich Nietzsche* (trans. Gillian C. Gill; New York: Columbia University Press, 1991).

— *Sexes and Genealogies* (trans. Gillian C. Gill; New York: Columbia University Press, 1993).

— *Speculum de l'autre femme* (Paris: Minuit, 1974).

— *Speculum of the Other Woman* (trans. Gillian Gill; Ithaca, NY: Cornell University Press, 1985).

— *This Sex which is not One* (trans. Catherine Porter with Carolyn Burke; Ithaca, NY: Cornell University Press, 1985).

Jack, A.M., 'Out of the Wilderness: Feminist Perspectives on the Book of Revelation', in Steve Moyise (ed.), *Studies in the Book of Revelation* (New York: Continuum, 2001), pp. 149–62.

— *Texts Reading Texts, Sacred and Secular: Two Postmodern Perspectives* (JSNTSup, 179; Sheffield: Sheffield Academic Press, 1999).

Janzen, E.P., 'The Jesus of the Apocalypse Wears the Emperor's Clothes', *SBLSP* 33 (1994), pp. 637–61.

Johnson, E.A., *She Who Is: The Mystery of God in Feminist Theological Discourse* (New York: Crossroad, 1992).

Johnston, H.W., *The Private Life of the Romans* (rev. Mary Johnston; Chicago, IL: Scott, Foresman and Company, 1932).

Jones, B.W., *The Emperor Domitian* (New York: Routledge, 1992).

Jones, D.L., 'Christianity and the Roman Imperial Cult', *ANRW* 11.23, pp. 1024–35.

Jordheim, H., *Lesningens Vitenskap: Utkast til en ny filologi* (Oslo: Universitetsforlaget, 2001).

Jung, C.J., *Answer to Job* (London: Routledge & Kegan Paul, 1954).

Keith, A.M., *Engendering Rome: Women in Latin Epic* (Cambridge, UK: Cambridge University Press, 2000).

Keller, C., *Apocalypse Now and Then: A Feminist Guide to the End of the World* (Boston, MA: Beacon, 1996).

— 'The Breast, the Apocalypse, and the Colonial Journey', in C.B. Strozier and M. Flynn (eds), *The Year 2000* (New York: New York University Press, 1997), pp. 42–58.

— *God and Power: Counter-Apocalyptic Journeys* (Minneapolis, MN: Fortress Press, 2005).

— 'Ms. Calculating the Endtimes: Gender Styles of Apocalypse', in *eadem, God and Power: Counter-Apocalyptic Journeys* (Minneapolis, MN: Fortress Press, 2005), pp. 53–65.

— 'Silly Women of the Last Days', in *eadem, Apocalypse Now and Then* (Minneapolis, MN: Fortress Press, 2005), pp. 224–72.

Kim, J.K. '"Uncovering Her Wickedness": An Inter(Con)Textual Reading of Revelation 17 From a Postcolonial Feminist Perspective', *JSNT* 73 (1999), pp. 61–81.

King, L.W., *The Seven Tablets of Creation* (London: Luzak & Co., 1902).

Kirk, K.E., *The Vision of God: The Christian Doctrine of the* Summum Bonum (London: Longmans, Green & Co., 1931).

Klausner, T., 'Aurum Coronarium', in Ernst Dassmann (ed.), *Gesammelte Arbeiten zur Liturgiegeschichte, Kirchengeschichte und christlichen Archäologie* (Münster: Aschendorff, 1974), pp. 292–309.

Klein, A.M., *Little Big Men: Bodybuilding Subculture and Gender Construction* (SUNY Series on Sport, Culture, and Social Relations; Albany: State University of New York Press, 1993).

Kleiner, D.E.E., *Roman Sculpture* (New Haven, CT: Yale University Press, 1992).

Koch, M., *Drachenkampf und Sonnenfrau: Zur Funktion des Mythischen in der Johannesapokalypse am Beispiel von Apk 12* (WUNT, 184; Tübingen: Mohr Siebeck, 2004).

Kraft, H., *Die Offenbarung des Johannes* (HNT; Tübingen: Mohr [Siebeck], 1974).

Kraybill, N., *Imperial Cult and Commerce in John's Apocalypse* (JSNTSup, 132; Sheffield: Sheffield Academic Press, 1996).

Krodel, G., *Revelation* (Augsburg Commentary on the New Testament; Minneapolis, MN: Augsburg, 1989).

Kugel, J., *The Bible As It Was* (Cambridge, MA/London: Belknap Press, 1997).

Laqueur, T., *Making Sex: Body and Gender from the Greeks to Freud* (Cambridge, MA: Harvard University Press, 1990).

Le Boeuffle, A., *Les noms latins d'astres et constellations* (Paris: Belles Lettres, 1977).

Leibowitz, N., *Studies in Bereshit in the Context of Ancient and Modern Bible Commentary* (ed. and trans. Aryeh Newman; Jerusalem: World Zionist Organization Department for Torah Education and Culture, 4th edn, 1981).

Levine, A.-J., 'The Disease of Postcolonial New Testament Studies and the Hermeneutics of Healing, with responses by Kwok Pui-lan, Musimbi Kanyoro, Adele Reinhartz, Hisako Kinukawa, Elaine Wainwright', *JFSR* 20 (2004), pp. 91–141.

Lewittes, M., *Jewish Marriage: Rabbinic Law, Legend, and Custom* (Northvale, NJ/London: Jason Aronson, 1994).

Lindijer, C.H., 'Die Jungfrauen in der Offenbarung des Johannes XIV 4', in *Studies in John: Festschrift Presented to J.N. Sevenster on the Occasion of His Seventieth Birthday* (NovTSup, 24; Leiden: E.J. Brill, 1970), pp. 124–42.

Lingis, A., *Foreign Bodies* (New York: Routledge, 1994).

Linton, G.L., 'Reading the Apocalypse as Apocalypse', in D.L. Barr (ed.), *The Reality of Apocalypse: Rhetoric and Politics in the Book of Revelation* (Atlanta, GA: Society of Biblical Literature, 2006), pp. 9–42.

Lohmeyer, E., *Die Offenbarung des Johannes* (HNT; Tübingen: Mohr [Siebeck], 3rd edn, 1970).

Lohse, E., *Die Offenbarung des Johannes* (NTD, 11; Göttingen: Vandenhoeck & Ruprecht, 1979).

Lovelock, J.E., *The Ages of Gaia: A Biography of Our Living Earth* (New York: Norton, 1988).

— *Gaia: A New Look at Life on Earth* (Oxford/New York: Oxford University Press, 1979).

Lutz, C.E., 'Musonius Rufus: The Roman Socrates', *Yale Classical Studies* 10 (1947), pp. 3–147.

MacGregor, J., 'The New Pop Hero: A Mirage of Muscle and Men?', *The New York Times*, 28 March 28 1999, Arts and Leisure, pp. 1ff.

Maier, H.O., *Apocalypse Recalled: The Book of Revelation after Christendom* (Minneapolis, MN: Fortress Press, 2002).

Malina, B.J., *New Testament World. Insights from Cultural Anthropology* (rev. edn, Louisville, KY: Westminster/John Knox Press, 1993).

— *On the Genre and Message of Revelation: Star Visions and Sky Journeys* (Peabody, MA: Hendrickson, 1995).

Margulis, L. and Dorion Sagan, *Slanted Truths: Essays on Gaia, Symbiosis, and Evolution* (New York: Copernicus, 1997).

Marshall, J.W., 'Collateral Damage: Jesus and Jezebel in the Jewish War', in E. Leigh Gibson and Shelley Matthews (eds), *Violence in the New Testament* (London: T&T Clark, 2005), pp. 35–50.

— *Parables of War: Reading John's Jewish Apocalypse* (Waterloo, ON: Wilfrid Laurier University Press, 2001).

— 'The Patriarchs and the Zodiac', in Richard S. Ascough (ed.), *Religious Rivalries and the Struggle for Success in Sardis and Smyrna* (Waterloo, ON: Wilfrid Laurier University Press, 2005), pp. 186–213.

— 'Postcolonialism and the Practice of History', in Caroline Vander Stichele and Todd Penner (eds), *Her Master's Tools? Feminist and Postcolonial Engagements of Historical-Critical Discourse* (Atlanta, GA: Society of Biblical Literature, 2005), pp. 93–108.

— 'Who's on the Throne: Revelation in the Long Year', in Ra'anan S. Boustan and Annette Yoshiko Reed (eds), *Heavenly Realms and Earthly Realities in Late Antique Religions* (Cambridge, UK: Cambridge University Press, 2004), pp. 123–41.

Martin, D.B., 'The Construction of the Ancient Family: Methodological Considerations', *JRS* 86 (1996), pp. 40–60.

Matthews, S., 'Thinking of Thecla: Issues in Feminist Historiography', *JFSR* 17 (2001), pp. 39–55.

McFague, S., *The Body of God: An Ecological Theology* (Minneapolis, MN: Fortress Press, 2004).

— *Models of God: Theology for an Ecological, Nuclear Age* (Philadelphia, PA: Fortress Press, 1987).

McGough, P., 'At the Court of King Dorian', *Flex* (September 1995), pp. 197–98.

— 'Hard Times', *Flex* (January 1994), p. 114.

McGuire, J. (ed.), *The Freud/Jung Letters: The Correspondence between Sigmund Freud and C. G. Jung* (trans. Ralph Manheim and R.F.C. Hull; Princeton, NJ: Princeton University Press, 1974).

McKinlay, J.E., 'Negotiating the Frame for Viewing the Death of Jezebel', *BibInt* 10.3 (2002), pp. 305–23.

Mellor, R., 'The Goddess Roma', *ANRW* 17.2, pp. 950–1030.

Mendenhall, G.E., *The Tenth Generation: The Origins of the Biblical Tradition* (Baltimore, MD: The Johns Hopkins University Press, 1973).

Mercadente, L., *Gender, Doctrine, and God: The Shakers and Contemporary Theology* (Nashville, TN: Abingdon, 1990).

Metzger, B.M., 'The Fourth Book of Ezra', in J.H. Charlesworth (ed.), *The Old Testament Pseudepigrapha* (2 vols.; New York: Doubleday, 1983), vol. 1, pp. 517–60.

— *A Textual Commentary on the Greek New Testament* (London/New York: United Bible Societies, 1971).

Míguez, N., 'Apocalyptic and the Economy: A Reading of Revelation 18 from the Experience of Economic Exclusion', in Fernando F. Segovia and Mary Ann Tolbert (eds), *Reading from This Place. Vol. 2: Biblical Interpretation and Social Location in Global Perspective* (Minneapolis, MN: Fortress Press, 1995), pp. 250–62.

Miles, R., *The Rites of Man: Love, Sex and Death in the Making of the Male* (London: Grafton Books, 1991).

Millar, F., *The Emperor in the Roman World (31 BC–AD 337)* (Ithaca, NY: Cornell University Press, 1977).

Miller, A.S., *Gaia Connections: An Introduction to Ecology, Ecoethics, and Economics* (Savage, MD: Rowman and Littlefield, 1991).

Moi, T., *'What is a Woman?' and Other Essays* (New York: Oxford University Press, 1999).

— *Hva er en kvinne? Kjønn og kropp i feministisk teori* (Oslo: Gyldendal, 1998).

Moore, S.D., *God's Beauty Parlor and Other Queer Spaces in and around the Bible* (Stanford, CA: Stanford University Press, 2001).

— *God's Gym: Divine Male Bodies of the Bible* (New York and London: Routledge, 1996).

— *Mark and Luke in Poststructuralist Perspectives: Jesus Begins to Write* (New Haven, CT: Yale University Press, 1992).

— *Poststructuralism and the New Testament: Derrida and Foucault at the Foot of the Cross* (Minneapolis, MN: Fortress Press, 1994).

— 'Revolting Revelations', in Ingrid Rosa Kitzberger (ed.), *The Personal Voice in Biblical Interpretation* (London and New York: Routledge, 1999), pp. 183–200.

Mounce, R.H., *The Book of Revelation* (NICNT; Grand Rapids, MI: Eerdmans, 1977).

Mowry, L., 'Revelation 4–5 and Early Christian Liturgical Usage', *JBL* 71 (1952), pp. 75–84.

Moxnes, H., 'Honor and Shame', *BTB* 23.4 (1993), pp. 167–76.

Moyise, S., 'Does the Lion Lie Down with the Lamb?', in *idem* (ed.), *Studies in the Book of Revelation* (Edinburgh: T&T Clark, 2001), pp. 181–94.

— *The Old Testament in the Book of Revelation* (JSNTSup, 115; Sheffield: Sheffield Academic Press, 1995).

Mueller, H.-F., '*Vita, Pudicitia, Libertas*: Juno, Gender, and Religious Politics in Valerius Maximus', in *Transactions of the American Philological Association* 128 (1998), pp. 221–63.

Müller, U.B., *Die Offenbarung des Johannes* (ÖTKNT, 19; Gütersloh: Gerd Mohn; Würzburg: Echter Verlag, 1984).

Nash, S.S., *Channel Surfing the Apocalypse: A Day in the Life of the Fin-de-Millennium Mind* (Penngrove, CA: Avec, 1996).

Ness, L., 'Astrology and Judaism in Late Antiquity' (Ph.D. Dissertation; Oxford, OH: Miami University, 1990) (http://www.smoe.org/arcana/diss.html accessed 21 January 2009).

Neumann, E., *The Origins and History of Consciousness* (German original: *Ursprungsgeschichte des Bewusstseins*, Zürich: Rascher Verlag, 1949; trans. R.F.C. Hull; New York: Pantheon Books, 1954).

Neusner, J. (ed.), *The Idea of Purity In Ancient Judaism* (SJLA, 1; Leiden: E.J. Brill, 1973).

Newsom, C.A. and Sharon H. Ringe (eds), *The Women's Bible Commentary* (London: SPCK/Louisville, KY: Westminster/John Knox Press, 1992; rev. edn, 1998).

Neyrey, J., 'Clean/Unclean, Pure/Polluted, and Holy/Profane: The Idea of the System of Purity', in R.L. Rohrbaugh (ed.), *The Social Sciences and New Testament Interpretation* (Peabody, MA: Hendrickson, 1996), pp. 80–104.

— 'Unclean, Common, Polluted and Taboo. A Short Reading Guide', *Forum*, 4/4 (1988), pp. 72–82.

Niditch, S., 'Genesis', in Carol A. Newsom and Sharon H. Ringe (eds), *The Women's Bible Commentary* (London: SPCK/Louisville: Westminster/John Knox Press, 1992; rev. edn, 1998), pp. 3–33.

Oakley, J.H., 'Nuptial Nuances: Wedding Images in Non-Wedding Scenes of Myth', in Ellen D. Reeder (ed.), *Pandora: Women in Classical Greece* (Princeton, NJ: Princeton University Press, 1995), pp. 63–72.

Økland, J., 'Men are from Mars and Women are from Venus', in T. Beattie and U. King (eds), *Gender, Religion, and Diversity: Cross-Cultural Approaches* (New York: Continuum, 2004), pp. 152–61.

— 'Why Can't the Heavenly Miss Jerusalem Just Shut Up?', in Caroline Vander Stichele and Todd Penner (eds), *Her Master's Tools? Feminist and Postcolonial Engagements of Historical-Critical Discourse* (Global Perspectives on Biblical Scholarship; Atlanta, GA/Leiden: Society of Biblical Literature/Brill, 2005), pp. 311–32.

— *Women in their Place: Paul and the Corinthian Discourse of Gender and Sanctuary Space* (JSNTSup, 269; New York: Continuum, 2004).

Okoye, J.C., 'Power and Worship: *Revelation* in African Perspective', in David

Rhoads (ed.), *From Every People and Nation: The Book of Revelation in Intercultural Perspective* (Minneapolis, MN: Fortress Press, 2005), pp. 110–26.

Olson, D.C., '"Those Who Have Not Defiled Themselves With Women"': Revelation 14.4 and the Book of Enoch', *CBQ 59* (1997), pp. 492–510.

Osiek, C. and David L. Balch, *Families in the New Testament World: Households and House Churches* (Louisville, KY: Westminster John Knox, 1997).

Paglia, C., 'Alice in Muscle Land', in *eadem, Sex, Art, and American Culture: Essays* (New York: Vintage Books, 1992), pp. 79–82.

Patai, R., *The Hebrew Goddess* (New York: KTAV, 1967).

Peerbolte, L.J.L., *The Antecedents of Antichrist. A Tradition-Historical Study of the Earliest Christian Views on Eschatological Opponents* (JSJSup, 49; Leiden: Brill, 1996).

Penglase, C., *Greek Myths and Mesopotamia: Parallels and Influence in the Homeric Hymns and Hesiod* (London/New York: Routledge, 1994).

Perry, P.S., 'Critiquing the Excess of Empire: A *Synkrisis* of John of Patmos and Dio of Prusa', *JSNT* 29 (2007), pp. 473–96.

Peskowitz, M., *Spinning Fantasies: Rabbis, Gender, and History* (Berkeley: University of California Press, 1997).

Peterson, Eric, *The Angels and the Liturgy* (trans. Ronald Walls; New York: Herder & Herder, 1964).

Peterson, Erik, *Heis Theos: Epigraphische, formgeschichtliche, und religionsgeschichtliche Untersuchungen* (FRLANT, 41; Göttingen: Vandenhoeck & Ruprecht, 1926).

Phelan, J.L., *The Millennial Kingdom of the Franciscans in the New World* (2nd rev. edn, Berkeley: University of California Press, 1970).

Pippin, T., *Apocalyptic Bodies: The Biblical End of the World in Text and Image* (London and New York: Routledge, 1999).

— *Death and Desire: The Rhetoric of Gender in the Apocalypse of John* (Literary Currents in Biblical Interpretation; Louisville, KY: Westminster/John Knox Press, 1992).

— 'Eros and the End: Reading for Gender in the Apocalypse of John', *Semeia* 59 (1992), pp. 193–210.

— 'The Heroine and the Whore: Fantasy and the Female in the Apocalypse of John', *Semeia* 60 (1992), pp. 67–82.

— 'The Joy of (Apocalyptic) Sex', in B.E. Brasher and L. Quinby (eds), *Gender and Apocalyptic Desire* (Millennialism and Society Series, 1; London: Equinox Publishing, 2006), pp. 64–75.

— 'Peering into the Abyss: A Postmodern Reading of the Biblical Bottomless Pit', in E.S. Malbon and E.V. McKnight (eds), *The New Literary Criticism and the New Testament* (JSNTSup, 109; Sheffield: Sheffield Academic Press, 1994), pp. 251–68.

— 'The Reproduction of Power: Feminism, Marxism and the Ideology of Reading', unpublished paper given at the Annual Meeting of the Society of Biblical Literature in New Orleans, 1990.

— 'The Revelation to John', in Elisabeth Schüssler Fiorenza (ed.), *Searching the Scriptures, A Feminist Introduction and Commentary* (2 vols; New York: Crossroad, 1993, 1994), vol. 2, pp. 109–30.

Potts, G.H., 'Imagining Gaia: Perspectives and Prospects on Gaia, Science and Religion', *Ecotheology* 81 (2003), pp. 30–49.

Preston, R. and Anthony T. Hanson, *The Revelation of Saint John the Divine* (London: SCM Press, 1949).

Price, S.R.F., *Rituals and Power: The Roman Imperial Cult in Asia Minor* (Cambridge, UK: Cambridge University Press, 1984).

Priest, J., 'A Note on the Messianic Banquet', in J.H. Charlesworth (ed.), *The Messiah: Developments in Earliest Judaism and Christianity* (Minneapolis, MN: Fortress Press, 1992), pp. 222–38.

Prigent, P., *Apocalypse 12. Histoire de l'exégese* (BGBE, 2; Tübingen: J.C.B Mohr, 1959).

Primavesi, A., *Gaia's Gift: Earth, Ourselves and God after Copernicus* (London: Routledge, 2004).

Prusak, B.P., 'Woman: Seductive Siren and Source of Sin? Pseudepigraphal Myth and Christian Origins', in Rosemary Radford Ruether (ed.), *Religion and Sexism: Images of Woman in Jewish and Christian Traditions* (New York: Simon and Schuster, 1974), pp. 89–116.

Quinby, L., *Antiapocalypse: Exercises in Genealogical Criticism* (Minneapolis: University of Minnesota Press, 1994).

— 'The Deployment of Apocalyptic Masculinity', in B. Brasher and L. Quinby (eds), *The Journal of Millennial Studies*, special issue, *Engendering the Millennium*, 2.1 (Summer 1999). (http://www.bu.edu/mille/publications/summer99/quinby.PDF).

— *Millennial Seduction: A Skeptic Confronts Apocalyptic Culture* (Ithaca, NY: Cornell University Press, 1999).

Rabine, L.W., 'Essentialism and its Contexts: Saint-Simonian and Poststructuralist Feminisms', in Naomi Schor and Elizabeth Weed (eds), *The Essential Difference* (Books from Differences; Bloomington: Indiana University Press, 1994), pp. 130–50.

Ramsay, W.M., *The Letters to the Seven Churches of Asia* (London: Hodder & Stoughton, 1904).

Rawson, B., 'From "Daily Life" to "Demography"', in Richard Hawley and Barbara Levick (eds), *Women in Antiquity: New Assessments* (London: Routledge, 1995), pp. 1–20.

— 'The Roman Family', in *eadem* (ed.), *The Family in Ancient Rome: New Perspectives* (Ithaca, NY: Cornell University Press, 1986), pp. 1–57.

Reekmans, L., 'La "dextrarum iunctio" dans l'iconographie romaine et paléochrétienne', *Bulletin de l'Institut historique Belge à Rome* 31 (1958), pp. 23–95.

Rehm, A., *Didyma,* part 2: *Die Inschriften* (gen. ed. Theodore Wiegand; vol. ed. Richard Harder; Berlin: Mann, 1958).

Rehmann, L.S., 'Die Offenbarung des Johannes: Inspirationen aus Patmos', in Luise Schottroff and Marie-Theres Wacker (eds), *Kompendium Feministische Bibelauslegung* (2nd edn, Gütersloh: Chr. Kaiser/Gütersloher Verlagshaus, 1999), pp. 725–41.

— *Vom Mut, genau hinzusehen: Feministisch-befreiungstheologische Interpretationen zur Apokalyptik* (Lucerne: Edition Exodus, 1998).

Reid, M.A., *Indecent Theology: Theological Perversions in Sex, Gender, and Politics* (London: Routledge, 2001).

Reimer, D.J., *The Oracles against Babylon in Jeremiah 50–51: A Horror among the Nations* (San Francisco, CA: Mellen Research University Press, 1993).

Resseguie, J.L., *Revelation Unsealed: A Narrative Critical Approach to John's Apocalypse* (*BibInt*, 32; Leiden: Brill, 1998).

Richard, P., *Apocalypse: A People's Commentary on the Book of Revelation* (The Bible and Liberation Series; Maryknoll, NY: Orbis Books, 1995).

Riches, J., 'Reception History as Literary History', lecture presented at the British New Testament Conference, 2007.

Rieger, J. and John Vincent (eds), *Methodist and Radical: Rejuvenating a Tradition* (Nashville, TN: Kingswood Books, 2004).

Robbins, T., *Skinny Legs and All* (New York: Bantam, 1995).

Robbins, V.K., 'Conceptual Blending and Early Christian Imagination' (http://www.helsinki.fi/collegium/events/Robbins.pdf accessed 21 January 2009).

Robinson, H.S., 'A Monument of Roma at Corinth', *Hesperia* 4 (1974), pp. 470–84.

Robinson, J. (ed.), *The Nag Hammadi Library* (San Francisco: Harper & Row, 1977).

Robinson, J.A.T., *Redating the New Testament* (Philadelphia, PA: Westminster Press, 1976).

Roloff, J., *The Revelation of John* (trans. John E. Alsup; Continental Commentaries; Minneapolis, MN: Fortress Press, 1993).

Rose, H.J. (ed.), *Hygini Fabulae* (2nd edn, Lugduni Batavorum: A.W. Sythoff, 1963).

Rossing, B., *The Choice Between Two Cities: Whore, Bride, and Empire in the Apocalypse* (Harvard Theological Studies; Harrisburg, PA: Trinity Press International, 1999).

— 'City Visions, Feminine Figures, and Economic Critique: A Sapiential Topos in the Apocalypse', in Benjamin G. Wright III and Lawrence W. Wills (eds), *Conflicted Boundaries in Wisdom and Apocalypticism* (Atlanta, GA: Society of Biblical Literature, 2005), pp. 181–96.

Rowland, C., 'The Book of Revelation: Introduction, Commentary and Reflections', *NIB* XII (1998), pp. 502–736.

— *The Open Heaven: A Study of Apocalyptic in Judaism and Early Christianity* (New York: Crossroad, 1982).

Rowlandson, J., (ed.), *Women and Society in Greek and Roman Egypt: A Sourcebook* (Cambridge, UK: Cambridge University Press, 1998).

Royalty, R.M., *The Streets of Heaven: The Ideology of Wealth in the Apocalypse of John* (Macon, GA: Mercer University Press, 1998).

Ruether, R.R., *Gaia and God: An Ecofeminist Theology of Earth Healing* (San Francisco, CA: HarperSanFrancisco, 1992).

Ruiz, J.-P., *Ezekiel in the Apocalypse: The Transformation of Prophetic Language in Revelation 16,17–19,10* (European University Studies Series, XXIII. Theology Vol. 376; Frankfurt am Main: Peter Lang, 1989).

— 'Praise and Politics in Revelation 19.1–10', in Steve Moyise (ed.), *Studies in the Book of Revelation* (New York: T&T Clark, 2001), pp. 69–84.

Ruthven, K.K., *Feminist Literary Studies: an Introduction* (Cambridge, UK: Cambridge University Press, 1984).

Saller, R.P. and Brent D. Shaw, 'Tombstones and Roman Family Relations in the Principate: Civilians, Soldiers, and Slaves', *JRS* 74 (1984), pp. 124–56.

Sals, U., *Die Biographie der 'Hure Babylon'* (Tübingen: Mohr Siebeck, 2004).

Sankovitch, T., *French Women Writers and the Book: Myths of Access and Desire* (Syracuse, NY: Syracuse University Press, 1988).

Sarna, N.M., *Genesis* (The JPS Torah Commentary; Philadelphia: Jewish Publication Society, 1989).

Satake, A., *Die Gemeindeordnung in der Johannesapokalypse* (WMANT; Neukirchen-Vlyn: Neukirchener Verlag, 1966).

Satter, B., *Each Mind a Kingdom: American Women, Sexual Purity, and the New Thought Movement, 1875–1920* (Berkeley: University of California Press, 1999).

Sauter, F., *Der römische Kaiserkult bei Martial und Statius* (Tübinger Beiträge zum Altertumswissenschaft, 21; Stuttgart: Kohlhammer, 1934).

Scapp, R. and B. Seitz (eds), *Eating Culture* (Albany: State University of New York Press, 1998).

Scharper, S.B., 'The Gaia Hypothesis: Implications for a Christian Political Theology of the Environment', *Cross Currents* 2 (1994), pp. 207–21.

Scherrer, S.J., 'Signs and Wonders in the Imperial Cult: A New Look at a Roman Religious Institution in Light of Rev. 13.13–15', *JBL* 103 (1984), pp. 599–610.

Schneider, L., *Beyond Monotheism: A Theology of Multiplicity* (London: Routledge, 2007).

Schneider, S.H., *Scientists Debate Gaia: The Next Century* (Cambridge, MA: MIT Press, 2004).

Schor, N. and E. Weed, (eds), *The Essential Difference* (Books from Differences; Bloomington: Indiana University Press, 1994).

Schüssler, Fiorenza, Elisabeth, 'Babylon the Great: A Rhetorical-Political Reading of Revelation 17–18', in David L. Barr (ed.), *The Reality of Apocalypse* (SBLSym, 39; Atlanta, GA: Society of Biblical Literature, 2006), pp. 243–69.

— *The Book of Revelation: Justice and Judgment* (Philadelphia, PA: Fortress Press, 1985; 2nd edn, Minneapolis, MN: Fortress Press, 1998).

— *But She Said: Feminist Practices of Biblical Interpretation* (Boston, MA: Beacon Press, 1992).

— *Feminist Biblical Interpretation in Context* (Boston, MA: Beacon Press, 1998).

— *In Memory of Her: A Feminist Theological Reconstruction of Christian Origins* (New York: Crossroad, 1984).

— *Invitation to the Book of Revelation: A Commentary on the Apocalypse with Complete Text from the Jerusalem Bible* (Garden City, NY: Image Books, 1981).

— *Priester für Gott. Studien zum Herrschafts- und Priestermotiv in der Apokalypse* (NTAbh Neue Folge, Band 7; Münster: Verlag Aschendorff, 1972).

— *Revelation: Vision of a Just World* (Edinburgh: T&T Clark, 1993; Proclamation Commentaries; Minneapolis, MN: Fortress Press, 1991).

— *Rhetoric and Ethic: The Politics of Biblical Studies* (Minneapolis, MN: Fortress Press, 1999).

— *Sharing Her Word: Feminist Biblical Interpretation in Context* (Boston, MA: Beacon Press, 1998).

— 'Visionary Rhetoric and Social-Political Situation', in *eadem*, *The Book of Revelation: Justice and Judgment* (2nd edn, Minneapolis, MN: Fortress Press, 1998), pp. 181–203.

— (ed.), *Searching the Scriptures: A Feminist Introduction and Commentary* (2 vols; New York: Crossroad, 1993, 1994).

Schwarzenegger, A. and Bill Dobbins, *Encyclopedia of Modern Bodybuilding* (New York: Simon & Schuster, 1985).

Scott, J., *Only Paradoxes to Offer: French Feminists and the Rights of Man* (Cambridge, MA: Harvard University Press, 1996).

Scott, K., *The Imperial Cult under the Flavians* (New York: Arno Press, 1975).

Segovia, F.F., *Decolonizing Biblical Studies: A View from the Margins* (Maryknoll, NY: Orbis Books, 2000).

— 'Postcolonial and Diasporic Criticism in Biblical Studies: Focus, Parameters, Relevance', *Studies in World Christianity* 5 (1999), pp. 177–95.

Selvidge, M., 'Powerful and Powerless Women in the Apocalypse', *NeoT* 26 (1992), pp. 157–67.

— 'Reflections on Violence and Pornography: Misogyny in the Apocalypse and Ancient Hebrew Prophecy', in Athalya Brenner (ed.), *A Feminist Companion to the Hebrew Bible in the New Testament* (FCB, 10; Sheffield: Sheffield Academic Press, 1996), pp. 274–85.

Setel, T.D., 'Prophets and Pornography', in Letty M. Russell (ed.), *Feminist Interpretation of the Bible* (Philadelphia, PA: Westminster Press, 1985), pp. 86–95.

Shaw, B.D., 'The Age of Roman Girls at Marriage: Some Reconsiderations', *JRS* 77 (1987), pp. 30–46.

Shepherd, M.H., *The Paschal Liturgy and the Apocalypse* (London: Lutterworth, 1960).

Sherk, R.K., 'The "Res Gestae" of Augustus', in *idem* (ed. and trans.), *The Roman Empire: Augustus to Hadrian* (Cambridge, UK: Cambridge University Press, 1988), pp. 41–51.

Simpson, M., *Male Impersonators: Men Performing Masculinity* (New York: Routledge, 1994).

Sjöö, M. and B. Mor, *The Great Cosmic Mother: Rediscovering the Religion of the Earth* (San Francisco, CA: Harper & Row, 1987).

Smith, J.Z., 'Fences and Neighbors: Some Contours of Early Judaism', in *idem*, *Imagining Religion: From Babylon to Jonestown* (Chicago, IL: University of Chicago Press, 1982), pp. 1–18.

— 'What a Difference a Difference Makes', in J. Neusner and E.S. Frerichs (eds), '*To See Ourselves as Others See Us': Christians, Jews, 'Others' in Late Antiquity*, Scholars Press Studies in the Humanities (Chico, CA: Scholars Press, 1985), pp. 3–48.

Smith, R.R.R. '*Simulacra Gentium:* The *Ethne* from the Sebasteion at Aphrodisias', *JRS* 78 (1988), pp. 50–77.

Soler, J., 'The Semiotics of Food in the Bible', in C. Counihan and P. van Esterik (eds), *Food and Culture: A Reader* (New York: Routledge, 1997), pp. 55–66.

Spencer, D.T., *Gay and Gaia: Ethics, Ecology and the Erotic* (Cleveland, OH: Pilgrim Press, 1996).

Spivak, G.C., 'Can the Subaltern Speak?', in C. Nelson and L. Grossberg (eds), *Marxism and the Interpretation of Culture* (Urbana: University of Illinois Press, 1988), pp. 271–313.

— *A Critique of Postcolonial Reason: Toward a History of the Vanishing Present* (Cambridge, MA: Harvard University Press, 1999).

Stauffer, E., *Christ and the Caesars* (trans. K. Gregor Smith and R. Gregor Smith; London: SCM Press, 1955).

Stenström, H., 'The Book of Revelation: A Vision of the Ultimate Liberation or the Ultimate Backlash? A Study in 20th Century Interpretations of Rev 14.1–5, with Special Emphasis on Feminist Exegesis' (PhD diss., Uppsala University, 1999).

Stern, D., 'The Captive Woman: Hellenization, Greco-Roman Erotic Narrative, and Rabbinic Literature', *Poetics Today* 19/1 (1998), pp. 91–127.

Streete, G.C., *The Strange Woman: Power and Sex in the Bible* (Louisville, KY: Westminster/John Knox Press, 1997).

Sugirtharajah, R.S., *The Bible and the Third World: Precolonial, Colonial and Post-colonial Encounters* (Cambridge and New York: Cambridge University Press, 2001).

— 'A Brief Memorandum on Postcolonialism and Biblical Studies', *JSNT* 73 (1999), pp. 3–5.

— *The Postcolonial Bible* (Sheffield: Sheffield Academic Press, 1998).

— *Postcolonial Criticism and Biblical Interpretation* (Oxford: Oxford University Press, 2002).

— (ed.), *Postcolonial Perspectives on the New Testament and its Interpretation, JSNT* 73 (1999), pp. 3–135.

Suleiman, S.R., 'Introduction', in *eadem* (ed.), *The Female Body in Western Culture* (Cambridge, MA: Harvard University Press, 1986), p. 1–4.

Swark, C., 'Jezebel', at *Caryn's Corner*, http://carynswark.blogspot.com/2007_08_13_archive.html (accessed 21 January 2009).

Sweet, J.P.M., *Revelation* (Westminster Pelican Commentaries; Philadelphia, PA: Westminster Press, 1979).

Tasker, Y., *Spectacular Bodies: Gender, Genre and the Action Cinema* (New York: Routledge, 1993).

Taylor, L.R., *The Divinity of the Roman Emperor* (Middletown, CT: American Philological Association, 1931).

Thimmes, P., 'Women Reading Women in the Apocalypse: Reading Scenario 1, the Letter to Thyatira (Rev. 2:18–29)', *Currents in Biblical Research* 2:1 (October 2003), pp. 128–44.

Thompson, L.L., *The Book of Revelation: Apocalypse and Empire* (New York: Oxford University Press, 1990).

Thompson, W.E. and J.H. Bair, 'A Sociological Analysis of Pumping Iron', *Free Inquiry in Creative Sociology* 10 (1982), pp. 192–96.

Treggiari, S., *Roman Marriage: Iusti Coniuges from the Time of Cicero to the Time of Ulpian* (Oxford: Clarendon Press, 1991), pp. 60–80.

Turcan, M. (ed.), *Tertullian: De cultu feminarum / La toilette des femmes* (SC, 173; Paris: Cerf, 1971).

van Dijk-Hemmes, F., 'The Metaphorization of Woman in Prophetic Speech: An

Analysis of Ezekiel 23', in Athalya Brenner and Fokkelien van Dijk-Hemmes, *On Gendering Texts: Female and Male Voices in the Hebrew Bible* (*BibInt*, 1; Leiden: Brill, 1993), pp. 167–76.

— 'The Metaphorization of Woman in Prophetic Speech: An Analysis of Ezekiel XXIII,' *VT* 43 (1993), pp. 162–70.

Van Kooten, G.H., 'The Year of the Four Emperors and the Revelation of John: The "pro-Neronian" Emperors Otho and Vitellius, and the Images and Colossus of Nero in Rome', *JSNT* 30 (2007), pp. 205–48.

Vander Stichele, C., 'Apocalypse, Art and Abjection: Images of the Great Whore', in George Aichele (ed.), *Culture, Entertainment and the Bible* (Sheffield: Sheffield Academic Press, 2000), pp. 124–38.

— 'Just a Whore: The Annihilation of Babylon According to Revelation 17:16', in *lectio difficilior. European Electronic Journal for Feminist Exegesis* 2000/1 (http://www.lectio.unibe.ch/00_1/j.htm accessed 21 January 2009).

Varner, E.R., 'Domitia Longina and the Politics of Portraiture', *AJA* 99 (1995), pp. 187–206.

Vermes, G., *The Dead Sea Scrolls in English* (2nd edn, New York: Penguin, 1975).

Visser, A.J., *De openbaring van Johannes* (De prediking van het Nieuwe Testament; Nijkerk: Callenbach, 1972).

Volk, T., *Gaia's Body: Toward a Physiology of Earth* (New York: Copernicus, 1998).

von Rad, G., *Genesis: A Commentary* (trans. J.H. Marks; OTL; Philadelphia, PA: Westminster Press, 1972).

Wainwright, A.W., *Mysterious Apocalypse: Interpreting the Book of Revelation* (Nashville, TN: Abingdon Press, 1993).

Wall, R.W., *Revelation* (NIBCNT, 18; Peabody, MA: Hendrickson, 1991).

Walters, M., *The Nude Male: A New Perspective* (New York: Paddington Press, 1978).

Warner, W., 'Spectacular Action: Rambo and the Popular Pleasures of Pain', in Lawrence Grossberg, Cary Nelson and Paula A. Treichler (eds), *Cultural Studies* (New York: Routledge, 1992), pp. 672–88.

Washington, H.C., 'Violence and the Construction of Gender in the Hebrew Bible: A New Historicist Approach', *BibInt* 5 (1997), pp. 324–63.

Weinfeld, M., *Deuteronomy and the Deuteronomic School* (Oxford: Clarendon Press, 1972).

Weinstock, S., *Divus Julius* (Oxford: Clarendon Press, 1971).

Wellesley, K., *The Long Year A.D. 69* (London: Paul Elek, 1975).

Wiggins, S., 'The Myth of Asherah: Lion Lady and Serpent Goddess', *Ugarit-Forschungen* 23 (1992), pp. 383–94.

Winkler, J.J., *The Constraints of Desire: The Anthropology of Sex and Gender in Ancient Greece* (New York: Routledge, 1990).

Wolfson, E., *Language, Eros, Being: Kabbalistic Hermeneutics and Poetic Imagination* (Bronx, NY: Fordham University Press, 2005).

Wood, S., 'Alcestis on Roman Sarcophagi', *AJA* 82 (1978), pp. 499–510.

Yee, G.A., 'Jezebel', *ABD* 3, p. 848–49.

Zamora, L.P., *Writing the Apocalypse: Historical Vision in Contemporary U.S. and Latin American Literature* (Cambridge, UK: Cambridge University Press, 1993).

Zane, F., 'Train with Zane: Bodybuilding in Future-World', *Muscle & Fitness* (June 1994), p. 247.

Zanker, P., *The Power of Images in the Age of Augustus* (trans. Alan Shapiro; Ann Arbor: University of Michigan Press, 1988).

Zell-Ravenheart, O., 'Theagenesis: The Birth of the Goddess', *Green Egg* 30, 123 (July–August 1998), pp. 16–20.

BIBLIOGRAPHY OF PRIMARY SOURCES

Augustine, *The City of God Against the Pagans* (trans. William Chase Greene; 7 vols; LCL; Cambridge, MA: Harvard University Press, 1960).

Catullus, in *Catullus, Tibullus and Pervigilium Veneris* (trans. Francis Warre Cornish; LCL; Cambridge, MA: Harvard University Press, 1962).

Dio Cassius, *Roman History* (trans. Ernest Cary; 9 vols; LCL; Cambridge, MA: Harvard University Press, 1914).

Hildegard of Bingen, *Scivias* (trans. Columba Hart and Jane Bishop; Mahwah, NJ: Paulist Press, 1990).

Livy, in *Livy* (trans. B.O. Foster; 14 vols; LCL; Cambridge, MA: Harvard University Press, 1919).

Martial, *Epigrams* (trans. Walter C. A. Ker; 2 vols; rev. edn, LCL; Cambridge, MA: Harvard University Press, 1978–79).

Ovid, *Fasti* (trans. James George Frazer; 2nd rev. edn, ed. G.P. Goold; LCL; Cambridge, MA: Harvard University Press, 1989).

Pliny, 'To Aefulanus Marcellinus', in *Pliny: Letters* (trans. William Melmoth; 2 vols; LCL; Cambridge, MA: Harvard University Press, 1915).

— *Natural History* (trans. H. Rackham; 10 vols; LCL; Cambridge, MA: Harvard University Press, 1971–1989).

Plutarch, *Advice to the Bride and Groom* in *Plutarch's Advice to the Bride and Groom and A Consolation to His Wife: English Translations, Commentary, Interpretive Essays, and Bibliography* (trans. Donald Russell; ed. Sarah B. Pomeroy; New York: Oxford University Press, 1999).

— *Quaestiones Romanae* in *Moralia* vol. iv (trans. Frank C. Babbitt; LCL; Cambridge, MA: Harvard University Press, 1936).

Suetonius, *Lives of the Caesars* (trans. J.C. Rolfe; 2 vols; LCL; Cambridge, MA: Harvard University Press, 1913).

Tacitus, *The Annals* (trans. John Jackson; 2 vols; LCL; Cambridge, MA: Harvard University Press, 1937).

Xenophon, *Oeconomicus* (trans. E.C. Marchant; LCL; Cambridge, MA: Harvard University Press, 1923).

Index of Biblical References

INDEX OF AUTHORS